CW00497988

A masterpiece. One of t~~he best~~
for a while. Carwyn James is one of the true
Welsh greats, without a doubt.

Jonathan Edwards MP

A thorough and intelligent biography
full of sympathy and literature.

Owen Martell, *O'r Pedwar Gwynt*

A politician, a teacher, a communicator and an
author, as well as the best rugby strategist in the
world. Carwyn is still inspiring us here.

Jon Gower

This is a Grand Slam of a biography, breaking
new ground in the field of sports literature.
One of the books of the year.

Professor Gareth Williams

To
Fiona,
Brian and Heather,
Lowri, Dean, William and Gregory.
With love and thanks.

INTO THE WIND: THE LIFE OF

CARWYN JAMES

ALUN GIBBARD

First impression: 2017

© Copyright Alun Gibbard and Y Lolfa Cyf., 2017

The contents of this book are subject to copyright, and may
not be reproduced by any means, mechanical or electronic,
without the prior, written consent of the publishers.

The publishers wish to acknowledge the support of
Cyngor Llyfrau Cymru.

Cover photograph: Colorsport
Cover design: Y Lolfa

We have made best efforts to contact the copyright holders
of all images and poems. If we have failed to acknowledge
any copyright holder, we should be glad to receive
information to assist us.

ISBN: 978 1 78461 404 1

Published and printed in Wales
on paper from well-maintained forests by
Y Lolfa Cyf., Talybont, Ceredigion SY24 5HE
website www.ylolfa.com
e-mail ylolfa@ylolfa.com
tel 01970 832 304
fax 832 782

Contents

Acknowledgements

MANY PEOPLE, WITHOUT whom this work would not have seen the light of day, need thanking. They fall into three groups.

Practical help was received from Owain Meredith, Archif Sgrin a Sain; Helen Glenister; Jane Davies; Caru James, Llanelli Library; Tim Hamill, Sonic One Studio.

The following need to be thanked for their consultations: Peter Hughes Griffiths; D Ben Rees; Russell Davies; Huw Tregelles Williams; Cenwyn Edwards; Robert Lewis; Peter Jackson; T James Jones; Martyn Shrewsbury. Thanks to Professor Gareth Williams and Jon Gower for reading the proofs of the Welsh version: your comments have been incorporated into this English version. I'm indebted to Professor Dai Smith CBE for reading the proofs of this English biography. I value his support and insight greatly.

Many trusted me with their archive material: David Rees; David Rogers; Les Williams; John Jenkins; David Meredith; Maldwyn Pryse; Alcwyn Deiniol Evans; Tony Cash and Dennis Mills from the JSSL; Dai Gealey and the staff at Llandovery College. Angelo Morello is to be thanked for accessing archives from Rovigo, Italy on my behalf and for many talks we've had about Carwyn, in Italy and via email. Thanks also to Rovigo Rugby Club, the town's Teatro and Accademia for their time when I visited them.

The fact that giants of rugby such as Willie John McBride and Colin Meads were prepared to have a chat on the phone with me about Carwyn says a great deal about the man himself. They were only two amongst many internationals, from many countries, who were so willing to talk about the man.

I acknowledge my debt to two volumes published on Carwyn's life. *Un o 'Fois y Pentre'* (One of the 'Boys from the Village'), edited by John Jenkins, was published less than a year after Carwyn died. It's a collection of essays by people from every walk of Carwyn's life. *Carwyn: A Personal Memoir* by Alun Richards is completely different. It's an account of a life through the eyes of a friend who was also an author. Both volumes have been invaluable sources. Alun Richards is unfortunately no longer with us, but I had many conversations with John Jenkins, for which I am extremely grateful.

Without the financial backing of the Welsh Books Council, this work wouldn't have happened at all. I thank them for their support. And equally the support of publishers Y Lolfa. It's been a long journey putting both Welsh-language and English biographies together. They have been supportive and patient in equal measure. I thank Carolyn Hodges in particular for her thorough and thought-provoking editing. That creative process has certainly polished my original work. Any weaknesses that may remain are mine.

Working on a project for over three years does have a bearing on family life. The subject of a biography can permeate the biographer's skin and take over every hour of the day. That might well be very difficult to live with! I thank my wife Fiona for putting up with this extra guest in our relationship. I thank her for practical and emotional support and for her insightful comments on so many aspects of Carwyn's life. My father-in-law was one of my English teachers at Llanelli Boys Grammar School and he was one of the five teachers that have shaped my life. He played no little part in setting me off on the journey that led to this book. He also gave me a wife, along with my mother-in-law of course! Quite a double debt! It was a particular joy to show the manuscript of the biography to my parents before publication. My father was at school with Carwyn and my mother met him later. Sharing this work with them was very precious. These personal, family connections made everything just that little bit more special.

Preface

JUST BEFORE CHRISTMAS last year my Welsh-language biography of Carwyn was published. This English biography is not a translation of that work, it's a restructured rewrite. The context into which this book will be released is different to the context of the Welsh biography and therefore the expression needs to be different also. But, to borrow from Led Zeppelin, the song remains the same.

There's a photograph of Carwyn in this book that captures much of the essence of the life that unfolds on these pages. He's standing near a piano, singing. An elderly lady wearing a Christmas paper hat is obviously accompanying him. The room, in Tumble Village Hall, is full of people enjoying their Christmas party. It's an important event in the community calendar. In the dim distance, the back wall of this room can be seen. It's lined with books from floor to ceiling, bought by the spare pennies earned underground and collected to form a village library; evidence of the coal miners' dedication to education and culture.

Carwyn would sing publicly, socially, throughout his adult life: in the student pubs of Aberystwyth, in the company of fellow National Servicemen, in Llandovery College staff gatherings and in rugby clubs throughout the world. This picture of him singing, in a hall next door to his birth village of Cefneithin, tells a story. Carwyn is in a crowd. Carwyn is also alone. Carwyn is singing. He has the attention of all in the room. However, as much as he is in the Hall, he is not of the Hall. It would be a safe bet that he was singing his usual 'Myfanwy' here, a song based on the Welsh legend of a man who thought he'd found love but was painfully rejected and then wandered aimlessly through fields and forests in his dejection. The song has permeated Welsh culture for over a century, predominantly through the Male Voice Choir tradition, and has found its way into films as diverse as *How Green was my Valley* and *Twin Town*. It's a song in that minor key much loved by the Welsh. Carwyn's own life would sing too often and too deeply in that minor key.

I've spent three years trying to understand the life of Carwyn James. It was always going to be a difficult task. A man who came as close as any to being a friend of his, the author Alun Richards, said of Carwyn that he was the man everybody knew about, but nobody knew. The process of trying to unravel the life of such a man is made all the more difficult when we consider that he played out his life on four stages: those of literature, broadcasting, politics and rugby. Add to this that by nature he was a very private person, and the task intensifies. But therein lies the fascination with the man who was Carwyn James. He really was unique, fascinating, stimulating, incisive, and a visionary whose view of the world went much further than the hedge at the bottom of the garden.

My research involved speaking to over a hundred people from Carwyn's four areas of interest and expertise, the geographical areas he was associated with and the institutions he was part of. It also meant long discussions with his family members. Their support has been invaluable for one main reason: they allowed me the freedom to come to my own conclusions. I never felt the weight of the family hand on my shoulders as I wrote. Carwyn's nephew Llyr James has been a strong support throughout, in allowing access to family photos and documents but also in many a discussion on various aspects of his uncle's life. Two of Carwyn's nieces, Non and Bethan, also contributed to the information and my understanding.

A shadow also hung over the enigma that was Carwyn's nature. On learning that I had started this work, many responded by saying, 'Oh, you're going to prove that Carwyn is gay, are you?' My answer was always, 'No, I'm not.' Why? Because, firstly, that wasn't ever the aim of writing the biography. The issue of his sexuality was only one aspect of his life, not the whole. And then, secondly, I cannot prove something that Carwyn had not resolved for himself. What I mean by this is dealt with thoroughly in these pages.

It's appropriate that Carwyn has had a biography commissioned in two languages. His Welsh dragon certainly had two tongues. He championed Wales and all things Welsh, and he championed the increasing use of Welsh in public life. But that was never to the exclusion of those who were Welsh but couldn't speak the language. He avoided the 'us and them' attitude that can so often be shown by many who campaign for the language and the Welsh nation, but either wilfully or subconsciously imply that the true Welsh are those who speak the language. Carwyn's speech as President for the Day at the pre-eminent Welsh cultural event, the National Eisteddfod, in Haverfordwest in 1972 shows that he did not take this standpoint. He stood firmly on an inclusive Welsh platform. He appealed to the Welsh of both languages, and was respected equally by both. More recently, a similar role was filled by the inimitable Welsh rugby international and British Lion, Ray Gravell.

So this is Carwyn, or at least my understanding of him. It was a life lived into the wind, not blown along by it. He faced the wind when it might well have been easier and more comfortable not to do so.

In the rugby world, he refused to go along with traditional rugby thinking and played into the wind every time. As these words are being written, the 2017 British and Irish Lions are preparing to go to New Zealand, under the leadership of Wales coach, New Zealander Warren Gatland. The question being asked as the present pride get ready to go to the southern hemisphere is: can they emulate what Carwyn achieved 46 years ago and beat the All Blacks in a Test series? There's no doubt that no one would be happier for the near 50-year record to be broken than the mastermind of that 1971 success himself, Carwyn James. It would have been against his spirit to think that no one else would lead the Lions to the success he achieved. Carwyn's legacy is certainly greatly appreciated in New Zealand, a legacy they have developed and nurtured from defeat.

In his personal life, he faced turbulent crosswinds and found himself walking in a different direction to almost anyone else. That proved to be a very isolated place to be. He liked that isolation, but he also suffered because of it.

This book answers many questions, contains new information and offers some definite conclusions. But I'm sure it leaves many questions unanswered. This fact may well be a reflection on the book itself for some readers, but the real, tragic relevance of such a statement is that the lack of answers was a living reality for Carwyn when he left this world at 53 years of age.

Alun Gibbard
May 2017

Artist unknown

In every man… there is one part which concerns only himself
and his contingent existence, is properly unknown to anybody
else and dies with him. And there is another part through
which he holds to an idea which is expressed through him
with an eminent clarity, and of which he is the symbol.

Wilhelm von Humboldt, *Autobiographical Fragment 1816*

Carwyn and the soil under his feet

> You never really understand a person until you consider things from his point of view… Until you climb inside of his skin and walk around in it.
>
> Harper Lee, *To Kill a Mockingbird*

THE GREATEST COACH Wales never had. The best Welsh coach ever. There's a certain significance to the fact that two such seemingly-contradictory phrases were said of the same man. Carwyn was a man of dualities. In his small, diminutive frame, opposites could sit quite comfortably. He was a chapel deacon who served in two prominent Anglican educational establishments; he took part in protests opposing Ministry of Defence plans in Wales and he did his National Service in the Navy; he showed his opposition to the apartheid regime in the sporting world, but in the name of the same sport, he travelled to Communist countries where greater physical atrocities were committed; this fervent Welsh nationalist led a team of rugby internationals to New Zealand under the British and Irish flag. More such dualities will unfold over these pages.

Through all this, he was never accused of duplicity, or of changing his views with the wind. Where others might have been criticised for being weak for showing such a characteristic, Carwyn wasn't. There was a consistency, an integrity to his view of the world that others respected, even if they couldn't always understand it.

And then, back to those two coaching phrases at the start of the chapter. They say quite a lot about the man lauded as the Maestro because of his achievements in world rugby. When he died, alone in Amsterdam in 1983, these two phrases were amongst the most common on the lips of those paying tribute to him. This firstly shows that the popular perception of him is of a rugby man. And of course he was, as historic and unprecedented successes on the field of play showed: the first and only Lions Test series win against the All Blacks in New Zealand, coaching his club to beat the same opposition and developing an innovative rugby philosophy that influenced the world game. Achievements indeed.

But this work will argue that we do Carwyn a disservice by reducing him to being a rugby man above all else. There was more to him than that, much more. It might well be the case that rugby wasn't even his first love, though there is certainly a correlation between the role that rugby played in his life at any particular time and the state of Carwyn's mind at those particular times. That correlation might be an unexpected one, as rugby, success and happiness don't necessarily relate to each other as might normally be perceived.

The phrases also show that things weren't quite as they should be. While one praises him as the greatest, the other says that he didn't get what many evidently believed he should have had: the opportunity to coach his country. Some had seemingly chosen to reject a greatness that others saw. Carwyn did have the opportunity to apply for the then-vacant job of Welsh coach, but contrary to popular perception, he wasn't rejected by the WRU – he withdrew his own application. This raises another question, which has answers on two levels. Firstly, he had already had a few battles with the WRU before the coaching vacancy appeared. Maybe he didn't fancy another one with people he didn't wholeheartedly respect. But then, on a deeper level, he had other struggles within himself that might well have made him battle-weary. Perhaps the fight wasn't in him anymore.

Into this arena of duality and identity come two new players: sexuality and community. There were some dualities which didn't sit comfortably at all in Carwyn's soul. Behind that warm smile and those kind eyes, battles raged; tormenting him, challenging the stillness he could otherwise exude. His body showed signs of this inner fight, glimpses of flaked and bloody skin to be seen under a risen trouser leg or shirt sleeve, signs of the psoriasis that was like fire on his skin, the outward blood of inner scars. The big question that burned inside him was that of his sexuality. He was having feelings that were diametrically opposed to the tenets of the faith he had been brought up in, as well as the particular values of the West-Walian heritage he came from. This was a very real duality and both sides fought inside Carwyn's head and heart.

Many might expect conclusive proof in this volume that Carwyn was gay. They will be disappointed. It's not up to an author to come to conclusions the subject himself didn't have an opportunity to arrive at. Many, on the other hand, will be appalled at the fact that stories relating to Carwyn's homosexuality are included at all, as they completely reject the idea that he might have been gay in the first place and hold that the whole story was nothing more than vicious gossip. The reaction of some to the Welsh-language version of this book suggests that this will be so, as some have reacted strongly to stories in the book relating to his gay encounters, saying that Carwyn never practised his 'problem'. What is to be found here is an analysis of the evidence available and a definite conclusion as to where Carwyn was on this issue when his life was taken from him.

These seeming dualities, contradictions, confrontations, battles and foibles were all different roots that fed the tree of Carwyn's life, bringing creative energy from many different directions to that one same central core. They created a man who was a broadcaster, a literature lecturer, a rugby coach and a political candidate; a man who loved theatre, opera, cricket, and snooker; a man who spoke four languages, had a fine singing voice and was a chapel deacon.

And so to community. 'What virtue has a tree without its roots?' asks rural Welsh poet and farmer B T Hopkins, whose own roots reached deep into the same soil as that of Carwyn James' family. A more renowned Welsh poet, and one who was to be a big influence on Carwyn James' life, put it another way. 'The influence of community is the greatest on each and every one of us,' said Gwenallt, one of the twentieth century's leading Welsh-language poets.

Carwyn knew the two individuals who shared those observations. He had come across one on the Eisteddfod (a competitive arts festival held entirely in Welsh) circuit, while the other was a poet whose works Carwyn studied at school before becoming one of his students at Aberystwyth University. He also knew the geography of these sayings. He was familiar with the Ceredigion of B T Hopkins, he knew of the industrial Glamorgan that was Gwenallt's birthplace and he lived in the rural Carmarthenshire that Gwenallt longed for, as he wrestled with the strong but often conflicting cultural pull of the two landscapes. Carwyn would have understood that tension.

But on a deeper level, Carwyn was also familiar with the sentiment behind the words. He felt the force of the psycho-geography they emanated from. He was very much a man of his patch; a man who had a constant basic need to feel a connection with his square mile. A man who was lost if such a connection to place, or at least an awareness of such a connection, either wavered or disappeared completely.

In this respect, he had an affinity with another prominent Welshman: Dylan Thomas. Walford Davies, fellow citizen of the same Gwendraeth Valley as Carwyn and leading Dylan academic, hails the Bard of Cwmdonkin Drive as a poet of place and not time. He too needed territorial connections and losing them brought disarray, especially in behaviour. The relationship between the individual and the land his feet stand upon is clear in Dylan's life.

As unexpected as it is to bring Dylan Thomas into Carwyn's life story, Walford Davies argues his point about the bard with a left-field quote from novelist George Eliot:

'A human life, I think, should be well rooted in some spot of a native land, where it may get the love of tender kinship for the face of the earth, for the labours men go forth to, for the sounds and accents that haunt it, for whatever will give that early home a familiar unmistakeable difference amidst the future widening of knowledge: a spot where the definiteness of early memories may be inwrought with affection, and kindly acquaintance with all neighbours, even to the dogs and donkeys, may spread not by sentimental effort and reflection, but as a sweet habit of the blood... The best introduction to astronomy is to think of the nightly heavens as a little lot of stars belonging to one's own homestead.'

It would be natural to think that the 'spot of native land' is the earth where we first saw the light of this world, the place from which we start and which we strive to arrive at. Normally it is, but it doesn't have to be. And maybe this was the greatest duality of all for Carwyn. His human life was rooted in two distinct areas of his native land. He was born in Cefneithin, in the industrial part of the Gwendraeth Valley. His family, parents, brother and two sisters came from the remote rural village of Rhydlewis in Cardiganshire (present-day Ceredigion), further north and further west than Carwyn's birthplace. Carwyn was the only one not born there and he felt that tear. One offered substance, the other the hope of substance. One 'spot of native land' was one of blood, the other was one of soil.

Unlike the three named bards, Carwyn was no poet, nor an author like George Eliot. But he had the heart of a poet, as described by American poet and essayist Ocean Vuong:

Every time we remember, we create new neurons, which is why

memory is so unreliable. I thought, 'Well, if the Greek root for "poet" is "creator", then to remember is to create, and, therefore, to remember is to be a poet.' I thought it was so neat. Everyone's a poet, as long as they remember.

Carwyn, the man of words, remembered, remembered well and needed to remember. He had a heritage that his memory could and would draw deeply from. His heart beat to a rhythm that was in step with men of words – much more than it was in step with men of rugby, even.

He had a strong sense of place. He would always look for the familiar through every difference he would come across. He needed to feel the soil beneath his feet because that was for him a formative force, the very essence of who a person was. He needed the 'definiteness of early memories' to be a 'habit of the blood'.

Every territory he placed his feet upon from then on was always seen in relation to the primal patch. He was a man who let the places where he lived and worked influence his memories, his feelings and his thoughts. Another Welsh poet, Waldo Williams, said that his beloved Preseli hills were always there for him as a support for every independent judgment he made. Carwyn needed that same awareness.

A clear question arises from the relationship between Carwyn and his human habitat. It's a question that permeates this biography. If we come to a sense of who we are through the land that we are a part of, and this work argues that we do, what happens when the connection with that land changes, weakens, complicates, loses focus, or disappears?

The pull of land is not a uniform influence. The relationship between it and an individual changes as that person moves away from the nursery soil and life happens to him or her. Sometimes the roots are stretched so far it's impossible to feel their force and their certainty. One of Wales' most prominent contemporary poets, Alan Llwyd, summed this up in describing leaving home to go to university as *'ennill gradd a cholli gwreiddiau'* (gaining a degree but losing his roots).

In 1970, the year that Carwyn stood as a candidate in a General Election, Welsh philosopher J R Jones commented:

> There is more than one quiet revolution happening in the world of men's thoughts at the moment, and not least among them is the new understanding, which is slowly gathering momentum, of the importance of the need for roots. And at the core of such a need there is the need for a foothold – for soil under the separateness that gives you the right for recognition and respect.

Carwyn needed such a recognition in his own life. He came to feel a profound sense of separateness, accompanied by an aching need to be respected and accepted. People respond differently to a sense of distance from the familiar. As his life and times progressed, the land and the roots it carried shook more and more. It became a less and less firm foundation for him. Before the end, the connection between him and the soil under his feet was very fragile: the foothold was shifting. The relevance of this will become evident, but before seeing the shifts in the land, we need to see the land itself.

CHAPTER 1

Cefneithin's cradle

Dyneiddiaeth y pwll glo, duwioldeb y wlad.
'The humanity of the coal pit, the divinity of the countryside.'
Gwenallt, '*Sir Forgannwg a Sir Gaerfyrddin*'
(Glamorgan and Carmarthenshire)

ACCORDING TO A saying probably African in origin, but popularised in recent times by Hillary Clinton, it takes a village to raise a child. Carwyn was born into a village where that would have happened literally. At the height of his success in world rugby, having led the Lions to their first ever series win on New Zealand soil the year before, he wrote a series of articles for the *Western Mail*. The attention of the rugby world was very much on him, but he was always his own man and didn't write what was expected of him. His articles weren't to do with rugby, or how he achieved his successes. He didn't share his sporting philosophy or his principles of excellence. He shared reminiscences about his childhood. Success hadn't changed him.

He had occasionally kept notes for a future autobiography throughout his adult life. The notes have disappeared and the autobiography sadly never materialised. Reading what writing we have of his reminds us again of Dylan Thomas, as Carwyn's words resonate with the spirit of Thomas' prose in *Return Journey* and other similar stories of his.

I'm afraid to watch on my own lest I fall through the gap in the hedge, my hiding place, on to the playing field, and I don't like the stinging nettles. I plead with my father to stop working in the garden, to stop admiring the grunting pig and to take me to watch the 'beetball'. I hold his large, warm, collier's hand and I feel safe, and I watch the huge men throwing the ball around. I enjoy watching them and I think my father does too, perhaps only because his three-year-old son is so quiet. Their voices, coarse and primitive, frighten me.

4   WESTERN MAIL, MONDAY, JULY 24, 1972

PERSONAL COLUMN
Carwyn James

A NEIGHBOUR'S turn to kill a pig, and we shall have the bladder to play with and faggots for supper. I like the aftermath, I hate the killing, but like a feast day it is in the air and, hiding behind my brother, I am drawn by fear to peer round the corner, to see and not to see, and I despise Dai Y Morchwr for his sharp knife, his butcher's apron, his boiling water, and I despise him even more for not being afraid.

The greedy animal, fat and over-fed by a few score pounds, maintains a piercing high screech as he fights to the death. Now it is all over, he is as dead as the last one, and as he hangs from the ceiling dripping red blood, he suddenly twitches nervously and I run away.

DAFYDD Jones kneels and gropes for his favourite Godly idioms, slowly, falteringly, seeking help from the occasional lengthy neighing cough, and I want to help him because phrase ... and I have heard them all many times before. With my left hand on my face I open two fingers just slightly to peer at the slow moving finger on the large face of the clock made in Birmingham, and note with relief, as he hits second gear, that 10 minutes have gone.

Another five and a whole torrent of words, of bits of hymns and scripture, coughless and unpunctuated, will pour forth into a mad over-drive crescendo, and I shall wipe the sweat from my brow. I like Dafydd Jones, and I practise his Wednesday prayer on my own, in private. Tonight it is hard going, the sun is still hot outside, and above the buzzing of claustrophobic bees I can hear the thud of ball on bat, of bat on ball, and the occasional recognisable soprano appeal. As William Rees kneels I wonder if I will still get a knock before going home.

I ATTEND my first funeral, a large funeral of men only, and the singing is loud and I feel small and glad that my father is with me. I look around the gallery of dark suits, white collars and black ties, and count the blue and black

Carwyn James, coach to the victorious British Lions rugby team last year, is to be admitted to the Gorsedd's white robed order of druids of the National Eisteddfod in Haverfordwest next month.

A frequent broadcaster on Welsh topics, he is a lecturer at Trinity College, Carmarthen.

scars on the faces and on the huge hands holding the white pamphlets.

I feel sorry for John and David crying in the front row of the mourners, and when Mr. Jones, the minister, refers to the passing of a young man, I do not understand. I look at the pamphlet again and find that he was quite old. He was 36. We leave the chapel and stand outside, and I listen to two strangers.

"Great pity, full of silicosis, poor chap, and so young."

"Let's hope his wife gets compo."

"Ai, more than his mother did. Old Ianto was full of it too, but they said he died of a heart condition. A bloody heart condition. I ask you. And there are thousands like him."

"It's about time they did something about it."

As we walk home quietly I think of the "they" and do not understand, and then begin to count the thousands, and by the time I have reached 500 we are home and tea is ready and I forget the thousands. And I soon forget John and David's father . . . and mother.

I DO not like the sickly smell of new leather or the fumes and welcome the break at Carmarthen and Pont Henllan to change buses. The rounded hills, the wooded slopes and the animals in the field are a joy, and to arrive in Rhydlewis is like entering the promised land. I had looked forward to it so much, keeping awake at night as I did on Christmas Eve and on the eve of the Sunday school trip, and I had travelled hopefully on many occasions, but those nocturnal journeys were as nothing compared with the real experience.

And here I am in Moelon, a dairy farm, and everyone speaks nervously and quickly in my mother's Welsh and in Moelona's Welsh and I feel at home as if it were Nantoer, a family novel which my mother was so proud to read to us during the long winter nights before we had a radio because she knew the author. I rush out to meet the cows and the calves, pretend to look at the bull and ride on my uncle's tractor, and savour the prospect of a month's holiday in the heart of South Cardiganshire away from the coal dust and not to be homesick.

Before going to the Y.M. to play ping-pong and snooker and renew friendships made last year, I call on Dan Teilwr and Ianto Bass and they tell me yet again about my grandfather whom I had never seen, a carpenter, a real craftsman and master builder, so they claim, and they go into ecstasies over another forebear who apparently was a poet or, as I suspect, a versifier.

I feel I belong, that my roots are here, and I feel guilty that I am the only one of the family not born a Cardi. Tonight I am not just a small boy, but the Romantic who has found his Ynys Afallon away from the realities of life, the school, the dread of the ambulance and the siren.

MONDAY, JULY 24, 1972.

PEOPLE do not keep pigs anymore. The same phrases fill the vestry every Wednesday night. The miner's widow still suffers, despite years of medical research and the feeble excuses of Members of Parliament. And Rhydlewis has changed.

23

He starts with an account of this incident that happened when he was three years old, an early imprint on the mind of an impressionable child. The scene is the bottom of his garden, which backed on to the patch of land the Cefneithin men used at that time to play rugby. This was to prove a lasting influence.

I'm nine. A Saturday afternoon in late March and Cefneithin are at home to Trimsaran. My job is to recover the ball from the gardens. The gardens are neat and tidy, and I've had strict orders from Dat [what Carwyn called his dad] and the neighbours to tread gently and to avoid the onion beds during the match. The touchline which I guard is only a yard from the hedge protecting the gardens, so usually I'm kept busy. This afternoon is no exception as Trimsaran play to their forwards, and their halves kick a lot. Geraint, our fly half, is playing well, whilst on two occasions, running like a corkscrew, Haydn *Top y Tyle* (Top of the Hill) almost scores. He eventually does, and in my excitement I fall and I'm stung by the nettles. I swear under my breath as I get back on my perch just in time to see Iestyn converting from the touchline. The Trimsaran full back drops a lucky goal, but we win by five points to four. I dash on to the field to collect the balls and to pat the players on the back as they make their way to the school to bath in the small tubs. I accept my threepenny bit from Dai Lewis, the ironmonger, who is the club secretary, and I look forward to spending it later in Eunice's fish-and-chip shop, which is opposite the Public Hall.

Iestyn James, one of my heroes, is out practising his place-kicking. I can hear the thud of the ball on the hard ground, I join him. He is a tall man with fair, wavy hair and freckles, and for the occasion, he wears large, brown shoes and has a kick like a mule. Standing behind the goalposts, miles from Iestyn, I try to catch the ball before it bounces and then I use all my strength to kick it back to him. I'm pleased when he says that one day I shall play for Cefen [Cefneithin].

These words echo a contribution he made to the first ever Welsh-language sports book of its kind, *Crysau Cochion*, (Red Shirts) published in 1958. In his chapter in that book, he says:

I heard my parents tell the story of losing me one Saturday afternoon – a shy lump of a three year old who wouldn't normally dare to wander out of sight of his house. They found me, following many anxious hours of looking, hiding quietly and peeping at the play on the park that was at the end of our garden.

A child's stone's throw away from the house in which he was born is the village school. His family's address was Heol (or Hewl, in the local dialect) yr Ysgol – School Road.

I go to school early in the morning. Vivi, Gwyn and Llyn are already there and we play soccer with a small, soft ball on the hard playground. The smallest and youngest, I play with Cliff because he is bigger and older, but we lose. I loathe playtime. I have to drink milk, which I hate, so I stuff my mouth with chocolate biscuits before gulping the cold milk down. I feel sick. I lose most of my break and most of the game and I'm very angry. I sulk in the lesson: refuse to listen to Miss Jones, Standard Two, who in her anger raps me on the knuckles.

The coarse and primitive voices of the rugby players and the anger of Miss Jones obviously left an impression on young Carwyn. His was evidently an active childhood, an outdoor one, full of fresh air.

Every evening after school, we play on our road, Hewl yr Ysgol. Two brothers versus two brothers: Meirion, the eldest and I, the youngest, against our brothers, Dewi and Euros. We play touch rugby but, as always, touch becomes tackle. We quarrel: Meirion fights Euros, and I kick Dewi on the shins, before bolting to hide in the *cwtch-dan-stâr* (cupboard under the stairs). In the afternoon we play again, and sometimes I can beat them with a side-step. I believe I'm Haydn *Top y Tyle* or Bleddyn. I love these games, but especially I love playing cricket on the road, for the ball somehow grips better on the road and I can bowl Peter round his legs. I think I'm Doug Wright and occasionally I'm Johnny Clay, but although I bowl better when I'm Doug Wright, I support Glamorgan and a photo of the team hangs in my bedroom.

On the shoulders of giants

The reference to Haydn *Top y Tyle* is significant. He, along with another Cefneithin man, Lloyd Morgan, were big influences on Carwyn throughout his childhood. The two men lived next door to each other in Heol y Dre in the village – or Heol y Baw (Dirt Road), as it's called locally.

Haydn was the star of the rugby team, the talented outside half who was admired by his fellow players and the young boys alike. Like Carwyn, all the other boys believed they were Haydn when they were at the heights of their flights of fancy, speeding through the long grass of the park. Carwyn reached the age when an important village rite of passage was bestowed on him: he was chosen to carry Haydn's rugby boots on match days. It was an honour not lost on the young Carwyn. Through this one simple, innocent task, Carwyn was established into the warp and weft of Cefneithin rugby club and into the deeper weave of Welsh rugby culture.

The Second World War arrived, and along with many Cefneithin men, Haydn had to leave the village to fight for the cause. He joined the Navy and was posted on the HMS *Hood*, the largest vessel in the Navy at the time. In May 1941, the ship was destroyed. It had been ordered to pursue two German warships out in the Atlantic: the *Bismarck* and the *Prinz Eugen*. HMS *Hood* was hit by German missiles and sank in three minutes, with 1,400 men on board. Only three managed to escape alive, and Haydn *Top y Tyle* wasn't one of them. The village and the surrounding area were rocked by this tragedy. They had lost a true star.

The other influence on Carwyn, Lloyd Morgan, was a collier who had gone to work underground at 14 years of age. Around the same time that Haydn lost his life, Lloyd came up from underground for the very last time and was given the label 'hundred percenter'. That was no comment on his ability or work ethic, but recognition that the 'niwmo' (pneumoconiosis) that had blighted hundreds of miners had taken a 100% grip on Lloyd and it was no longer possible for him to work in the pit. He was 30 years old.

Carwyn would have seen quite a lot of Lloyd when he was growing up in Cefneithin. Lloyd was the man who would go from house to house collecting betting slips for the local bookie, and was known as Lloyd *y Bwci* (the Bookie). Michael James, Carwyn's father, liked a bet and Lloyd would call for his slips weekly.

Lloyd's sister lived in the same village. She had six children and when a new council estate was built in Cefneithin, she moved there, to Heol y Parc. Her home backed on to the park, directly opposite where Carwyn's home backed on to it. Colliers lived in 21 of the 24 houses in Heol y Parc. When Iestyn James' words came true and Carwyn did play for Cefneithin, one of Lloyd's sister's six children was given the honour of being boot-carrier to Carwyn James. He was Barry John.

Barry John begins his autobiography, *The Barry John Story*, by saying that he regretted the fact that his Uncle Lloyd didn't live long enough to see his nephew play for Wales. When Lloyd died, the entire village went to the funeral. That says a great deal about Lloyd Morgan. Such a sight would not be seen again in Cefneithin until Carwyn's death.

According to Llyr James, Carwyn's nephew, Haydn and Lloyd were two large presences in his uncle's life and Carwyn would speak of them often and admiringly. The lives of Haydn and Lloyd tell us a lot about the life of the village they were a part of. The two men embodied the values and the life patterns that formed Cefneithin.

A killing and some plays

There were many threads to such a pattern. One of those was an immediate link to the natural world, one that meant they experienced nature red in tooth and claw. Where coal was king, there was no hiding from the fragility of life, as an ambulance siren would often remind them. But even in an industrial world, the natural world was never far away in Cefneithin. In most houses, it was at the bottom of the garden.

Today it is our neighbours Rhys and Menna's turn to kill the pig, so their uncle JP is there, fretful and fussy, to cast a critical eye on the operation. Soon we shall have the bladder to play rugby, and faggots for supper. I hate the killing. Hiding behind my brother, I'm drawn by fear to peep round his legs, fearful, even while eager to see. How I despise Wil *y Mochwr* (the Pig Man) for his sharp knife, his scraper which I shall hear and feel for a long time to come, perhaps forever. I despise him even more for his not being afraid. The fat creature, overfed by a few score pounds, maintains a piercing, high-pitched screech as he fights for life. His hind legs hang from the ceiling in a vanquished V formation, his warm, red blood drips on the cold, stone floor. It is all over, he is dead as the last one. Suddenly, in defiance of death, he twitches and I run away.

Another entry says more about his love of cricket and shows his awareness of the shadows that lurked under the surface of Cefneithin life.

Cricket on the road and I'm batting. The ball runs down the hill from an immaculate Emrys Davies drive over the bowler's head. An ambulance, the one vehicle feared by a miner's son, turns the corner and is coming towards us. We step on to the pavement. I can feel the uneasy silence. The dreaded ambulance comes slowly up the slope, over the pitch and the three stones, our wickets, and, at least, passes my home. In relief, I hit the next ball wildly on the leg side into Ffynnon Cawr's hayfield, and I'm out.

The boys mentioned are farm boys from the Ffynon Cawr farm, backing on to Heol yr Ysgol. The connections in those early days were with boys of the land, not the colliers' boys who would have been far more numerous in Cefneithin. Meirion and Euros were the only two boys whose fathers didn't work underground. They were also older than Carwyn, as was his brother Dewi. He chose to play soccer in school with Cliff as he said, because he was bigger and older.

Rugby, school and street play were only three sets on the Cefneithin stage. Other cultural influences came into his life too.

> In Standard Five my favourite afternoon is Friday, an afternoon of drama, music and games. I like drama except when the teacher asks me to do something on my own in front of the class. I feel proud that our teacher, Mr Evans (we call him Gwyn Shop behind his back because his parents run the combined Post Office and shop opposite the school), writes plays and is a drama producer. He also helps Cecil James, a fine local musician, to produce the opera, and once I was invited to take part in Smetana's *The Bartered Bride*. I thus prefer the Welfare Hall to the Cinema, and I often go with my mother to the Hall to see the plays of Dan Mathews, Edna Bonnell, Gwynne D Evans and Emlyn Williams, and on one memorable occasion, I even went to see Lewis Casson and Sybil Thorndike.

The Welfare Hall was the official name of an important building in Carwyn's life. Locally however, it was always referred to as Neuadd y Cross (Cross Hall) In writing the history of the Hall, Lyn T Jones says that the occupations of the Hall's founding members reflect the nature of the changing community at the time: two doctors, a shopkeeper, a colliery manager, a furniture maker, two checkweighmen, a stone mason and seven colliers.

After the hall opened in 1932, it soon became a busy focal point for the area. Before that, plays and various shows were popular social events staged in primary schools, but when the Hall opened, the appeal of theatre broadened significantly. As his words show, Carwyn was caught up in this at an early age.

Another Cefneithin resident, Nan Lewis, has written about the influence of the Hall.

Cross Hands Hall's 1932 Art Deco facade, preserved to this day
Alun Gibbard

> We would go to Neuadd y Cross to see every drama. Apart from the
> local drama company, other companies would come to visit us in
> turn – Dan Matthews' Company from Pontarddulais, Ivor Thomas'
> Company from Pont Henry and Edna Bonnell's Company from
> Llanelli. We didn't watch a drama; we lived it, disappearing into
> oblivion from our own little world.

In this context, local playwright Gwynne D Evans, a former
teacher of Carwyn's, refers to one aspect of Carwyn's life that is
not so well known, and one which was not developed.

> I remember him writing a play based on the romantic story of
> Llyn y Fan. I saw it performed and I believed that it showed great
> promise. But I failed miserably to persuade him to persevere. The
> desire to write hadn't gone completely though, and not too long
> ago, we agreed to work together to write a play from the point of
> view of the players, not the spectators. Following much discussion,
> we produced a promising outline, but because of how busy he was,
> that was it. And now...

Not long after his childhood recollections appeared in
the *Western Mail*, Carwyn was the guest on a BBC Wales

programme called *Holi Hynt* (Questioning Progress). In that programme he elaborates on the influence of Gwynne D Evans mentioned in those recollections. Carwyn refers to his former teacher as the 'Sean O'Casey of Wales', who was always aware of his own heritage as part of the bigger picture of cultural heritage outside Wales.

An excerpt from one of Gwynne D Evans' recorded-for-television plays was shown on the programme. *Angladd i Bawb* (Funeral for Everyone) won a BBC drama competition in 1972. One of the actors in it would also have been familiar to Carwyn. Ernest Evans was a Cefneithin man who would go on to be a regular favourite in Welsh-language soap *Pobol y Cwm*. He was the nephew of W J Jones, Carwyn's primary school headmaster, who had won a cap for Wales. WJ was the man who started the move that led to the famous Ernie Finch try for Llanelli against the 1924 All Blacks, 'The Invincibles', as they were called. WJ was a hooker for Llanelli, and Ernie Finch played on the wing for the same club.

In the Welsh-language collection of tributes and reminiscences about Carwyn, published within a year of his death, called *Carwyn: Un o 'Fois y Pentre'*, (One of the 'Boys from the Village') WJ himself recalls the rugby links between the two.

> Occasionally, Carwyn would introduce me as the man who'd taught him to play rugby. That was a little private joke of course, as both of us knew that I didn't do such a thing. It is true that I did try to introduce some of the basics of the game to the boys in the school on a Friday afternoon and I remember Dewi as being a slippery little runner, but his brother was too young and small to make any mark amongst the giants of Standard 7. Gwendraeth School was the outside half factory, and by the time Carwyn went there, he had at least seen proper rugby, and I will take some of the credit for that.

Carwyn's square mile was both sporting and cultural. His love of theatre was cemented early in his childhood days. He would know the names of rugby stars and classical singing stars equally well and would treat them both the same. Carwyn, under the influence of his father particularly, immersed himself in the musical heritage of Cefneithin life.

Mr Jones, the Schoolmaster, is strict and we have to develop a liking for the Modulator because he likes the Modulator. We touch the notes gently to 'lah' as we race up and down the ladder, and then, at the command of his ruler, we leap dangerously from 'doh' to 'sol' to 'doh' and leap down again. WJ is enjoying himself, already seeing in us members of the Choral Society singing 'Worthy' or 'Man is born of woman', but the boys are just hanging on, holding on, producing half-hearted inaudible treble notes in case he detects a wrong one. How we pray that we are not made to sing on our own, and long for the afternoon break, for the games lesson is to follow. The Modulator, even, grows on one and I have it in the Band of Hope on Tuesdays as well. I have to practise sol-ffa at home, for Dat, who sings for the village Male Voice, communicates in *sol-ffa* with the confident air of a man conversing in his mother tongue, and insists that I read the tenor line to harmonise with his bass. I enjoy listening to the Male Voice, and often on a Saturday night I lend my support at an Eisteddfod, feeling so proud when I watch my father, Lloyd Low, WJ and the demonstrative conductor, Tom Asa Williams, the barber, singing 'Comrades in Arms'. How eagerly I long for them to win, which they usually do.

Gwynne D Evans is an all-round sportsman, while W J Jones played for Llanelli and had one cap for Wales as a hooker. I love the games lessons, particularly when we play rugby, for like WJ I also want to play for Wales.

Shadows

But aspiration and ambition were tempered by matters of more eternal significance, even for a little boy.

I attend my first funeral, a large funeral composed of men only. Consequently, the singing is loud, incredibly loud even for a chapel, and I feel small, glad that my father is with me. I look around the gallery of dark suits, white collars and black ties and I'm compelled to count the blue and black scars on the faces and on the large hands holding the white pamphlets. I count Dat's as well.

I feel sorry for John, Mair, and David crying in the front row of the mourners, but when the Reverend LLywelyn Jones refers to the passing of a young man, I don't understand, for I look at the pamphlets again and find that he was quite old. He was 36. We leave the chapel and stand outside and while my father lights his Woodbine. I listen to the two miners I had never seen before.

'Pity, full of silicosis, poor chap, and so young.'

'Let's hope his wife gets Compo.'

'Aye, more than his mother did. Old Ianto was full of it too, but they said he died of a heart condition. A bloody heart condition, I ask you. And there are hundreds like him.'

'It's about time THEY did something about it'.

As we walk home quietly, I wonder who 'They' are, and since Dat won't tell me I don't understand, and so I start counting them by the hundreds. By the time I have reached fifty we are home, tea is ready, and I forget the hundreds. And I soon forget John and Mair and David's father… and mother. I'm no better than 'They'. Perhaps Dat won't get silicosis.

Thoughts of immortality directed Carwyn to the transcendent, which would have been an integral part of the Welsh village culture that Carwyn was brought up in. This is seen clearly in his recollection of a weekly ritual he shared with the man who lived in number 1, Heol yr Ysgol.

Dafydd Morris next door, with whom I go to the prayer meetings in Tabernacl, kneels and his mind gropes for his favourite godly idioms, slowly, falteringly, seeking delay from the occasional lengthy neighing cough. I feel nervous and want to help him as phrase leads to phrase, for I have heard them all so many times before. With my left hand over my face, I open two fingers slightly enough to peer at the slow, moving finger on the large face of the clock – made in Birmingham – and note with relief, as Dafydd hits second gear, that ten minutes have gone.

Another five, and the whole torrent composed of bits of hymns and scriptures, but coughless and unpunctured, will pour forth in a mad overdrive crescendo, and as he ends I shall wipe the sweat from my brow. I like Dafydd Morris, and I practise his Wednesday prayer on my own in private. Tonight, in the Chapel vestry, the going is hard: the sun is still hot outside, and above the buzzing of claustrophobic bees I can hear the thud of ball on bat, of bat on ball, and the occasional recognisable soprano appeal. As in turn Thomas Evans kneels, I wonder if I shall have a knock before going home.

Dafydd Morris family owned the house that Carwyn was born in. The old man held some sort of spell over Carwyn. Not only did he go to the prayer meeting with his elderly neighbour, but Carwyn also visited his house regularly. The two, man and boy, would sit together listening to the morning service on the radio. One of Carwyn's sisters, Eilonwy, remembered her younger brother disappearing next door. On the BBC documentary made two years after Carwyn's death, she says,

> When he was a little older, he would leave the other children and he wouldn't say where he was going. But it was to the prayer meeting that he went.

Later in life, friends and family expressed no surprise at all that the young Carwyn would disappear to go to a prayer meeting. Carwyn, they say, would do what he wanted to do anyway, regardless of his friends' reaction. He was accepted as a full member of Tabernacl Chapel in 1946, while he was still at school. By 1955 he was a deacon and the correspondence secretary, a responsibility he held for nearly a quarter of a century. According to Eifion Lewis, son of Tabernacl minister Morley Lewis:

> It was obvious from his body language during a service that Carwyn enjoyed listening to the proclamation of the Word and that he was keen to learn more of Christ and His Kingdom. He would lean forward when listening, resting his chin on his hand, and after

the service he was keen to discuss points raised in the sermon. He would often refer to sermons he had heard in the past and every preacher received words of appreciation from him.

Carwyn was occasionally aware of the times in which he lived, as much as the place. It's no surprise that a world war triggered such temporal thoughts.

I'm ten and in Standard Four. The war is on, we have gas masks in cardboard boxes, air-raid shelters in the gardens and a talented Dad's Army in the village of which my father, trained as a marksman on rabbits in Cardiganshire, is a devoted member. I read Rockfist Rogan, RAF, in the *Adventure*. Suddenly, in the middle of sums, at eleven o'clock exactly, the hooters of Cross Hands, Blaenhirwaun and Tumble collieries combine like massed brass bands at the National to sound the alarm, and at the sharp command of Miss Rachel Ann Jones we dive dutifully under our desks, so we miss all the fun.

For a German bomber, flying very low, is driven by a Spitfire towards the sea at Cefn Sidan. The Germans panic and drop their bombs over Gwendraeth Grammar School, just off-target, fortunately, so no one is hurt. That night, as I listen to my friend Aeron, an eyewitness, bragging about what he had seen, I'm consumed with envy, feeling cheated of a memorable experience, of witnessing with my own eyes the skill of a Rockfist Rogan finding his prey, a real German bomber to the kill. To be a pilot, a fighter pilot, is now my only ambition. Goering is the enemy, God is on our side (the Minister told us so yesterday) and we dutifully hang 'our washing on the Siegfried Line' every Monday. I don't sleep well, for I plunge bomber after bomber into the sea at Cefn Sidan. How I long for the war to last until I'm old enough to join the RAF.

The Gwendraeth Valley saw its World War action on the morning of Thursday 10 June 1940. Grammar School pupils recall it was towards the end of the third lesson. The sound of aeroplanes and machine-gun fire was heard in the skies above the rolling pastures. Carwyn and his friends might well have been ordered to hide under their desks, but Gwendraeth Grammar School boys didn't all run to hide. Those who ran into the open air to see what was going on saw three Spitfire planes attack a German Heinkel III bomber. Occasional bursts of gunfire were followed by empty cartridge cases falling from the sky, which eager schoolchildren collected as mementos.

Bombs also fell on this quiet and remote part of West Wales, as Carwyn rightly recalls. Seven bombs in total fell in his locality, as the Heinkel III released its bombs in order to lighten its load, enabling a quicker getaway from the Spitfires. He succeeded in doing so, and Carwyn vividly remembered this fragment of history experienced by Cefneithin.

This happened before Haydn *Top y Tyle* was killed on HMS *Hood*. We have no account of how that wartime tragedy affected Carwyn's Standard Four RAF ambitions. He was however, to enlist in the Navy himself in the years between his ambitions to be Rockfist Rogan and writing the story for the *Western Mail*.

Carwyn's early world then, is one of fresh air, rugby, theatre and God telling them that He's on their side. A world of cricket and funerals, Miss Jones and Dafydd Morris, Haydn *Top y Tyle*, Lloyd *y Bwci*, Gwynne D Evans and W J Jones. And it was the world of a shy boy, who needed to feel safe and to feel the warmth of his father's hand when rugby players were shouting. He looks back over the shoulder of 1972 with fond, warm, vivid memories, but not through rose-tinted spectacles. He hadn't forgotten the shadows that crossed his skies, just as those menacing wartime planes had done in his Gwendraeth days.

CHAPTER 2

Rhydlewis over the rainbow

I am what time, circumstance, history, have made of me,
certainly; but I am also much more than that. So are we all.

James Baldwin

BUT IN ORDER to understand Carwyn fully, we need to get to
know a community in which Carwyn never lived, yet one which
was always a part of his living perception wherever he lay his
head at night. His childhood recollections also take us to this
place, that haven somewhere over the rainbow; the place of
hope and eternal, unfulfilled longing. He writes of Rhydlewis, a
small rural village tucked away in a forgotten fold of Ceredigion.
He would be sent there every school holiday when he was at
secondary school, for many reasons. His mother, for one, was
insistent that her boys would not work in a coal mine in any
capacity and sending them away for the summer would mean
that they would not be tempted, like other boys their age, to
work the school holidays in the pit. There was also a deeper
reason, relating to the irresistible pull of ancestry, history and
roots.

> I hate the sickly smell composed of new leather and the fumes of
> the Western Welsh bus, so welcome the break at Carmarthenshire
> and Pont Henllan to change buses. The rounded hills, the wooded
> slopes and the placid, leisurely animals in the field are a joy, and
> to arrive in Rhydlewis, a little village in south Cardiganshire where
> my mother was born, is like entering the promised land. I always
> look forward to it so much, keeping awake at night as I used to

on Christmas Eve and on the eve of the Sunday School trip, but
those nocturnal journeys on which I travelled so hopefully were as
nothing compared with the real experience.

It's impossible to understand Carwyn James without
understanding Rhydlewis. That's where his family came from
before moving to the Gwendraeth Valley. It was, and still is, a
traditional rural Welsh village. It lies on the banks of the River
Ceri, which joins the Teifi at the end of its journey. One glimpse
of *Atlas Hanesyddol Ceredigion* (Ceredigion Historical Atlas)
shows that Rhydlewis took its place alongside a plethora of
similar communities throughout the county which depended
on small cottage or traditional craft industries for their life
blood. Just that one small community would have flourmills,
lime kilns, sawmill, wood turner, clockmaker, hide worker,
candlemaker, coracler, hat maker, brickworks, stone quarries,
ironworks, saltworks, printer, bookbinder and more than one
blacksmith. Local workers and craftsmen stayed at home, and

A former Rhydlewis blacksmith's forge
Alun Gibbard

stayed close to their roots. They knew to whom they belonged. Grandfathers and great-great-grandfathers weren't strangers.

These craftsmen, the small industrialists, were responsible for their own clock. The saying that the Welsh don't have a word that conveys the urgency of the Spanish *mañana* was nowhere more true than in Rhydlewis. They have two post boxes in the village, one bearing the insignia of Victoria, the other that of George – the passing of time doesn't seem to have much effect. The rhythm of life was governed by grass and milk and not much else. The milk would feed every Rhydlewis generation and also be sent to feed those in foreign parts.

At the centre of village life was an old ramshackle, favourite uncle of a corrugated red tin building which sold all provision needed for life. It's still there, even if the supplies available have depleted substantially. It keeps an eye on all those who go left and right, as it has always done. It watched Carwyn's ancestors and it still watches over his family members who still live in the village.

Conflicting interpretations of village life

For such a small, out-of-the-way village, which wasn't even visited by the great railroad revolution, it has inspired two prominent works of literature. Carwyn referred to one in his childhood recollection: the novel *Teulu Bach Nantoer* (Nantoer's Little Family) by Moelona. Elizabeth Owen, as she was christened, took the name Moelona from Moelon, the family farm on which she was born. Published in 1912, her book became the most popular children's novel in the Welsh language and still holds on to that title. In spirit, it's related to Enid Blyton and the *Little House on the Prairie*.

> Here I am in Moelon, a dairy farm, where everyone speaks nervously and quickly in my mother's Welsh and in Moelona's Welsh, so I feel at home as if it were *Nantoer*, a family novel which my mother was so proud to read to us during the long winter's nights, before we had a radio, because she knew the author.

I rush out to meet the cows and the calves, pretend to look at the bull because I'm afraid of him, ride on my Uncle Tom's tractor, and savour the prospect of a month's holiday in the heart of south Cardiganshire away from the coal dust and the black pyramids of waste. I finally decide not to be homesick.

The other book, equally well known in its circle, couldn't be more different. Caradoc Evans' *My People: Stories of the Peasantry of West Wales*, stirred strong critical, judgmental emotions as he exposed the dark side of the Welsh chapel village life he experienced growing up in Rhydlewis. There's no reference to Caradoc Evans' work in Carwyn's recollections. Evans and Moelona were contemporaries, but they didn't see the place in the same way.

The characters in both novels are the flesh and blood that moved through Rhydlewis in the first dozen years of the twentieth century. They were the people who worked those cottage industries as well as the minister, the shopkeeper and the tailor. But primarily the tales and observations put down on paper came from the family experiences of both authors. Both families were friends and neighbours of Carwyn's family, going back a long way. This is how Moelona describes the Nantoer of the title:

Bwthyn bach to gwellt oedd Nantoer, fel y rhan fwyaf o dai bychan yr ardal honno. Nid oedd ond dwy ystafell ar y llawr a math o daflod uwchben. Llawr pridd oedd iddo, wedi'i wneud yn galed a gloywddu gan fynych gerdded arno. Ceid ambell i lech yma a thraw tua chyfeiriad y tân. Isel oedd y muriau a bychain y ffenestri, ond oddi fewn ac o gylch y tŷ, roedd popeth yn lân a threfnus odiaeth.

'Nantoer was a small thatched cottage, like most of the small houses in the area. There were but two rooms on the ground and some kind of loft above. It had an earthen floor, hardened and shiny black from the constant walking on it. There was an occasional slate here and there near the fireplace. The ceilings were low and the windows small, but inside and around the house, everything was most clean and tidy.'

Moelona, *Teulu Bach Nantoer*

40

Moelona presented her stories of clean and tidy life to the Eisteddfod in Wrexham in 1912 and the work was published the following year. The cottage of the title, in her time, was situated near the Nantoer stream, on the slopes overlooking the village itself. As a young girl, Moelona would have been familiar with this building, passing it regularly on country walks with her parents. For Moelona, fictional life was milk and honey.

Not only would Carwyn's mother read the novel to him, but the family would gather round the radio to listen to Moelona's work being broadcast. Childhood friend and neighbour Grant Peregrine remembers one such occasion. He recalls Carwyn enthusing about listening to someone from Rhydlewis on the radio. In May 1937, one of Moelona's stories, *Y Lleian Lwyd* (The Grey Nun) was adapted for *Awr y Plant* (Children's Hour) on the BBC.

Caradoc Evans' world on the other hand, was devoid of any milk or honey. It was a world of wormwood. It was social criticism at its most raw. His was a world of incest, death and suffering, usually within the same family. He highlighted what he saw as the hypocrisy of chapel life and how it had a corrupting influence on people's lives. Its publication in 1915 created a storm. The *Western Mail* referred to the book when it came out as 'the literature of the sewer'. Evans was accused of bringing clouds of disrepute down on his own people.

> Nanni's income was three shillings and ninepence a week. That sum was allowed her by Abel Shones, the officer for Poor Relief, who each pay-day never forgot to remind the crooked, wrinkled, toothless old woman how much she owed to him and God.
>
> 'If it was not for me, little Nanni,' Abel was in the habit of telling her, 'you would be in the House of the Poor long ago.'
>
> At that remark Nanni would shiver and tremble.
>
> Caradoc Evans, *My People: Stories of the Peasantry of West Wales*

Moelona and Caradog were born in the same year. They

went to the same school, under headmaster John Newton Crowther. He was an Englishman who had learned Welsh and a prominent member of the James' family chapel in Rhydlewis, Hawen. But it was Moelona, and not Caradog, who was chosen by him to be the pupil teacher of the school, even though both tried for the position. Because her mother had died in 1890, she couldn't fulfil her ambition of going to university as she was needed at home to care for her father. She stayed at the Rhydlewis School until she gained a teacher's certificate. Caradog left school at 13 to work in a draper's shop in Carmarthen, before moving on to become a journalist on the *Daily Mirror*.

The work of the two Rhydlewis residents is relevant to Carwyn's life story because of the picture their works paint of the Rhydlewis life that Carwyn's forefathers would have lived. When both novels were being published, Carwyn's parents were settling into a new life together in the village. Between the publication dates of the two novels, they had married, set up home and had their first child. The first three years of Carwyn's parents' married life happened between the covers of two seminal Welsh publications.

Carwyn's family would collect their daily provisions from the red corrugated tin shop on the square, and make their way to Pendre, their detached home on the outskirts of the village, towards Llangrannog. They would pass the tailor's shop, Moelon Farm, a mill and the blacksmith's. On their walk to the chapel, in the other direction, they would have walked past the public house too, but only until the early 1920s. The Gwernant Arms closed its doors for good following a petition gathered by the minister, the Reverend John Green. He was a zealous teetotaller and he collected enough names to close the Gwernant. Today it's a private residence, and no other pub has opened in the village since then.

The family tree

Michael James came to Rhydlewis from the neighbouring village of Beulah, arriving to work on the farms. His wife-to-be, Annie Davies, was a member of a long-established Rhydlewis family. The way the two met is part of the ebb and flow of Rhydlewis life at that time, and for generations before that. Individuals would up sticks to look for work when times were hard. Having found work, they would then also find love.

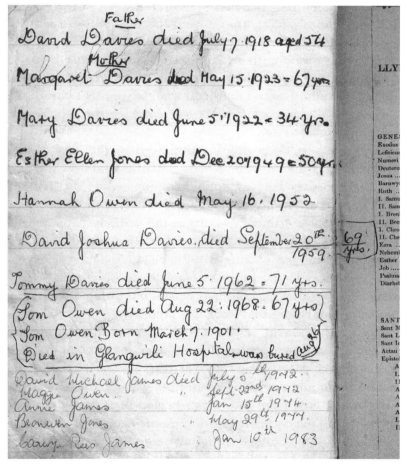

Carwyn's family Bible

Way back in time, Annie's family came from Llanarth in the same county. David Davies and his wife Elinor had settled in Rhydlewis in the early part of the nineteenth century. Their first child, Thomas, was born there in 1836 in the family home Bronallt, near Hawen chapel. He became a cooper, making barrels and the metal bands needed for the wheels of the carts or the gambo. Thomas married another Annie from the village and they had a son in 1864 called David. But everyone knew the man that was Carwyn's grandfather as Dafi'r Saer (Davey the Carpenter). Dafi married Margaret, also from the village, and they had two sons, Tommy and Joe, also both carpenters, and a daughter, Annie – Carwyn's mother.

Carwyn's grandmother Margaret's family had also come to the village from somewhere else within the county. As the one side of the family moved to Rhydlewis from another part of the county, so Margaret's ancestors were making the same move from somewhere else.

Margaret's story begins in Brongwyn in the Teifi Valley. Thomas Rees and Elizabeth Rees left their home village to live in Rhydlewis. He had secured employment at the Brithdir Mill, one of two in Rhydlewis. They had two sons, Rees Arthur and David. Rees Arthur was born in 1837, and he became well known as a poet under his bardic name, Rhys Dyfed. He was a regular and successful competitor at eisteddfodau. At 29 years of age, he was in the process of collecting his poems with a view to publishing his collected works, but an illness took his life from him before that work was complete.

His brother, David, stayed in Rhydlewis throughout his life. He too became a carpenter. He was born in 1824 and married a village girl, Mary Evans. In 1880 he built a home for the two of them and named it Pendre. As was the custom at the time, many men from the village helped in the building, but David did all the carpentry work himself. Their new home was a detached stone cottage in its own land, on the outskirts of Rhydlewis. The front door was in the middle of the front of the house, with two rooms either side of it. There were two bedrooms upstairs. Traces of David Rees' handiwork can be seen in the house today, where a part of one interior wall has been left bare, exposing some wooden beams and stone.

David and Mary Rees had a daughter, Margaret, and throughout her life, she was known as Margaret Rees Pendre. This carpenter's daughter married another carpenter: David Davies. They moved to a cottage on the other side of the village called Llain, which has now changed its name to Bronwylfa. It was in this home that they had their first child, a daughter whom they named Annie.

It's into the life of this Annie that a young man from nearby Beulah walked. Michael was looking for farm work. He fell in love with Annie and they set up home together back in Annie's birthplace, Pendre, built by her grandfather. Annie's grandmother, Mary, died in 1912, making it possible for Annie and her husband to move into her old home. Michael and Annie had their first child there: Gwen, born in 1914. Eilonwy was born there in 1918 and their first son, Dewi, was born there in 1927. The three children would have had a thoroughly Welsh upbringing, in terms of language, culture and way of life generally. The parents were chapel people who participated in the social and cultural events of their community.

Formative forces and tensions

One particular building in the village would have been an important social gathering place for the Jameses, as for every other villager: Dan's tailoring shop, known locally as *Siop Dan Teiliwr*. Amongst the rows and strips of folded fabric and the apparatus for making suits and curtains, the men of the village would gather to put the world in its place. The burning issues of the day – political, religious and so much more – would be discussed for hours. Michael James would take his rightful place in this forum of local democracy. In the evenings, the younger men and women of the village would go there to be taught how to recite.

Dan Teiliwr's shop

Poetry and prose were high on the debating agenda in Dan's shop. Many of the men there were poets, and many others competed in eisteddfodau. The tradition that had nurtured Moelona and Caradoc Evans hadn't disappeared. A regular visitor was the most influential Welsh-language children's author of the last century, T Llew Jones, who, like many others, would walk over from a neighbouring village to be part of the discussions. Such occasions would have been rich pickings for a man who would become such a prolific children's author.

It was in this small tailor's shop that the genealogy of all involved would be kept alive and handed on, because knowing to whom you belonged was as important as life itself. On those long, sunny school holidays in Rhydlewis, the young Carwyn would be one of the little boys winding through the legs of the adult men as they talked, and as he did so, he would have subconsciously taken in snatches of Welsh folk culture. He had an awareness, if an incomplete one, of his own literary connections.

> Before going to William Thomas' YM [YMCA] to play ping-pong and snooker and renew friendships made over the years with Terwyn Maesyfelin, Dai Dolanog, Albie and others, I call on Dan Teiliwr and Ianto Bach, still busily making suits, who tell me yet again about my grandfather – whom I had never seen – a carpenter, a real craftsman and master builder, so they claim. Later they go into ecstasies over another forebear who apparently was a poet, or, I suspect, a versifier.

The YMCA was a wooden hut, just up the road from the corrugated tin shop. It had been transported there during the First World War, when many carpenters in the village, Carwyn's relatives amongst them, travelled to Pembrokeshire to rescue the unwanted shed and bring it back over the border to Cardiganshire. The friend Carwyn mentions, Dai Dolanog, still lives in the village, and in the house that gave him his nickname.

> Carwyn and Dewi would come to us every summer holidays when they were in their teenage years. They were here from the day after school finished until the day before it started again. The two were part of our lives as village boys. We would do everything together. But we never played rugby in the village mind, never. Football was our game and Carwyn could take his place in whichever team he was chosen for. Other than that, we would play cricket in the field near the river, behind Dan Teiliwr's shop.

Other roots are still to be found in Rhydlewis soil. The house built by Carwyn's grandfather, Pendre, is now owned by Dai Rees Davies, the son of Carwyn's mother's brother. It has been in the family since it was built. Dai remembers his cousin Carwyn visiting in those summer days, and staying in many different houses on such visits.

When he came and stayed on the Moelon farm, he would be staying with his aunt, Maggie, his mother's sister. She was farming there then. He would love being on the farm, contrary to what we might expect, maybe. Maggie then moved to a small cottage, Ffynnon Wen (White Fountain), across the road from Pendre. He would also stay with her in Tŷ'r Capel, (the Chapel House) when she moved there. If (for whatever reason) there was no room to stay with Maggie, he would stay in Melin Brithdir, which was still a working mill then.

Every summer, throughout Cardiganshire, a Summer Football League was held. Many teams from throughout the county would compete for a prestigious Cup. Carwyn played for the Rhydlewis team in these competitions.

Carwyn's Rhydlewis was a land of milk and honey. A promised land that resonated with the life Moelona describes in her children's novel and that Carwyn would have heard about as a child before going to stay there during summer holidays. There wasn't one black sheep grazing in the fields of his memory and his family wouldn't know of such an animal. Rhydlewis was a constant, emotional presence for Carwyn. When he was there, he would insist that he would not be homesick for Cefneithin.

In his childhood recollections, we get a clear picture of Carwyn James. His aspirations, interests and fears, family habits and village rituals. It might well have been rugby that catapulted him to worldwide renown, but he was very conscious that things could have been so different.

I have been one of the most fervent supporters of Cefneithin ever, and my debt of gratitude to the club is immense. My roots are in Cardiganshire: that's where my sisters and brother were born, but the family moved to Cefneithin about two years before I was born. It's a worry for me to consider how much interest I would actually have in rugby if I had been born and brought up in Rhydlewis, Cardiganshire.

Later in his life, we hear a similar message:

> My father left the farm and came to work as a miner in the
> Gwendraeth Valley, and so, like Dai Hughes and later Barry John
> – like most of the boys living in the village – I was doomed to play
> rugby.

It's evident that Carwyn the adult would reflect regularly
on how different his life would have been if his family had
stayed in Cardiganshire. A man with an acute sense of fate sees
that he was doomed to play rugby. Another excerpt from his
recollections gives us another word that reflects the feelings of
this young boy, looking two ways at once.

> I know I belong, that my roots are here, and I feel guilty that I am
> the only one of the family not born a Cardi, not born in Rhydlewis.
> Tonight, I am not just a small boy, but the Romantic who has
> found his *Ynys Afallon* (Avalon) far away from the realities of life,
> the school, the black pyramids, the dread of the ambulance, and
> the disturbing siren.

He doesn't feel sorry that he wasn't born in Rhydlewis, he
feels guilty. A man with the heart of a Romantic, a man of
poetry and prose, feels the guilt and sees his Avalon at the same
time.

CHAPTER 3

When coal was landlord

The fellowship of the chapel and the charm of the choir, the fun of the pub and the fury of the fighting places; and the brotherhood of the coal face melting everything else, creating a warm neighbourhood despite the dust and the mist. The day and night danger of the pit, the massacre of the explosion, uniting people together, with strike and Union weaving through everything. Truly, the life of the valley had its own charm.

James Griffiths MP, first Secretary of State for Wales

SO MUCH HAD happened to Carwyn James before the second day of November 1929, when he first saw the world. The James' guilty youngest was born in the family home in the Gwendraeth Valley: Rose Villa, 2 Heol yr Ysgol, Cefneithin. Michael, Annie and their children Gwen, Eilonwy, and Dewi had moved from Rhydlewis to Cefneithin when Dewi was a baby. They set up a new home that was two different worlds within four walls.

It might well have been the saccharine Rhydlewis of Moelona's work that tugged at Carwyn's heart strings and brought the family round the radio, but it was the harsh realities of Caradoc Evans' Rhydlewis that drove the Jameses out of their square mile. It was nirvana only in retrospect and aspiration.

In reality, Caradoc Evans' and Moelona's family lives were very similar, even if that didn't transfer to the page. The farm that Moelona took her writing name from, Moelon – the farm where Carwyn stayed on his summer holidays – wasn't her family home for long. Her father ran into financial difficulties and had to leave the farm. Her parents suffered heartaches and hardships. On one tragic day, one of their children died as they were burying another.

Caradoc Evans' father made a living from collecting the debts owed by the poor of the village. He was the enforcer who would visit to take furniture away from those who couldn't pay with money. Ironically, after he died, his widow and son lived in abject poverty, necessitating Caradog's departure for the drapery world of Carmarthen at 13 years old.

Both families were living victims of a far greater trend, as were the Jameses. Day-to-day life in the first two decades of the last century was not comfortable in Cardiganshire. It was a time of increasing economic hardship throughout the county, as agriculture hit very hard times. The county's economy was changing. The wool industry was not thriving and the county became increasingly focused on other areas of agriculture, flooding that particular sector with new labour. Then, after the First World War, many larger estates were sold off, triggering an increase in the number of small landowners. It was farming at a time of depression and life was tough.

The county was changing in other ways too. Statistics might not bleed, but they can show a picture that suggests that people suffered considerably. This is true of censuses relating to Cardiganshire between 1851 and 1921. They show a decline in the county's population of 18.5%. That's a considerable drop, which reflects both the scale of the exodus, the situation that led to it and the impact on those left behind. The first ever drop in the number of those speaking Welsh was also seen in the 1921 census. In that census and the next, ten years later, the number didn't drop below 80%, but such change as was seen showed that the county and its way of life were changing. Despite the Twenties being the decade in which Plaid Cymru was formed, and despite the strength in numbers of the language and the dominance of its culture in the county, Plaid Cymru didn't field one candidate in the county in those early years.

People were leaving the county in increasing numbers, looking for work. Not better work, just work. Not just one, but all three core trades in Cardiganshire were affected – sea trade, lead mining and agriculture. The movement of people in and out over county borders was seen as a threat to the traditional way of life, as much as it changed the economy. Insecurity made its first appearance, threatening the core value of 'this is how it's always been'. One published article shows that a significant source of such insecurity was the motorbike. Using this mode of transport, young men and women could travel to meet partners in faraway communities at the other end of the county, and even, God forbid, in other counties, thus fragmenting the familiar.

Change was happening and it wasn't good change. It was something that Michael and Annie James had to respond to. Around the fire at Pendre, they discussed the harsh reality that blights married couples to this day. How should they respond to the lack of work coming Michael's way? He was one of five brothers. Each one had had to leave the family community to look for work – one having to go as far as Australia. Many of his contemporaries had left their supposed rural idyll to find work in the dark dust of the Rhondda. Finding work that paid enough to keep things together normally meant leaving the county.

One option was available to the Jameses that seemed to be viable, and at the same time only across the county border in Carmarthenshire. This was a county that experienced the polar opposites of what was happening to its neighbours in Cardiganshire on one side and Glamorganshire in the other. One was in decline. The other, which contained the world-changing Rhondda Valleys, experienced a rapid boom. Carmarthenshire experienced both within its boundaries, and as such serves as a microcosm for what was happening in pre-war South Wales. There was coal in Carmarthenshire too – the county next door was the western periphery of the South Wales Coalfield. Annie and Michael decided that it was worth a try.

Michael made his way to the anthracite coalfield of Cross Hands in east Carmarthenshire. He secured work in the New Cross Hands Colliery and through the effective network of chapel life, he sorted a room for himself in a house four doors down from Tabernacl Chapel, Cefneithin. He stepped out from the wide-open expanse of Cardiganshire countryside to take his place shoulder to shoulder with coal miners in the darkness underground. He stayed in his new surroundings during the week, returning to his wife and children at weekends – that was the rhythm of life for a good few years in the 1920s. In so doing, Michael James typified the socio-cultural trend of the time. It was the men who were on the move, leaving women and children behind, even though they were well-provided for. Historian Russell Davies sums up this move:

> This process created an imbalance in the distribution of men and women across Carmarthenshire.

New Cross Hands Colliery
Aerofilms Ltd

The South Wales Coalfield was the best in the world, they said. The coal was really good, and so were the working conditions. Michael walked from a changing world into a world which was also changing, but for completely different reasons. When Michael arrived in the new county, less than half of its population lived in agricultural parishes. In 1871 that figure would have been three-quarters of the county's population. Times were changing. If there were quiet periods at the pit with not much work, Michael could return to the fields of Rhydlewis and use his former skills, knowing full well that when things picked up, he could return to the coalface, secure that his job was waiting for him.

Even through the hardships of the 1920s, a decade which saw a depression in industrial areas of Britain and a General Strike, as well as a little-known but significant strike in the anthracite coalfield of Cross Hands in 1925, Michael succeeded in securing plenty of work. It says a great deal that despite the economic hardships that coal and heavy industry saw in the 1920s, they offered Michael and his family better prospects than agriculture in Cardiganshire at that time.

The year after the General Strike of 1926, there was another new step for the James family. Michael decided that travelling back and forth from the Gwendraeth Valley to Cardiganshire was too much, as was living in one room, away from his family. They decided to move permanently. In 1927, Michael, Annie, Gwen, Eilonwy and Dewi moved to Cefneithin. Michael was now a coal miner and nothing else. They brought with them a caseful of influences and traditions that Carwyn would spend his lifetime unpacking. Five individuals who had been moulded by Cardiganshire values moved to Cefneithin, and lived out these values and traditions in the Gwendraeth Valley. Into such a world, Carwyn was born.

But as much as he was born into a world of growing industrial prosperity, it wasn't all paradise. In his work *Secret Sins: Sex, Violence and Society in Carmarthenshire 1870–1920*,

Russell Davies quotes the findings of the Minister of Health's report on Carmarthenshire in the 1920s:

> The diet lacks a sufficient proportion of protein, mineral salt
> and vitamins… The inevitable sequel of the prolongation of such
> conditions must be deterioration of physique… and the prevalence
> of rickets which we have mentioned is, in our opinion, the first
> manifestation of such a condition.

Such comments must be taken into consideration when assessing Carwyn's later life.

The name of the Jameses' new home in Cefneithin was a plaque on a brick wall which showed they were in a different world. There were no Rose Villas in Rhydlewis. The name of their home was an indication of a shift towards the respectability and status that English offered the native Welsh. The same was true of Christian names. Gwen, Eilonwy and Dewi moved into the world of Bernard, Derrick, Brian and David. Robert Rhys, from Swansea University's Welsh Department, notes these names as those of prominent Welsh-language poets and authors, born in the same cauldron of Welsh culture as Carwyn, but given names that would be alien to Welsh-language culture.

That wasn't true of Carwyn, of course. Michael and Annie were brought close to a family from a neighbouring village through tragic circumstances. Dewi, Carwyn's brother, contracted diphtheria, as did the son of the Reverend Berian James, the minister of a chapel in nearby Penygroes village. Dewi survived his illness, but the minister's son didn't. When Carwyn was born, he was given the name of the minister's dead son, which as fate would have it, meant he inherited both his Christian name and his surname.

As Carwyn was born while Dewi was still suffering from diphtheria, the eldest James child, Gwen, who was 15 years older than Carwyn, was given the task of looking after her newborn brother while his parents tended to the son who needed constant care. From early days therefore, Carwyn experienced maternal care from two women. Not long after, Eilonwy, 11 years Carwyn's senior, would also do her share of caring for her brother. Little wonder that the family often said that Carwyn had three mothers.

Cwm Gwendraeth

The epicentre of the Gwendraeth Valley is Llangyndeyrn Mountain, where the granite rock tears through the fertile pastures of the common land, separating the coal from the soil of agriculture. It's an area as rich in history, myth and legend as it is in grazing pasture and black diamonds. Village names honour men of God from the sixth-century Age of Welsh Saints, such as Cyndeyrn (Saint Mungo) in Llangyndeyrn, at the foot of the mountain of the same name. Llanddarog is named after one of the men who worked for tenth-century king and lawmaker Hywel Dda (Hywel the Good). Indigenous military leaders who resisted invading Normans and English, such as Rhys ap Gruffydd, and immigrant landowners who settled large estates in the area, such as Baron Cawdor, shaped both the architecture and the landscape of the Gwendraeth. Kidwelly stands in tribute to one of only two women in Celtic history who led revolts against invading armies. Boudica made her stand against the Romans; Gwenllian faced the Normans in a battle near Kidwelly castle. Her army was heavily defeated and she was beheaded.

The Gwendraeth Valley gets its name from two rivers called the Gwendraeth, the *Fawr* (Large) and the *Fach* (Little). Both have their source near Llyn Llech Owain (The Lake of Owain's Stone), in the hills immediately above where Carwyn was born. Llyn Llech Owain is a nature reserve today, but it gets its name from the neglectfulness of Owain Lawgoch (Owain of the Red Hand), a man who led an army of French mercenaries against the English. On his return from France, he regularly took his horses and soldiers to a well in the hills above where Cefneithin sits today. One day, however, he fell asleep and forgot to put the stone back on top of the well. According to the legend, the well overflowed and created the lake that's there to this day.

From their shared beginnings, the two rivers make their individual ways to the sea, where Kidwelly lies. The Gwendraeth Valley is therefore actually a combination of two smaller river valleys: the little and the large. As with the rivers and the valleys, so too with the way of life. The Gwendraeth Fach is very similar to rural Rhydlewis but the Gwendraeth Fawr is far more industrial, and that's where Cefneithin lies.

But this isn't a duality that has led to any tension or schism. There is a strong spirit of co-operation between the two Gwendraeth Valleys; a social cohesion and a strong sense of knowing what belonging to the valley means, and of who doesn't belong to it.

Within this unity lies the diversity created by two such different areas coming together under one identity, creating a whole greater than the sum of its two parts. Carwyn's father entered a Gwendraeth that was rapidly changing as life in the communities around the Gwendraeth Fawr faced the industrialisation of labour and culture.

Author Bernard Evans, a friend of Carwyn's, gives us a clear picture of such a life in the two novels he wrote based on life in the Gwendraeth Valley, *Glaw Tyfiant* (Irrigating Rain) and *Y Meini'n Siarad* (The Stones Speak), both published after Carwyn's death. This paragraph from *Glaw Tyfiant* captures the spirit of the community in which they both grew up.

Dau grwt sy yno'n eistedd ar ben wal yn yr heulwen. Maen nhw'n ddigon ifanc, yn ddigon heini, i fedru eistedd ar ben y wal er ei bod hi'n uchel. Y tu ôl iddynt, mae'r fynwent lle mae 'Er serchus gof am...' yn glos, glos, at 'Er cof annwyl am'... Mae sodlau'r ddau'n taro'n ysgafn ar gerrig y wal, a'r tu ôl iddynt, mae gorffennol y pentre yn gorwedd boch wrth foch, ystlys wrth ystlys, morddwyd wrth forddwyd, a'r tip glo'n gwgu ar yr heulwen sy'n gwenu'n llawen oddi ar 'ymdrechaist ymdrech deg'.

'Two lads sit there, on top of the wall in the sunshine. They're young enough, fit enough, to be able to sit there, even though the wall is very high. Behind them, the graveyard where "In fond memory" lies very close to "In loving remembrance"… The heels of the two boys lightly kick against the stones of the wall, and behind them lies the village past, cheek to cheek, flank to flank, thigh to thigh; and the coal tips frown at the sun, which in turn smiles happily on "you have fought a good fight".'

Carwyn would have rejoiced in the heritage of his hinterland. It would have been shared with him through primary and secondary education, in conversation with the unschooled but educated older residents of Cefneithin, informing his view of Wales and the Welsh.

But through every change and challenge, the spirit of place – the spirit of what it was to be a Gwendraeth native – was dominant. This one valley made from two is replete with dualities. It was, and is, a spirit moulded by farm and pit, by a culture formed from soil and coal, one drawing from the other. It was a simple life, where poverty meant slicing bread transparently thin, making balls from anthracite ash mixed with clay and water to supplement the coal, and the staple Welsh cake – flatbread, fat, sugar and dried fruit baked on a griddle – a daily presence.

This was the safe world that Carwyn was born into. The unique world that Carwyn experienced in a formative, first-hand way, being the only one of the children born in that village. Two old Welsh ways of living came together on Rose Villa's hearth and lay together in unity. It was Carwyn's first and foremost actual safe place.

Michael James' Gwendraeth

The face of industry changed in the Gwendraeth in the 1920s. Cross Hands was the centre of the valley's industry, right next to Cefneithin. The area soon gained the name 'Land of Pyramids', because of the pyramid-shaped slag heaps that punctuated the skyline. They shaped the backdrop of

Carwyn's upbringing, and one in particular were an obvious presence in his life. Behind the posts on the pitch where the men played rugby, loomed one such large black pyramid. In one television programme, Carwyn is seen walking across the pitch, cigarette in hand, then resting against the rugby posts, with the pyramid behind him. If we freeze-frame on this image, there could not be a better image of the world that shaped Carwyn's early years.

The landscape couldn't be more different today. One road sign offers a link between the Cross Hands of old and the village as it is today. The main road through the retail park is Heol Stanllyd, and it leads to Leekes department store, having passed McDonalds. Stanllyd is a tribute to the New Cross Hands Colliery – it was one of the seven veins of coal worked at the colliery, which opened in 1869 and stood on the site where Leekes is today. In the early decades of the last century, a new drift mine was opened side by side with the parent deep mine. It's to the New Cross Hands that Michael came from the fields of Cardiganshire, to become one of 850 men who worked there. Both pits dominated an area and a life far greater than the footprint they made.

The Cross was only one pit amongst many in that area. When Michael James first arrived there, 4000 miners would have worked in pits such as the Emlyn, Blaenhirwaun, Mynydd Mawr, Dynnant, Gwaith Bach, Glyn Hebog, Capel Ifan, Carway, Pont Henri and Trimsaran, in the furthest reaches of the South Wales Coalfield. It's easy today to forget their presence and their influence, as they lived under the shadow of better-known pits further east.

Most Cefneithin men would walk to their work. One of the village's children, Nan Lewis, remembers the daily pattern.

It's almost as if we children believed that every man in the world was a coal miner, every village had a hooter and every day was split into shifts. We would hear the morning shift – hear the noise of the hobnailed boots dragging across the road while it was still dark.

We would see the afternoon shift – see the unrecognisable men coming home, coughing, up the hill. They would come home in clusters, with one or two stopping on the way to pull on a cigarette, while others would bend over as they drew breath. Each one had his food box and his tea bottle in his pocket, and a block of wood, to light the fire, under his arm. These were the men of the works, and these were our fathers.

This was the heartbeat of the community into which Carwyn was born. The late Reverend Gareth Davies started his working life underground, and his father was a collier in the Cross.

In the coalfield, you could tell the time without any watch or clock. The hooters would mark the passage of time three times a day – the morning shift, the afternoon and the night – and of course, they announced the end of every shift. The only exception would be when there was an accident in the pit. At some time on the morning of 18 February 1928, the Cross hooter sounded, and it was to our house that the sad news was brought. My father had been killed. Following the Great Strike of 1926, there were many periods of unemployment in the pits and that was the case in February 1928. Those officers who had responsibility for safety had to go into work, in order to keep the pit in working order, ready for the return to work. That morning there was a fall, and my father was caught under it. There weren't enough men around to save him.

Michael James and his family were already in Cefneithin in February 1928. Only a few months before Gareth Davies' father's accident, they had come to a world that offered new hope. Such a tragedy in the pit where Michael worked, so soon after he arrived there, would be a reminder that hope could be very fragile. Little wonder that Annie James swore she would never send her two boys underground – and she kept her oath, with Dewi going on to be a bank manager and Carwyn to excel in many fields far away from the coalfield. That's why both were sent to Rhydlewis every summer, in case they followed the other Cefneithin boys to the coalmine for summer holiday work. One of Carwyn's heroes, the previously-mentioned Gwenallt, was also sent from his family home in the industrial Swansea Valley to stay with relatives in farming Carmarthenshire. They had mothers of the same spirit.

Michael was 30 years old when he started work as a coal miner. His new work circumstances couldn't have been more different from his previous experience in the fields of Rhydlewis. When Michael arrived there, the miners' union officer in that area was Jim Griffiths, who became an MP and then the first Secretary of State for Wales. One of the *cryts* (lads) who didn't avoid working underground in his teenage years was Peter Rees. He is the oldest-living former Scarlets rugby player, having won his first cap for Wales in 1947.

> My father told me regularly, 'If you don't work hard in school, it'll be moleskin trousers for you!' That was the constant threat and it was a real one. I was at Gwendraeth Grammar School at the time, but I had no interest in schoolwork at all. My only interests were chasing a rugby ball and chasing girls! I didn't listen to my father, and at 14 years old, I started to work underground, wearing those hard-wearing, rough moleskin trousers.
>
> Before long, I worked alongside Michael James, as one of the *cryts* helping him. I would gather the coal that he had dug out of the face, so that it could be put in the drams and taken to the surface. Michael was a quiet man, who was kind to each one of us boys.

As the Gwendraeth area changed, with the arrival of heavy industry and other incomers to work in it, there was an obvious impact on the language of the area. Like Rhydlewis, it was naturally a predominantly Welsh-speaking area. In the case of people like the Jameses, inward migration was no threat to the Welsh language. But many came who didn't speak Welsh. In *A Study in Nationality*, published in 1911, J Vyrnwy Morgan refers to this linguistic shift. The process identified by him intensified as the First World War years gave way to the 1920s and 1930s.

> It's true to say that there are more people speaking Welsh today than in any other previous era. But it is equally true to say that more Welsh speakers now speak English as well, which is a far more important consideration.

That would have been something completely new for Michael and Annie, and their two eldest daughters too. Gwen moved to the Gwendraeth Valley when she was 13, and Eilonwy was 11. Their new home gave them another language to contend with, another way of looking at the world. Interestingly, this also had an effect on the Welsh that they spoke. Its rhythm and cadences were those of Cardiganshire Welsh, which intensified when they moved to Cefneithin. They sought to hold on to a certain purity of Welsh, as they perceived it, when many around them were losing theirs.

Carwyn's Gwendraeth

Cefneithin didn't look like what would be considered a typical mining village when the Jameses arrived, and it still doesn't today. It's far too stretched out for that, with very few rows of the terraced houses that shape the mining village stereotype in our minds. There were occasional terraced houses, but more common was the row of a few houses here and there, separated by a field or two, a cluster of buildings on the square, a school, a park, only one chapel, some detached houses, all alongside the one road that was the village artery. For such a small village, it sustained eight shops. There was a farm, some streets beginning to make their way from the main road, but at both ends of the village, a definite end. Like Rhydlewis, it had no pub.

There were two shops on Heol yr Ysgol, including Siop Morris on the corner of High Street, a few yards away from Carwyn's house. It was a shop that sold a little bit of everything, but it was also the social gathering point for Cefneithin people, as the shop of Dan Teiliwr was in Rhydlewis. But the focus in the Cefneithin shop was more pastime than culture. In the passage on the way in there was a dartboard, and in the shop itself, a small table in the corner where the men of the village played cards, Michael James included. Around this table, the conversation would turn to things that had happened at the pit and the burning issues of the day for coal miners – the hardships, the incidents, the strikes – and the comments made by the chapel minister from the pulpit the previous Sunday. Commerce, not culture, was the heartbeat of the social cauldron of Cefneithin life amongst the counters, jars and bottles of Siop Morris, and that's what the children would hear as they ran in and out of the shop to buy their sweets.

Across the road, the cobbler's shop stood. But unlike many other Welsh villages, this particular cobbler's wasn't the social hub of the village as he certainly wasn't open all hours. This cobbler's main delight was to play the violin, and he played in many an orchestra, including the one that played in Swansea's Grand Theatre.

Next door and attached to the cobbler's was the ironmonger's, and then next door up again, Siop John. This John made his living mainly from selling chicken feed and food for other animals, and he also had a delivery service and a petrol pump outside his shop. John also owned many houses in the village, renting them to colliers who came to the area in search of work. And naturally, his tenants made up a significant proportion of his customers as well.

Bread for the village was baked across the road, in Siop Get. A little further down the road, the Swithybank shop was a sign of expanding commerce in the Western edge of the South Wales coalfield. The Swithybanks were a family who had moved into the area 'from away', and they opened a small chain of local shops in their new community, having shops in Ammanford and Capel Hendre as well. And then a mile or so outside the village, in neighbouring Gorslas, stood the Co-op. Once a week, an army of Cefneithin housewives would be seen marching back from the Co-op with bulging shopping bags swaying by their sides. Maybe Cefneithin had as many shops as Rhydlewis did, but the Cefneithin eight reflected and shaped a significantly different society.

Michael James rented a new home for his family, but not from John the Shop. The owner of his new Rose Villa home lived next door to him in number 1, Heol yr Ysgol. The father of the family had died in 1920, when his son Eifion was only eight months old. At the end of the Second World War, Eifion married Nancy Williams and she moved into her new husband's family home. She remembers:

> They were very tough times on Eifion's mum. When her husband died, she faced many hardships, but the rent from Rose Villa helped a lot. When Michael arrived next door, her father [Dafydd Morris, who Carwyn went to prayer meetings with] and three of her brothers lived in number 1 as well, so there was a houseful of neighbours to welcome the Jameses.

Eifion's uncles all worked in the coal mine and Carwyn's male neighbours along the street were all colliers too. In number 5 lived Grant Peregrine and his family. Grant remembers:

> Carwyn and I were back and forth in each other's houses all the time. His dad Michael used to call on us regularly as well. My dad worked the night shift, and after he came home in the mornings, Michael would pop in to find out what had happened in the pit during the night. He wanted to know what the men had been talking about and if anything had happened during the shift. He was in our house for a chat before the rest of us had breakfast!

There was a houseful at the Peregrines' as well. Every bedroom was occupied, with more than one sharing them; family members needing board and lodging while they worked on the coal. In order to make room for everyone, while maintaining the sanctity of the Welsh parlour under lock and key, the living-at-home hours for the Peregrines, as for the Jameses too, happened in one specific cosy room. Grant continues:

The living room was the shed in the garden, right opposite the back door. There was a Rayburn in there and a large table, which is where we would eat our food. The Jameses had the same in number 2 and many other houses in Hewl yr Ysgol as well. It was a very warm and comfortable place.

He also explains that he and Carwyn shared a favourite pastime.

There weren't many rabbits in our area, because of the coal mines, I'm sure. So what we did then was shoot crows. We both loved that. We would go round to each other's gardens and shoot the birds when they landed on the shed roof, or the roof of the house sometimes, too.

When Carwyn was one of the older boys in the primary school, he would receive a special request every Christmas. Grant Peregrine says that the Postmistress would only ever ask Carwyn to help deliver the Christmas mail. One of Carwyn's teachers in that primary school, Gwynne D Evans, was the son of the Postmistress and remembers the impression this little boy made on the village.

As there was only one house and the school between my home in the Post Office and Carwyn's in Rose Villa, I could probably say that I knew Carwyn from when he was a little child. But the first time I paid particular attention to him was when my mother mentioned a little boy who would do the shopping for the elderly and the sick in the village, with every item put to memory and every account correct to the halfpenny.

This continued until Carwyn was older as well. My mother would always try to help students get some cash during the holidays. Carwyn took his turn behind the counter of the Post Office, and he soon realised that it was so much more than a space for Post Office business. It was, under my mother's jurisdiction, the unofficial citizen's advice bureau for the village and beyond. I heard her say more than once how surprised she was that such a young boy as Carwyn was at the time could win the trust of other people so quickly and so completely. He was always ready to listen and offer advice, but politely and without giving the impression that he was being nosy. Wasn't it that ability to engender empathy that was the secret of his success as a coach? By the time of the 1971 tour to New Zealand, he had perfected that art.

Such was the cradle of Carwyn's upbringing: an industrial yet rural village where the fresh smells of farming and the taste of coal dust dominated daily living. It was a village of bustling new commerce and an emerging middle class; hymns and prayers formed the soundtrack to every village activity; centuries-old established cultural forms filled their free time, as well as the new cultural forms of the day where the hard-earned pennies of coal could be spent. The boy Carwyn settled into this life, taking his active place in the life of its people as well as on its streets and fields.

CHAPTER 4

Yellow socks and Miss Dora

The sacrifices demanded of the parents of the late Twenties
and early Thirties so that their children could have a
secondary education were really intolerable.

Wynford Davies, *Gwendraeth Commemorative
Volume 1925–1975*

WHEN IT CAME to schooling, Michael and Annie James were
keen for their eldest boy Dewi to fall under influences similar
to those he would have felt in Rhydlewis, had the family not
moved from there. When he was 11 years of age, therefore,
he was sent to the secondary school in Llandeilo, not the
Gwendraeth School in his own valley, where coalminers'
children went. Llandeilo was far more rural in spirit. That's
where the farm boys would go.

Dewi was two when the Jameses left Cardiganshire, and
would not have had any schooling in Rhydlewis before the
family left. It might therefore seem strange that his parents
wanted to maintain a Rhydlewis influence that was seemingly
so tenuous. But he had tasted a certain way of life in those
first couple of years which would then have been nurtured to a
certain degree in the mixed atmosphere of farming and mining
Cefneithin, and so his parents wanted it sustained even further
throughout his secondary school days.

Carwyn's brother travelled to Llandeilo with other boys
from Cefneithin whose parents had made the same decision,
on a bus run by local company LCW – the initials of the owner,
a Mr Williams. But to the boys who used it, the letters stood

for Llandeilo Cattle Wagon! If the bus broke down, or if Mr Williams needed to take boys who had missed it to the school later in the morning, he would use another of his vehicles: a hearse.

The same considerations weren't pressing on Michael and Annie when it was time for Carwyn to go to the Big School. He was sent to the one down the road: Gwendraeth. In the book published to commemorate the fiftieth anniversary of the school, Carwyn refers to the choice available to him at 11.

> Like everyone else in Cefneithin, I had a choice between Llandeilo or Gwendraeth. Despite the fact that Dewi my brother was already at Llandeilo, the choice for me was easy and painless.

Carwyn doesn't elaborate on why the choice was so simple for him. The one life-changing event that happened between Dewi going to secondary school in 1938 and Carwyn doing the same in 1941 was the outbreak of World War II. It might well be that Annie James wanted her youngest closer to home at such troubled times. There's certainly no reason to suggest that the two brothers didn't get along and wanted to be in separate schools. Carwyn's account of his childhood memories and their relationship through adult life suggest the opposite.

By the time he put on his Gwendraeth school uniform, his two older sisters had left home. Gwen and Eilonwy were both in their twenties by then and home life was considerably different to the one they had enjoyed when they first settled in Carmarthenshire. Now, as the guns of World War II sounded across Europe, the family in Rose Villa was only father, mother and two secondary-school boys.

When Carwyn walked through the gates of Gwendraeth School for the first time, he trod on soil central to the development of the Gwendraeth Valley in the last century. The deep-seated need to open a new school in the Gwendraeth Valley first surfaced as the guns of the previous World War were falling silent. At that time, in the village of Drefach, Cwm

Mawr House stood in splendid elegance behind railings and trees. Its imposing presence in such a small West Wales village bred myths and legends. Carwyn would not have been aware that those gates he first walked through were called the White Gates in Drefach, because of the firm belief that ghosts lived in the house. Someone had even seen the Devil himself fall down the chimney of Cwm Mawr House.

Carwyn had been in the school earlier that year, in order to sit the entrance exam. He passed with flying colours. On his first day proper, he said that he was ready for a ducking in a washbasin of cold water from the older boys. It was, after all, the accepted initiation – and one to be privately proud of, despite any insecure fears. But what actually troubled him was a surprise.

> My worry was the socks I had to wear. A mother of a friend of mine, so chuffed that her little Gwyn had passed his scholarship, worked diligently through the summer to knit two pairs of socks: yellow socks with navy blue tops. In those days of short trousers, the socks would reach up to the knees, so they were prominent enough. How embarrassing! …If I had had to venture to the Gwendraeth as naked as the day I was born, I wouldn't have felt more uncomfortable! It was as if two Man U fans (although the colours would be different) had ventured into the Spurs camp, and every one of [the boys at school] in their turn made some comment about how pretty the wool, the knitting and the wearer was. Talk about drawing attention to yourself!
>
> My dear mum was as endearing as ever when I got home at the end of that first day, but she had an unexpected, abrupt, curt reply to her question, 'How did it go then?': 'No more of those bloody socks for me!'

The fact that Carwyn felt he needed to resort to swearing in front of his mother was an indication of his unease. That didn't happen often.

Carwyn didn't have to worry too much about his uniform throughout his school days. In those days of rationing, while short boys didn't have too many problems, the choice for taller boys was more limited and they would receive clothes vouchers. PE teacher Gwynfil Rees was the master in charge of measuring the boys to see if they were eligible for extra vouchers because of their height. He wouldn't ever have had to measure Carwyn for this reason.

In this relatively new secondary school, the old Cwm Mawr House was the focal point of the school. When Carwyn started there, it was called the Gwendraeth Valley Secondary School. In 1946 it changed to Gwendraeth Grammar School. On the lips of the people of the valley, however, it was referred to as Cwm Mawr School for years.

Educationally, it was a pioneering school, and had been from the day it opened. First headmaster Llywelyn Williams was a trailblazer. When establishing the curriculum for this new place of learning, he adopted a controversial educational plan that had originated in the United States: the Dalton Plan. In the school's commemorative volume, former pupil D Leslie Williams remembers that plan.

> Forms, except for registration purposes, were abolished; timetables were abolished; even lessons were abolished – which is where the plan came in. On the first Monday of every month every pupil was issued with a work-programme in every subject; they were called 'assignments', and had to be completed by the last Friday of the month... It was the pupil's choice which subjects he proposed to study at any particular time; and it was to that subject room he would go, where the teacher would be at his desk to give individual help. 'Individual Attention' – that was the psychological basis of the Plan, plus free access to the subject library, which was always left open for use.

Llywelyn Williams was still the headmaster when Carwyn started at Gwendraeth. The active implementation of the plan had ceased by 1941, but its driving force and many of its central principles were still active and influential.

In 1941 in the Gwendraeth, then, there was no fear of the new. It was a time when parents in this coal community had to sacrifice so much to give their children a secondary education, thus giving the young ones opportunities they themselves could only dream of.

Carwyn placed his writing pen, his pencil, his ruler and his clean blotting paper on the Gwendraeth desks. Over the following seven years, he absorbed everything that came his way and, of course, contributed so much to school life himself. This immersion in all that Gwendraeth stood for included an acute awareness of the role the school played in the life of the wider community and the symbiotic relationship between the two. These were shared values that he put down on paper.

> I would think that the Gwendraeth School reflected the local coal-mining community, one which had a huge respect for the value of education. It's a warm, close-knit community, where everyone knows everyone. It's friendly, everyone greets everyone else and nearly everyone is prepared to wear their hearts on their sleeve. There was no snobbery of any sort, and every person knew their size. If such a feeling was not inherent in someone, then they would soon be told.

Carwyn started at the school when the world was at war, but that wouldn't have been much of a day-to-day reality in his particular corner of Wales. He might well have remembered hiding from the Germans under his school desk, but reminders of a world at war would have been few and far between for Carwyn and his schoolmates.

There was however, one incident that changed the pattern of Gwendraeth School life. In 1941, the Germans bombed Swansea in three days of relentless blitz. Many were killed and the town was flattened. One consequence of this carnage was that Swansea children were then sent out of the area for their education. Many were sent to the relative calm of rural West Wales, and Swansea High School pupils were sent to the Gwendraeth Valley.

The order of the school day was changed to accommodate the new visitors. Gwendraeth pupils would start school earlier in the day and finish earlier, and then Swansea pupils would start their school day. After an initial period of following this plan, it was decided to educate the pupils of both schools together. The Carwyn of split-level rural and industrial Gwendraeth also came into contact with pupils from faraway urban Swansea.

One of Carwyn's fellow pupils was John Meurig Thomas, the now-knighted eminent chemistry scholar, a world leader in his field. He recalls a homely, happy school environment, with only one or two aloof teachers. He remembers Carwyn's contribution to the school:

> When it was school Eisteddfod time, Carwyn was right there in the middle of everything; leading the victorious recitation party, disciplining the most melodious choir or assisting the teachers in the leading of events. I can see and hear him to this day singing songs such as '*I Blas Gogerddan*' and '*Yr Aderyn Pur*', or reciting from *Samson Agonistes*.

When Carwyn cast his mind back to the same days, he remembers the cultural activities more than anything. But he does so in a far more unassuming way than his friend John Meurig Thomas.

> I'll never forget the Eisteddfods. I was in the Red house team, under the influence of some of the older children at first, but then accepting the responsibility for continuing the tradition. I was given the opportunity to take part in public speaking events in the Urdd (The Welsh League of Youth) meetings, to perform a drama or two and to sing in a choir... And I had the opportunity to broadcast for the first time as well. Tysul Jones (one of the teachers from Swansea who had come to the Gwendraeth) took four of us to the studio in Carmarthen to record an interviewing competition, with Hywel Davies presenting.

The teacher in charge of the pupils who moved from war-torn Swansea to the relative pastoral peace of the Gwendraeth Valley was Tysul Jones. This is how he remembers the same occasion that Carwyn recalled:

> I remember a request for four boys to take part in an Interviewing Competition in the Studio. I remember the names of two of the four I took – two from Gwendraeth and two from Swansea. Two became quite prominent in Welsh life: Carwyn James and Urien William [who went on to become a leading academic and author]. Was it Gwendraeth School that gave them the first opportunity to broadcast?

Flowers, feathers and faith

In the days of petrol rationing, travel had to be restricted. In school terms, trips far afield weren't possible. This meant that pupils were taken to local sites of historical interest, such as Kidwelly Castle and Carreg Cennen Castle. There was no shortage of significant historical sites well within the rationed catchment area of the Gwendraeth School. The confines of war therefore gave Carwyn and his classmates an immersion in local Welsh history. They had an acute awareness and appreciation of the heritage of their hinterland. This enriched the soil of Carwyn's roots, secured his sense of place and the personal identity that brings with it.

Quite often there was no need for any vehicle to take them on their educational school trips: they could be done on foot. This was particularly true of the visits to the Hall in Cross Hands. It was a trip of about three miles – though Carwyn lived nearer to the Hall than the journey from the school – and they would be taken there to see films and plays. As willing as the school was to go to the cinema, and as popular as such visits were with the pupils, it was not a move without opposition. The cinema's worth in the community was questioned rigorously by many chapel and church leaders and members. A popular verse of the time was often heard thundering from the pulpit:

O cadw fachgennyn o'r sinema ddu.
Mae rhwyd gan y gelyn
Dan flodyn a phlu.
Athrofa drygioni yw'r sinema i ni.

'Stay away, young boy, from the dark cinema.
The enemy has a net
Hidden under flower and feather.
To us, the cinema is a college of evil.'

It was a time of tension between traditional and new values – as in every age, of course. The cinema was the battlefield in Carwyn's day: the emergence of popular culture. He would have heard the objections when he took his regular place in the chapel pew, but he succeeded in keeping flower, feather and faith in happy equilibrium.

A tension between the chapel and another central societal institution reared its head at this time also. Faith and politics clashed head to head. As the material situation of the colliers deteriorated, throughout the locust years of the Twenties initially and then in following decades, some chapel ministers felt it was right to challenge the circumstances that placed their collier chapel members in such dire economic situations. The affairs of this world took over in many a religious gathering, causing those who opposed the emergence of such a radical faith to say that matters of the next world were being neglected.

Such a political religion had firm roots in the village next door to Carwyn's Cefneithin. For daring to support the miners in the great strike of 1926, Reverend Tom Nefyn Williams was thrown out of the pulpit and stripped of his ministerial responsibilities in Tumble. He fuelled the flames by criticising his chapel members severely for not siding publicly with him. Such a controversy was a major talking point at the coalface in all the Gwendraeth Valley pits, and pits throughout South Wales, for many a year. Michael James would have been involved in such talk, no doubt carrying summaries home with him at the end of a shift. Another popular verse at the time sums this up.

Dyw Dai yn licio dim yn y capel nawr
Ond ambell i bregeth ar gyflog a thai.

'Dai likes nothing in the chapel now
Other than the occasional sermon on pay and housing.'

The heat of this storm no doubt had cooled by the time Carwyn was of an age to understand the issues, but he lived and worshipped in its legacy.

The tension and sometimes the fission between cinema, politics and faith were certainly not influences that Carwyn would have experienced had he grown up in Rhydlewis. These were very much Cefneithin, Gwendraeth Valley forces that gave Carwyn a taste of popular culture and politics mixed in with his hymns and prayers.

Two tongues

Back at school, English was the official language. It was however, a naturally Welsh-speaking school, like so many other schools in similar areas throughout Wales. For former Gwendraeth Grammar pupil Wynford Davies from Pontyberem, the two languages existing side by side was never a problem.

One thing we took for granted at the time was that the language of the playground was Welsh, whereas the language of the school was English. We saw nothing strange in this.

Lynn Griffiths, who was a pupil there between 1928 and 1935, remembers things a little differently.

The constant struggle with the English language appeared to be the bane of our lives. Prior to entry to a grammar school, the majority had been taught through the medium of Welsh, and the need to avoid the pitfalls of English grammar and the acquisition of a fair style became almost a nightmare.

30 years later, the situation hadn't changed. In the Gwendraeth of the Sixties, this is how one of its most famous sons, Barry John, remembers the language of the school.

> The language of education is largely English, although in my day the colloquial language of playground and corridor was Welsh. A master would teach you in English, but if he wanted to talk to you personally, or if he called out 'Be quiet!' or 'Sit down!', he usually used Welsh.

If Carwyn's written work, as well as his later broadcasting, is any indication, he was completely comfortable in both languages and could express himself equally well in both. Again, this was very much a Gwendraeth Valley influence, in stark contrast to the almost exclusively monoglot Welsh of Rhydlewis. The people of the Gwendraeth could express their Welshness in two languages.

The language was a real issue for one teacher who was a significant influence on Carwyn. But it wasn't the Welsh-English balance that troubled Miss D E Williams, or Miss Dora as she was called. Her worry was the purity of the Welsh that the Gwendraeth pupils spoke. For her, a North Walian who had sat at the feet of leading Welsh academic Sir John Morris Jones at Bangor University, the Welsh in the part of Wales where she secured a teaching job was a trampled language, and its speakers were to be pitied.

In his chapter on Carwyn in *Heart and Soul of Welsh Rugby*, Professor Gareth Williams says:

> It is a commonplace that the 'best' spoken Welsh – that is, the purest, most idiomatic form of the language, uncontaminated by English borrowings and insertions – is to be found on the borders of north Carmarthenshire and south Cardiganshire. It was certainly a belief to which the James household subscribed,

and the children were encouraged to avoid the vulgar street patois of the Cefneithin natives in favour of the unpolluted vernacular the family had brought from Rhydlewis, and which could be revitalised by summertime return journeys.

This is true, but it must be noted that Carwyn did use many local Gwendraeth Valley words in his conversations and in his writings.

Miss Dora and other teachers

The influential Miss Dora lived in the former Cwm Mawr House, within the school grounds. The dining hall was on the ground floor of the house, as was the Domestic Science department and the headmaster's study. Upstairs there were two sewing rooms either side of the bathroom which served the two teachers who rented the flat on that floor: Miss Dora and senior teacher, Miss A M Williams, known as Miss Maud.

Miss Dora and Miss Maud held positions of power within the school hierarchy. One central duty was the transmitting of messages from the headmaster to the rest of the staff – a key role indeed. Miss Dora had her own inimitable way of fulfilling this task. If she agreed with the contents of the head's message she would begin her announcement by saying 'Mr Williams says…' If, however, she was displeased with the message, she would say 'He says…'

She started at the school when it first opened in 1925, and stayed there until 1963. The pupils had nothing but respect for her. Towards the end of her years, when she was in ill health, Carwyn would visit her at her home in Criccieth, North Wales. Unfortunately she was not well enough to be able to appreciate the triumphs of her former pupil with the Lions in 1971. No doubt she would have been very proud of him, even though she detested rugby when she was a teacher. 'That cursed football!' was her usual way of referring to it, and she was particularly displeased when her pupils, Carwyn amongst them, were taken from her Welsh lessons in order to play rugby for the school, or

77

Miss Dora

worse still, so that pupils could go to watch a game of school rugby.

Her main contribution, without doubt, was nurturing her pupils to understand Welsh literature. She had a natural, infectious ability to bring pages of literature to life, as one former pupil, M Auriol Watkin-Griffiths, recalls:

> She was an inspired Welsh Literature teacher. When broadcasts to schools on novels were few and far between, she arranged a weekly visit for her sixth formers to a nearby house, Glyn Gwendraeth, where, comfortably seated in front of Mrs Jones' blazing fire, we listened enthralled to T H Parry-Williams' first broadcast lessons on *'Barddoniaeth Gymraeg'* (Welsh poetry).

T H Parry-Williams was a giant of Welsh literature, a formative force in its development in the early part of the last century. In 1933, he presented a series of 12 BBC radio programmes on Welsh poetry. He would broadcast on the radio regularly while Carwyn was at school, as did many other leading Welsh poets of the time, such as Gwenallt. Carwyn would come across both in the days after the Gwendraeth. Miss Dora would ensure that her pupils had the opportunity to listen to these Welsh literary greats as often as possible. This quite often meant that she would take groups of her pupils to homes near the school so that they could listen to radio broadcasts in various parlours. She would also take them to hear the poets themselves, if they happened to be speaking anywhere in the vicinity of the school.

T H Parry-Williams was a particular influence on the

young Carwyn. On a 1973 BBC television programme, Carwyn explains how the influence of T H Parry-Williams changed the course of his life:

> I was supposed to study Chemistry, Physics and Maths in the sixth form. That was the intention. But suddenly, I came across the poetry of T H Parry-Williams and was enchanted at a young age by this new style. He ploughed a new furrow, where the traditional was open to be enchanted by the new.

He then studied English, Welsh and Geography for his Higher School Certificate (the A-Level equivalent at the time), thus ensuring the continued influence of both T H Parry-Williams and Miss Dora. Her philosophy and spirit was more in tune with the Dalton approach than the traditional grammar school way of educating. Quite often, she would give her classes a one-word task: 'Compose!' M Auriol Watkin remembers this:

> And we did. What a wealth of three-act plays, short stories and poems emerged. This was a period of creativity indeed.

Miss Dora would have been one of the teachers who organised the trips to the Hall in Cross Hands, as well as to other halls in the area. She would also produce her own school plays, to be performed in the Gwendraeth and in local public halls.

Carwyn's own recollection of her, in the school commemorative volume, is very concise.

> Miss Dora: the most endearing of teachers, extremely cultured, an excellent teacher in the sixth form. My debt to her is indeed great.

Without doubt, she nourished Carwyn's soul and enriched both his cultural appreciation and expression. This was to be the strongest heartbeat throughout Carwyn's life, stronger than any other, including rugby. The field of Welsh literature, at least, was one that would never present him with any disappointments or rejection.

Carwyn evidently discussed Miss Dora's influence on him with his friend, the author Alun Richards, as Richards recalls:

> It is not difficult to understand how Carwyn came to revere Gwenallt, nor indeed to understand his gratitude to the teacher who introduced him to such a writer. Miss Dora, of course, would have none of the snobbish indifference, if not the total ignorance of Welsh writers frequently found amongst teachers of English Literature in Wales, an ignorance that extended and extends to Welsh writers in both languages. The feeling, extraordinary to outsiders – if it's Welsh it can't be much good! – is a part of the anglicised provincial intellectual's inferiority and remains lurking like a deep mist in a good deal of Welsh life, particularly in towns and cities. It was always a matter of astonishment to Carwyn, who frequently discussed it.

Carwyn would strongly disagree with Richards on matters of Welshness and Welsh identity, both culturally and politically, but it's evident that Richards understood how confident Carwyn was in his bilingual Welshness.

Miss Dora wasn't the only influential teacher in Carwyn's school days, and it would be remiss to neglect two other members of staff. Carwyn himself regularly praised the contribution of his English teacher, Gwilym John Evans. He was also one of the teachers responsible for rugby at the school, but Carwyn reacted very favourably to the way he taught English Literature, again as succinctly as he summed up Miss Dora's contribution:

> ...not the set books, but the way he developed our critical abilities and tastes. I must thank him for his vision.

One other teacher was a major influence in directing the course of Carwyn's life. Gwynfil Rees was the PE teacher and was responsible for rugby at the school. He was a Welsh

Gwynfil Rees

graduate from Aberystwyth University, where he had studied under the two leading poets, T H Parry-Williams and Gwenallt. Carwyn told him quite clearly that he wanted to follow in his footsteps and do the same degree with the same two lecturers. No doubt Miss Dora would have been very pleased with this, even if she thought that Carwyn played too much rugby. The oval-ball game and the literary culture of Wales came together in the person of Gwynfil Rees.

Rees wrote a poem to commemorate his former pupil after Carwyn's death.

Teithiodd y byd a phrofi gwin a gwermod,
Ond daliai'r wên mor hynaws ag erioed.
Yn Seland Newydd cyrraedd brig awdurdod
A'r meistri gynt yn plygu wrth ei droed.
Y llednais ŵr a'r gŵr bonheddig rhadlon,
Heddwch i'th lwch ymhlith yr anfarwolion.

'He travelled the world, tasting wine and wormwood,
But his smile would always remain true.
In New Zealand he reached the summit of authority
As the former masters kneeled before him.
An enigmatic man, a generous gentleman,
Peace to his ashes in the company of immortals.'

A rugby teacher in those days, and in that geographical area, was in a very strong position indeed. Gwynfil Rees was well aware of that, as he wrote in 1983, over 40 years after he would have first met Carwyn.

There was very little work needed to coach these boys – the boys of Cefneithin, Cross Hands, Tumble and Pontyberem. Rugby was in their blood and every one of them could run, kick and pass the ball before coming to school. I was delighted by such talent, and proud to be able to count them as friends to this day.

His comments also show the strong social and societal bonds of rugby.

As with clothes and school trips, rugby was also affected by the war. Not only did petrol rationing affect rugby trips as it did those to the cinema, but in this case also, there would have been a shortage of men to take teams to away games as many teachers were serving their country on the battlefield. It seems that perhaps the young Carwyn was not fully aware of this:

At the time I don't think that we were aware of the restrictions imposed by the war effort, we simply took it for granted that organised games could not be played. I spent many a pleasant afternoon playing soccer for the local youth club. My tenuous claim to fame during this period was an offer by a smooth-talking Cardiff City scout to take part in a soccer trial, which I declined.

When the Cefneithin ex-schoolboys side [football, rather than rugby] began playing matches in the season 1945–46, I became a playing member, and I was barely 16 when I played my first cup final against Pen y Banc.

If circumstances didn't allow one thing to happen, Carwyn would find a way to do something else. He would develop this ability throughout his life. This was the beginning of a new routine in his life, which meant that he would play rugby for the school on Saturday morning and then for the Cefneithin team in the afternoon.

Gwynfil Rees remembers Carwyn's weaknesses as well as his strengths. He would readily say that Carwyn was more talented than his contemporaries, but also tell Carwyn regularly to be aware of one deficiency in his game – an attempt by the wise educator, no doubt, to rein in some of the natural enthusiasm.

> He was a master at the drop goal (he kicked one for Wales at the Arms Park), and I would preach at him sometimes that he was using such a kick far too often. But then, maybe in a game the following Saturday it was a Carwyn drop goal that would win us the game, and he would walk off the pitch and look at me with a mischievous smile!

Gwynfil Rees also saw another weakness in Carwyn's game:

> He wasn't too keen on tackling. I would therefore have to make him practise. With the help of another member of staff, Mr Gwilym Evans, we would take Carwyn out on to the pitch, along with the team's vice-captain, Dilwyn Roberts. He was a strong, solid hooker, and when he had the ball in his hands, he would hurl himself towards opposing players without any fear in his body. That's the task I gave Carwyn: to tackle Dilwyn Roberts time and time again. Carwyn would walk from the pitch bruised and tired, but his tackling became far more secure and solid.

Carwyn certainly didn't forget this instruction. He recalls the incident in his contribution to the school's 50th anniversary commemorative volume.

> I shall never forget the painful afternoon when I had to tackle my friend, Dilwyn Roberts, a tough hooker, whose brief was to run hard and straight at me, and mine was to knock him flying. As far as I could make out, Gwynfil Rees was the only one who enjoyed the sadistic proceedings. I certainly didn't, but, in turn, I must confess that I enjoyed the rewards.

Many of Carwyn's school friends recall an incident when Carwyn made sure that his teacher knew that the pupil had learned his lesson. Carwyn had just played for the Welsh Schoolboys team and in a report on the game, the *Yorkshire*

Post referred to 'a brilliant last-minute tackle by the Welsh Secondary Schools captain.' Carwyn's response on reading the report is not surprising. He posted a copy of the *Yorkshire Post* to Gwynfil Rees!

Welsh Schoolboys rugby

It was no surprise that Carwyn was chosen to play for the Welsh Schoolboys team and that he captained his country at that level. This is how he recalls his time with the Schoolboys.

> I had two seasons and six caps for the Welsh Secondary Schools Rugby Union, and in my second year captained the side. It was a thrill to wear the Welsh jersey. The first time was at Ynysangharad Park, Pontypridd, versus Yorkshire. The Headmaster, half his staff and half the school, it seemed, were present at the match, and people like Dai Lewis and Lloyd Morgan had seen to it that the village was well represented.

As a sixth-former, Carwyn went on his first foreign trip, to France, with the Schoolboys. Until then, the furthest he had travelled was Cardiff, but that game took him to Paris. He said that he enjoyed the experience of playing in Stade Colombes very much. Alongside him in that team were Roy Bish, Ken Jones and Lewis Jones, and Clem Thomas was the captain. This was the beginning of a lifelong friendship between Carwyn and Clem, and also the beginning of Carwyn's enduring admiration of the playing style of the incomparable Lewis Jones, who shone brightly for Wales before leaving to play Rugby League. Carwyn said that Lewis Jones was one of the most exciting attacking players Wales had ever produced, and he influenced Carwyn's whole philosophy of rugby.

> The boring coach will continually preach that mistakes must be cut to a minimum. The creative coach on the other hand, will invite his players to go out there and make mistakes. They will achieve little unless they make mistakes. We must introduce the spirit of

adventure. I loved the Lewis Jones approach – 'I may concede two tries but I'll score four!'

Carwyn's time with the Schoolboys saw significant building on the foundations laid by Gwynfil Rees and Gwilym Evans. He learned further lessons and gained further experience under coach Eric Evans, who would be the Secretary of the WRU in years to come. On that journey to Paris, he addressed his players in the Palais D'Orsay hotel. His words left an indelible mark on Carwyn's rugby brain – he could recall the main points of that speech in 1975, nearly 30 years later.

> 1. Never, ever question the decision of the referee.
> 2. Don't throw the ball around haphazardly in your own 25, but when the occasion allows, we want you to play the running, attacking game which is essentially our style of play.
> 3. When you score, don't make an exhibition of yourself; rather, start thinking about your next score.

It's difficult to think of a clearer summary of Carwyn's own rugby principles, both as a player and as a coach. He also acknowledges another influence that being part of the Schoolboys squad had on him.

> I was so nervous at having to make my first speech at the dinner which followed our game against Yorkshire at Abbeydale Park, Sheffield, when Bob Oakes spoke brilliantly, that I vowed that night that I would study the art!

The next step in Carwyn's rugby development is no surprise. School rugby turned to village rugby, which turned to playing for his country as a schoolboy. Next, Llanelli rugby club came knocking at his door at 17, before he threw his school uniform away.

He wore the outside half shirt for the first time in an away game on the Brewery Field in Bridgend. It was number 6 in those days, before it changed to the now infamous number 10, as in those days they started their counting with the full back as number 1. He then played in Pontypool.

His inside half in those games was Handel Greville, a former pupil of Gwendraeth School, and a member of the family who kept the shop in the village of Drefach where the boys would go for their sweets.

These early Scarlets appearances also gave him another of his rugby principles. Particularly in remembering the game against Pontypool, when he played against the two leading flankers of the day, Allen Forward and Ray Cale, he shows clearly that he saw the wider significance of putting a schoolboy up against players of calibre and experience.

It speaks volumes for the lack of foresight of the club's 12-man selection committee in the late Forties that they should have given such a baptism to a raw 17 year old. The following season, after a pleasant tour of Cornwall with Llanelli, I learnt my lesson at the Gnoll, in the form of a late tackle by a 14-stone centre which shattered my confidence and put a temporary end to my first-class

C James' first appearance on a Scarlets team sheet

career. Ever since, I have had strong reservations about blooding young players too soon.

Snooker, cricket and the Urdd

Outside the school grounds, Carwyn was also a popular and active figure in sporting and cultural circles alike.

Sir John Meurig Thomas remembers Carwyn's snooker ability. As noted above, this was a talent he practised when on school holidays in Rhydlewis.

> Snooker was very popular indeed when we were in school. There were regular league competitions throughout the area, and quite often special Exhibition events in the Hall in Cross Hands. I remember one such occasion, when the renowned Sydney Smith made an appearance there. The organisers asked one of the local men to come forward to challenge Sydney Smith and Carwyn was chosen. He was thrashed, it must be said, but it has to be noted that it was Carwyn who was chosen by all the local men.

Sir John also recalls Carwyn's love of cricket.

> I remember him playing for the Tumble village cricket team, Lower Tumble to be precise. He was a really good all-rounder who could bat and bowl. He was a right-arm bowler, and fairly slow. He would also play cricket for Tumble when he was home on his University holidays too, or on the occasional weekend.

His primary school teacher and local dramatist Gwynne D Evans remembers noticing Carwyn's cricketing talent and hearing him speak on how much he loved the game.

> The first time I saw Carwyn with a cricket bat in his hands, I realised that he had a natural talent for the game. As he was eager to learn, I was happy enough to give him a few tips. When he was only nine years old, I ventured to choose him for the team to play against the older boys of Tumble School. I remember him scoring a tidy six runs and he kept his place in the team. Not long ago, I

heard him say that he would have liked a career as a professional cricketer. If he had followed such a path, Welsh rugby would have suffered terribly. But at least Glamorgan would have had their Brearly way before England did.

Away from sporting fields, Carwyn took full part in the activities of the Urdd, the Welsh League of Youth. One of the organisation's leading lights in the Gwendraeth, Stella Treharne, the first head of Kidwelly Welsh Primary School, remembers Carwyn the Urdd member.

From the 1930s, Urdd activities were organised in the region known as Mynydd Mawr, covering the area on and around the Great Mountain which gives it its name. Carwyn's primary school headteacher, W J Jones, was one of the active teachers who was responsible for organising Urdd activity in the region.

Carwyn fell under the influence of the Urdd in another place close to his heart.

The minister in Carwyn's chapel, Tabernacl, was Morley Lewis. He started an Urdd group which met in the school nearby on Friday evenings. Carwyn was asked to be its leader, and the minister's son, Elfed Lewys, who would become a popular ballad and folk singer, was the secretary.

Carwyn was insistent that his Urdd group had to prosper from day one. He was someone who understood the value of culture, not only entertainment, and this drove the group. He also had a personal appeal – through his rugby playing of course, but also through his snooker and cricket. This meant that Urdd members threw themselves wholeheartedly into every activity and it was a very popular group. Every village had its own Urdd group, and we met regularly with each other as well.

Closing the classroom door

Carwyn James' school days came to an end in 1948. His time at the Gwendraeth Grammar School had been prosperous and fruitful on many levels: from his first school report at the end of his first year, when he had an A for every subject, to the very last results when he secured enough A Levels to go to university; from the day he first played for his school team to the day he captained the Welsh Schoolboys; from the day he sang his first song at school to the day he took a leading part in one of Miss Dora's productions – Carwyn shone. This is not the whitewashing of a biographer. His own headmaster, Llywelyn Williams, said so.

> He is the most able of the pupils who have passed through this school. Indeed, should the opportunity ever arise, I shall be pleased to offer him an appointment to my staff.

Praise indeed. Alun Richards also recognises the value of the Gwendraeth days to Carwyn:

> If he became one of the most confident Welshmen of his generation, it was because in his early years he had an education of which he could be proud.

But if he was a hero in his school and in his community, he was a hero with feet of clay. The talents and abilities flourished, but under the surface, the pounding heart was that of the poet rather than the sporting star – he was a sensitive soul, who felt too deeply. The first clear indication of this came at a time when he was being considered to play for the Welsh Schoolboys team. On his first attempt to make the squad, he was not chosen. He showed his disappointment by writing a poem.

Siom

Minnau'n llawn hoen, ac mewn hwyl anghyffredin
Chwaraeais fel arwr y gad.
Disgwyliwn yn awchus am glywed y newydd,
A'm dewis fel maswr y wlad.

Drannoeth a minnau'n llawn hyder a sicrwydd
Ces gerdyn ar drothwy y drws –
Yr hyder a'r sicrwydd yn araf ddiflannu
Pa newydd – ai cas ynteu tlws?

Oedais am funud gan feddwl drachefn
Ai arwr neu lwfryn ow'n i?
Wel, do'n eithaf sicr chwaraeais fy ngorau
A'r maswr oedd – neb ond myfi.

Ond syrthiodd fy nhrem ar air annymunol
A syrthiodd fy ngwep yr un pryd.
I lawr daeth fy nghestyll fel castell ar dywod
A llanwodd fy nghalon â llid.

'Disappointment

Full of vigour and unusually good spirit
I played like a hero of war.
I then waited excitedly for the news
That I would be the nation's outside half

The day after, full of confidence and surety
A card came through the door –
Confidence and surety wavered
What news – was it ugly or good?

I hesitated a while, thinking.
Was I a hero or a coward?
Well, yes, I certainly played my best
And the outside half should be no one but me.

But my gaze fell on an unpleasant word
And my face fell at the same time
Down came my castles as if on sand
And my heart filled with rage.'

In the documentary BBC Wales produced to mark Carwyn's death, Gwynfil Rees refers to this poem. Over footage of Carwyn the adult standing on the touchline during a rugby game in Gwendraeth School, the poem is read. His former rugby teacher then explains the background to the poem.

His brother Dewi got hold of the poem. Carwyn didn't show me that he had written it or indeed, that he felt the disappointment it contained. At the time, I thought he took the fact he hadn't been selected very well – in fact, he appeared very casual about the whole thing. But it's now evident that he felt the rejection deeply.

This was the first, but it would not be the last time that Carwyn would feel disappointment in the rugby world. His reaction shows us a great deal about Carwyn the human being. To those all around him, he took not being chosen for the squad very well, with hardly a break in his stride. But he had kept his true feelings to himself. He was not a schoolboy who revealed his emotional complexities. He would remain such a person throughout his life.

The school tie

By the time Carwyn left Gwendraeth Grammar, the pieces that would shape his life had been shaped, formed and carved. Over the next very short 35 years, they would slowly, sometimes painfully, fall into place, giving us the jigsaw picture that was the life of Carwyn James. From the many-faceted tensions and influences of hearth, classroom and community, Carwyn created his own heritage, the central thread of which can be summed up in the way that Carwyn himself evaluated the influence of his hero, poet T H Parry-Williams. In describing why the poet had captured his imagination, Carwyn said that in Parry-Williams' work, the traditional is open to be mystified by the new. That's how Carwyn read his life.

CHAPTER 5

A student by the sea

Roedd Aberystwyth mor bell o'r byd nes gorfodi ei fyfyrwyr i fyw ar eu hadnoddau eu hunain. Nid oedd ganddynt wrth eu drysau ddinas fawr, yn llawn o chwaraedai na chyngherddau na llyfrgelloedd, bob un ohonynt, cofier, yn cystadlu â'r coleg.

'Aberystwyth was so far from the world that it forced its students to live on their own resources. They didn't have a big city at their doors, full of playhouses, concerts and libraries – each one, remember, competing with the college.'

R T Jenkins, *Edrych yn Ôl* (Looking Back)

CARWYN'S FEET LANDED on new soil in October 1948. For the first time, he was to leave Rose Villa. The tight formative arms of the Cefneithin mining and farming community loosened their grip on him and let him go. A new vista awaited him, one which now had a shoreline and a horizon.

His Aberystwyth University registration card shows that when he left his family home, his father Michael was unemployed. His brother Dewi had followed the two sisters into the world of work, having just begun a lifelong career in banking. Carwyn was the first in the James line to go to a university. He did so in the year that saw the formation of the NHS and the Welfare State, when the people of United Kingdom were becoming the generation who had 'never had it so good'.

When Carwyn stepped from the train that brought him from Carmarthen to Aberystwyth on that first day as a student, he walked into a town that was experiencing change of its own. The seaside resort was just starting to be the place to go for day trips, as opposed to the week or two-week holiday which had been the tradition until then. Holidaymakers and day trippers alike now filled the streets. The town's officials were in the process of preparing an application proposing Aberystwyth as the capital of Wales. That honour was eventually given to Cardiff, of course, but the decision to apply for such a lofty status says a great deal about the self-confidence and ambition of the people of Aber, and their sense of identity. Carwyn would have warmed to such positive expressions and the outward-looking attitude they conveyed.

However, even though Aberystwyth was experiencing a certain kind of flourishing in those post-war days, the county of Cardigan as a whole was not. The same forces that had driven Michael James out of the county over 20 years earlier were still active. The population of Ceredigion as a whole was declining rapidly as economic forces drove its citizens to look for greener, or maybe blacker, pastures.

For Carwyn personally, it was indeed a significant new beginning, but he was also on old soil. His was a return to a place he'd never lived in before. Ceredigion had taken a firm grip of Carwyn's ankles as he left his mother's womb. So in Aberystwyth he was in a new place, a new home, but his boundaries were still Carmarthenshire and Ceredigion, as they had been from the day he was born. They were days of the juxtaposition of the new and the traditional, befitting the influence that T H Parry-Williams had had on Carwyn in his Gwendraeth days.

Carwyn shared his new home with some fellow former pupils of Gwendraeth in a house called Roxborough, 12 Elm Tree Avenue, near the train station in Aberystwyth. The house looked out on to the walkway from the area of Plascrug into the town centre – a popular, social, thoroughfare.

In his first year, Carwyn studied Geography, Philosophy, Welsh History and Welsh. In his second year, he studied Welsh

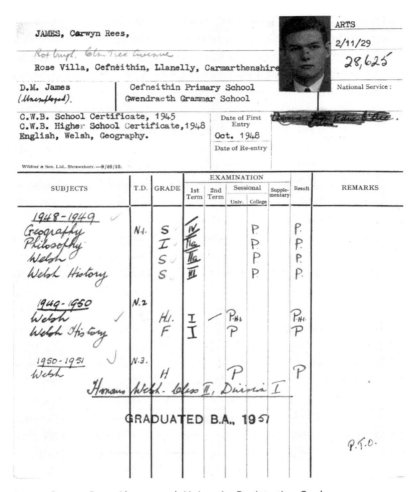

James, Carwyn Rees. Aberystwyth University Registration Card

History and Welsh, and then the third year was his honours year in Welsh. That final year, nine students sat for their honours in Welsh, a high number. Three of the nine were sitting for their degree following their years in the military. They were Thomas Jones from Penuwch, J Roderick Rees, a future influential poet in Wales, and R I Dennis Jones, a future head of Llanelli Boys' Grammar School. Carwyn was one of the six who had gone straight from school to university. What was true of Carwyn's Welsh class was true of the University as a whole – it would have been a new mix of younger and more mature students. As in his village life and in his chapel life, Carwyn was a young man in the company of older people.

At the feet of giants

In his Aber days, Carwyn fulfilled a dream and was in his seventh heaven. Aberystwyth was Carwyn's only choice of university, with him refusing to fill in a second and third choice of place to study. Aber was exclusively number one for one simple reason, or should that be two: T H Parry-Williams and Gwenallt. Two prominent, influential poets and academics, and two of Carwyn's heroes. Miss Dora had immersed her pupils in the work of these two giants. Gwynfil Rees had studied under them. Carwyn himself loved their work, identified with their main themes, and was so eager to sit at their feet. Meeting such highly-esteemed heroes, however, would prove to be a different prospect to what Carwyn might have expected, as fellow student Dafydd J Bowen remembers.

> Such literary giants would have been very distant to us in those days. They would have been in their ivory towers, away from any connection with so-called ordinary people. I remember the thrill of seeing them for the first time. Carwyn showed a particular curiosity in seeing T H Parry-Williams in the flesh for the first time, as he did when he saw Gwenallt. For Carwyn, Gwenallt's work represented the dual forces that he felt pulling on his own personal life, the humanity of the coalfield and the divinity of rural Wales. But I think T H Parry-Williams was his greatest hero.

These recollections of a close friend echo Carwyn's own words about T H Parry-Williams when he recalls hearing his radio broadcasts during his school days. On a TV programme in the 1970s, Carwyn recalled his Aber days and the influence of his hero in particular.

> In Aber, I remember being enchanted by his lectures. They were so interesting, as he brought both historical issues and Old Gaelic to life.

Carwyn's course would have taken him into the depths of the literary tradition of Wales, back across many centuries, and would have introduced him to poets and scholars long gone from the popular Welsh cultural consciousness. This study would have enriched and deepened Carwyn's idea of Wales and being Welsh, as he became increasingly aware of the heritage that he was part of.

But there was a drawback to such studies. Carwyn would not have heard either of his two literary heroes discuss their own work with the students. Work as current as theirs was not on any curriculum. His was a course involving the history of literature, medieval texts, grammatical studies, Gaelic, Latin and other ancient academic fields. There would not be one text from the twentieth century on the course, with very few from the nineteenth either. There would be very little thematic or critical literary study of any text on the course. Carwyn, therefore, would have been more familiar with the works of T H Parry-Williams and Gwenallt themselves when he was in Gwendraeth with Miss Dora. No doubt the inquisitive Carwyn would have made the most of any opportunity to discuss their work with either one of the two if he had the chance, though.

Gwenallt's work explored the tension between the industrial and the rural manifestations of the nation that can be called Wales. Carwyn noted his liking of Gwenallt's ability to be a 'realist in the way he dealt with the heavy-industrial world'. Gwenallt grasped Carwyn's immediate family circumstances as they moved from one part of Wales to another. T H Parry-Williams caught the spirit of the Carwyn who had been brought up in that world.

Carwyn's encounters with T H Parry-Williams would have been far fewer had it not been for the poet's late but significant life decision a few years before Carwyn arrived at the University: he married. Up until then, he had been a very private man, conspicuous by his absence from University social gatherings. In a biography of Parry-Williams by R Gerallt Jones in the *Dawn Dweud* (Talent for Telling) series, a student, Menai Williams, recalls this change in the Professor:

> Even though he was always politely friendly with us all, he was never to be seen amongst us, the students, at any social occasion, such as the meetings of the Celtic Society. Before I left college, however, things changed. After he married, we would regularly have the company of Sir Thomas and Lady Parry-Williams at many a happy gathering.

The two married in August 1942. Amy Thomas came from the same part of the world as Carwyn – the village of Pontyberem in the Gwendraeth Valley. Even though she was a lot older than him of course, Carwyn and Amy Thomas would have mixed in the same circles and known the same people. He can be grateful to her for drawing her husband out of the shadows and into the warmth of the students' company, with the added bonus of having direct association with her himself, which would have forged associations quicker. Carwyn had many more conversations with TH than he would have had if TH had remained a single man.

Friendship and new teams

A shortage of textbooks in post-war Aberystwyth led to a lasting and significant friendship for Carwyn. Professor Thomas Parry was a lecturer at Bangor University and would visit Aber to give lectures on the life and work of medieval Welsh poet, Dafydd ap Gwilym. There weren't enough copies of *Cywyddau Dafydd ap Gwilym a'i Gyfoeswyr* (The Cywyddau of Dafydd ap Gwilym and his Contemporaries) in Aber, so Carwyn shared a copy with third year student, Dafydd J Bowen. The two became very close friends, as Dafydd Bowen mentions in his contribution to the memorial volume to Carwyn, *Un o 'Fois y Pentre'* (One of the 'Boys from the Village').

> Throughout the following terms, we would meet regularly for lengthy discussions in the Quad or in town, and by the summer of 1950, when Carwyn had his Travelling Scholarship, we were close enough as friends for Carwyn to ask me to go with him to Brittany.

T H Parry-Williams organised trips from Aberystwyth University to Brittany, in order for students and lecturers alike to experience another Celtic country. It's not clear if Carwyn went on one of these trips or a separate one. Carwyn's need to go is an indication of his outlook on life as a whole. He had the need to look outward, to look beyond the more immediate confines of the Welsh world he was a part of. Carwyn referred to this trip in a Welsh-language broadcast on the BBC in 1960:

> When life is intense and cross-currents are at their most fierce, I am always jealous of little children and old people – the old, old people such as the women I saw in Brittany who had to all appearances survived life and the grave. I had very little opportunity to speak to them, but I think about them often when I'm in conversation with an elderly lady who lives near me at home.

As is typical in Carwyn's writing generally, he sees the local in a wider context. It's the human experience in its totality that's important to him, not the parochial manifestation of it. His creative mind could see and develop connections that were not immediately evident. This ability of his no doubt contributed to the perception of him as a man full of dualities, holding two opposing thoughts or opinions at the same time. But for him, they were not dualities at all. Only connections.

He felt no need to fly with birds of the same feather when it came to making friendships, either. Dafydd Bowen is a case in point. Carwyn himself said that Dafydd Bowen was such a good friend because he didn't know anything about rugby.

Alun Richards, in his book, *Carwyn: A personal memoir*, quotes Dafydd as saying that Carwyn described the friendship in this way: 'I like your company because you don't know anything about rugby – and can't impose on me.' Dafydd Bowen's version of the same quote in *Un o 'Fois y Pentre'*, in the chapter he wrote, doesn't include the last phrase, 'and can't impose on me'. Is the omission of those five words significant? Dafydd Bowen's emphasis in the chapter he wrote is on the fact that it was the friendship that was important and the fact that Carwyn didn't like rugby to get in the way of that. Alun Richards, on the other hand – more detached, more analytical and a man who did know his rugby – was sensitive to the fact that many had imposed on Carwyn, particularly in the rugby world. That was worth noting for him.

Carwyn the Welsh Schoolboys captain obviously did take his place in the rugby world at Aberystwyth, but not at the University. Carwyn explained why:

> John (Alfie) Brace, brother of Onllwyn, both products of Gowerton Grammar, was the resident college fly half, so I had to be content with playing for the Second XV and Aber Town until Alfie decided to play for the town side.

Alfie was evidently a very good player to keep someone like Carwyn out of the team. But there was another determining factor, as John Brace himself explained:

> I was the fly half at the time and, of course, I had heard quite a lot about this talented youngster who had arrived at Aber. But he had no hope of being selected. By virtue of being the captain of the team, I was also the chairman of the selectors. Carwyn couldn't get into the first team for a year.

Carwyn went from being captain in his school, captain of the Welsh Schoolboys, chosen to play for Cefneithin and Llanelli, to failing to secure a place in his university's First XV.

He had already expressed his disappointment on not initially being chosen to play for the Welsh Schoolboys, in the poem that revealed his inner thoughts. He must have felt the same level of rejection at not walking into the University First XV. He also mentioned how he felt it wrong that he had been thrown in to play against grown men when he was only a schoolboy. Not getting in to Aber Firsts then, was a third knock-back in the rugby world within the space of a year or two. The adult Carwyn would go on to experience disappointment and rejection in rugby circles more than in any of the other worlds in which he moved. It started early, and it was there again in his uni days. The poet's heart beating in Carwyn would surely have felt this, though we know of no poem this time.

Just as he knocked the schoolboy disappointment to one side and used it as an inspirational driver to succeed next time, he didn't settle for second best in Aberystwyth either. He did play for the Second XV, but he also, as he said, joined the town rugby team. In doing so, he was taking part in what was a brand new venture. Aberystwyth Rugby Club's first ever game was against the University's Second XV in 1947, with the town team losing 24–3. Ellis Davies was one of those who formed the club in 1947, and is still involved with it.

> Lots of us young men at the time liked our rugby, and we thought it would be a good thing for us to form a team. In those early days, including when Carwyn joined us, we played on some land near the Gasworks – I could never call it a rugby pitch! It was obvious that the young lad who came to us at the beginning of the 1948 season was extremely talented. I played in the pack, and as was the case then, it was anywhere in the pack. It was a pleasure to see this gifted outside half doing what every good outside half should do, which is side-stepping and passing his tacklers. He was younger than most of us in the team, as a boy straight from school, but his ability was more than obvious.

The town rugby team's opponents in those early days were the university teams, Lampeter University and town teams, and teams from the Military Services. Carwyn went back to his university team for his second year, playing for the first team as captain. Wherever he played, he enjoyed his rugby.

> The trips from College to the mining villages of Tumble, Llandybie, Pontyberem, and the wonderful hospitality laid on were occasions we looked forward to with relish. When the ex-servicemen at last disappeared from the College scene, and there was a little tightening on discipline, Dr Lily Newton, the new Vice-Principal, was most understanding of the problems facing the captain of the wild young men of the Rugby Club!

Alun Richards recalls one specific incident that shows the nature of the relationship between Carwyn and Dr Lily Newton. Usually the team would return from away games in the early hours of Sunday morning on the milk train. Dr Newton didn't think that was appropriate behaviour for her students and felt that it would give the College a bad name. She introduced a new rule insisting that all teams would be back in Aberystwyth by midnight on Saturday, without fail. Not long after introducing such a rule, Carwyn's team were playing in Birmingham – though Carwyn was not with them, as he was injured. The team returned at five o'clock the following morning. Alun Richards recounts what happened next.

> The captain was summoned, and although not personally involved, held responsible. It was a confrontation which is not hard to imagine, and those involved feared the direst consequences – perhaps the prohibition of away games, a firm and understandable act on the part of a new vice-principal determined to impose a more stringent rule now that most of the ex-servicemen had left. But Carwyn, made completely innocent by his own absence, emerged from the interview an hour later as silent victor and no restrictions of any kind were placed on his team.

The story goes that in his argument, Carwyn made a great deal of the negative influence of the ex-servicemen on their younger, more naïve teammates. If this did influence the decision, that raises one point. In his statement above about enjoying travelling with the team, he mentions the fact that the ex-servicemen had gone and that Lily Newton at the time was new. Either that part of the story is not accurate, or Carwyn managed to persuade the College Vice-Principal that students who were no longer there had been a bad influence! It would not be difficult to believe that the charming, persuasive Carwyn had indeed succeeded in doing such a thing.

Carwyn was involved with another team as well during this period, an involvement that could well go some way towards making some sort of claim that Carwyn was the first rugby professional!

Cefneithin RFC, quite a force in the Llanelli League in the late Forties, only achieved full WRU status in the 1948–49 season thanks to the drive and influence of Ivor Jones and Ewart Davies. During my first year at Aber, I occasionally travelled home to play for Amman United in the West Wales league competition. I don't think Lloyd Morgan approved me playing for the Amman at all. I have a sneaking feeling as well that he was displeased by the dramatic effect achieved by his opposite number in the Amman Valley, an equally strong and well-known personality, Bertie Davies. Bertie headed a deputation of five Amman United high officials and committee men which came to see me at my home one dark evening to persuade me to play for the 'best and richest team in Wales', as Bertie put it. The others said very little – I think they were there for the theatre. In turn, with my transfer back to the Club [Cefneithin], I insisted on the Amman prima donna treatment when it came to a midweek cup match. But after losing in the first round, Lloyd, in front of many of the local pundits, had the last word as I boarded my hired, chauffer-driven vehicle bound for Aberystwyth: 'Make the most of it. That's the last bloody taxi you'll have.'

He was lured by another club, and for financial gain as well! Carwyn himself was quite happy to call himself a prima donna, not a phrase we would usually associate with him. But there's

Carwyn not being predictable again. His willingness to play for Amman United shows that however strong his loyalties were, his ambition could be stronger. That took him outside expected boxes.

Carwyn's visits back home would cause quite a stir. All the young lads would flock to see him at every opportunity. He would willingly share his time with them, helping with passing or kicking a rugby ball in the park. One of these young lads, Elwyn Jenkins, became a coalminer, then a Presbyterian minister. He also played rugby for Llanelli and Swansea. He remembers being a 16-year-old lad when Carwyn came back to Cefneithin during his third year at Aber.

> I had been playing snooker one Saturday night, in Oswald Evans' little hall on Cross Hands square. A short man called Maldwyn came up to me and tried to persuade me to go for a trial on Cae Pownd (Pond Field), Cross Hands, as there were plans to form a new team in the village. But because I came from a poor family, and times were hard, I didn't have proper togs. But, to my surprise, I was chosen as full back.
>
> When I think of that occasion, I realise that my enthusiasm was far greater than my understanding of the game. But I do remember that the famous Carwyn James, who lived nearby, gave me advice and helped to coach me. I had no idea at the time that I would be playing with Carwyn in the Welsh Trials. He hadn't long been captain of the Welsh Schoolboys and there was a lot of demand for his services.

Carwyn sums up his rugby days in Aber in a very positive way. This wasn't only confined to the field of play.

> I thoroughly enjoyed my rugger at Aber; mainly I suppose, due to the marvellous spirit of the team. We were a cliquish lot – we drank coffee together every morning in the refectory and we took over The Ship for our after-match sing-songs. Big Roy Williams, who later became a professional with Wigan, would sing 'I wonder who's kissing her now?', Lem Evans would give a fair impression of Al Jolson, and dear 'Myfanwy' was always popular.

Carwyn's innate modesty prevented him from saying that it was he himself who would sing 'Myfanwy' on such occasions, after the ex-servicemen had sung their own particular brand of songs that knew nothing of the world Myfanwy lived in. Alun Richards describes the world of The Ship pub on rugby evenings.

> As the night wore on and the singers wore out, Carwyn's turn would come: a time for sentiment. In the sweetest of light tenor voices, he would sing the Welsh love song 'Myfanwy', hands crossed in his deacon pose, bringing a reminder of the years of innocence which he was to carry with him all his life. This was the chapel Carwyn, carrying the pulpit in his voice; often changing the mood of the assembled company so that hymns followed, very probably sending the singers home with a beery glow of maudlin satisfaction at this raising of tone before 'time' was called by the indispensable Treorchy landlord.

It's a touch sentimental to suggest that one rendition of 'Myfanwy' would change the entire mood of a lively pub heaving with rugby muscle and banter. Suffice to say that he always made his own contribution and didn't feel the need to totally compromise by letting the more carnal songs rule the day.

Politics and protest

It wasn't all rugby for Carwyn in Aber. It wasn't all Welsh literature either. Aber Uni team captain John Brace remembers an incident where rugby had to take second place.

> He let me know in midweek on one occasion that he wouldn't be available for a game the following Saturday. He was going with the University branch of Plaid Cymru to Tregaron, to lie on the railway tracks there as a protest against British Rail's proposals to end the Carmarthen to Aberystwyth service. Carwyn said that it was important for him to be there. That act of lying down on the rail track showed how strong his principles were.

Politics was the one new aspect of Carwyn's life that began in Aberystwyth. The traditional Liberal winds of Cardiganshire would have blown across him on the Rose Villa hearth and the red hot socialism of the Gwendraeth Valley would have seared his skin as soon as he walked out on to the streets. But it was the nationalism of Plaid Cymru that succeeded in luring him into party membership and activity. Carwyn was his own man.

His first link with Plaid Cymru, in terms of membership if not perception, also involves his friend Dafydd Bowen, as he recalls:

> I was already a member of Plaid Cymru before going to Aber, having joined the party in my fourth year of secondary school in Fishguard, under the guidance of one of my teachers, the Welsh author and activist, D J Williams. When I arrived at Aber, it was obvious that Welsh was more than a subject. It was a mission. Welsh was a political subject as well in those days, because of the crisis the Welsh language faced. There was a guiding conviction that every activity in the name of the language had to include the desire to fight for the continued existence of the language and its culture.

Because Dafydd Bowen had Carwyn's confidence, he was in a position to build on the work carried out by Miss Dora and others in the Gwendraeth. There Carwyn had formed a specific historical, cultural and literary view of what it meant to be Welsh. In Aberystwyth, this perception of nationalism took on a more political form. Carwyn would not have seen much difference between the subject he studied for his degree and the principles that his new political party stood for.

In 1972, in a TV interview on Welsh-language programme *Cywain* (Gathering), he explained his move towards party-political nationalism. The presenter, Ednyfed Hudson Davies, asked him if it had been a wrench for him to turn his back on the socialism of his upbringing when he turned to Plaid Cymru.

INTO THE WIND: THE LIFE OF CARWYN JAMES

No, there wasn't any wrenching at all to be honest... at college in Aberystwyth, I came face to face with politics. I don't think I was aware of it when I was a little boy in the village... The most important thing, I suppose, when I was in Aber, was studying Welsh history. We will not be truly Welsh until the schools of Wales teach Welsh history. And the fact that I combined Welsh History and Welsh at Aber is what made me join Plaid Cymru.

In Carwyn's own words therefore, there is a clear statement that his nationalism was more cultural than overtly political or economic.

Fellow Welsh honours student, and later Professor, Brynley Roberts remembers the activities of Plaid Cymru in Aberystwyth in those days.

We used to meet in a coffee shop a little up the road from where the Welsh bookshop Siop y Pethe is today. There's a chemist's there today. In the upstairs room there was a café. That's where we would meet as the Plaid Cymru group, in meetings that could be called rather sedate, over coffee and cakes. The discussions were always lively and energetic, but all within fairly conservative confines.

The political emphasis might well have been strong within literary circles, but it would not have been deemed to be a particularly strong political emphasis within the more purely political groups in Aber at the time. Theirs was a social, cultural politics. But nevertheless, Carwyn's political awakening, however that might be defined, happened at Aberystwyth.

He became the President of the Plaid Cymru student branch in 1951 and was re-elected in 1952, two years that bridged his third-year honours and his fourth-year teacher training. Plaid Cymru was without doubt the strongest political party, numerically, amongst the students.

With all that said, it was a period when protest in the name of Plaid Cymru was beginning, and the quiet, private Carwyn played his part. He first did so in his first term at Aber. Manny

Shinwell, a leading Labour MP and the Government Minister who had overseen the nationalisation of the coal industry, was to visit Aberystwyth. At that time, he was Secretary of State for War and then Defence Minister. It was as a Minister that he went to Aber. The organiser of the protest against the visit, because it was in the name of war, was Gwilym Prys Davies, who would go on to stand against Gwynfor Evans in the historic 1966 by-election at which Plaid Cymru won their first seat in Parliament, and he was later made a Lord. Dafydd Bowen remembers the protest:

> For me personally, it was as exciting a time as that famous march in Grosvenor Square against the War in Vietnam, or the march through Swansea as part of the protest for Welsh language road signs. Carwyn would have many a fine hour as a Welshman, but the Shinwell day proved to be a significant day for the young nationalist from Cefneithin.

The protest does seem to have awakened something political in Carwyn. He also took part in a protest in Trawsfynydd against the proposed firing range on Bronaber, 8,000 acres which had been bought by the Ministry of Defence. At the end of the Second World War the military camp on the site was used to fire explosives and bullets not used in wartime action. The Ministry of Defence wanted to extend its activities in Bronaber, arguing that the land there was of no value for agriculture or tourism. The protest against these plans was held in 1951, with protestors – Carwyn amongst them – sitting across the entrance road, stopping vehicles from entering the camp. Dafydd Bowen was there as well.

> Carwyn was never easy to drag from his bed in the mornings, but on that morning, he was up and ready at 4 a.m., the same time as me, in our digs in Plascrug. We had a quick breakfast and we walked over to meet Derec (The Reverend F M Jones) and Islwyn Lake near Seilo Chapel and then onwards and forwards from there to the battlefield.

The Secretary to the Plaid Cymru branch when Carwyn was President was Elystan Morgan – Baron Elystan Morgan today, but a student in the Law Department at Aber in the early Fifties. He contested three general elections and a by-election for Plaid Cymru in the Fifties and early Sixties. In 1966 he did become an MP, for Ceredigion, but for the Labour Party, having defected to them. Like Dafydd Bowen, Elystan Morgan had become a member of Plaid Cymru when he was still at school – in his case, in Aberystwyth. He remembers one particular occasion when Gwynfor Evans, then President of Plaid Cymru, visited the party's University Branch:

> We heard a sparkling speech by him, as was to be expected. And then, after the meeting, he went back to the house where Carwyn was living at the time, to have some supper. Many others went back to the house as well of course, because Gwynfor was there. Carwyn was completely comfortable in such company, involved in conversations and holding his arguments better than most there.

Elystan Morgan clearly admired Carwyn and the two worked closely together as leader and Secretary of the Plaid group for a good two years. That political and practical closeness gave Elystan an insight into his colleague's political abilities.

> I don't think that it's correct to say that Carwyn was an instinctive politician. That wasn't his heartbeat as he led Plaid Cymru at the University. The literature and the history of his country was more of a driving force than any political policy.

In showing such an approach, Carwyn's political motivation was in keeping with the general spirit of Plaid Cymru under the leadership of Gwynfor Evans. There were times of internal tensions within the party, with new forces from the industrial Valleys pulling at the interpretation of nationalism as propagated by Gwynfor Evans. People such as Emrys Roberts were calling for a more solid economic basis for Plaid's political philosophy. He, and those like him who saw

Wales more through coalfields and steelworks than through history and books, wanted a change of emphasis that reflected a broader Wales. Carwyn would have sided with Gwynfor in any such discussion, drawing on the Wales that he had come to know through Cefneithin, Gwendraeth Grammar lessons and Dafydd Bowen.

Plaid Cymru's approach also differed from the interpretation of nationalism across the water in Ireland. Elystan Morgan recalls one story that illustrated this very graphically.

> A very esteemed guest was invited to the college: Professor David Green, a scholar and fervent Irish nationalist. He was a large man with a big red beard, and he wore corduroy trousers. The image he conveyed, the spirit he exuded, made you think of Dylan Thomas. He made it clear that he deeply resented the very respectable, non-violent, diluted form of nationalism that was to be seen in Wales, through Plaid Cymru. The high point of his talk were these words: 'Plaid Cymru is not sincere. As a nationalist movement it hasn't shot one policeman yet. I am serious.' The audience were astounded and there's concise summary of the difference between nationalism in Wales and in Ireland at the time.

It would be unfair however, to suggest that Carwyn didn't apply his nationalistic principles, whatever they were based on, to particular issues. He did conscientiously work out and apply what he believed. One article he wrote in the University Magazine, *Llais y Lli* (The Voice of the Ocean), gives us an example of this. He argues for the need for a Welsh College. Later in his life, when he was on the Council of Aberystwyth University, these were also his guiding principles then.

> The ideal therefore, is for a university to create broad and cultured minds, in contrast to narrow and burdened minds. In other words, personalities equal to the philosopher Plato, the esteemed figure Aristotle and the gentleman Henry Newton. The three stand on the same ground when they say that one of the main functions of a university is to develop good citizens...

Let us consider the fact that we belong to a Welsh society which has its own particular culture. The heritage that is ours is a spirit, a personality, a nature, that is Welsh. If that is so, we elevate our esteemed language and insist that it's through the language that we will enjoy the living experience of touching the general culture of the world at its best. In our particular community, the clearest mirror that we can look through is our language, in order to discover both the highest muse and the universal culture of the world.

Sea air and fresh winds

Carwyn left Aberstwyth with an Honours Degree in Welsh and a Teaching Certificate. Many of his contemporaries had Carwyn down as a First-Class Honours student, but this wasn't to be the case. One or two of his final papers – Old Gaelic and Cornish – proved to be the stumbling block, giving us a rare example of Carwyn failing to reach expectations. There is an interesting explanation for that failing. His natural ambition would have made him push himself for that First-Class Honours. In fact, he pushed himself too far. It was common for students at that time to turn to any method possible to help them study better. One such popular aid was a tablet that would keep the student awake all night in order to revise. Carwyn turned to these tablets, but they didn't agree with him and made him ill. He was unwell over the days of the two exams that let him down.

Aberystwyth was a good, influential period in Carwyn's life. He was amongst those of like mind. Rugby, literature and politics were all there together. Alun Richards says that Carwyn's rugby acumen benefited from his time in Aber:

Carwyn's spell in quieter waters undoubtedly taught him much that was later to be of value to him as a coach, and those who saw him play regularly and played with him have special memories of his style, his immaculate kicking and the safety of those long tapering fingers above all, the grace of his movements and his willingness to take risks.

Those quieter waters did Carwyn good. Their relative isolation meant that he could develop his rugby there outside the main circuit of rugby culture and without the prying eyes of rugby officialdom. His time there would be echoed again later on in his lifetime, when he would again be in protected environments. One would be another academic institution, the other a foreign town. Comparative isolation turned into protection for Carwyn. At such times, he could keep his eyes firmly on the soil from whence he came.

The fresh sea air gave Carwyn the open space he needed to open his mind. It gave him the headspace to expand the influences of both Cefneithin and Rhydlewis. In this new-found space he intensified his knowledge of and love for Welsh literature; he developed a political awareness. Again, his friend Alun Richards could see this:

> In Aberystwyth, it is probable that Carwyn himself developed, perhaps unwittingly, for himself the qualities he was to ascribe to his most famous Welsh Lions, Barry John and Gerald Davies: 'I love an inner calm, a coolness, a detachment, a brilliance and insouciance which is devastating. Some sniff the wind – they created it.'

Carwyn did make many friendships during his university days that he kept throughout his life, including one particularly lasting one. Like many other students, Dafydd Bowen would go with Carwyn on his occasional weekend visits back home to Cefneithin. On one such occasion, Carwyn's mother confided in Dafydd Bowen that she found it difficult to get Carwyn to share his thoughts and feelings and that he tended to keep himself to himself. He was, she said, so different to his brother Dewi in that respect. Dafydd Bowen knew exactly what Annie James meant. But he gives the maternal observations some further thought. What she said was true, he says, but it wasn't the whole truth:

It would be a mistake to assume that he could not share his thoughts. During our time lodging together in our college days, he would share many of the secrets that young men would whisper to each other, and over the years since then, he would be as full of trust as anyone else.

This is in stark contrast to Alun Richards' observation. It's evident that Carwyn and Dafydd Bowen's friendship included more trust and openness than all others. Dafydd Bowen concludes the above thoughts with one short but penetrating sentence. It's one they lived going forward with their lives, and one we understand far more clearly looking backwards at it.

Many things remain now that no one else will know.

CHAPTER 6

Special Coder James

Белеет парус одинокий
В тумане моря голубом!
Что ищет он в стране далекой?
Что кинул он в краю родном?

'The lonely sail grows white
In the fog of the blue sea!
What does he pursue in a foreign land?
Why does he leave his homeland?'
Mikhail Lermontov, 'The Sail'

THE 1950S HAVE been described as the decade with an identity crisis. They fell between two decades that saw seismic changes throughout the world, albeit for very different reasons. The Fifties were a waiting room of a decade, holding those who had been through the war of the Forties and who were on their way to the revolution of the Sixties. It was a decade of conformity and consensus following destruction, as its people tried their best to hold on to familiar values whilst embracing the new world order that was emerging. It's into such a decade that the graduate Carwyn stepped when he left the shores of Aberystwyth as a 23 year old.

It's a strange anomaly that the first step that Carwyn took on that journey was to become part of the very institution that he had protested against as a student. He did his National Service. As a student, he protested at least twice against military expansion in parts of Wales. Now he was enlisting in a military organisation. And in doing so, the nationalist was also doing his British duty.

He didn't seem to question this move in any way. He had options. He could have deferred his National Service by two years through opting to do research at Aberystwyth University. A contemporary of his on the same degree, Brynley Roberts, did just that. T H Parry-Williams discussed this possibility with Carwyn, as he did with Brynley Roberts. But not even his hero's attempts at persuasion succeeded. This might well have only delayed his National Service, but those extra two years could have bought him time, allowing for the possibility that the National Service system could change in that time. It would also have kept Carwyn in the world of Welsh literature that he loved.

He could also have declared himself a conscientious objector. Many students at Aber at the same time as Carwyn took this step, but he chose not to accept either alternative and followed what he felt to be his duty. Having made that decision, there was little doubt as to which one of the Military Services he would enlist in. His brother Dewi had been in the Navy. As an 18 year old, he had gone to the Far East and to Australia, being away from Rose Villa for a long time. Their uncle, the father of Dai Rees Davies, Rhydlewis, was also a sailor. The family tradition, then, was to go to sea. There was one obstacle however: the family teased him constantly because he couldn't swim! On his journey across the Channel to Brittany, he had been very ill, and on arriving on the other side, he immediately requested to go home straight away on the next available boat. He didn't in the end, but his most immediate experience on the sea before National Service hadn't been a pleasant one. This didn't hold him back, and off he went to sea. There was no sign of a desire to follow his childhood dream of joining Rockfist Rogan in a fighter plane!

In the Navy

Carwyn headed for the Victoria Barracks in Davenport, near Portsmouth. Once there, he was again in a minority group for more than one reason. The Army was the Service that recruited the largest number of civilians on National Service – over 1.2 million between 1951 and 1960. Only 40,000 joined the Navy. Navy top brass believed that two years would never be enough to train a large number of men properly for Naval service. They were, therefore, more particular in their recruiting. Only the best would do.

Once in Davenport, Carwyn was chosen for a selective group within the Navy. In doing so, he would play a far more active part in his National Service than the majority of the others doing the same. That majority were training for something that might happen. Carwyn was involved with what was actually happening, in the name of the Cold War. He was part of an active military strategy, the direct result of government intervention.

There was a growing concern in government circles at the start of the 1950s that they should know more about Russian life and thought in order to understand their 'enemy' better. This included needing to understand the Russian language. A Ministry of Defence publication in March 1951 puts it like this:

> The existing resources of reliable Russian linguists for service
> under HM Government in the event of war are hopelessly
> inadequate... The requirement is unanimously described by the
> Intelligence Service as essential.

The response was to teach British citizens Russian in order for them to serve the government. The largest language scheme ever devised by a British Government was put into action, using those who were on National Service. This training programme led to the formation of the Joint Services School for Linguists, the JSSL. Only 1,500 were chosen for the JSSL from the Navy – Carwyn was one of them.

Recruitment was, of necessity, strict and confidential. In recounting the story of Leslie Whithead, a fellow JSSL member of Carwyn's, this is said of what happened to him before he was enlisted:

> …when he'd been accepted for the Russian course, his neighbours had been quizzed about his background by strange men in macs.

There are no stories of men in raincoats on the streets of Cefneithin or Aberystwyth, but the scrutiny must have been the same for all being considered for the JSSL.

Tony Cash, who would go on to be a television producer, establishing *The South Bank Show* with Melvyn Bragg, for example, started in the JSSL at the same time as Carwyn. He remembers the timetable they all had.

> It was four to six weeks' basic and other training; four weeks at sea; ten months on the principal language course; three to four months at RAF Wythall learning military terminology and radio and tape-recording technology. A total of four weeks – two times two weeks – annual leave; possibly three or four weeks' hanging around waiting for courses to start.

Following his basic training in Davenport, Carwyn went to the Army base in Coulsdon, Surrey, as a member of the fourth group to be recruited to the JSSL. The Russian lessons were co-ordinated there on behalf of the joint Services, as well as in Bodmin, Cornwall. Once in Coulsdon, they would learn the Russian alphabet, grammatical forms and pronunciation. These were formal lessons within a disciplined military environment. There was a definite structure to Carwyn's days, within which he was coming into contact with new and varied world views and ways of living.

Their Russian lessons were based in a building opposite the Guards' Headquarters in Caterham. The servicemen's home was a row of concrete cabins, with the inside open to the beams in the roof. Each man had his single bed, with a small cupboard by its side. There was one charcoal-burning heater in each cabin, and only one table and six chairs for the 24 men to share between them. Consequently, most of the men did their homework on their beds.

There was a strict emphasis on cleanliness, order and discipline. Each cabin was inspected at nine o'clock every night, and then again after breakfast the following morning. Amongst the tasks that Carwyn would have to perform were shining the bin lids, black-leading the stove and cleaning the windows with newspaper.

He would regularly have been woken at 6 a.m., even though the first parade wasn't until 8 a.m. Marching exercises were deemed necessary in order to maintain a military discipline alongside the patterns of teaching. But there was a problem: they were members of the joint services and each individual service has their own particular marching style, so trying to get them all to march as one proved quite a task. The parades were subsequently a combination of chore and amusement.

The backbone of the teaching was a series of 45-minute sessions between 8.30 and 12.30, with a break in the middle. The full group of 30 would have their grammar lessons together and then break into groups of ten for the oral practice. In the afternoon, they would have a combination of lectures on a range of related topics and other activities such as watching films. The working day would end at 4 p.m., when they would have their tea, and then supper at seven. Quite often there would be a lecture or a presentation in the evenings, on any topic that linked with Russia. Any spare time the servicemen had would usually see them on a bus to Croydon or even to London. Theatre shows and pub visits were the order of the day on such occasions. Carwyn would have benefited greatly from these social events, with his natural ability to hold conversation and his genuine interest in people supplied with new wells to draw from.

On the whole, the tutors on the JSSL course were former

JSSL Staff. Front row (L to R): Brigadier E K Page (principal at Coulsdon 1954); Wing Commander Edgar J Harrington; Flight Lieutenant A Heath-Bullock; Professor Elizabeth M Hill; and Marshal of the Royal Air Force, Lord Tedder (Chancellor of Cambridge University). Row 2: Dr Jan Horvath; Princess Natasha Naumova; Mr Alexei Plyushkov; Mme Alexandra Hackel; Mr Vladimir Saulius. Row 3: Mme Chernysheva; 2nd Lt L Gemson; Mr Goodliffe; Mr Boris Ranevski; Mr Cameron; Ms Doris Mudie; Mr Courtney Lloyd; Princess Elena Lieven.
Courtesy of Peter Robbins (Army)

Soviet citizens, with a fair number of Poles and citizens of the Baltic States, but there were a few British amongst them. The émigré majority divided into two. Brynley Roberts, a fellow student of Carwyn's at Aber, but who deferred the start of his National Service till two years after Carwyn, remembers this:

> Many of the older Russians had served in the First World War and then left Russia after the revolution. The others served in the Second World War. The attitude of the two camps towards their motherland was very different. The older ones tended to offer a more sentimental picture of the Russia they had left, feeling a strong longing for the Russia of old and wanting to return to it. The view of the younger Russians was much harder and more negative. We would therefore have two opposite and sometimes conflicting views of what Russia was. I'm sure that having both views enabled us to form a more balanced opinion for ourselves, somewhere in the middle between the two.

This was another pushing of the boundaries for Carwyn – a step further again from Aberystwyth, which had in itself been a step away from Cefneithin, not just in terms of geography but in opening up new cultures as well. He would come across attitudes and opinions that had until then been alien to him. But it also offered a strange continuity. He had been war-aware from the last days of primary and through grammar school. Ex-servicemen had been amongst his fellow students at Aber. Now he was doing his National Service. Warfare and things military would be a presence in his life, to varying degrees and in different forms, from 1939 until 1956.

Carwyn felt the effects of war in one very practical way in the JSSL. They might well have had all the latest technology on their innovative course, but there was a distinct shortage of set books, writing paper and biros, and copies of Russian literature. The tutors would quite often lend their own books to their students. This is something that Carwyn would have taken advantage of without any hesitation. This was his introduction to the world of Russian literature, which would prove to be a strong influence on him throughout his life. He fell under the spell of Chekhov and discovered Lermontov, Tolstoy, Pushkin and Dostoyevsky. Extracts from the works of these literary giants were read regularly to the JSSL members and they were expected to read the works for themselves too – in the original language of course. This is how the British men would get into the mindset of the Russians the government wanted them to understand. To the same end, Russian films were shown regularly – both features and propaganda.

As Carwyn was a good singer and liked his music, Russian songs appealed to him instantly. He learned many of that country's popular and influential songs. We have a record of one such instance on the YouTube social media channel. In 1973, he recorded an item for a BBC network programme with a choir of eight other ex-JSSL members. They sang '*Stanochek*' (The Spinning Loom), and Carwyn was the soloist. It's a song about a factory worker falling in love with a fellow factory worker who doesn't want to know and goes with someone else, leaving her to her spinning loom. The two presenters

The '*Stanochek*' choir
Tony Cash

were Melvyn Bragg and ex-JSSL member Tony Cash, who remembers the impression Carwyn made on them during their JSSL days:

> He made such an impression on us at Coulsdon that he was not going to be forgotten very easily. He was a kind man, very considerate. And his singing voice made him a prominent part of the choir that was established at the camp. The programme in 1973 was the first in a series of what I called Documentary Entertainments on specific themes. It contained poetry, elements of drama, song and spoken word and was filmed in front of a live audience. There was no way that Carwyn wasn't going to be a part of it.

Tony Cash shared a cabin with Carwyn when the two arrived in the Surrey camp in October 1953, staying there for ten months.

> If there was any one singer in the 1953 Coulsdon choir who stood out, it was the late Carwyn James... Carwyn was blessed with a

sweet tenor voice, which coupled with his very slight build made his hugely successful career in club and international rugby union difficult to envisage – until you saw him in action, that is.

The song *'Stanochek'* is in a book of Russian ballads used by the JSSL, *The Samovar Songbook*. It includes folk songs, ballads, Cossack songs, Gipsy songs, popular Russian songs and the *chastushki*, satirical songs. Fortune favoured Carwyn when he was placed at Coulsdon, as the choral tradition grew more quickly and strongly there than in other camps. The man from the Male Voice Choir tradition was in his element. Informal singing sessions were held regularly in the NAAFI, but there was also a formal choir, with proper rehearsal times and performances. Again, the choir would sing Russian songs, a further way to immerse the men in the Russian way of life.

Carwyn left Coulsdon and then went to the Midlands, to RAF Wythall, for four months. This is where his knowledge of Russia and Russian would be applied specifically to a military situation. He learned to use sophisticated radio equipment in order to listen to secret Russian messages, for analysis at GCHQ. They would have been given a specific list of call signs, the secret one-word pseudonyms given to tanks, ships, aeroplanes etc. to identify who was communicating with who, as Tony Cash explains:

> Call signs were changed regularly and GCHQ was particularly interested in learning who had become what; 'Hawk' becoming 'Pig-Iron' for example, or 'Eagle' changed to 'Bucket'.

If those names or call signs were heard, the JSSL men were to note what time the name was heard, where the person was at the time and what the content of the message was.

The next step was applying the military and linguistic training in a more direct military situation. JSSL members were more active than most other National Servicemen. It has been believed that Carwyn went back to his base in Davenport

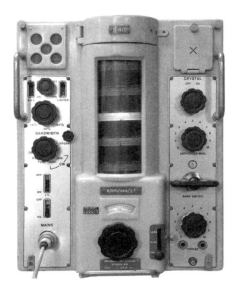

A Murphy B40 short-wave receiver, as used by Carwyn at Cuxhaven

after Wythall – he did, but only as a stopover on his way to Germany, as one of his fellow JSSL members confirms:

Selection for the Navy [rugby] team was almost inevitable if you were half fit and reasonably sober. We had only about 120 Navy men in Germany at the time, whereas the Army and RAF could choose from minimally 60,000 each. We were annihilated in both games… so where was the magic in these grotesque encounters? Simply playing alongside Carwyn James, the greatest coach Wales ever had and so intelligent and innovative that many rate him as the best the world has ever seen.

More later of Carwyn's rugby experiences in the Navy. This comment was made by Ian Wooldridge, who was to become a highly-respected sports journalist. He was a part of the third group of men accepted into the JSSL. Being older than Carwyn, he would have been in a position of leadership and was a leader in the cabin in which Carwyn lived in Coulsdon. The significance of this comment is that it places Carwyn in Germany. He did not go back to Davenport therefore, but more importantly, it shows that Carwyn did travel abroad with the Navy. He was constantly teased by family and friends that he had been a Navy member who had never been to sea. But he had. Tony Cash affirms this:

Everybody had to have their time 'at sea', without exception, even if it was in the seas around England.

Ian Wooldridge moved to the Naval Camp in Cuxhaven, near Hamburg, Germany at the same time as Carwyn in 1954. He mentioned his time there in a story for the *Daily Mail* in 2001. Carwyn's responsibility in Cuxhaven was to listen to messages transmitted from Russia, specifically in his case to East Berlin. On his Murphy B40 receiver, he would listen in to Soviet military radio traffic, particularly voice messages between ships, planes, control towers and even occasionally, Red Army conversations involving tanks, etc. A specially-designated building, the Watch Room, accessible only to men who had signed the Official Secrets Act, housed these receivers. Probably not more than 20 were manned 24/7. It was intense, detailed work, with the pressure of government expectations bearing down on them. British Intelligence services needed to know the whereabouts of Russian soldiers, planes, ships and submarines, as well as what weapons Russia might have at the time and which weapons were being developed by them. As at RAF Wythall, Carwyn's instructions in Cuxhaven came from GCHQ in Cheltenham, who needed to know what was happening in Eastern Europe as the Cold War intensified.

Rugby in the Navy

Tony Cash sums up Carwyn's place in the JSSL:

> Of all Coders who could call themselves sportsmen, undoubtedly the greatest was Carwyn James. And he had a very pleasing disposition. Every one liked him, there's no doubt about that. That says quite a lot, because we were after all in a massed group of men, in a military context, living closely together for quite a long time with everyone having their own agenda.

There was one fellow Navy member who would have

understood Carwyn's particular background and upbringing very well. Terry Davies was in the Navy at the same time as Carwyn, as a member of the Marines. He's from the village of Bynea, on the eastern outskirts of Llanelli. He played his club rugby for Swansea and Llanelli and he reached the highest level with Wales and the British and Irish Lions. He is regarded as one of the best full backs Wales has ever produced. He remembers seeing Carwyn before their days in the Navy.

> I had seen him around in about 1950–51, when the West Wales XV were playing on Swansea's St Helens ground. I played for Swansea at the time. This young little outside half made quite an impression on everyone. He was only a student at the time but he was a very mature player. I didn't meet him on that day – that didn't happen until we were both in the Navy.
>
> Both of us had been chosen to play for the Navy team against the RAF, in Twickenham. As neither Carwyn nor I were officers, we weren't allowed to stay in a hotel and we had to stay in barracks nearby. That's where I met Carwyn for the first time.

Facing Carwyn and Terry Davies in that game was another man who would become a rugby giant. R H Williams played for the RAF team. Before the end of the decade, R H Williams, Terry and Carwyn would be playing for the same club team, Llanelli, and RH and Terry would be touring with the British Lions. Carwyn would have to wait a little while longer before making his own distinctive mark on Lions history. For that Services game in Twickenham, Terry Davies dared to challenge the officer responsible for selecting the Navy team.

> For some reason he had decided to chose Carwyn as full back and myself as outside half. Having seen Carwyn play for West Wales, I knew beyond doubt that he was an outside half and a very talented one at that. I approached the coach and told him, 'I think you've made a mistake, Sir. Carwyn should be outside half and I should be full back.' The reply came like a bullet from the posh mouth of the officer: 'Are you suggesting that I am wrong, Davies?' And that's how it stayed. Carwyn played at full back and I was outside half.

It goes without saying that history would prove the officer to be wrong. Carwyn also refers to this gentleman, Captain H C Browne, when he recalls the process of choosing the players for the Navy team. A trial game had been arranged in order for Captain Browne to select the final XV. The favourite for the full-back position was Frank Fenner. Carwyn had evidently been told that he was being considered for the full-back role and he decided that he would play to the best of his ability, with nothing to lose, even if someone else was a favourite for that position. He played really well, attacking at every opportunity, and dropped three goals. Captain Brown had to choose him.

> What I remember vividly is receiving a part-congratulatory, part-briefing letter from Captain Browne, who was obviously uneasy about a certain facet of my game, the gist of which I can recall, if not the exact wording. 'Dear James. There are three things I want you to do on Saturday. Number one, tackle. Number two, tackle. Number three, tackle.'

Captain Browne could stand with Gwynfil Rees in identifying Carwyn's rugby weakness. Carwyn's response to such comments usually referred back to his Lewis Jones observation: that a team he was playing for might well concede two tries, but they would then score four.

The relief from the routine and intensity of JSSL life for Carwyn was undoubtedly his rugby. His colleagues at the language school remember this aspect of Carwyn's time there more than anything else. Mike Williams, for example:

> I have but a few memories of Carwyn James, yet even after 62 years, they remain clear. Unfortunately, my rugby wasn't good enough to enable me to gain a place in the JSSL camp rugby team, but I clearly remember at a training session playing on the opposing side to Carwyn. His positional play, sense of territory and handling of the ball were exceptional, but the most outstanding thing about him that I recall was his unbelievable body swerve.
> We were of similar build so I expected to be as nimble as

him. I went to tackle him as he approached me, carrying the ball, but he simply wasn't there! Picking myself up, I realised what a superb rugby player he was and why I should stick to cycle racing. I remember Carwyn as a rather quiet, introverted man, but one whose deep thinking was matched by instant action.

Geoff Sharpe remembers playing rugby in Germany:

I admired him enormously and followed his rugby career with Wales over the years. I always thought it a shame he was playing at the same time as Cliff Morgan. One rugby memory I have is playing rugby with him. Needless to say, we won! Our tactics were simple. Whenever we had possession we handed the ball to Carwyn and watched him jiggle and dummy and spurt his way to the end zone. It was amazing to watch! A great memory of a wonderful person.

A wonderful person, let it be noted, not just a wonderful player. William Heatherington, another fellow JSSL member, remembers a story that places Carwyn in Scotland.

In Invergordon in the late summer of 1953, all kinds of sporting activities were laid on for the hundreds of sailors assembled, including a sailing regatta and rugby trials. As a scrum half, I volunteered for the home fleet selection and I found myself playing in the number 9 shirt with Carwyn at 10. I don't know which ship he was on, but we met for the first and only time on that field. I look back on that day as my finest moment in rugby. Carwyn far outshone anyone else on the pitch: all I had to do was feed him a long accurate pass from the base of the scrum and he made me look like the best scrum half in Scotland! Happy memories.

It was impossible not to be aware of Carwyn's presence on the rugby pitch in his Navy shirt. His colleagues suggest that Carwyn would have been excused some usual Naval duties in order for him to be released to play rugby. William Heatherington says that this was the case when he was in Invergordon. Alun Richards elaborates on this issue, confirming that the Naval authorities would do their best to make sure that Carwyn was always available for rugby duty. There was one man who was particularly influential in this process, Gwyn Walters. He would become a leading Welsh rugby referee and was influential in the Navy hierarchy during Carwyn's days, as Alun Richards sums up:

> Mr Walters had an arrangement to divert promising players to an unnamed naval officer in Devonport.

Some have suggested that this means that Carwyn was excused all duties in order to protect him to play rugby. That takes the issue too far and is a rather naïve interpretation. He would have to have fulfilled his responsibilities like everyone else, as exceptional rugby talent would not be reason enough for Carwyn to be absolved of all National Service duties. But within that system, there was an understanding that they would do everything possible to develop his rugby. Others have also suggested over the years that he was chosen for the JSSL in the first place because of his rugby. That again, is incorrect. The leading criterion for JSSL inclusion was to have good language qualifications. The majority of Coders entered with good A Level language results. The rest either had O Levels or their equivalent or, as in Carwyn's case, a degree.

Reference to Gwyn Walters brings to mind another future Welsh referee that Carwyn came into contact with in the JSSL, in this case at Coulsdon. With reference to the attempts at unifying the parading traditions, there were times when they marched separately, within the discipline of their own particular service. As Carwyn's Navy group drew near to the Army parade, the Army leader, Cennydd Thomas, whispered to Carwyn as their paths crossed, 'You're playing Saturday!' That is now in the annals of rugby folklore, whether it be true or not.

Carwyn did find an escape in rugby. Coulsdon's geographical

location offered him a rugby escape outside Naval confines as well.

> It was a great joy to be able to escape on Saturday mornings, away from the parades and the divisions and the bull, to a reasonably civilised community at Herne Hill where the feeling at the ground and at The Half Moon, their social headquarters in those days, was intensely Welsh – far more so than at any rugby ground in Wales.

He played his first game for London Welsh in 1952, against the Old Cranleighans. The *Western Mail* noted the occasion, if rather underwhelmingly:

> The schoolboy international, in his first match with London Welsh, created a favourable impression.

London Welsh offered him a complete break from the JSSL over the Christmas period in 1953. The club went on a tour of South Wales, their first since the end of the Second World War. The first game was against Maesteg, during which Carwyn threw what was described as the most unreasonable dummy pass that led to a try for the visitors. This team secured a double victory against Neath on that tour for the very first time, and then they played Swansea. But the best encounter for Carwyn, no doubt, was that at Stradey Park against the team he had played for as a schoolboy. Whatever happened on the pitch, returning to home soil while he was doing his National Service must have been a tonic for the young Carwyn. It would have been ointment for his soul.

London Welsh note one game in which Carwyn shone more than usual. Cardiff were visiting Old Deer Park and in one particular move, Carwyn picked up a loose ball in his own half, ran effortlessly past two tacklers and started a sequence of passing between himself and Dudley Pope that ended in Carwyn himself finishing the move with a try under the posts. At the end of that same season in 1956, Carwyn captained

London Welsh to their first victory in 25 years in the Middlesex Sevens. They beat Emmanuel College Cambridge 24–10 in the final. While he was with the Exiles, he was also chosen to represent Surrey in county rugby.

His time with London Welsh ensured that he played rugby at first-class level and in so doing, kept his name in the minds of players, coaches and officials alike. It kept him from the anonymity that might well have been his lot if he had been restricted to Services rugby.

He certainly was in the shop window, as he received an offer from Rugby League team Oldham to play for them professionally. But like his friend Terry Davies, he turned down the opportunity to play professionally, choosing to stay with the amateur code of the game.

Two years

He only did his National Service for the required two years, but they are an important two years in his life. The fact he played such an active military role is one that has caused surprise and curiosity to many who are only aware of the most

Watering hole for the Welsh Exiles, The Half Moon, Herne Hill
Matthew Black

basic details of his involvement. He was quizzed about this on a Welsh-language TV programme, *Cywair* (Tone), in the 1970s. Presenter Ednyfed Hudson Davies asked him about his Navy days:

> EHD: Remembering your background in the chapel world and with Plaid Cymru, was there any barrier for you in joining the Navy?
>
> CJ: I would say that immaturity was the reason for me going to the Navy. I don't think, maybe, that I heard enough about pacifism from the pulpit. In Wales, during the War years (I was about 10 years old when war broke out) and in the years after, we constantly heard that 'our side' was good, was healthy. I would like to have heard more about the definite, strong objections to war. There's no doubt that I am a pacifist today – and I have a little bit of a conscience that I served in the Navy. But at the same time, I'm glad that I did so, because I learned another language.

This is consistent with his childhood recollection that the minister had said in chapel that God was 'on our side'. It might well be easy to assume that a Welsh-Nonconformist upbringing would be inherently pacifist, but the wartime reality was obviously different. That being said, he did stand shoulder to shoulder with pacifist demonstrators when he was a student. The naivety he mentions would appear to have blurred the lines between his chapel upbringing and the more radical nature of student life.

Having joined the Navy, Carwyn fully engaged with what was required of those on National Service – even more so as a member of JSSL – but also there was a constant pull to step away. Rugby gave him that opportunity. The escape the game offered Carwyn is to be understood on a deeper level than just offering an occasional diversion. He always had that need to escape; the need to channel his energies somewhere other than towards the main focus of what he was doing at any given time. School, university and now National Service clearly showed this aspect of his personality. Rugby was always the escape, the change of world, the easing from the pressure of the familiar, the change of routine. It's where he went when he wanted to remind himself where he came from. Later in his life, rugby was to lose that role.

He stepped outside his square mile. He learned a new way to live. He understood a new country's language and the curtain was lifted on a whole new literature and culture. And like the characters in the plays of the Chekhov that he grew to love, he continued to look towards his own personal Moscow, wondering if he would ever get there.

CHAPTER 7

Chalk and whistle

Like a clock the tide regulates life:
The hawk feeds from the sky
The same shadow of necessity;
Salmon swim old, known ways to the sea.

Tony Curtis, *Towy*

HAVING LEFT THE Navy, Carwyn was free to look for work in his chosen profession of teaching. When he left Aberystwyth, he had a letter from T H Parry-Williams in his pocket, to be shown to whoever he might apply for a job with. It was a short letter, but heartily recommending Carwyn for any teaching job he might try for. It was akin to having a reference from John Betjeman for a teaching job in England.

There was one headteacher, however, who wouldn't need to see such a reference: Carwyn's former head, Llewellyn Williams. He knew of Carwyn's abilities and there was a vacancy at Gwendraeth Grammar School when Carwyn was looking for a job. It would appear that was a situation perfect for Carwyn. Gareth Williams sums up what most people who knew of the situation thought at the time, and what Carwyn's former headmaster himself thought. Everyone was:

> …confident that if Carwyn were to canvas the support of one or two councillors, the post was safely his. It was an expectation that was not met; that slightly superior detachment prevailed, then and later. Carwyn would not canvas and that was that.

COLEG PRIFYSGOL CYMRU
UNIVERSITY COLLEGE OF WALES
ABERYSTWYTH
TEL. 346

June, 1952

It gives me great pleasure to bear testimony in favour of Mr. Carwyn Rees James, B.A., a student of this College. He pursued courses of instruction in the Department of Welsh Language and Literature as far as the Honours Stage, which he completed in June, 1951, by passing the University Examination of that grade. He was placed in the First Division of the Second Class.

I found Mr. James to be an intelligent and hardworking student. He made rapid progress, and his work at the Honours Stage was most creditable. He has taken a very prominent part in the various activities of College life, having held offices in the Students' Representative Council and achieved high distinction in athletics (College and University).

Mr. James has a charming disposition and a pleasant manner. I beg to recommend him most heartily for a suitable post.

T. H. Parry-Williams

Reference letter from professor and poet T H Parry-Williams

Canvassing was a crucial dark practice at the time, with candidates paying a clandestine visit to councillors central to the appointments process in schools, asking for their support in their application. Some – a few – refused to follow such a practice, preferring to depend on their own abilities and the interview process alone, without going cap in hand to any councillor. Carwyn was one of those. Gareth Williams puts the reason for that down to Carwyn's innate 'superior detachment', and there's no denying that he could manifest such a trait. Others might suggest that it was down to his high moral standards. This is what Alun Richards says:

> What is clear, after this experience, [is that] Carwyn never applied for any post as an ordinary schoolmaster where there was the slightest chance that he might be rejected.

But before he could decide where he was going to work, there was an unexpected turn for Carwyn. He was involved once more with Eastern Europe a matter of weeks after leaving the JSSL.

Swansea Rugby Club asked him to play for them on their tour of Romania. They were the first club in Britain to tour behind the Iron Curtain. Carwyn accepted the offer, but only after going through the official channels to obtain clearance to go. Having only just left his work with the JSSL, he was still bound by the Official Secrets Act.

The group left Wales for Amsterdam on a Sabena Airlines flight in August 1954. His former Navy teammate Terry Davies was also on the tour. He remembers the sight that faced them when they arrived at Amsterdam Airport.

> In front of us were three Dakota aeroplanes. This is what the Romanians had sent to take us from Amsterdam to Bucharest. It looked as if the war was still on, with each one painted in camouflage colours. There was a lot of discussion on that Dutch tarmac as to whether we should go on the planes at all. There was

quite a bit of panic. But we didn't have a choice, of course, and off we went.

No fears were assuaged when they boarded the planes. The Dakotas were usually used to carry goods, so there were no fixed seats. The passengers were to sit on loose chairs, scattered here and there. This proved to be a particular challenge on take off, with the chairs and their occupants hurtling towards the back of the plane as it reached towards the vertical.

We were all in one pile at the back of the plane!

Once airborne, they came into atrocious weather. Soon, they were in the throes of a thunderstorm.

Every time lightning flashed across the sky, the whole inside of the plane would be fully lit, as well as the ground beneath us. That's when we could see how close we were to the mountains – far too close! I'm sure there was something wrong with our pilot. It was as if he had something to prove by taking us all through the storm and safely to our destination, come what may. It was a reckless determination!

Terry's fears were confirmed when they touched down in Bucharest. Theirs was the only plane to have made it, the other two planes having turned back to Amsterdam because the weather was so bad. Carwyn was on one of the planes that turned back.

When the others arrived in Bucharest the day after, Carwyn was full of panic and fear as he told us the story of how they feared for their lives and had to turn back. You could see the fear in his eyes.

The team stayed in a hotel in the centre of Bucharest, but their official headquarters was the British Embassy in the city. The man from the Embassy responsible for looking after them was a short, bespectacled diplomat. It was evident that he wanted to make the most of the visit of a group from the West to his communist environment.

> We all had an invitation to go and see a military air show. We all felt that this was an opportunity for the authorities to flex their military muscles in front of a Western audience. The little man from the Embassy had his own agenda though, and the fact he was short all of a sudden became relevant. He came with us, but hid in the middle of our group, out of sight, and took photographs of all the planes in the show.

The players had very little sleep in their hotel as it was on a cobbled road which tanks and other military vehicles would use constantly during the night until about 4 a.m. Russian manoeuvres were evident enough.

They played two games in Romania, against the capital's team, Bucharest, on a football pitch in a very big stadium. Their most challenging opponent was the heat.

> It was over 100° in the stadium, as it was the middle of August. They were considerate enough to move the game from its original

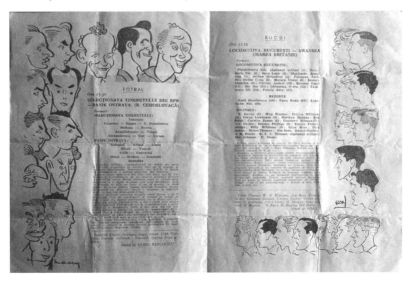

Swansea vs. Locomotiva Bucuresti match programme

afternoon kick-off time to the evening, but it was still unbearably hot. By half time, sweat was running down our faces in white lines.

Carwyn played in the second of the two games, but had to leave the field of play because of an injury. There were no substitutes allowed in those days, so Swansea had to play the remainder of the game with 14 men. Shortly before Vivian 'Matty' Davies' death a couple of years ago, he mentioned that he was Carwyn's scrum half in that game.

The Swansea club were clearly impressed with the way that their tour had been organised and the way they were treated while in Romania. Dave Dow, the club's current archivist, explains why:

> From what players who went on that tour said in the years after their visit, the coaching methods used were those of the Russians. But the main thing that the players noted was the standard of medical care in that country at the time. It seemed to be far in advance of the way things were in this country. They seemed to suggest also that our players were more unfit than they were.

In his book, Alun Richards claims that Carwyn had been told not to show that he spoke Russian. Carwyn's former JSSL colleagues see no reason why this should be true, in fact suggesting it would have been advantageous for him to do so.

In a context broader than that of the oval ball alone, this was a bold venture by Swansea Rugby Club. From 1947 until 1989, Romania was known as the Romanian Socialist Republic. Stalin might well have died a year before Swansea's tour, but he still cast an iron shadow over communist countries surrounding the USSR. Any attempt in Romania to oppose the Communist regime would be stamped on heavily. Millions were exiled, entire communities were displaced within their own country and tens of thousands were killed. It was a country under oppression.

It was into this political environment that Swansea Rugby

club sent their team. In discussing this with those currently at the club, there's an ambivalence as to the reason why this step was taken at the time. It's as if the tour itself is remembered, though the reason for it isn't.

It also raises the question of Carwyn's involvement on the tour. He had spent the year before the tour eavesdropping on the conversations of Russian intelligence, which would have included references to Romania. He would therefore have had a clear idea of what was happening there. If there were questions relating to reconciling National Service with anti-military protests at university, it would seem natural to ask the same question of his decision to accept Swansea's invitation to tour an oppressed Communist country. This becomes even more relevant if we turn the clock of Carwyn's life forward a decade or so, when he would make a strong public stance against the apartheid system. But why didn't he make the same kind of stance against oppressive, godless Communist power?

But there were cultural forces influencing Carwyn's view of Russia that weren't the same as those prevalent during the apartheid confrontations. Such forces were active, if not dominant, 20 years before Carwyn went to Romania with Swansea. In the 1930s, Gareth Jones, a fellow Welshman, journalist and former secretary to Lloyd George, had tried to tell the world how Stalin was causing suffering and death amongst his own people, specifically in Ukraine. Even though Jones would be proved right, he faced worldwide opposition, including vociferous opposition from his fellow Welshmen. In open rejection of Jones' claims, a series of letters in Welsh-language weekly publication *Y Cymro* (The Welshman) in 1933, for example, shows that there was a deeply-ingrained sympathy from the Welsh towards Russia. They said that the issues with Stalin's regime paled into insignificance when compared to the kind of world that Hitler wanted to create. Russia was acceptable – it was a more humane regime as it was based on the equality of all, on sharing. It was a world view more in step with the socialism of the coalfield in which

Carwyn was brought up. It was the dominant voice, with Gareth Jones' assertions being a lone cry in the wilderness at the time. Carwyn was always more likely to follow the dominant public perception than the lone voice.

In the valley next to Carwyn's Gwendraeth, the Amman, Communism itself was a very strong political force. Two Ammanford men, Communist members, were killed in the Spanish Civil war. Their town was the home of Y Tŷ Gwyn, ironically named The White House, which was a centre for Communist studies and activities. This, added to the previously-mentioned radical theological tradition Carwyn would have inherited, gave him a political and social subconscious that leaned naturally to the left. Into this mix we must also put his two years of intense Russian Studies. In this context, perhaps we can understand why he felt no need to take a stance.

Carwyn the family man brought gifts back with him from Romania. His niece Bethan, Eilonwy's daughter, remembers what she received from her uncle. She had had to go to live with her grandparents, Carwyn's mother and father, for a while as her mother was ill and unable to look after her.

> I was in Rose Villa for a school term at least. I remember Carwyn giving me a gift from Romania. It was made from wood, a kind of two-figure weather-forecasting toy, where the man and woman would pop in and out of their home according to what the weather was like. At that time, I have a vivid child's memory of Carwyn's rugby shirts drying in front of the fire in my grandmother's house and hearing the sound of the studs on the rugby boots like horses' hooves on the pitch at the bottom of the garden.
>
> Carwyn had a special way with us children. He would look at us in a loving way. He always had a smile on his face, even when he wasn't smiling.

Looking for work

Having returned from Romania, Carwyn could begin to look for work in earnest. He didn't have to wait to long for his first job. He was appointed as a Welsh teacher at the Queen

Elizabeth Grammar School, Carmarthen, one of the oldest schools in Wales. It had been a part of the grammar-school establishment for centuries. As for Carwyn, he was back in Carmarthenshire, back in Cefneithin, back in the Rose Villa of his cradling years.

One of his pupils at his new school remembers the arrival of their new teacher. Carwyn James would come face to face with Denzil Davies again when the two were candidates in the same constituency in the General Election of 1970, but their first encounter was as teacher and pupil in Carmarthen.

> Queen Elizabeth was a grammar school in the traditional interpretation of the word. Discipline was strict. It was very anglicised in spirit. And Carmarthen itself was a county town in the true sense of the word. There were three different classes [in each year]. The 'A' stream for the best of the Welsh and non-Welsh speaking pupils, the 'E' stream for the non-Welsh speaking boys not good enough for A and the 'W' for the Welsh-speaking boys not good enough for the 'A' either. In direct contrast to what can happen today, Welsh was the language of the schoolyard and English was the language of education.

Educationally, it was amongst the best schools in Wales. It was also a major rugby school, playing against teams from Haverfordwest to the west and Neath to the east.

> But strangely enough, looking at it now, we didn't play against Llandovery College. They weren't deemed good enough for us to play them. There was no football in the school at all, only rugby.

A rugby legend born 13 years after Carwyn, and who went to school less than ten miles from Carmarthen, had a totally different experience. Three-time British Lion Delme Thomas went to St Clears Secondary School, where there was no rugby at all. It was only football, until one teacher arrived to change everything. An individual teacher could have a huge influence on the sporting direction of the school he was in.

Other pupils who were at Queen Elizabeth at the time remember the contribution made by Carwyn.

The boys at the Gramm didn't have the opportunity to see Carwyn's real greatness as a Welsh teacher. The Head of Department taught the sixth form and the pupils in the best streams in other years, the 'A' stream. Carwyn taught pupils in the second stream, the 'W', and the Welsh-as-a-second-language pupils in the 'E' stream.

Naturally, Carwyn assisted the PE teacher in the rugby coaching, including the first team. He would bring players from the Llanelli club [which he had started playing for again by this point] to contribute to the training sessions as well. In these sessions, the pupils would aim to tackle Carwyn as hard as they could and floor him in the process, so that they could have the bragging rights of having tackled him. Very few boys succeeded in doing so. Usually Carwyn's famed side-step meant that he could avoid them completely, leaving the aspiring tackler on his face in the mud.

As a teacher, his most notable characteristic was his gentleness. He would hardly ever lose his temper or discipline us severely. With Carwyn, correction was a gentle word of admonition, which was far more of a punishment than anything else. On one rugby trip, to an away game in Tenby, one of the boys was smoking in the back seat of the bus. Carwyn caught him, and told him off in his usual style, 'Do you think you will play better today if you smoke that?' That pupil remembers that telling off to this day and admits that it was far more effective because he felt that he had offended Carwyn.

In one school exam, which Carwyn was supervising, he went up to one pupil who he knew was a good Welsh student even though Carwyn didn't teach him, and whispered in his year, 'If you study Welsh at university, remember to study Welsh Literature and try to do as few language courses as possible.' Such was his concern for pupils and his love for literature.

Carwyn was only in Carmarthen for two years. He left just before a future world rugby star started at the school. But this young boy, Gerald Davies, was used to seeing Carwyn playing for Llanelli.

For me, like every other rugby player in the village, Saturday afternoon when the Scarlets were playing at home inevitably meant a journey to Stradey. Whilst there were many Scarlets heroes, it was Carwyn James who stood out for me. There were those who admired his drop kicks, or his subtle, canny kicks to touch; I thrilled to his side-steps, his running with the ball... He teased opponents, almost daring them to tackle him, persuading them to go one way when he had made his mind up to go the other. By many people's standards, the measurement of a player's contribution to the game is in direct proportion to the amount of mud he has managed to accumulate on his kit. For Carwyn, the reverse was true: he hardly needed to shower at the end of a triumphant game.

Following a break of not playing for the Scarlets while at University and on National Service, Carwyn started playing for the club again in 1954. He played for them about 50 times while at the Carmarthen school. He went on to play for them over 100 times more after he left Carmarthen and started as a teacher at Llandovery College. The club records for this period aren't complete, but there's definite proof that he played at least 133 games for them, in a period when the Scarlets played 237 games. The probability is therefore that he also played in a fair proportion of the 100 or so games for which the team-sheet details are incomplete.

In moving from Carmarthen to Llandovery, Carwyn was moving to another old Welsh educational establishment, one that would have a significant influence on his life.

CHAPTER 8

Floreat Landubriense

Sic, cara Mater Landubriensum,
Te laude digna concelebrant tui
Conclamet assurgens beatam
Te pia progenies parentem.

'Thus, dear Mother of Llandoverians,
May your men together hymn you with deserved praise,
And may your rising pious progeny
Acclaim you as their blessed parent.'
John Williams, 1848

LLANDOVERY COLLEGE WAS formed as a result of a backlash to the publication of a government report nearly 200 years ago. Carwyn's appointment plays directly into the reasons why the College was formed, and it's worth summarising those early formative factors before looking at Carwyn's arrival at Llandovery.

The report's official title is 'Reports of the commissioners of enquiry into the state of education in Wales', and it was published in 1847. But its publication is noted in Welsh history as 'the Treachery of the Blue Books' because of the colour of the covers of the volumes that contained the report and its damning indictment of Wales and the Welsh. It criticised educational standards and noted that this was partly due to teaching being in English even in areas where Welsh was the dominant language. But it also said that the Welsh were lazy, ignorant and immoral, and that the cause of this was the

Welsh language and Nonconformity. The report's three authors were non-Welsh-speaking English Anglicans. The response to this report was strong and vociferous, with many prominent Welsh people showing their indignation by publishing books, pamphlets and newspaper articles and speaking out publicly.

One man who was moved by this criticism of the Welsh was Thomas Phillips, a prominent surgeon from Radnorshire, who had worked for the East India Company in India. At the time of the report he was 88 years old and lived in London. He decided that he wanted to open a new Welsh-medium school back in Wales. He coupled this with another perceived need, which was to offer a higher standard of training for Anglican clergy than was available at the time. He did not take long to accomplish this, opening Llandovery College on 1 March 1848. Amongst the first Trustees of the college was Lady Llanover, a significant patron of the arts and champion of maintaining Welsh traditions, such as the Welsh costume. Two years after Llandovery opened, she published *Y Gymraes* (The Welshwoman), the first Welsh-language publication for women. Her husband was Benjamin Hall, after whom Big Ben is named.

Llandovery College's Welsh credentials are firm, both linguistically and culturally. For the first time, a classical, liberal education was available in Wales and in Welsh. This secured its academic credentials as well. Over a century later, Carwyn was appointed the College's Head of Welsh, placing him on the same line as founder Thomas Phillips. But he was the first to be given the official title of Head of Welsh in over a hundred years. This could indicate that such a position had not been thought necessary as the College was deemed to be Welsh in language anyway, and denoting a Head of Welsh would therefore be superfluous. It could also mean that giving Welsh official status had not been considered necessary.

The application of Thomas Phillips' founding principles fluctuated considerably after his days, and the status of the Welsh language at Llandovery depended on whoever was

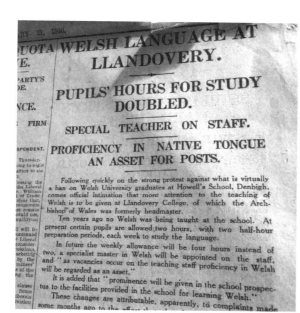

WELSH LANGUAGE AT LLANDOVERY.

PUPILS' HOURS FOR STUDY DOUBLED.

SPECIAL TEACHER ON STAFF.

PROFICIENCY IN NATIVE TONGUE AN ASSET FOR POSTS.

Following quickly on the strong protest against what is virtually a ban on Welsh University graduates at Howell's School, Denbigh, comes official intimation that more attention to the teaching of Welsh is to be given at Llandovery College, of which the Archbishop of Wales was formerly headmaster.

Ten years ago no Welsh was being taught at the school. At present certain pupils are allowed two hours, with two half-hour preparation periods, each week to study the language.

In future the weekly allowance will be four hours instead of two, a specialist master in Welsh will be appointed on the staff, and "as vacancies occur on the teaching staff proficiency in Welsh will be regarded as an asset."

It is added that "prominence will be given in the school prospectus to the facilities provided in the school for learning Welsh."

These changes are attributable, apparently, to complaints made some months ago to the

Western Mail
and South Wales News.

TUESDAY, JULY 30, 1929.

WELSH AT LLANDOVERY.

ATTENTION has been drawn, in Wales and in Parliament, to the position of the Welsh language at Llandovery College and to the requirements of the foundation deeds regarding the use of the language. The PRESIDENT OF THE BOARD OF EDUCATION has instructed the Chief Inspector of the Welsh Department of the board to visit the college and investigate, but the report of the inspector is not to hand. Possibly some resentment

Warden at the time. Many chose to ignore the Welsh provision completely and ran the College along more traditional Anglican/anglicised lines. From time to time, this tendency would be attacked in the Welsh press, as those concerned by the lack of Welsh at the College sought to remind those who ran the school of their heritage. The way Welsh was taught was also a reflection of how the Warden viewed the role of the language in the school. There were times when it was a subject passed around from teacher to teacher, or random guest teachers were called in to teach Welsh – including at one time the Vicar of the nearby village of Myddfai.

But Llandovery's location counterbalanced this to a certain extent. However Welsh was or was not used in the College, Llandovery has always maintained a singularly Welsh image or ethos. Being tucked away in a rural, agricultural corner of the Carmarthenshire countryside plays a big part in this. The area around it was Welsh-speaking, and pupils were sent there because of the perception that it was more Welsh-speaking than any similar establishment. Most of the children who went to Llandovery were sent there from rural Welsh-speaking schools, and six pupils every year were sent there on a scholarship from Carmarthenshire schools.

A century after the College was founded, after the Second World War, a new Warden was appointed: G O Williams, who went on to become Archbishop of Wales after leaving Llandovery. He arrived at the College with a clear vision. His philosophy was as one with Thomas Phillips': he wanted to develop the teaching of Welsh, and he wanted to increase the use of Welsh in the daily, social and cultural life of the College. Having been there nearly eight years, he decided that he needed to create the role of Head of Welsh as part of his plan. He asked some respected colleagues, one of whom was Sir T H Parry-Williams, if they could recommend anyone. It's obvious who he recommended, and Carwyn was appointed. Two references, one written and one verbal, from his former Professor had helped secure Carwyn's first two employments.

G O Williams also sought to develop the Christian emphasis in College life – again, more in keeping with the vision of its founder, who said:

> Christianity is here not merely a subject... but a way of thinking, living, and worshipping that alone makes sense of all the school's activities.

G O Williams introduced specific changes to the curriculum which facilitated his linguistic and theological aims, as summed up by Gareth Evans in *A History of Llandovery College*:

> All boys were taught Welsh during their first three years at the school, with special classes for those learning it as a second language. It was then made optional in forms IV to VI. Some pupils were taught Divinity through the medium of Welsh and successful efforts were made to acquire a Welsh-speaking French master. Welsh societies were formed, a St David's Day Eisteddfod was held, Cerdd Dant [vocal improvisation over a given melody] was taught and Sunday evening services in the Welsh language as well as Welsh plays performed.

These were big changes to college life and work. Carwyn would have identified with them immediately and would have relished the opportunity to develop new ideas. Other changes would follow, some evidently needed urgently. The College's current Head of Rugby, Iestyn Thomas, was a pupil there in Carwyn's days and he recalls the ethos of the college:

> The first years of the Sixties in the College could still be called the Dark Ages. It was a very harsh regime. The cane or the gym shoe were very common tools of discipline. But more than that, the whole atmosphere of the school was old fashioned and oppressive, almost.

One specific change helped break this suffocating atmosphere: the introduction of the House system at the

College. This happened in the very early Sixties, as one other former pupil, Geraint Eckley, remembers:

> The House system developed as a means of welfare within the school. During the time I was there, the authority to discipline was transferred from the prefect to the teacher who was the head of a house. The system was getting more civilised.

Carwyn was appointed as one of the Heads of House.

A change of world

Carwyn did teach other subjects, not just Welsh. He taught English, for example. But his main responsibility was Welsh. In his first year he was the form teacher for a class of Welsh-speaking pupils, the result of another change to school life. Until that time, pupils had been divided into their classes alphabetically, but G O Williams changed the emphasis and made Welsh the determining factor.

One teacher on the staff when Carwyn was there remembers a particular Carwyn effect on the developing emphasis on the Welshness of the school. Iwan Bryn Williams was a rare North Walian in a school of South Wales staff.

> There's room to believe that the College stance on teaching Welsh caused some parents to keep their children away from Llandovery. But this is where Carwyn excelled more than any other teacher at the College. Those parents who might have considered keeping their children from the college would end up sending them if they thought that there was a possibility of their son being coached by Carwyn James.

This perceived influence would have increased with Carwyn's rugby stature as the years went by.

In settling at Llandovery, Carwyn settled into another specific, clearly-defined pattern of living, following the previous, opposite patterns of life as student and serviceman. Needless to say, his Llandovery life evidently resembled his JSSL days more than his student ones. In the College, as in the Navy, he was bound by a timetable inside and outside the classroom. In both he was also part of an establishment almost alien to the upbringing he had had in Cefneithin. These are important factors to consider when we remember Carwyn as a Maestro, a pioneer, a leader. He was all of these things. But his innovation needed foundations. He needed to feel safe before he could take risks. He needed to know the rhythm of the comfortable before he could improvise.

From such emotions the dualities previously noted could also rise. He created another such tension when he walked through Llandovery gates. This socialist Nonconformist was on the staff of a private, Anglican college. But he would have taken comfort from the fact that it was an establishment where there was order and tradition, even if that wasn't directly his tradition. He played his part in re-establishing the Welsh traditions.

When Carwyn was made Housemaster, on the introduction of that system to the college in the early Sixties, he was given a room on the first floor of the College in a part of the building that overlooks the Quad. Two concrete courts stood to one side, similar to today's squash courts, but they were Fives courts in Carwyn's days. The boys played their free-time games in the Quad itself, before returning to their lessons through the door below Carwyn's window. On their way they would pass Carwyn's grey Morris 1000, and then later, his Riley.

In the room itself there was a fireplace with a gas fire in it, two or three comfortable chairs, and one black-and-yellow sofa. To the right of the fireplace there was a television, and a large gramophone stood to the left. There was a table behind the sofa, completely covered with papers of various descriptions, and there was a box full of records on the floor. At the back of the room, the left-hand door opened into his bedroom and the door on the right was to the bathroom.

Leading from the entrance door to his accommodation was

a long corridor where nearly 60 pupils aged between 13 and 18 would sleep. Carwyn was responsible for their welfare as Housemaster. Pupils from successive intakes while Carwyn was at Llandovery all say that the door to his room was always open to them. Year in, year out, these boys would walk into his room to watch television, to play his records, to read a book or to chat with Carwyn.

His day would start to the sound of a bell at quarter past seven. A second bell would sound 15 minutes later. The eight o'clock bell was far louder than the previous two, and it was the one calling them to breakfast. As a Housemaster, every three weeks Carwyn would have to supervise breakfast. This involved asking the Blessing on the food, which Carwyn did in Welsh. The other two Housemasters did so in Latin.

Prayers said, he would then walk amongst the tables, making sure the boys were eating their breakfast and not misbehaving. Breakfast over, Carwyn would then ask for silence, so that the register could be called. The boys would reply to the calling of their names in Latin, 'Adsum!' (I am here). Then, when the boys had gone, it was the teachers' turn to have breakfast. His breakfast over, Carwyn would collect his newspaper, the *Western Mail*, not the *Daily Express* of his upbringing, and go back to his room to read it, with a cup of tea and his ever-present cigarettes.

Hearing rushing footsteps in the Quad below would shake Carwyn from his morning newspaper ritual as he then knew that the boys were on their way to the church in the College grounds for their morning devotions. Carwyn, wearing his cap and gown, would need to follow them there. After church, lessons. Lunch at one, followed by a rugby session, before a couple of hours of further lessons. Supper was at seven, and while the boys were doing their work in their rooms, the staff would meet to put the school and the world to rights. The younger boys would go to sleep around nine o'clock but all prep work would end by quarter past ten.

When numbers allowed, Carwyn would hold many of his

lessons in his room, more often than not in his slippers and with a mug of tea in his hands. Sometimes he would teach in his dressing gown. The boys had one particular way of assessing what sort of a mood Carwyn was in on any given day. If he had woken up on time and was out of bed in good time, he would wear his brown shoes. But if he got up at the last minute, he would put black shoes on. Black shoes meant he'd overslept, had to rush to get ready and was therefore likely to be in a bad mood. No doubt this is a myth; or at least, a truth exaggerated. But it's one old boys stick to to this day. At the end of the day, with everyone else in bed, Carwyn would take off his shoes – black or brown! – put on his slippers and boil the kettle. He'd do some marking, write some letters or an article for a newspaper or magazine. Read. Listen to some of his records. Make some phone calls. And then to bed.

These were the bones of Carwyn's time at Llandovery. Five days a week, twelve weeks a term, three terms a year for twelve years. It was a routine which gave him reassurance.

Historian and education academic Sir Deian Hopkin was a pupil at Llandovery for Carwyn's first five years. Carwyn taught him Welsh in his last year there, along with two other pupils from the same year and two from the year below them.

> Carwyn was an exceptional teacher. It certainly enriched our education to be taught in a mixed-year class like that. It was possible to have broader discussions and see things in a different way. He would always try and encourage his pupils to try and write poetry. But he didn't have much success with this particular pupil on that front!

Others remember Carwyn's approach to discipline, working within the House system that had changed the way the school dealt with such issues. Former pupil Geraint Eckley suggests that Carwyn wasn't averse to the more old-fashioned ways of discipline:

I remember him telling me once that he had lost his temper with a pupil in Carmarthen, to the point that he punched him in the stomach until the boy folded like a penknife before falling to the floor.

That is not the picture that comes to mind in thinking of Carwyn and his gentle disposition. But it does show that he was not someone you could take advantage of. Geraint Eckley goes on to say that Carwyn's approach had changed by the time he arrived at Llandovery.

When it was time to punish someone by giving them the school's accepted method of the cane or plimsoll three times on the backside, Carwyn was a very reluctant practitioner. He would loiter and procrastinate for as long as possible before completing the task. Until I started to write these words, I thought that he did so in order to prolong the agony for the recipient as long as possible. Today however, I'm not so sure.

Through conversation with other former pupils, it's evident that Geraint Eckley isn't the only one who thinks that Carwyn did try to make them more uncomfortable by delaying the punishment. Some say that they found it difficult to warm to him, because he could be nice and approachable to them one day and then authoritative and distant at other times. They are a small minority, but it would appear that Carwyn's attitude to discipline was more akin to the old-fashioned Llandovery at the start, but that he changed with the College. One story in particular shows Carwyn's early attitude, which made him unpopular with the boys.

It was a tradition for the boys to walk into the town and visit the sweet shop near the college. Some of them would ask the old lady who owned the shop for something they knew was kept at the back of the shop. While she was distracted, they would fill their bags or pockets with all kinds of sweets, chocolates and pop for free. The College soon found out about this activity. Carwyn was given the responsibility of discussing it with the pupils. On Carwyn's very sympathetic pleading, the boys readily admitted their crime. They were shocked, however, to learn that Carwyn had already prepared a punishment for them, which was to perform various duties around the College campus in full view of staff and pupils, who knew exactly why they had to do what they were doing. The boys labelled the punished: 'thieves'. It was an early form of community service. This course of action enraged the boys who had been caught. They had firmly believed that they would be excused punishment because they had voluntarily confessed. Confession, they thought, was in itself a virtue which negated punishment, or so they thought they had been led to believe. The fact that Carwyn had, in their view, misled them and then shamed them publicly created a bitterness towards him.

But old traditions were coming into increasing conflict with new ideas – Carwyn's arrival at the College was proof enough of that. The year that saw the greatest changes was 1960–1961. The introduction of the House system has already been mentioned. Linguistic considerations also governed this change. David Gealey was a pupil at the school before Carwyn's time, but returned there as a teacher while Carwyn was there. He was Carwyn's deputy in the Welsh department.

> When I returned I found out that Tŷ Cadog existed on the campus. The idea of establishing a House system, whereby pupils were put into separate teams called Houses, was a completely new idea for the College. Tŷ Cadog was established specifically as the Welsh House, where the Welsh-speaking boys would be placed. It wasn't there when I was a pupil. There were about 200 pupils in the College at that time, and about 50 of them lived in the Welsh House. That change was down to Carwyn.

Sir Deian Hopkin summarises the changes introduced that year in the context of the Welsh Society. He was editor of the College magazine, *The Journal*, at the time, and in an article looking back at the year just gone, he gives this summary – evidently aware of words used by the Prime Minister of the day, Harold Macmillan:

> We hear so much these days about the winds of change. It's not a wind that fell upon the activities of the Welsh Society this year, but a whirlwind. Officials were elected and a committee of four established. But in truth there was very little for us to do, as a comprehensive programme of events had been arranged by Mr James.

Carwyn had obviously used all his influence and contacts to invite many prominent people to address the Welsh Society. Welsh Rugby international Clive Rowlands, for example; politician Gwynfor Evans; author T Llew Jones, whose conversations he had eavesdropped on in Dan Teilwr's shop in Rhydlewis; psychiatrist Harri Pritchard Jones; actor and entertainer Ronnie Williams, half of the comedy duo Ryan and Ronnie, who was from Cefneithin. The presence of *Western Mail* journalist J B G Thomas as a guest shows that the activities weren't exclusively in Welsh, but even when the guest speaker was speaking in Welsh, all non-Welsh-speaking pupils were always invited. 'Carwyn did his best to be inclusive' is the

Victorious drama group (Sir Deian Hopkin 4th from left)

phrase used by one non-Welsh-speaking pupil who attended some of the Welsh Society events.

The science laboratory and the gym quickly became the busy focal points for Welsh Society activities. In the labs, the boys would watch films of Wales and British and Irish Lions rugby matches. The Society regularly turned the gym into a theatre. English drama productions had been held there for some years, but under Carwyn, Welsh plays were performed there, to be seen by pupils and public alike. These were school productions with the boys taking part, or performances by guest drama companies. There was no shortage of amateur drama groups in Carmarthenshire as a whole, and in the Swansea Valley also. Edna Bonnell's drama group from Llanelli and the Swansea Welsh Drama Group were regular visitors. These were the groups that Carwyn would have seen in the Hall in Cross Hands. He continued and extended that particular part of his heritage.

Carwyn also arranged trips to see plays in other theatres. He regularly took groups to see plays performed in Trinity College, Carmarthen, and a particular favourite of his was to take pupils to see the plays of Welsh playwright Saunders Lewis. These trips also included going to see English productions, in the name of the English Department. Twice a year they would go to Stratford to see some of Shakespeare's plays. Sir Deian Hopkin appreciated those visits.

> We had an opportunity to see some of the greats on those trips.
> I remember seeing Laurence Olivier, John Gielgud, Michael
> Redgrave, Vanessa Redgrave and Judi Dench when we went to
> Stratford with the school. The significance of those visits, however,
> didn't dawn on me, or the other boys, until we had long since left
> Llandovery College.

Another Carwyn innovation was the formation of the Sixth Form Society. This gave the senior pupils an opportunity to appreciate culture, politics and issues of the day in a more mature way. The Society was also a forum to show international films – very innovative for the time. Pupils recall discussing the poems of Ezra Pound with Carwyn in one of these meetings.

The spirit of the words of both Harold Macmillan and Bob Dylan was being felt in this educational and establishment corner of Carmarthenshire. The winds were blowing and the times were indeed changing. Both the College and Carwyn worked through their traditional attitudes, including discipline. The ethos of the College certainly changed – there was a change of heart and a change of tongue. David Gealey sums it up:

> The changes were completely visible. G O Williams started to change some of the College's basic structures, and then his work was continued by R G Tree [the next Warden]. Into this process, Carwyn introduced his own changes. He increased the number and profile of the Welsh-language activities and in so doing, he changed the whole tone of the College.

A rather unexpected innovation, and one which caused quite a stir in this boys' private school, was the introduction of Folk Dancing. Through his friendship with Rita Morgan, a teacher at Pantycelyn Secondary School in Llandovery, the two began Folk Dancing evenings in the College. No doubt the introduction of Secondary School girls was a very welcome distraction for the Llandoverians.

Carwyn linked Llandovery's increased activities in the name of the Welsh language to similar activities organised by other national Welsh groups and societies. The Urdd, the Welsh League of Youth, was the main link between the College and the Welsh-speaking Wales outside its gates. The personal link between Carwyn and Rita Morgan was the catalyst for this. In Carwyn's early days at the College, she was the regional organiser for the Urdd and approached Carwyn initially in this capacity, wanting to form a branch of the Urdd at the College. This coincided conveniently with the work that Carwyn was doing there anyway. Rita Morgan, now Williams, explains her reasons for contacting Carwyn:

> I had heard of Carwyn James before contacting the College. He was an international rugby player as well as being Head of Welsh at Llandovery. Contacting such a person was an obvious step for me to take, therefore, in the name of an organisation that served young people throughout Wales. He was, quite simply, a hero.

Rita had been in many a meeting where Carwyn was the guest speaker, and would have warmed to his charms and talent. She admits, however, that the College was a frighteningly strange place when she first went there. That visit, in 1957, was to invite Carwyn to be the guest speaker at the Urdd's New Year's Eve Party in Pantyfedwen. Carwyn began to visit the Urdd's Camp in Llangrannog regularly from 1958 onwards. Amongst the young boys camping there for a week that year was a certain Gareth Edwards. Once again, therefore, Carwyn was back in Ceredigion's fresh sea air, albeit for a few days or a week at a time. Two years after that first camp, he was still a regular visitor to Llangrannog. A young girl from neighbouring village Coed-y-Bryn was working in the kitchen there during school holidays. She would later be one of Wales' foremost broadcasters on radio and television, Beti George:

> Because we lived so close to Llangrannog, we would regularly volunteer to work there while the camps were on. That particular year, 1960, we were all excited that Carwyn James would be there. Without doubt, he was a hero. He'd played for his country and he spoke Welsh. You could almost say that he was a god to us! On one weekend, which fell in the middle of the two week camp, I remember having a lift home with him, as he was going to Rhydlewis for a few days.

Coming from the same Ceredigion stock as Carwyn, she understands the Rhydlewis markings on Carwyn's character.

For one thing, Carwyn's family looked like Ceredigion people. The word 'cadaverous' comes to mind – the pale, thin, boney faces. Although that changed in Carwyn's case in later years. Emotionally, in terms of personal characteristics, there was a toughness and a need to be separate; a shyness but a firmness as well.

Many fellow Llangrannog visitors remember Carwyn's reluctance to go into the sea when the campers and the officers went down to the beach. They also remember his contributions to the camp's *Noson Lawen*, the entertainment evenings. Rita Williams certainly does:

> It's in those entertainment evenings that we would all see Carwyn, the witty entertainer, at his exuberant best. He made adjudicating on the various performances of each House at the camp into his own form of entertainment. He was equally unforgettable when he was master of ceremonies at the impromptu dinner to honour the injured captain of the Officers' team. It's a surprise that all the children weren't raised from their beds by the raucous noise that came from the Officers' quarters!

As Carwyn and the Urdd grew closer and closer, so did Carwyn and Rita. This relationship developed further when Rita left the Urdd to start a job as a teacher in Pantycelyn Secondary School, Llandovery. They were now in the same town. The friendship grew and grew between Rita and the one she was soon to call 'Jâms':

> Those of us who were from 'the workers' wouldn't use the words 'friend' or 'colleague' in our everyday living. In the coal communities we came from, the word 'partner', or 'pantner' in the vernacular Welsh, was what we were used to hearing. From my first days of meeting Carwyn, he became my 'pantner' in the true collier sense of the word. He proved to be so when I started as a young, inexperienced teacher in a secondary school in Llandovery and he was a 'pantner' to me throughout his life.

Rita Williams would experience one particular Carwyn

trait more than others did, as she well remembers:

> Carwyn would invite many prominent Welsh people to the College, to address the pupils. Soon it was the turn of Kate Roberts, popular author and the one deemed to be the Queen of Welsh Literature. It was a big invite. There was great expectation for her visit. As the day drew ever nearer, Carwyn told me – yes, told me, not asked me – that I would need to put her up, and look after her from the moment she arrived until the moment she was to speak at the College. He was more than ready to delegate responsibility to others. At the time, I had just bought a cottage in Cil y Cwm, and had building work going on there. I said that I would help, of course, and Kate Roberts came as expected. As soon as she did, Carwyn disappeared! I had to look after her on my own. And to make matters worse, I wasn't allowed to go and hear her speak at Llandovery College!

On a different linguistic note, Carwyn did not waste any opportunity to influence his pupils through his knowledge of the Russian language and culture. One guest at the Welsh Society was Owen Edwards, future Controller of BBC Wales and first Chief Executive of S4C. He was invited to share his stories of a recent visit to Moscow and Leningrad. Carwyn also tried to teach Russian to some of his pupils, as Sir Deian Hopkin remembers.

> He tried his best to teach me some basic Russian. He would share some words and phrases with me occasionally and sometimes would lend me some books on Russian as well as some of the country's literature.

Sir Deian, along with two others who studied A Level Welsh with him, Geraint Eckley and Iolo Williams, were chosen by Carwyn to take part in a BBC broadcast from their Swansea studios. They were to contribute to a discussion programme chaired by Professor Jac L Williams from Aberystwyth University. Carwyn, like Miss Dora, would constantly try to push the boundaries of teaching away from just the set texts.

CHAPTER 9

Renaissance

Games, especially football, cricket and athletics,
became moral correctives, instruments of
character formation and social control.

Dai Smith and Gareth Williams, *Fields of Praise:
The History of the Welsh Rugby Union 1881–1981*

BEFORE THE DECADE ended there would be another complete change as a new warden brought in an altogether new spirit. According to those who were there at the time, the arrival of R Gerallt Jones in 1967 caused nothing short of a Renaissance in Llandovery College. That description is one used by Iestyn Thomas:

> That's the effect that appointing Gerallt Jones had. It was a change of world and a change of way of thinking. Carwyn was delighted with this change and was one of the most enthusiastic to implement any change the new thinking brought with it, in order to move the College forward.

Carwyn had settled. When he had arrived at Llandovery, the new teacher had fallen into the long-established way of doing things, their way of thinking, as his disciplining exploits show. But as the years went on, he found his own feet. This gave him the confidence to be himself more and more, and as this process caught hold, he could assert himself more and more. So by the time R Gerallt Jones arrived, he was open to any change and would often drive that change forward himself.

The new warden was certainly a complete departure for the College. Both his predecessors would be considered in the usual tradition of Llandovery Wardens, however much they changed and developed college life. R Gerallt Jones was completely outside the box. He did have an Anglican upbringing, being the son of a clergyman. He had also had a private education, but his outlook typified neither establishment, and he was the first non-ordained Anglican to be Warden at Llandovery. He was an influential poet and novelist. He came to Llandovery from Jamaica, where he had been working as the first principal of Mandeville College on the island. He had taught in a secondary school and also a university. His obituary in *The Independent* newspaper in January 1999 says this of him:

> To all these appointments he brought balanced judgement, a dryly witty manner, and a broad spectrum of interests which, though deeply rooted in Wales and the Welsh language, looked out at England, Europe, and the wider world with a mixture of fascination, amusement, sympathy, and sometimes consternation.

This was also Carwyn's heartbeat. The two of them were kindred spirits.

R Gerallt Jones saw Llandovery more as a university than a school, and set about making changes that reflected that belief. He introduced, for example, a rag week at the beginning of each academic year. No previous Llandoverians had been seen wheeling a bed from the College to the nearby town of Llandeilo! He cut a different dash to previous Wardens on Campus too. He was the first, without doubt, to be seen on the back of a tractor rolling the cricket pitch in preparation for a match. These two images paint a picture of the change of attitude and approach that permeated every aspect of college life under the new Warden, but without any drop in academic standards.

Rugby master

In 1964, a few years before R Gerallt Jones was appointed Warden, Carwyn was appointed Head of Rugby at the College. He took over from a man who was himself an institution within the Llandovery College establishment. T P Williams, known as Pope, was a master highly respected and very influential. He was an icon on the campus, an embodiment of the values and attitudes that made Llandovery what it was, but specifically, the embodiment of Llandovery as it had been in the 1920s and 1930s. His influence on the development of rugby in the College is immense. In 1952, for example, he led Llandovery to win the Rosslyn Park Seven-a-Side tournament, the first educational establishment outside England to do so.

It's intriguing to think then, how this influential man reacted to the arrival of a former Welsh Schoolboys captain and a man

Carwyn and T P 'Pope' Williams

who was playing regular first-class rugby for Llanelli, something Pope had never done. Former pupils who were there at the end of the Fifties, in Carwyn's first years at Llandovery, say that Pope had a begrudging respect for this talented young man. He admired his achievements, but didn't seem to sure as to how to use them within the school context. He didn't turn to Carwyn for advice in any way. It was Pope's way or no way. A successor of Pope and Carwyn's, Iestyn Thomas, was taught by both.

> It was very old school but he employed some methods which were unusual and quite forward-thinking. We had a scrummaging machine, which was very unusual for a school. It was very basic, mind, with blocks of wood for us to put our heads between, but with no foam on them, only thin linoleum to protect the front row from the impact of a whole pack pushing. I'm fairly certain that we would have been the only school in the UK to be weight training in the Sixties – even if it was only baked-bean tins filled with concrete and sawn-off scaffolding poles.
>
> TP also saw the benefit of spreading the ball wide across the three-quarter line, as was central to Carwyn's philosophy. But Carwyn did so much more with that, moving players deeper and more off the ball. His approach was far more scientific.

When he took over as Head of Rugby, Carwyn immediately extended the list of schools the College would play against. He added Hereford Cathedral School, Atlantic College, Rydal, Whitgift, St John's Leatherhead, Merchant Taylor's, Belmont Abbey, Dean Close, Cheltenham and then, in 1968, Millfield. He wanted to stretch the team by making them play against a greater variety of teams and against the best. Until then, their main regular fixtures were against Monmouth School and Christ College Brecon. These games were rituals. They were more than 80 minutes on the pitch – they were heritage. They were warfare. One of Wales' current rugby superstars, George North, is a former Llandoverian who went to the College through a Carwyn James Scholarship:

About 6,000 people would come to see our games against Brecon. These fixtures had a central place in the entire school calendar but also playing in these games was a major rite of passage for us boys. Usually we would wear black or navy socks. But if we were chosen to play against Brecon, we were allowed to wear the red socks. This was a huge honour which had to be marked in a very formal way. The night before the game, there would be a ceremony to present us with our socks, if it was the first time we had been selected for this game.

We were then expected to wear the socks to bed that night. They were not to be taken off until after the game. But because it was such an honour to receive them, the boys would not take them off for a very long time after the game. The pride we felt overcame any strong smell that came from the socks after being on our feet for 24 hours or so. Those socks were a significant symbol!

The first time Iestyn Thomas played against Millfield, Llandovery were hammered. The next game between the two teams was back on Llandovery soil.

The night before, we were all in Carwyn's room for a team talk. The talk started with a silence which went on for a long time. Then Carwyn chose to speak. He inspired us all to be the best players we could be against Millfield the following day. By nine o'clock that night, I was ready to walk out of his study through the wall and take Millfield on. I had never experienced anything like that before, nor since. He was unique; very, very, special.

In the game the following day, Millfield hardly got near the ball and the home team secured a very comfortable victory.

When Dai Gealey returned as a teacher, he also helped Carwyn with rugby training. He too had a room of his own, like Carwyn, and there was an intercom system between the two. One day, Dai received a message through the intercom. Carwyn asked him if he could assist in the training session that evening.

By the time I got to Carwyn's room, I realised that I had forgotten my rugby shirt. 'Don't worry,' said Carwyn, 'you can borrow one of mine to save you going back to your room.' With that, he threw a rugby shirt at me. I looked at it and saw straight away that it was a French international shirt. Carwyn had just played for Wales against France and had swapped shirts with his opposite number after the game. 'I can't wear this!' I said. 'Wear it and be quiet,' was Carwyn's reply. So I did. I'm sure I'm the only person ever in the history of Llandovery – and many another College probably – to wear an international rugby shirt for a school training session!

Rugby trips were a more central part of the rhythm of college life than the drama trips were. Rugby would often necessitate going outside Wales and more than once this meant going to Ireland. Iwan Bryn Williams recalls one happy occasion when Carwyn took him to a bar in a Dublin College on one such trip, and he found himself deep in conversation over a pint with Irish rugby legend Ronnie Dawson.

Rugby at Llandovery took significant strides forward under Carwyn. There is a certain significance in the fact that Carwyn played this central role in the College's rugby development. According to the earliest rugby documents in Wales, the first rugby game played in the country was played between Lampeter University and Llandovery College in 1856. This is not far off 20 years before clubs such as Llanelli and Swansea were formed. The Welsh Rugby Union wasn't formed until 1881. It seems fitting that Carwyn was involved in an establishment central to the development of the game in Wales. In *The History of Llandovery College* by W Gareth Evans, one sentence sums up the College's ownership of Carwyn:

> One would like to think that the seeds of Carwyn's success as assistant manager and coach of the British Lions in New Zealand in 1971 were sown on Tredegar Close [the College's rugby pitches].

Who can blame the College for thinking in such a way? There's no doubt that the most exciting, expansive rugby in

Llandovery's history was played in Carwyn's days. He left his contemporary, innovative stamp on the old regime he became a part of. This process also fuelled Carwyn's own fires of ambition, the sparks of which would be felt the world over in only few years' time.

Ever thinking of the future and laying solid foundations, Carwyn started an Easter Rugby Course in order to focus on developing the ability of the younger boys, ready for the season that was to follow. Carwyn's rationale for these courses was: '... there are new laws to be faced and new schools to be played.' There was no room for complacency in Carwyn's world.

Choir, chapel and cricket

In 1967, Carwyn was given another responsibility when he was made Head of Cricket. This was a sport that had been close to Carwyn's heart since he was a boy on the school holiday fields of Rhydlewis. He referred to this in his written childhood memories.

> One of the great thrills to me as a boy was to watch Glamorgan play: a greater thrill was to anticipate the game and play in it. I would always put the Aussies in first, feed them with lots of runs, take the occasional wicket, and then, moment of moments; HE would come in, the great man himself.
>
> How I used to hate him! I would attack his off peg, give the ball a lot of air and make it turn towards second and third slip, and I allowed him to thump the occasional one square and through the covers. But at the right psychological moment, I always got him with a straight quick low one and I appealed arrogantly and confidently – and he was out. Bradman D lbw James C 23.

Staff members and friends alike say that he delighted in cricket as much as in rugby. He was often heard quoting Neville Cardus, *The Guardian*'s cricket correspondent and a hero of Carwyn's because he was also that newspaper's music correspondent. Two of Carwyn's worlds, sport and music, collided in Cardus' form. Carwyn would follow his mentor by combining music and opera in his writing about sport. Carwyn added his own Welsh twist to this, as rugby legend Gerald Davies sums up:

> His, a scholars' mind, was academic in its precision, though not dryly so. He had a passion for Welsh poetry and literature generally and in his writing brought a poet's sensitive mind to bear on a rugged and boisterous game.

Like rugby, cricket had also been played at Llandovery since very early on in the College's history, having started there in the 1860s. And also as with rugby, Carwyn immediately extended the list of schools the College would play against.

He would regularly stand in the cricket nets with many cricket balls at his feet, which he would then bowl at the batsman in front of the stumps from all angles and at all speeds, in order to test his reactions and skills. The Carwyn who would do this was the same person who had won a Welsh Schools competition for throwing a cricket ball. His aim and strength were therefore not to be questioned. He would persist with this practice until he was satisfied that the batsman at the crease had perfected the stroke needed to deal with the ball he was bowling at them. He had top-quality assistance: Emrys Davies used to stay at the College for fairly long periods in order to help Carwyn with the cricket coaching. He had played first-class cricket for Glamorgan and was also a Test Umpire. He was from Llanelli and Carwyn from nearby Cefneithin, both were Welsh-speaking chapelgoers and both had a similar, forward-looking mentality towards their sport. Iwan Bryn Williams remembers Carwyn's cricketing days:

> Cricket probably took more of Carwyn's time than rugby did. Matches were longer, to start with. It was also a tradition that the coach had to officiate as umpire in every game the school played, apart from those against Brecon. He was therefore entirely caught up with every game for their duration.

On the College campus as well as his teaching cap and gown, Carwyn would wear his rugby tracksuit, his cricket whites but also one more uniform: his choral robes. It's no surprise that the man noted for his fine singing voice by chapelgoers, students, rugby players and sailors alike should take his rightful place in the church choir that contributed to the devotional life of Llandovery College. But his choral involvement wasn't only about singing. He identified with the Anglican spirit of contemplation and worship. The simplicity of the services, the routine, the comfortable predictability touched his heart. It reached his quiet, central core.

He became good friends with the Chaplain of the College, the Reverend Wyndham Evans, who took up his responsibilities around the same time as Carwyn. He was a High Churchman, and as a Nonconformist deacon, Carwyn could have had a great deal to disagree with him about. But once again, Carwyn could break bread with those who were diametrically opposed to his own convictions. This was also true of the Bishop of St Davids, who was a member of the Llandovery board of Governors and a regular visitor to the College as well as a regular participant in the services.

Communion was held three times a week at 7.15 a.m. The Compline Service was every Saturday evening, and then on a Sunday, it was Communion, Morning Prayers and then Evening Prayers. When religious feast days fell midweek, such as Ash Wednesday, lessons were postponed in order to celebrate in an appropriate manner.

A central part of any devotion was the contribution of the choir. An essential part of College ritual and tradition was the procession from the main school building to the Chapel. The leader, in his red and white robes, would carry a cross lifted high, and a row of boys, two by two, would follow him reverentially. Carwyn was one of these cross-bearing, robed leaders. They needed to wear different robes for the Evening Prayers. In this service, the Second Lesson would be read in Welsh, and the reader was expected to wear their cap and gown to do so. Carwyn was a regular contributor, genuflecting to the altar before and after each reading. This Nonconformist played more than his part in the Anglican worship of Llandovery, as Iwan Bryn Williams recalls:

> I am not surprised at all that Carwyn appreciated these services: he could identify with the richness of the language, he was enough of a musician to appreciate what came from the organ and the choir and he was sensitive enough to the whole service to be able to immerse himself in it. On the other hand, he very rarely complimented the sermons in these Sunday church services.

Such was the life of Carwyn James, teacher at Llandovery College. He took his place in its long-established corridors, but he opened many doors and windows as well. While he was there, he also lived a full life outside the College walls, in many different fields. It was a time when he extended his influence and contribution to the public life of Wales.

CHAPTER 10

The world beyond the gates

A dizzying round of games, conferences, parties and carnivals
The New York Times on the World Youth Games, 1957

CARWYN'S FIRST CONTRIBUTION to the wider world outside Llandovery was a step back behind the Iron Curtain once again. In July 1957, less than a year after starting at the College, he went with Llanelli Rugby Club to Moscow. This was another first for Carwyn, as the club were the first to visit what was then the Soviet Union.

The Cold War that Carwyn had eavesdropped on was still ongoing, but the Soviet leader who had taken over after Stalin's death had a different outlook towards the West. Khrushchev wanted the rest of world to admire his country. One expression of what was called the Kruschev Thaw was his decision to invite the sixth World Youth Games to Moscow for the first time. He wished to show how hospitable his country was.

Countries throughout the world were invited to send teams to compete in a wide range of sporting events. 130 countries accepted the invitation and on 28 July 1957, the opening ceremony was held in Moscow. Amongst the 30,000 or so competitors and officials at that ceremony were members of Llanelli Rugby Club, who had been invited to represent Great Britain in the rugby competition. The way that happened and how they eventually got to Moscow is in itself the meeting of a Cold War spirit and rugby politics.

Once Khrushchev had announced his intention to host the Games, the machinery of the Communist Party in Britain

VI World Youth Games Opening Ceremony, Moscow
David Rogers collection

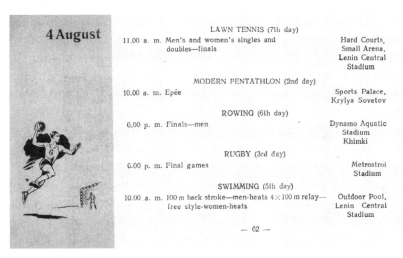

4 August

LAWN TENNIS (7th day)
11.00 a. m. Men's and women's singles and   Hard Courts,
doubles—finals   Small Arena,
                                        Lenin Central
                                        Stadium

MODERN PENTATHLON (2nd day)
10.00 a. m. Epée   Sports Palace,
                                        Krylya Sovetov

ROWING (6th day)
6.00 p. m. Finals—men   Dynamo Aquatic
                                        Stadium
                                        Khimki

RUGBY (3rd day)
6.00 p. m. Final games   Metrostroi
                                        Stadium

SWIMMING (5th day)
10.00 a. m. 100 m back stroke—men-heats 4×100 m relay—   Outdoor Pool,
free style-women-heats   Lenin Central
                                        Stadium

— 62 —

Itinerary for part of one day at the VI World Youth Games

was immediately put into action. They convened a meeting in London, and amongst the delegates were two councillors from Llanelli who were members of the Communist Party. One of them was a man named Alan Oakley, who had been at the fifth World Youth Games in Warsaw in 1955. When the topic of who should represent Great Britain in the rugby competition arose, the councillors wasted no time in saying that Llanelli should be asked. That recommendation was accepted. Handel Rogers, Chairman of Llanelli RFC, received a phone call telling him the good news. But it wasn't from the councillors or the Communist Party, as Handel Rogers' notes of the time show:

> The first information received by Llanelli RFC of the invitation to the Festival of Youth Games 1957 was by telephone call from Mr Reg Pelling, sportswriter in the *Daily Mail*, who had received the information from his London office.

There was very little time between the phone call and the day they would have to leave for Moscow. Llanelli needed to move quickly. They were expected to pay £1,000 for the tour, but the club could not pay such a large sum. Following intense negotiations between East and West, the Russians agreed to pay the travel expenses from London to Moscow and Llanelli managed the costs from West Wales to the UK capital. The official invitation did come eventually, by telegram from Moscow. Once that arrived, Llanelli officials though that it would be right and proper if they informed the Welsh Rugby Union and, more than that, offered the Union the opportunity to take the Welsh team to Moscow instead of Llanelli going as a club. The Union's response was that they didn't have time to arrange anything and that Llanelli should go. No doubt they felt that there was no time to organise the necessary committees.

Preparations on the pitch were put in the hands of club captain R H Williams, and Carwyn was asked to assist by preparing the backs. This was Carwyn's first proper coaching role. Club officials say that the encouragement of the WRU was conspicuous by its absence, as Handel Rogers' notes suggest:

> On the day of departure, 20 July, I did receive a telegram from the WRU, but this turned out to be instructions not to wear the Scarlet jersey, as we could be mistaken for the Welsh team.

This was an early encounter with the WRU for Carwyn. There was no official recognition or blessing for the Scarlets' trip, and no one from the Union was there to see them on their way the day they left for the USSR. There was one exception, however, as Handel Rogers remembers:

> Lord Heycock was at the Port Talbot railway station to wish us well. He was conspicuous in a solitary act by friendly officialdom at the outset of our journey, apart from the truly rousing send-off at Llanelli Station, headed by our [WRU] District Representative, Mr D Hopkin Thomas and his wife.

Llewellyn Heycock was a lifelong Trade Unionist and leading Labour politician. His wish to stand on the platform to wave bon voyage to the Llanelli team is a gesture indicative of the attitude towards Russia amongst many in Wales already referred to. This might well have been 1957, but the Welsh still felt as they did in 1932 when the warnings of journalist Gareth Jones about Stalin's atrocities were ignored. Russia was alright. Wales had an industrial and a philosophical affinity with the USSR and on this particular occasion, it was an honour for Wales to send a team to the World Games. Heycock's stand embodied this way of thinking.

But attitudes were beginning to change, and those who were showing a willingness to support events and visits to the USSR were being questioned. This was partly due to more details of Stalin's actions coming to light, confirming what Gareth Jones had claimed at the time during which the atrocities were being committed. Academic and author Kate Bosse-Griffiths captures this 'Shall we? Shan't we?' dilemma in a book she wrote following a visit to Russia and Berlin, *Trem ar Rwsia a Berlin* (A Glance at Russia and Berlin). After admitting that she had pondered for a long time about whether she should go on such a trip, she explained why she did:

> Some people will think that a visit to a country behind the Iron

Curtain is a betrayal of Christianity. In trying to understand the enemy, they say, you are giving them an opportunity to spread their ideas. Worse still, they say, your money will support the spies that undermine Western civilisation.

It wasn't love or hatred that drove me to visit Russia, nor was it a Communist or anti-Communist conviction. It was the irresistible urge to compare rumour and truth in the Soviet world.

The fact that an academic and author like Kate Bosse-Griffiths had to seriously consider whether to go or not shows the strong pull for and against the Soviet forces. Chapel deacon Carwyn did not feel that this visit was a betrayal of Christianity any more than his previous visit to Soviet-dominated Romania had been, nor that his embracing of his National Service had been a betrayal of his pacifist heritage. It was neither love nor hate that sent Llanelli to Moscow either, just an irresistible urge to play a game they loved, with no thought for political or religious implications. The wider political context was also of a different nature to the future volatile and overtly-political conflict between apartheid and sport. Llanelli could go to the Soviet Union either unopposed or indeed actively heralded. That did not happen in the early Seventies when they came face to face with apartheid, as we shall see.

18 players went, and two officials: Handel Rogers and club Treasurer Ron Harries. The journey to Moscow would take them six days. They went by train to Dover, ferry to Ostend and train again from Ostend to Berlin. They were to stay in East Berlin, as it was the Russians who had organised the trip. They did not expect what they saw when they arrived in that part of the German city, as Handel Rogers explains:

I shall never forget the strange atmosphere in the railway station there, when there must have been two or three hundred people queuing for tickets and yet one could have heard a pin drop. It was odd, after London, to observe the grim, sad, silent figures here – it was breathless and gripping.

Also on that trip was former Navy and Swansea teammate, Terry Davies, who had joined Llanelli shortly after the Romanian trip. He too, will never forget the arrival in Berlin:

> We arrived in the middle of the night. It was strange to see one side of the city lit, but the other in darkness. We went to the dark side. Before we could get off the train, the soldiers came on board to check and search everything. We were then allowed to go to where we were staying. When we awoke in the morning, it was like looking out over a war zone. The roads were really clean, but the buildings were ruins, many without roofs or windows, walls missing and piles of rubble everywhere.

Their short stopover in Berlin had a very negative effect on the players. In Handel Rogers' words, '...the team, all of us, had lost heart and a little spirit.'

Mid-afternoon that day, they caught a train to Moscow. They stopped at Brest, on the Polish-Russian border, so that the passengers could stretch their legs. Under the leadership of Carwyn James, the Llanelli squad gave an impromptu rendition of 'Sosban Fach' on the platform. Terry Davies remembers one particular aspect of that journey:

> The only other passengers on the train with us were Red Army officers. They were obviously very familiar with that journey as every one had brought his own food. We hadn't and were given were given black bread and sausages. We all hung our sausages outside the window as they smelt so badly. As a result, we pretty much went without food for the two-day journey.

At 4 p.m. on Thursday 25 July, the Llanelli players arrived in Moscow station. They received a warm, affectionate welcome. Young girls in traditional costume placed garlands of flowers around each of their necks, as they did to everyone arriving in the capital for the Games.

The bus journey from the station was their first opportunity to see this iconic city. Carwyn had reached at least the physical

Moscow of his beloved Chekhov. He also saw some of the buildings from which the messages he listened in to in his JSSL days would have been transmitted. They were taken to the university buildings where they were to stay, and in the university grounds a marquee was erected as the refectory for the duration of their stay.

The teams in the rugby competition were France, Italy, Romania, Czechoslovakia and Llanelli. The WRU's fears had come true. The organisers thought that Llanelli were the Welsh national team and, for one of their games at least, put 'Wales' on the scoreboard. Everybody who knew the game of rugby knew exactly who Llanelli were, and had no problem about facing such an illustrious rugby club. Everyone, that is, apart from France. Having seen Llanelli play one of their games, they refused to play them in the next round as they weren't an international team. They evidently didn't want to face the possibility of losing to a mere club side. As a result, Llanelli had a bye into the final of the World Youth Games rugby competition. They were to face Romania in that final, with Carwyn James and Terry Davies coming face to face with some players they had played against on the 1954 Swansea tour. The game ended in a draw. But that wasn't the end, as Terry Davies explains:

> The organisers weren't happy with that draw. Somebody had to win, they said. There had to be a replay. That happened a few days later and Romania won, following some completely unreasonable decisions by the referee. It was obvious that decisions were made along political lines, not rugby ones – a bit like the Eurovision today!

A jury of officials sat in a row at the side of the pitch in order to adjudicate on any unclear incident. It was the TMO system without the television.

The replay caused big problems for Handel Rogers. It ruined their return travel arrangements, which had to be cancelled and

Postcard from Moscow
to his parents

other arrangements made to get 20 people back from Moscow to Llanelli. Not an easy task in the late Fifties. Handel Rogers' first port of call was the Youth Games organisers. It was they, he said, who had caused the situation in the first place. How did they suggest it could be resolved? Negotiations led to an agreement that the organisers would contribute to the costs of flying the Llanelli men back, instead of them taking the train and boat as planned, to make them less late in getting home. That having been agreed, there was no guarantee as to which day they could fly back. It could be any one of two or three. Many of the men subsequently missed a day or two's work because of the late arrival home. Carwyn was lucky, as he came back during what was Llandovery College summer holidays.

While he was in Moscow, Carwyn enjoyed the city's life immensely. Handel Rogers remembers a night out with him:

> A few of us went to the Bolshoi Theatre: myself, Carwyn and Ron Harries. We had a memorable night there, seeing an opera. The conductor was Alexander Shamil'evich Melik-Pashayev [renowned Soviet-Armenian conductor]. We saw the opera *Ivan Susanin* [*A Life for the Tsar*], composed by Glinka.

Susanin was one of the first Russian operas to be known outside the country. It's a patriotic work, heroic but also sad. In 1939, the poet S M Gorodetsky was commissioned to rewrite the libretto, removing references to the Tsar and adjusting the remainder of the work to be politically acceptable.

Terry Davies also remembers going with Carwyn on a trip to the city centre, but to somewhere quite different to the Bolshoi:

> Carwyn, R H Williams and myself went one day to Red Square. After a while we saw a long row of people and asked what it was. We were told that it was the queue to see the embalmed bodies of Lenin and Stalin. The three of us decided that we wanted to join the queue. After a while, we were inside the mausoleum,

III МЕЖДУНАРОДНЫЕ ДРУЖЕСКИЕ СПОРТИВНЫЕ ИГРЫ МОЛОДЕЖИ
III INTERNATIONAL FRIENDLY SPORTS GAMES OF YOUTH
III JEUX SPORTIFS AMICAUX INTERNATIONAUX DE LA JEUNESSE
III. INTERNATIONALE FREUNDSCHAFT-SPORTSPIELE DER JUGEND
III JUEGOS DEPORTIVOS AMISTOSOS INTERNACIONALES DE LA JUVENTUD
29 VII — 10 VIII
МОСКВА—СССР 1957

| Командная заявка | Team Entry List | Engagement d'équipe | Mannschaftsanmeldung | Inscripción del equipo |

| Печатать на машинке | Please, use typewriter | Rédiger avec machine à écrire | Mit Schreibmaschine ausfüllen | Utilizar la máquina |

СТРАНА — COUNTRY — NATION — LAND — PAIS   WALES   GT BRITAIN

Национальная федерация — National Association — Fédération nationale — Nationale Föderation — Federación Nacional
Клуб — Club — Klub

Фамилия Name Nom Familien Apellido	Имя Surname Prénom Name Nombre	Игровой номер Number on the back Dossard N Spielnummer Número en espalda		Фамилия Name Nom Familien Apellido	Имя Surname Prénom Name Nombre	Игровой номер Number on the back Dossard N Spielnummer Número en espalda
1. TERRY	DAVIES	1	12. Bryan	THOMAS	19
2. PETER	DAVIES	18	13. MIKE	PHILLIPS	5
3. Cyril	DAVIES	4	14. REES	WILLIAMS	11
4. Howard	LEWIS	8	15. LLOYD	BOWEN	15
5. Wynne	EVANS	7	16. JOHN	MILES	13
6. JOHN	EVANS	17	17. JOHN	BROCK	12
7. GEOFF	HOWELLS	2	18. RAYMOND	WILLIAMS	5
8. Glynn	JENKINS	14	19. Aubrey	GALE	16
9. Cledwyn	JAMES	6	20.		
10. HENRY	MORGAN	10	21.		
11. Bryn	THOMAS	9	22.		

Подпись Президента или Секретаря Клуба
Signature of the President or Secretary of the Club
Signature du Président ou du Secrétaire du Club
Unterschrift des Präsidenten oder Sekretärs des Klubs
Firma del Presidente o Secretario del Club

Подпись Президента или Секретаря национальной федерации
Signature of the President or Secretary of the National Federation
Signature du Président ou du Secrétaire de la Féderation Nationale
Unterschrift des Präsidenten oder Sekretärs der Nationalen Föderation
Firma del Presidente o Secretario de la Federación Nacional

Дата, Date, Datum, Data.

Дата, Date, Datum, Data

2 экземпляра должны быть получены 1 июля 1957 г. по адресу: СССР. Москва Г-227. Центральный стадион имени В. И. Ленина

2 copies to be received by the Organizing Committee before July 1st, 1957.   USSR. Moscow 227, Lenin Central Stadium

2 exemplaires doivent être reçus avant 1 juillet 1957 à l'adresse: URSS. Moscou 227, Stade Central Lénine

2 Abschriften sind 1.VII 1957 zu bekommen. Die Adresse: UdSSR. Moskau 227, Zentrales Lenin-Stadion

2 ejemplares han de ser recibidos hasta el 1 de julio 1957.   URSS. Moscú 227, Estadio Central Lenin

For Llanelli, read Wales!

standing before two coffins, covered by glass. There they were, Lenin wearing a dark suit and Stalin in full military uniform. Both had yellowed considerably, Lenin more than Stalin of course. I turned to RH and said quietly, 'Look at these two. Between them, they have killed more people in the world than anyone else!' And there they were, in such respectable and majestic surroundings. It was a strange, strange feeling to stand there in front of them, and Carwyn hardly spoke a word the whole time we were there.

The team went to many events together, including a visit to a concert by the Siberian People's Choir. Handel Rogers mentions one song in particular from that concert, 'The Song of the Young People'. It refers to the futile efforts of young people from the eastern USSR to plough barren soil. There was a strong inference, said Handel Rogers, that young people needed to be taught how to live.

In a surprising comment, Handel Rogers says that the Russians were amazed as to how much the Llanelli players could drink before a game. In their country, athletes were prohibited from doing any such thing. On this trip, it was Leningrad Beer that was available for the Llanelli boys, a beer so strong that it was almost black in colour. One evening, under the influence of Leningrad Beer, the Llanelli players entertained some of the other competitors through song. Soon it was Carwyn's turn, as Terry Davies recalls:

> For a while, he refused to sing anything. But he changed his mind, no doubt wanting to share a little of his country's heritage and feeling it was right to do so in Russia. He sang 'Myfanwy'. As soon as he started to sing, the rowdy crowd became quiet and soon you could hear a pin drop. By the end, everyone was quite emotional. The Llanelli boys were a mix of emotion because of the song and a huge pride that the singer was one of us. He'd had such an effect singing a song in Welsh as a Llanelli man. That was special.

The view on Carwyn's use of Russian on this trip varies. Some say he used his Russian, others say he didn't. The probability is that he did, as there was no reason not to. The team were given an official interpreter, Maphua. Again there is disagreement here about one basic fact: whether Maphua was a young man or a young woman! Some say one, others say the other. Whatever the gender, all who recall her existence are agreed: Carwyn spent a great deal of time with the translator, and she asked him constant questions about life in the West. Maphua was more than ready to give an opinion on the answers received to her questions as well, expressing shock, for example, that girls in the West were so willing to dress in order to please men. Maphua was impressed, however, by many other aspects of Western life. According to Terry Davies, in gauging the response to so many conversations, it was as if Maphua had a brief taste of being free.

The day after Carwyn sang 'Myfanwy', the team were on the plane back home. As they walked across the tarmac to their plane, Maphua stood on the balcony of the terminal, enthusiastically waving, with tears in her eyes. Her brief glimpse of freedom was soon to depart.

A Welsh cap

Less than six months after returning from Russia, Carwyn received a call that most in the Welsh rugby world had known was inevitable. He was chosen to play for Wales. He wasn't likely to have received a letter or a phone call to inform him of the good news. In those days, the method of communication was the authoritative voice of the man at the BBC, though there would be a strong indication of who was in the team before that. Rugby myth has *Western Mail* rugby correspondent J B G Thomas as the man who actually chose the Welsh team in those days, and long after. He was an influential man, of that there is no doubt. To such an extent that the saying was, 'If you want to know who's playing for Wales on Saturday, read J B G Thomas' column a few days before.'

Carwyn was chosen to play his first game for Wales against Australia in January 1958. It wasn't likely to be the start of a long international career, as he was already 29 when he first pulled on the Welsh jersey. Traditionally, the reason given for him having had to wait so long for that first cap was the fact that the first-choice outside half in those days was star player Cliff Morgan. Cliff won his first cap in 1951 and was well-established in that position by the time Carwyn started playing rugby again in 1954. Carwyn, it could be said, was unlucky to be playing in the Cliff Morgan era. That is true. But it is also true that Carwyn actually was not as equipped physically to play in that position as Cliff was. Cliff was aware of that:

> Why did I play for Wales more times than Carwyn? I think it was because I was stronger. I'm reminded of one school report I had (in Tonyrefail Grammar School). It said '... not very good in class. His biggest asset is his buttocks!'

He was stockier and more firm-set than Carwyn. He was consequently stronger in his tackling and more aggressive in his attacking. The two men would become very good friends. They played against each other many times, in Cardiff-Llanelli games and in the Welsh trials. Cliff certainly admired him:

> I loved playing against him. He always had a smile on his face on the pitch – a cheeky little thing he was.

On the Saturday morning of 4 January 1958 then, Carwyn pulled on the Welsh jersey for the first time. Cliff Morgan was injured and Carwyn had been called upon to replace him. Also winning their first caps that day were Carwyn's Llanelli teammate, inside half Wynne Evans, and also John Collins, Don Devereux and Roddy Evans. In front of a capacity crowd of 55,000, Wales beat Australia 9–3, with Carwyn dropping a goal to secure the victory.

That day was the first time a young schoolboy from Tregaron would see his hero in action live. In years to come, Carwyn would work in the same BBC Sports department as respected sports reporter John Evans. On that day in 1958, John Evans was there as a schoolboy and he wrote about his experience in Welsh-language magazine *Blodau'r Ffair* (The Flowers of the Fair):

Still on the wall of a pub in Llanelli

CARDIFF ARMS PARK

CARDIFF RUGBY FOOTBALL CLUB

AUSTRALIA v. WALES

CARDIFF ARMS PARK — JANUARY 4th, 1958

There was a school trip from Tregaron to see the match. We had heard that Carwyn would be playing as Cliff was injured. Our Welsh teacher, John Roderick Rees, told us, 'If you see Carwyn, give him my regards'. The two were fellow honours students in Aberystwyth. There was very little chance that we would be able to do so, but as fate would have it, one of the first people we saw, outside the castle, was the man himself, with a duffel bag over his shoulder. We greeted him excitedly. If Owain Glyndŵr himself had acknowledged us that day, it wouldn't have compared with the experience of speaking in Welsh with our hero, who would be representing his country in a couple of hours' time.

So the Cefneithin boy played for his country. There was much rejoicing on the streets of that particular village. There was an excitement that the little boy who used to deliver Christmas mail and groceries was now playing rugby for Wales. Villagers of all ages felt pride, and the children felt a particular cause to rejoice. This is how the next boy from the village to play for Wales, Barry John, remembers Carwyn's first cap:

Cefneithin is a small village, like so many other villages throughout Wales. But after 4 January 1958, we knew a boy from our small village who had played for Wales. That changed everything. It made us different from so many other of those small Welsh villages. But not only had he played for Wales, he scored as well. This is the man who would play with us in the park. It's very difficult to appreciate the effect something like that can have on a village unless you've actually experienced it.

He was capped for Wales a second time that same year, but he was chosen to play as a centre, not an outside half this time, as Cliff Morgan was fit to play. He played against France on 29 March of that year, in Cardiff. Wales lost, 16–6. This was not the first time that Carwyn and Cliff had played on the same team, though. That had happened in the April of the previous year. The sixth Commonwealth and Empire Games were to be held in Cardiff in July 1957, and in order to raise money to build a new stand at the Arms Park for that major sporting event, an exhibition rugby match was arranged. It was between a Welsh XV and an International XV. Rees Stephens captained the Welsh team, and Englishman Eric Evans led the International XV. It was a field packed with stars. Wales won 17–16, which was the biggest combined score at the Arms Park since the Welsh victory there against England in 1922. Carwyn and Cliff played their part in the victory, and in the entertainment as well. They swapped positions frequently throughout the game.

In between playing for Wales and Llanelli, Carwyn was of course back at his duties as teacher in Llandovery College, and rugby coach under Pope. Any uncertainty as to how the Head of Rugby at the College reacted to having to work with Carwyn must have intensified when he attained the status of an international player. Carwyn continued to play for Llanelli, but in the last season of the Fifties and the first of the Sixties, he returned to his village club, Cefneithin. With Carwyn leading them, needless to say they won their League Championship in 1960–61.

In the period between leaving the JSSL and leaving Llandovery, Carwyn's rugby career followed a definite course, albeit an unusual one. He coached the boys at the College; he played for Llanelli, for West Wales and for an invitation Welsh XV; he visited Romania with Swansea and Moscow with Llanelli; he was capped for Wales; he captained Cefneithin to Championship victory; he was made Head of Rugby at Llandovery. All in an eight-year period. Cutting across this line of progression was Carwyn's pioneering involvement with the developing rugby coaching culture that was happening in world rugby at the time, led by Wales. Coaching was actually a new concept outside the school world.

In Dublin in 1964, an event took place that played a significant role in that development of rugby coaching, and Carwyn was there. The Leinster branch of the Irish Rugby Union organised a rugby-coaching school in Dublin. The decision was made to invite those involved at different levels of coaching in countries outside the Irish Republic to take part. They were together for a week. One who was also there was Syd Millar, a future Irish international player:

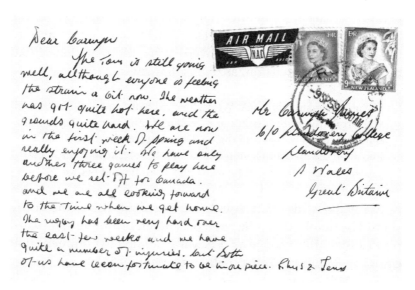

A postcard from Lions R H Williams and Terry Davies to Carwyn, Lions New Zealand Tour 1959

185

We were based at Mosney, about 30 miles outside Dublin, in the Butlins camp there. Carwyn arrived a few days after me. My impressions of him then were that he was quite an enigma at the beginning. He was obviously an intellectual, very well read and not just in sport. By the time we left, Carwyn was highly regarded by all of us.

Also there were Julien Saby and René Deleplace from France, two men who were at the forefront of the development of coaching in their country. Chris Laidlaw, a member of the All Blacks touring team in 1963, was there, and also Cadfan Davies from Wales. This Bridgend man is not very familiar to many in the Welsh rugby world, but he is a key individual in the development of Welsh rugby coaching. He was, without doubt, a formative influence. He was appointed by the WRU in 1963 to lead a working committee on the state of rugby in Wales at the time, and to suggest specific ways the game needed to improve in order to move on. The WRU were the first rugby union in the world to commission such a report. During his research period, he was appointed coach of Bridgend Rugby Club, the first appointment of its kind. He contributed significantly to the week in Dublin. All who were there thought that it had been a valuable occasion, as Syd Millar says:

It was an invaluable week. We all learned from each other. Carwyn was prone to aiming banter at myself and other forwards, saying that we were donkeys and the backs were thoroughbreds! But I know, on his own admission in the end, he left Mosney with a far greater understanding of forward play than he had before.

Many forwards that Carwyn was to to deal with in the future should be thankful that he gained as much insight into forward play as Syd Millar suggests. Forwards tended to comment that Carwyn sometimes didn't really understand them.

Syd Millar says that the time that those on the course spent together socially was as valuable a contribution to understanding coaching as the formal sessions. It was at such times, Millar says, that they came to understand the part that appreciating the particular characteristics of individuals played in coaching. Carwyn would not have only contributed to this, he would have been leading the others. His man-management is something that players would consistently and regularly praise him for.

The value of that course can be measured in many ways, and no doubt other benefits came from it that can't be measured. Suffice to say that three of the delegates went on to play leading roles not only for their countries but for the British and Irish Lions as well. Ronnie Dawson would be the Lions' first coach on their 1968 tour, and later became the first Irish coach. Syd Millar coached the undefeated Lions on their tour of South Africa in 1974 and also coached his country, Ireland. And of course Carwyn led the Lions to their first ever series victory against the All Blacks – to this day still the one and only series victory. He of course, did not go on to coach his country.

Carwyn would have been in his element in such expert company. He would have loved the intense tactical talk and analysis, the working out of moves on the training pitch, the mind games in the classroom and the chats over a G & T in the bar. The door to the wider rugby world had started to open for Carwyn. It was only a few years later that he left Llandovery and less than two years after that he was coaching the Lions.

CHAPTER 11

Small screens and pages

People don't notice whether it's winter
or summer when they're happy.

Anton Chekhov

THE SAME YEAR he stepped on to the international playing field, he also began what was to be a long asssociation with the broadcasting world. The earliest record of Carwyn presenting a programme for the BBC is on 2 March 1958, in between his two appearances for Wales. That programme was called *O Fon i Fynwy* (From Anglesey to Monmouth). It was described as a St David's Day magazine programme, and in it Carwyn visits various communities throughout Wales and speaks to colourful characters in each. This would have been a natural extension of his upbringing in Cefneithin, where he would mix with people of all ages and spend time with them talking about everything and nothing.

His love of music soon found expression on the airwaves. He was given a radio programme called *Wrth y Ford Gron* (At the Round Table) in which he would choose a variety of songs and music to play on the turntable. Rita Williams remembers his preparation for these programmes:

> It was quite common to see him in his room with a pile of records all around him, as he tried to choose his music for the programme. But he would also use my record collection as well.

When he was losing the battle in juggling all his increasing responsibilities and commitments, Carwyn would enlist the help of some sixth form boys in this selection process. One of these was John Jenkins:

> On more than one occasion I chose the playlist instead of Carwyn, while he was away speaking somewhere or on other duties. It was a pleasure to sit in his study and pore through his record collection. Quite an honour for a schooolboy!

Carwyn was one of the guests on TV discussion programme *Ddoe a Heddiw* (Yesterday and Today) in 1959. The presenter was actor Emrys Cleaver, who had recently been in three films: *The Wind of Heaven* (1956), *The Rescuers* (1956) and *The Druid Circle* (1957). The programme's other guests were also rugby internationals, Dewi Bebb and R T Gabe, with contributions from Mair and Elinor Jarman.

Carwyn was the one asking the questions on another programme the following year. *Troi a Thrafod* (Talk on Topics) was recorded in Powis Castle, Newtown and his guests were author, literary critic and Liberal Nationalist politician Glyn Tegai Hughes, the historian Glanmor Williams and playwright John Gwilym Jones. The following year he turned to religious broadcasting when he presented *Nesau at Dduw* (Drawing Nearer to God), which was a devotional programme. Fellow Welsh international Dewi Bebb, the Welsh winger at the time, read a Biblical passage on this programme. Unfortunately, not one of these programmes has been kept in the BBC Archive, and nor have any of the many other broadcasts he made throughout the Sixties.

Rugby commentator Huw Llywelyn Davies remembers a series Carwyn presented called *Wrth Fynd Heibio* (In Passing). This was again broadcast while Carwyn was a teacher at Llandovery:

> His official title for *Wrth Fynd Heibio* was presenter and he would travel from place to place week in, week out, meeting people as he

went along. I remember programmes coming from Craig y Nos and Dr Williams' School, Dolgellau, and another, bearing in mind he was a pacifist, from the army base at Crickhowell.

Broadcasting gave Carwyn more than one opportunity to meet and interview people he admired in various fields. This was never more true than when he interviewed D J Williams. He was the author and teacher who had enrolled his pupil and Carwyn's close uni friend Dafydd Bowen to the ranks of Plaid Cymru. He was a prolific and popular Welsh author, and also a political activist in the name of the nationalist cause. On the programme with Carwyn he discussed his role as one of the three imprisoned during the attempted arson attack on Penyberth, a farm on the Llŷn Peninsula that had been taken over as a training camp and aerodrome for the RAF. There was strong opposition to this move and protests were held at what its opponents had dubbed 'The Bombing School'. In 1936, the three leaders of Plaid Cymru – dramatist Saunders Lewis, chapel minister Lewis Valentine and Williams – set about burning one of the buildings at Penyberth. All three were imprisoned in Wormwood Scrubs for their act.

Carwyn's first venture into sports broadcasting was through a series of sporting items on children's magazine programme *Telewele*. He appeared over a dozen times on this programme between 1961 and 1963. His first item was directed by Cliff Morgan, who had embarked on what was to be a long broadcasting career after hanging up his rugby boots. The sports bulletin was often presented by Ronnie Williams and then later by the man who would become his other half in the most famous Welsh double act, Ryan Davies.

Early in his broadcasting career, Carwyn came into contact with two men who would be leading lights in Welsh broadcasting for the next few decades. The first was a man who pioneered sports broadcasting in the Welsh language: Thomas Davies, a future Head of BBC Wales Sport. In the memorial service to Carwyn in Tabernacl Cefneithin, Thomas

Davies was one of four who spoke. With reference to Carwyn's sports broadcasting, he said this:

> I worked with him for over 20 years in the television and radio world. Apart from the period he was at Rovigo, we were close throughout that whole time. I feel that his big contribution to broadcasting was his programme ideas, his care over the items he was responsible for and his care for the use of language, in both languages.

Such characteristics were evident from the very early days of Carwyn's broadcasting. In his Welsh-language broadcasting, Carwyn was involved in the process of creating Welsh sporting terms in those early days. There were regular meetings and informal discussions in order to create these terms. The main men involved in this process were Thomas Davies, who had an old-fashioned purist's approach to the language; Eic Davies, father of Huw Llywelyn Davies; and Carwyn. Huw Llywelyn Davies, who would himself do so much to continue this legacy as the premier Welsh rugby commentator of the last 20 years or so, remembers a specific example of creating a Welsh rugby term and its instant application:

> My father had gone to Llandovery College to visit Carwyn, as he often did. He wanted to discuss some rugby terms with him. The main issue that day was to come up with a term for reverse pass. After much deliberation, a term was agreed on. Carwyn promised that he would do his best to use that specific rugby move that afternoon when he played for Llanelli, and my father would be commentating. And that's what happened. During one particular move Carwyn threw a reverse pass, which was described by my father using the newly-created phrase. Having done so, Carwyn then turned towards the stand and gave my father a knowing smile! The term didn't exist that morning, but by the afternoon it had been used in a match commentary for the first time ever.

The other broadcasting great Carwyn worked with,

future Head of BBC Wales News Gwilym Owen, saw other qualities:

> The programme *Campau* (Sports) was predominantly aimed at children and broadcast in the afternoon. I would contribute football stories to this programme, which Carwyn presented. Occasionally I was asked to present the programme, and every time this happened, the following morning I would receive a letter from Carwyn congratulating me on my work and thanking me for taking over from him. In that period, I had the distinct impression that he was a painfully shy creature, and that he didn't mix well with others.

Carwyn might well have been well suited to visiting communities throughout Wales and having fleeting chats with their people, but a more sustained exposure with work colleagues showed a different side.

At this time also Carwyn began to contribute to the *Y Maes Chwarae* (The Playing Field) Wednesday evening radio programme. Between *Y Maes Chwarae*, *Campau* and *Telewele* therefore, Carwyn contributed to 13 sports programmes in 1962 alone. Most were to do with rugby, but not all, as he prepared stories on other sports as well. These early years of the Sixties were pioneering years for sports broadcasting generally, not only in the Welsh language. Carwyn played his part.

In 1966, he made a programme for Network BBC on the trend for Welsh Rugby Union players to go to the north of England to play professional Rugby League. *Gone North* was broadcast on 9 March 1966 and featured the inimitable Eddie Waring, the voice of Rugby League. Carwyn would broadcast in Welsh and English until the end of his life, with the BBC and HTV, often at the forefront of new developments. In 1970, for example, Carwyn commentated on the first broadcast of a Seven-a-Side Competition for Under-15 year olds. It was unusual for anyone to broadcast on both channels, such was the rivalry between them. Carwyn transcended this.

Angels unaware

Carwyn would not have been able to address so many societies, go to so many rugby matches and various other events if it hadn't been for the generosity of the many friends who would drive him to these places. It was at this time in his life that he perfected the art of using others to drive him around, even though he had passed his test.

Rita Williams was a particularly helpful friend who would not only drive him from place to place, but also had a cottage in Cilycwm, on the outskirts of Llandovery, which was a welcome bolthole for Carwyn. Another of Carwyn's designated drivers, Iestyn Thomas, remembers this in the context of social evenings as opposed to public functions:

> He used to enjoy a good night out in the Railway, Llandovery and at the end of such evenings he would often ask me to drive him to the cottage in Cilycwm. I would drop him off there and it was obvious that he had a key of his own to get in. He had forgotten the key one night, and he climbed in through the window. As you can imagine, there was plenty of talk in the College about him staying at this young woman's house and having a key of his own. But we saw no evidence of anything more than that. That didn't stop the talking though!

Sir Deian Hopkin was one of those boys who did the talking about Carwyn and Rita:

> She was a very attractive woman. We all tried our utmost to put her and Carwyn together in a relationship. In fact, I think that we managed to convince ourselves that they actually were an item. She was in the College a great deal and always with us when we went on any excursion.

Rita herself, having already acknowledged Carwyn as her 'partner' in the colloquial working-class-culture sense of the word, had a clear view on Carwyn's relationship status:

> I'm sure that he had no girlfriend at all during our friendship
> in the days of the Urdd and the Llandovery days after that. The
> reason for that is that if he was interested in anyone, he would
> have sought my advice about her first!

Carwyn's closest friends, at that time and later, say that Rita was the closest Carwyn ever got to having a girlfriend.

Her friendship with him highlights a common thread in Carwyn's life. Many strong, independent women played a prominent part in it. His mother and especially his sister Gwen fulfilled such a role on the hearth. Miss Dora dominated the classroom days. The role was not fulfilled by anyone in particular in his Aberystwyth or National Service days, nor at Queen Elizabeth Grammar School. But from Llandovery onwards, until the end, there would be no shortage of influential women once more. As well as Rita in his Llandovery days, for example, a regular visitor to see Carwyn was BBC Wales producer Ruth Price. She had produced the first TV programme that Carwyn ever presented. She would be a continuous presence in his life from that moment onwards.

Red shirts

In the same year that he won his two Welsh caps, he contributed

to another ground-breaking project. As with the contribution to the very early days of Welsh sports broadcasting, he also played his part in the first Welsh-language sports book, *Crysau Cochion* (Red Shirts).

The editor's original intention was to discuss, for the first time in Welsh, the history, technique and tactics of many different sports that the Welsh had made a great contribution to. That intention was kicked into touch very early on – as the editor says,

'...the spirit of each game caught the pen of each contributor.' What was published in the end, therefore, is a colourful, lively, often personal account of their sport by many leading Welsh sportsmen. There are articles by prominent golfers, cricketers, rugby players and track-and-field athletes. Carwyn's chapter is entitled *Dawn a Disgyblaeth* (Talent and Discipline). He mentions the abilities needed to be a good rugby player, and his artistic temperament is evident as he describes his rugby. In translation it reads:

> It is the open hand of the artist that fingers the ball, and the energy to pass it comes from the wrists and not from his arms, and his every movement is clean and complete.

The same temperament is also needed to kick a rugby ball:

> Even when the rugby player kicks the ball, there will be sympathy between him and the ball and he knows every twist and turn in the air, and its bounce on the ground, having studied the ball's movements intimately. Every different type of kick needs to be studied. How many times have we heard the cry, when the ball bounces neatly into the lap of the winger, 'How lucky!' Lucky? Maybe.
>
> Natural talent and ability is innate in many children, but we must fan the flames at some stage and in some place. The sooner the better. We must encourage the child to love the game first, and even though the radio and television are fairly effective mediums by now, neither one nor the other can be as effective an influence as watching your village or school team play the game.

What would he say in these days of constant rugby coverage? The primary influences of village and school meant more to him than any rugby broadcast. He develops the relationship between community and rugby further, in the same chapter:

> These boys were brought up in the sound and fury of the game. They heard chatter about rugby and cricket daily. They came from coal communities where people were hot-headed about sport of

all kinds. Last Saturday's game was the main topic of conversation on the hearth, the roadside, the village square and the cobbler's workshop, while playing snooker, having a pint and even after the Sunday morning service in chapel. It will indeed be a sad day in the history of rugby when villagers lose interest in their team, the team that no other has the right to judge but they themselves.

Carwyn then applies these thoughts to his own situation, back in Cefneithin, by referring to two of his heroes, Haydn *Top y Tyle* and Iestyn James. In the year he wins his two caps for Wales, this is what he puts in print as being important to him. He talks of Iestyn James specifically:

It was an honour to be Iestyn's helper when he was practising his kicking. He had an important role, as he was the one who would kick every conversion and penalty for the team. I used to stand behind the posts as he would kick from every conceivable angle from all distances up to the halfway line. He would very rarely wear his rugby boots for these practice sessions – that would be showing off. I can see him now, in his large, wide, brown shoes. He was six foot of a strapping, muscular young man (in the eyes of a child at least) and he could run faster than a greyhound. When he ran along the wing, you could swear that his red wavy hair challenged anyone to come anywhere near him, and I knew that his hand-off was as potent as a donkey's kick. The War was cruelly brought home to me, in fact to all of us in the village, when we heard that Iestyn was lost.

He gives an example of the kind of inspiration young boys could have from watching their heroes in the flesh on the touchlines when he recalls the inspirational play of Haydn *Top y Tyle*:

Then, suddenly, in his own half, the ball lands in Haydn *Top y Tyle*'s hands, with many of 'them' all around him. He kicks, no, he dummy kicks, and away he goes like a bolt, weaving this way and that between his opponents like an eel, his running artistically balanced. The top half of his body would move effortlessly from one side to the other and his feet wove wonderful patterns as he side-stepped now and again on his victorious quest.

He then discusses the merits of Welsh rugby stars at the time. He would love to travel far and wide to watch Bleddyn Williams play, he says – 'the best player I ever saw'. Cliff Jones (a former pupil of Pope's at Llandovery) was 'one of the best outside halves Wales ever saw'. Onllwyn Brace's virtue was noting the importance of discipline alongside natural talent. Carwyn elaborates on this point:

> In Wales, to a large extent, we have depended too much on a player's natural ability, to play 'as it comes', and not enough emphasis has been placed on discipline and thorough training.

Onllwyn, he says, learnt that attitude while he was at Oxford. What is common to these three rugby stars, Carwyn says, is that they were aware that:

> Practice, fitness, understanding and discipline were as important as natural ability. This is the goal the true [rugby] footballer should aim at.

In rugby as in life for Carwyn, individual expression had to spring from a firm foundation. Many stars of Seventies Welsh rugby would smile to hear Carwyn's emphasis on fitness. They wouldn't have thought that he was a coach big on fitness in any way. But his words are relevant for the time in which they were written.

Words he wrote at the end of one particular season at Llandovery add to the points he made in *Crysau Cochion*:

> The new laws and the concept of the modern game have laid far more responsibility on the forwards: gone are the days when the forwards automatically fed the ball to the backs. The emphasis now is on forwards crossing the advantage or the attacking line, and when stopped, they set up a platform for a secondary attack...

Few first-class clubs in Great Britain manage to play the modern game. The modern game calls for new skills and new skills take a long time to master. They have to be taught at an early age.

Hence Carwyn's Easter Rugby schools for example, to meet that early-age need.

His contribution to *Crysau Cochion* is significant in that it's the first time he outlines his rugby philosophy at length and in print. His principles are clear in his chapter. His analytical mind, applied to individual players and to the state of rugby in general at the time, offers a penetrating analysis that would be rare in any rugby-playing country in the world. These words take on further significance considering they were written long before any form of formal coaching set-up was adopted by the WRU or anyone else in rugby, indeed when coaching (outside the schools set-up) was considered anathema.

The call of the Navy

As the Fifties drew to a close, Carwyn returned to two institutions he had been a part of earlier in the decade. The first was his return to the Navy. Having completed his National Service, he was required to meet further such obligations for a few years, as Tony Cash explains:

> We were all required to do reserve training after our National Service, which meant we were liable to recall in case of emergency; but, more importantly, we had to do three weeks' radio monitoring in Germany in each of the three successive years. Carwyn would have done likewise. I suppose it's possible that if for some reason he missed reserve training one year (he was in Moscow in the summer of 1957) his return to Germany could have been postponed till later.

A colleague of his on this second stint of Service, fellow Welshman Billy Davies from Bridgend, goes further. He was responsible for activities at Harlech College later in his life, but in the late Fifties, he was in the Navy with Carwyn:

I was familiar with the name Carwyn James as a rugby player. Then in about 1957 or 1958, I was with him in Kiel, Germany, where we had both been sent to work with the Navy Reserves. It was quite an honour for someone like me to meet Carwyn. After completing our duties, I had the opportunity to invite Carwyn to come to Harlech College to address the student body and to take some coaching sessions.

Carwyn was therefore back in Germany once again. His duties were the same as before, eavesdropping on Russian messages from the other side of the Iron Curtain.

The call of academia

He also returned to his old university at Aberystwyth. His registration card shows that he started an MA degree in November 1959, and in a subject that would take him back to the Welsh Literature of the Middle Ages. He embarked on study to prepare a 'Critical Text on the poetry of Raff ap Robert, and Edward ap Raff, including an Introduction, Notes and Glossary'. Raff ap Robert was a lesser-known Welsh poet born in around 1550, and Edward ap Raff was his son. Carwyn's close friend Dafydd Bowen recalls his return to Aber:

> Nothing came of the proposed thesis. As in his earlier Aberystwyth days, Carwyn liked to sleep in in the mornings, and after arriving at the National Library of Wales, he would far prefer to have discussions with Dr B G Charles about any sporting matter than study the documents he needed to look at. He would also be more than happy to be distracted by Mac, R W McDonald, as they discussed various world events in the Catalogue Room.

Carwyn stayed with Dafydd Bowen in the summer of 1959 and the following summer.

> He stayed with me at my home in Plasywrugen, at the top end of Brynymor Road. Living together once again was an extremely pleasant experience, and we enjoyed two serene summers together.

Remembering that serenity was the clearest of very few memories that Dafydd Bowen shared with me in his care home on the outskirts of Aberystwyth. He remembered very little of the undergraduate days, the protesting, nor very little else. He did remember Carwyn, Welsh poet and activist D J Williams and himself going for a pint in Fishguard. But the strongest memory by far was of those two summers, and they brought a warm smile of recognition to his face.

Leaving Llandovery

As the Swinging decade drew to a close, Carwyn had decisions to make. Thoughts were turning towards leaving Llandovery. But, true to the pace of both Llandovery life and Carwyn's own mind, such a change would happen slowly. The arrival of new Warden R Gerallt Jones in 1967 no doubt gave Carwyn a dilemma. On the one hand, such a kindred spirit at the helm of the College might have encouraged Carwyn to stay there and work with him. They were both literary men and independent thinkers, ready to try the new within the context of their love for tradition. Gerallt Jones said on many an occasion that Carwyn had been a great help for him in settling at the College and understanding a world that was so different. For all his Anglican upbringing, Gerallt Jones was the first layman in the College's history to be appointed Warden and Carwyn had arrived there as a Chapel deacon.

In long, deep discussions in Carwyn's study or the Warden's house, often late into the night, Gerallt Jones caught many glimpses of Carwyn's genius temperament:

> During our discussions, I came to feel the unrest that lay below his contemplative, gentle quiet and the fact that his looking, as tentative as it was, was towards a distant horizon. I believe that he, like some of his political and literary heroes, in the depth of his being, longed for the Wales of Middle Ages myth, the Wales of Gwyn Jones' poetry, an organisational Wales, a civilised Wales

– the patrician element to his personality somehow welded tidily with the folk integrity of his upbringing in Cefneithin.

The other side of the dilemma for Carwyn was the assurances that Gerallt Jones' arrival gave him. If Carwyn was contemplating leaving, he would not have to worry about what would happen to the Welsh language and heritage of the College. Similarly, on the rugby field, there would be no cause for concern. That legacy was also in good hands. In addition to Gerallt Jones' appointment, the College had also appointed Goronwy Morgan as a PE teacher. He was a former international player with the same rugby philosophy as Carwyn. If Carwyn left, therefore, his two great loves would be in safe hands.

As this thought process was going through Carwyn's mind, he had started to receive invitations to lecture occasionally at Trinity College, Carmarthen. The link between Trinity and Llandovery has already been established, with College pupils visiting Carmarthen regularly to see various productions. Also, in 1969, he had been selected as a candidate for Plaid Cymru in the General Election of 1970. He had promised Gerallt Jones that he would resign from the College if he was chosen as candidate. He didn't want his selection to be a stumbling block to his College work nor to be a reason for people to criticise the College itself.

One other factor contributed to his decision to leave Llandovery. Carwyn told some of his friends that he wanted to leave the College to make it easier for him to be considered as the coach for the 1971 Lions Tour. That really is ambition.

Living as he was in a small corner of West Wales, in close College circles against the backdrop of small coal-community village life, it was only a matter of time before the word got out that Carwyn was thinking of leaving Llandovery. A Cefneithin man, a member of the famous John family – not Barry in this case but one of his brothers – informed Llanelli Rugby Club Chairman Peter Rees of Carwyn's unrest. That was enough to spark Peter Rees into contacting Carwyn, the son of the coal miner who Peter had been a helper to as a boy in the Cross Hands Colliery. Llanelli coach Ieuan Evans was leaving the club and a replacement was needed.

The Sunday afternoon arrived when Peter Rees, with his wife and son, travelled from Llanelli in order to meet Carwyn at Llandovery. They had afternoon tea in Carwyn's study. It was a very traditional Welsh scene, but one that would have far-reaching consequences.

Carwyn accepted the invitation to coach Llanelli. He also accepted an invitation to be a full-time member of the Trinity College staff. A major period in his life was to come to an end. He played an active part in the appointment of his successor as Welsh teacher at Llandovery, Huw Llywelyn Davies.

> Carwyn was in the College when I went for my interview. When it was over, Carwyn and Warden Gerallt Jones came up to me and said that the three of us were going to Stradey Park there and then to see a seven-a-side competition. And that's how it was.

Huw Llywelyn Davies had known of Carwyn since he was a young boy, going with his father Eic to watch Carwyn play rugby. Eic would later work with Carwyn in the BBC and now Huw was his successor in Llandovery.

Carwyn looked back at his time in Llandovery as an influential part of his rugby life:

> Without doubt, I count the 12 years I spent at Llandovery as the most practical period of my career. The desire to coach had started to germinate as far back as 1960 and I was fortunate to work with early pioneers such as Cadfan Davies, Bridgend, on CCPR courses. But the most significant step was taking the reins at Llanelli.

After Carwyn's death, former Warden R Gerallt Jones summarised his thoughts on Carwyn's time at Llandovery:

> Probably the most typical memory of him is the lone figure in his overcoat, his head uncovered, walking up and down the touchline

on Tredegar Close fields, turning his back to the wind in order to light his cigarette, boiling with internal excitment and expecting every day that his team , this time, would deliver that perfect performance, that they would show him the game not as it was, but as it should be.

Carwyn's successor, Huw Llywelyn Davies, remembers words that Carwyn shared with him that show a deeper significance to his departure from the College:

> When it was confirmed that I had been successful in my application for Carwyn's job, he came up to me to congratulate me heartily. But then he added some far more poignant words, 'Congratulations, but don't make the same mistake as me and stay here too long, or you will find it very difficult to leave.' The impression that those words had on me at the time – and what happened to him later in his life has not changed that – is that he felt safe at Llandovery and maybe not so safe afterwards, when the arms of the College loosened their grip on him. As warm as the welcome was for him at Trinity College, I think he had quite a shock as to how different life was outside the Llandovery walls. Life there was a little tougher than the life experienced in a world where everyone worshipped him, even the most anti-Welsh.

The door from Llandovery had opened a little bit in 1968, when he started some part-time lecturing at Trinity. He resisted calls to go full-time that year, because he didn't want to disappoint his A Level pupils halfway through their course. That obligation met, the door to Trinity opened fully. In 1969, Carwyn started on a new path that would take him to Higher Education, and to a new world. Time alone would tell if that was indeed going to be a move that was detrimental to Carwyn, and would be the cause for him to turn his back into the wind once again.

CHAPTER 12

Coaching, Springboks
and politics

In Wales, what is special is small country psychology –
a special kind of need for heroes that could reassure
us of our existence as a country.
Rhodri Morgan, Former First Minister of Wales

ONCE OUT THROUGH the Llandovery gates, Carwyn's feet were
back in Cefneithin and on the hearth of the home in which
he had been brought up. He moved back into Rose Villa full-
time. He had been away for six years while doing his degree
and his National Service, back for two years while teaching
in Carmarthen, and away again for the twelve years he spent
at Llandovery before returning at the end of the Sixties. There
were times, of course, when he stayed at home for weekends
or during school holidays throughout the years away. But now,
in a physical way, Cefneithin was his home once more. He
was back living with his parents, in his fortieth year to heaven.
Metaphorically, it could be argued that he had in fact never left
Rose Villa.

Before long, Michael and Annie would have a second
child back home. Gwen had decided to curtail her career as
a psychiatric nurse in order to look after her ageing, failing
parents. Michael by then was suffering considerably from the
effects of years working underground. He needed a constant
oxygen supply at home. Annie too was showing signs of years
of hard work, as a wife and mother who had brought up four

children with little or no support and at a time that was austere and challenging.

When Gwen arrived back home, she contributed significantly to Carwyn's adaptation to life outside the idyllic world of Llandovery. Her sisterly arms were there to catch him if he was ever to fall. The sister replaced the caring institutional structure of a private school. The family once again had cause to say that Carwyn had more than one mother looking after him. As the Seventies approached, he was back under the care of two of those three mothers.

One of the early decisions that the siblings took was that their parents needed a new home. 40 years after moving into Rose Villa, they were to move out. Carwyn and Gwen had decided that their parents needed a home more suitable to their age and condition as Michael and Annie approached the shores of the Golden Pond. They had a bungalow built on the main road through the village, opposite the present site of Maes y Gwendraeth Comprehensive School. Their choice of name for the new family home is significant: they called it Hawen, after the family chapel back in the village of the Rhydlewis that Michael and Annie had moved from to start a new life in Cefneithin. As they approached the end, they returned to the beginning. They put down new roots in old soil.

This was the very beginning of the period in Carwyn's life when everyone thought they knew who he was. He was to achieve so much from this revived homely grounding, but he was also to prove that bright lights cast long, dark shadows. They were to be years of accumulating difficulties.

If in terms of geography he stepped from Llandovery to Cefneithin, in terms of his career, he stepped from a well-established institution of the establishment into two separate worlds whose currents were changing rapidly. He would both create and help define those new developmental currents in the rugby and educational seas.

Who needs a coach?

The rugby-coaching culture was in as much of a state of flux as
the popular culture of the Swinging decade that was nearly at
an end. The story begins back in the days when Carwyn was at
primary school, although he wouldn't have known much about
what was going on at the time from his little classroom. In
1935, an organisation called the Central Council for Physical
Recreative Training was formed, which later changed to
Central Council for Physical Recreation. The aim was simple:
to improve the standard of as many sports as possible within
the countries of the United Kingdom. It was soon the turn of
the Welsh Rugby Union to talk to Council representatives. The
WRU's goodwill was evident enough, but their enthusiasm was
not so forthcoming. The initial WRU response was to form a
Coaching Consultative sub-committee. Such a typically Welsh
response, to form a sub-committee!

Many years later, events on the field of play forced the
WRU's hand and their response to the whole coaching issue was
dramatically different. When Carwyn was still in Llandovery,
assuming responsibility for the College rugby team, Wales were
on tour in South Africa. In Durban, they suffered their heaviest
defeat in 40 years, losing 24–3 to the Springboks. That was in
1964. Carwyn himself mentions the significance of that defeat
for rugby in Wales in his book, *The World of Rugby*, co-written
with John Reason and published to coincide with a series of
the same name for the BBC.

> Wales collapsed in the last 20 minutes and returned home not
> only chastened but uncomfortably aware that they could no longer
> survive on the cult of the individual.

Carwyn, of course, knew better than anyone how to use the
abilities of the individual, but he knew how to do so within a
team context.

The WRU President at the time, D Ewart Davies, who was
due to retire that year, understood the situation clearly:

It was evident from the experiences of the South African Tour that a much more positive attitude to the game was required in Wales. Players must be prepared to learn and re-learn, to the point of absolute mastery, the basic principles of rugby union football. The importance of correct coaching at all levels cannot be overemphasised. The Schools and Youth Union shoulder a special responsibility in this connection.

The Training Committee's Chair, V J Parfitt, was clearly frustrated, according to Davies:

> V J Parfitt complained about the lack of interest being shown by clubs towards the coaching courses that were available. Elvet Jones, a British Lion of 1938, remarked that clubs and the WRU had shown scant attention to coaching; and that unless there was a far more radical approach, future AGMs would degenerate into a gathering of social, not rugby, clubs.

As a direct result of pressure from rugby clubs, a Coaching Working Committee was established in the wake of the discussions relating to the South African defeat. Cadfan Davies was a leading member of this committee, along with Cliff Jones, the genius outside half in 1930s Welsh rugby, and Alun Thomas. On 16 July, 1964, this group asked Carwyn and a number of others involved in coaching, as well as some former international players, to join them on the Working Committee under the Chairmanship of Cliff Jones. This was the first official link between Carwyn and the WRU structure.

In 1966 a coaching course was organised by the WRU in Aberystwyth, for prospective Welsh Secondary Schools and Welsh Youth Internationals. Taking these young, promising players through their paces were Dai Nash, Geoff Whitsun, Grahame Hodgson, Cadfan Davies and Carwyn James. Many of the players on the course would go on to have long careers with top clubs: Malcolm Swain with Aberavon and Moseley; Roger Lane at Cardiff; Ian Lewis at Bridgend, Elis Wyn Williams at London Welsh; Jeff Thomas at Swansea; Selwyn Williams, the scrum half who would play under Carwyn at Llanelli; and future Llanelli and Wales coach, Allan Lewis.

The previous year, 1965, the Committee had suggested that Wales needed a full-time coaching administrator. The recommendation was accepted, and in 1967 Ray Williams was appointed as the world's first full-time professional rugby union coach and national coaching coordinator. Former Welsh international and leading rugby journalist Clem Thomas said of this appointment:

> The appointment of Ray Williams in 1967 was the best decision made by the WRU in my lifetime, and, in my view, was fundamental to the ensuing success of Welsh rugby... It was now apparent that there was a need for a professional with considerable ability to guide and structure the new conceptions of coaching.

Slowly, as change happens in Wales, individual clubs started to appoint coaches. Wales sought to set an example and in 1967, the first coach was appointed to the national team: Dai Nash. Carwyn was considered for that job, a full nine years before his famous tangle with the WRU for the job of Welsh coach. In 1967 it was deemed that he was too inexperienced for the job. In their volume *Welsh Rugby: The Crowning Years 1968–1980*, co-authors Clem Thomas and Geoffrey Nicholson sum up the choice of the first Wales coach in this way:

> The more logical choice would have been Carwyn James, who, apart from Ray Williams, was the only rugby intellectual mind in Wales.

Three members of the Coaching Working Committee were given broader responsibilities than merely coaching clubs. In 1967, David Harries was asked to coach a Monmouthshire representative team to play against the All Blacks and Dai Hayward was asked to coach an East Wales team against the same opposition. Carwyn was asked to coach a West Wales representative team. Carwyn's captain for that game at St Helen's rugby ground in Swansea was Clive Rowlands. The two would meet again.

Carwyn's feet were moving further and further under the WRU table. The coaching world was changing. But it wasn't moving everything with it as it swept along. Many clubs still resisted the whole concept of coaching, and as much as the WRU had formed their sub-committees and working committees, the Welsh international team still went on a tour of Argentina in 1968 without a coach, a decision which triggered the resignation of the incumbent Dai Nash and led to the appointment of Clive Rowlands.

That was the year Llanelli appointed their first ever coach. Ieuan Evans was a well-known figure in the area, the son of a leading Communist affectionately called Ianto Coch (Red Ianto). He was a leading light in schools-rugby circles and a fellow member with Carwyn of the WRU Coaching Working Committee. Llanelli had shown their forward-thinking attitude to coaching by inviting Tom Hudson to develop the club's players' fitness. He had made a name for himself outside the rugby world, training Swansea Town football players and competing in the pentathlon at the 1956 Olympic Games. It was a bold step indeed to bring him into the Llanelli rugby fold, and he was still there when Carwyn joined Llanelli as coach.

1968 was also the same year that the British and Irish Lions had their first ever coach. Ronnie Dawson had played for Ireland and the Lions and had been at the same coaching conference as Carwyn in Dublin in 1964.

Despite all this innovative momentum, many still refused to accept the idea of a coach. The first Welsh international coach, Dai Nash, was more than aware of this, having heard many comments to that effect on the terraces:

'Oh we've never had coaching, you know, we all pick it up, we're all natural players you know; oh no, you'll stifle flair. No, we don't want coaching.'

This blatant opposition to coaching led to considerable antagonism between clubs. Those who opposed coaching accused those who embraced it of nothing short of cheating. They were going against the spirit of the game, if not in fact breaking the rules of the game, and that in order to gain unfair advantage over the opposition. But it wasn't as if the concept of coaching was alien to the entire Welsh rugby culture. It was totally acceptable in one particular area of Welsh rugby – in fact it was warmly embraced and encouraged, as Wales' second national coach, Clive Rowlands, remembers:

> When I say there wasn't coaching in Wales, every school side in Wales was heavily coached. Every school had a school teacher, didn't have to be the PE teacher, but they would be involved in rugby football over 70, 80 years ago.

Boys needed coaching then, not men. Once a rugby player reached a certain age, it was argued, he didn't need coaching any more. It was argued that planning and preparing for games went against the spirit of the game, according to Rowlands:

> Cadfan Davies described a conversation with the then Chairman [sic] of selectors: 'I'm sorry,' he said, 'we were delighted with the last match but one or two of my colleagues are concerned that the coach will become the selector of the team and therefore we won't be continuing this experiment.'

There was a palpable fear of the whole idea of coaching – a fear that coaches would usurp the traditional role of the selector, and that without being a proper member of the Welsh Rugby Union.

Llanelli didn't nurture such fears, and appointed Ieuan Evans as coach. When Carwyn took over from him, he settled into the spiritual home of West Wales rugby, Stradey Park. It was a venue with a significance that resonated far beyond the county boundary. The spirit of Stradey was perfectly described by Carwyn himself in an article for one particular match-day programme. That was in 1973 when his old university, Aberystwyth, were celebrating their centenary. One of the celebratory events was a rugby game against Llanelli in March of that year. The man responsible for selecting the Aber representative team was Welsh international John Dawes, also a former Aber student. The match was given the title the Dr Idris Jones Memorial match, in honour of a Llanelli man who had also been a member of the governing body of Aberystwyth University. In that match-day programme, Carwyn encapsulates the significance of Stradey, but not before quoting his former lecturer and poet Gwenallt. He then moves on:

> Stradey Park is the National Park of Carmarthenshire, Pembrokeshire and Cardiganshire as well as being the National Park of Welsh-speaking Wales. It's a delight to hear the accents of the three counties at Stradey, in addition to the hardening of some consonants by visitors from the Swansea Valley and West Glamorgan, as people flock here on a Saturday afternoon to support or criticise, or in midweek as they look out for evening respite from a hard shift in the pit, the tinplate works and the steel foundry. Llanelli is a rural industrial town, a large village reluctant to be a town. A central hub for a collection of villages and that centre, through lack of vocabulary, being called a town. The heart of that community is to be felt here, where the quickening beat soon turns to fever. And if the eyes of the supporters are red and scarlet, much is expected of the team and woe betide them if they fall short. This is the open-air theatre of West Wales rugby, the folk theatre of Dyfed. It must be better than any other, better than Twickenham, Murrayfield and Lansdowne Road and a hundred times better than the child's play on Cardiff Arms Park and St Helen's.

In the same article, he showed that he was was very much aware of developments in Aberystwyth town centre at that time as well. He applies something that was going to happen in Aber a few weeks after that celebratory game at Stradey to his central point about Stradey being the folk theatre of Dyfed:

On 19 April, a centre for drama will open in Aberystwyth and its name, Theatr y Werin (The People's Theatre) is significant. This is an educational establishment of some importance, and close to the hearts of many of us, acknowledging its gratitude to the common people of the land and hoping that they will then take advantage of the facilities and services, remembering that the hope of a civilised society is exactly this involvement with each other.

Rapid changes

This new chapter in Carwyn's life could not have been more diametrically opposed to his previous life in Llandovery. They were indeed, revolutionary days for Carwyn. No sooner had his feet touched the Stradey turf than he had to prepare his team to face the mighty Springboks, he was chosen as the parliamentary candidate for Plaid Cymru in Llanelli and then he was chosen as the coach of the British and Irish Lions. All this happened within six months, the first six months of his lecturing responsibilities at Trinity College, Carmarthen. They were indeed an extremely significant few months in Carwyn's life. The Springboks' visit was sure to be a difficult fixture with political implications far beyond the game itself. The Lions, Plaid Cymru and Trinity would all take him to brand new worlds. But he did face all these new challenges and opportunities from the comfort of his parental home. It was, once more, a case of Carwyn pushing boundaries, but from the vantage point of the comfortable. Within some of these triumphs, however, were the early seeds of fragmentation.

The Springboks arrive

Carwyn would have known of the impending Springboks visit when he was asked to be the coach of Llanelli Rugby Club. The game was arranged for January 1970. That would no doubt have excited the coach in Carwyn, being an opportunity to apply himself against international opposition, which in turn would further his coaching ambitions.

But it wasn't all positive. Any visit by a South African team in those days would bring with it political fallout that quite often overshadowed the game itself. Throughout the Sixties, every team representing that country, in whichever sport, faced protests on their arrival in Britain and at each venue they were to appear at. The country's apartheid system – open, legal and public discrimination against black people – was abhorred in most parts of the world. No black player would have been considered for the South African rugby squad.

Many in the UK saw sport as an ideal arena in which to make those objections known. Countries refused to send their national teams to South Africa and many refused to accept South African teams to their countries. This sporting withdrawal, it was said, was a clear statement to the South African government that apartheid wasn't tolerated. But in many other countries, the situation wasn't so clear-cut. Some saw that continued engagement with South Africa was a way of influencing from within, of persuading the powers that be, by being in their company on these sporting tours. The fact that the Springboks were allowed to tour Britain shows that no boycott had been enforced by the British government, however strong their opposition to apartheid was. Protest and objection was therefore left to local groups wherever the South Africans were to play.

One of the Springboks party on the 1969–70 tour, Tommy Bedford, remembers the welcome they had when they arrived in Britain. His words are those of a man denied the captaincy of his country because he was deemed to be too liberal.

> Instead of proudly stepping out at Heathrow wearing our Springbok blazers, we were smuggled out in a coach to a golfing hotel. You feel you haven't got a friend in the world.

In 1964, the International Olympic Committee decided to ban South Africa from competing in the Tokyo Olympics. In 1968, as an indication of the reverse standpoint, South Africa cancelled the proposed England cricket team tour in their country, because England had selected Basil D'Oliveira: a man born in South Africa, but not to a white family.

There was increasing pressure on the Welsh Rugby Union to disown South Africa. In 1967, two member clubs, Brynamman and Llangennech, put forward a proposal suggesting that all rugby ties between the WRU and South Africa should be severed. It was put to the vote. The result was very close, but the motion was defeated.

Carwyn's personal views were clear enough. He strongly opposed the apartheid system on moral, religious and political grounds. His stance on this issue was far clearer than his involvement with National Service and Communism, the former a challenge to his pacifist chapel heritage, the latter the challenge of a godless belief system to his Christian faith, also including human atrocities committed in its name. Carwyn discussed his views on apartheid with the Llanelli Rugby Club hierarchy. He was realistic enough to accept that the game had been arranged before he was asked to be coach and that cancelling wasn't an option, but he still needed to make his stand. He agreed to prepare the team for the game, but said that he would not be present at the match itself. He was therefore, to make a clear definite stand, but without any show or bravado. The players walked on to the pitch without their coach. He stayed in the dressing room, under the stand, listening to the game on the radio. His absence on the touchline was a clear political statement. His presence under the stand was a clear statement of his commitment to his team.

It is of no great surprise that the South Africans noted the game against Llanelli as the game that tested them the most on the whole tour. They only won by one point. The game is remembered in rugby folklore for the fact that Llanelli came so close to defeating the Springboks, but also for one particular try the home team scored. It was one of the best tries that Stradey ever saw, the culmination of a 21-pass move by 14 of the Llanelli players. No doubt the one player who didn't manage to be involved in that move was given quite a hard time by his teammates for a long time after the game! But that move, and the game as a whole, was an early indication of the James philosophy that was to develop over the next six years or so.

Carwyn the politician

Carwyn the rugby man, Carwyn the literary man, Carwyn the broadcaster were all Carwyns that Wales, and sometimes the world, knew about. Carwyn the politician was a lesser-known being. The seeds of his politics were sown in Aberystwyth, as we have already seen. They took firmer hold in his Llandovery days, and in the early Sixties specifically. Plaid Cymru had already formed a branch at Llandovery when Carwyn arrived there, but it was very small – about half a dozen members. Sometimes the group would meet in Carwyn's room at the College. 1961 proved to be a significant year for the Party in the town, as well as for Carwyn the political being. A *Noson Lawen*, an evening of popular entertainment, was arranged in order to raise funds for Plaid Cymru. The entertainment was led by singing group Parti'r Ddraig Goch (The Red Dragon Party) from Llangadog, with prominent Plaid Cymru politician Gwynfor Evans, later to be elected the party's first MP, as MC. Party members went from door to door, distributing leaflets publicising the event and selling tickets for it. Everyone in the town knew it was happening. The evening was a huge success, gaining Plaid Cymru an increased profile and following.

Carwyn's next high-profile involvement with Plaid Cymru came after 1963, the year in which Dr Richard Beeching published his report, *The Reshaping of British Railways*. He recommended that 55% of British railway stations be closed, along with 30% of the tracks. Llandovery station was on the list of stations to be axed and the Mid-Wales Line, which ran through the town, was on the list of tracks to be closed. The townspeople formed a group to protest against such proposals. Beeching's axe had to be stopped.

The protest group was a cross-party one. Lady Megan Lloyd George, the Carmarthen Labour MP, was involved, as was Gwynfor Evans. Carwyn also played a prominent role. According to the secretary of the group, Cyril Jones, Carwyn's presence had a definite effect:

> Carwyn's presence in that group, and at other Plaid activities, gave a certain credibility, an authority, to our work. It gave us a respectability. People saw this teacher from Llandovery College standing in the name of Plaid. It was easier for many to accept Plaid once they saw that Carwyn was involved.

The group won their fight. The line and the station were kept open and they still are, unlike the line that took Carwyn from Carmarthen to his university in Aberystwyth. Carwyn's role in this campaign saw him develop economic arguments as well as cultural ones, which had been his political leaning previously. He argued for the jobs that would be lost, as over 100 people were employed in the Llandovery goods depot.

When the General Election of 1964 was announced, Carwyn was a more seasoned political campaigner than he had been before. He campaigned vigorously on behalf of the candidate, Gwynfor Evans. Twice a week he walked miles and miles, knocking on doors and engaging in persuasive conversations in Rhandirmwyn, Cilycwm and other remote rural areas around Llandovery. Cyril Jones remembers Carwyn's activity:

> He would often use his rugby during these political conversations. He would ask, for example, who people would support on Wales-England international days. 'Wales, of course!' was the reply, without exception. Carwyn's response then was more political. 'In that case, in this election, who are you going to support: Wales or England?'

As well as walking the country lanes, Carwyn would also stand on public platforms under the Plaid Cymru banner. Hundreds of meetings were held during that campaign, and the largest crowds in East Carmarthenshire were always at the ones in which Carwyn was speaking.

By the 1966 General Election, Plaid Cymru were strong enough in Llandovery to be able to afford to rent a shop in the town. That year would prove an historic one for the party, with Gwynfor Evans elected its first ever MP, and in that constituency. However, that didn't happen in the General Election held in March that year. He lost that battle to the incumbent Lady Megan Lloyd George. But she was not well, and many of her own Labour Party had thought it unwise for her to be selected as candidate in the first place. Their fears proved correct: Lady Megan died from breast cancer in May 1966. A by-election was therefore needed, and was called for 14 July. The night before election day, on the Wednesday, there was a public meeting in Llandovery and Carwyn was there.

When the by-election result was announced, Gwynfor Evans had defeated the Labour candidate, Gwilym Prys Davies, by 2,436 votes – a swing of 12% from Labour to Plaid in a matter of a few months. Carwyn had travelled down to Carmarthen by train for the announcement and managed to secure a lift back to Llandovery later that evening, amidst scenes of celebration and euphoria. Back in his study, the party continued!

The following morning, the victorious Gwynfor Evans and his supporters went on a cavalcade around the constituency. When the car procession reached Llandovery, Gwynfor's agent Cyril Jones remembers seeing Carwyn and Rita Williams standing side by side in front of the Castle Hotel, waving enthusiastically.

Carwyn not only led the growth of Plaid Cymru in Llandovery, he also widened the party's appeal amongst young people. Without doubt, rugby was the lead factor here.

Carwyn's political awareness developed significantly in those first six years of the Sixties. It was more political than it was in Aberystwyth, less cultural. In this respect he was bringing the spirit of Rhydlewis and the values of Cefneithin ever closer together.

In 1968, he was given an opportunity to formulate his political views and to present them to a British audience. In a programme called *A Disunited Kingdom?*, presented by the young Robin Day, the whole issue of independence for Wales and Scotland was discussed on a lengthy BBC programme. It was a combination of studio discussion, with a panel and audience, and contributions on film by various individuals. Carwyn was one of these individuals. His film contribution was almost ten minutes long.

It opened with archive footage of him dropping a goal in his first game for Wales in 1958. Carwyn's nationalism is put firmly in the context of rugby culture. Carwyn is then introduced, through voice-over narration, as believing that the Welsh should govern Wales. Carwyn begins to present his argument:

> To be Welsh today is to be aware of an old vital tradition that has survived. It is also to feel a new sense of nationhood which is at last finding full expression. No real serious attempt has been made by successive London governments to plan the Wales of today. Our people, our young people are leaving the countryside. But depopulation is not confined to the rural areas. It is becoming more and more apparent in the industrial valleys as well. It is the duty of government to govern responsibly and to provide alternative industries in the mining valleys now facing doom. But day by day, the people of Wales are realising the futility of a government in which they had put so much faith.

The pictures we see after this are as stereotypical as they can be. An old Welsh farmer sits on the back of his horse, two sheepdogs scurry back and forth in the yard of an old Welsh farmhouse which nestles on the slopes of a hill. Carwyn explains that the spirit of Wales is to be found in such mountain farms, in the cottage by the stream, and on the hearth of the coal miner. He leaves us in no doubt that his sense of Wales, and therefore his nationalism, comes from a very definite perception of Wales, the one he would have learned about in his school days from those popular textbooks, reinforced and embellished by conversations and experiences on the streets of Cefneithin and Rhydlewis. He then turns to the language. He is seen to be walking across the yard of another farm and begins a conversation in Welsh with the farmer. We are not told as part of the programme, but he is at Pantycelyn Farm, home of William Williams, the prolific and influential eighteenth-century hymn writer. The farmer Carwyn is speaking to is a sixth-generation descendant of William Williams. The canvas of Carwyn's nationalism is nearing completion: the rugby, the farm, the hills, the chapels and the hymns. Carwyn explains that Welsh is the oldest language in Europe and Wales needs to protect its language. He moves on to say that people are leaving rural Wales, schools and train stations are closing and communities are suffering. The pictures change to a village scene where three old men sit on a bench at the side of the road. Flat caps, scars and a shortage of breath evident in all three. Carwyn is back in Cefneithin. This is where his more economic and political analysis starts.

> I was born and brought up in the industrial village, Cefneithin, located literally under the shadow of the coal tips. As the son of a miner, I feel more at home here than I do in the agricultural area of North Carmarthenshire. The black pyramids are part of the scenery, a symbol of economic wealth. It is sobering to think how much mineral wealth has left this valley, and today there is so little to show for it. And the future is bleak and uncertain.
>
> What is the future for these close-knit communities, in the Rhondda Valley, in the Dulais Valley or in my own Gwendraeth Valley? Already the unemployment figures are high in these areas, often four times the average for Britain as a whole. In the White Paper on the Welsh economy, the completely unrealistic figure of 15,000 new jobs needed in Wales by 1971 was given. Professional economists put the figure at a minimum of 60,000. It may well be more.

And then, as if in a reflective break from outlining policy, he breaks off into Welsh and says, '*Mae dyn yn rhy fawr i gardod*'

– man is too big to beg, though no translation is offered on the programme.

> A nation needs institutions to foster and develop its interests. Sadly, the institutions of Wales are mainly cultural. But even culturally we are found lacking. It is typical that Wales has produced so many world famous opera singers and yet it has no opera house, so many world famous actors and yet has no national theatre. The present Labour government at last fulfilled a long-standing promise and established a Welsh Office and gave Cabinet status to the Secretary of State. The office needs power to act and to govern.

Here he brings his piece to a conclusion by saying that there are signs of an awakening in Wales, an increasing awareness of what it is to be Welsh and what the Welsh nation actually means. There is, he continues, an increasing desire to transfer this new perception into political power by taking a full part in the democratic process and by Wales being allowed to govern its own affairs.

In a long, walk-and-talk piece to camera in the Civic Centre in Cardiff, he explains that the buildings around him were originally designed with housing a future Welsh parliament in mind. He ends his contribution:

> The central government in London has failed badly and the only alternative is to see fulfilled the vision of the city fathers. And I feel that the ultimate decision is in the hands of the Welsh people – in our hands. If we will it, it is ours. Nothing can stand in the way of the power of the nation.

Carwyn the parliamentary candidate

Having worked with Gwynfor Evans on the rail-closure campaign in Llandovery and in the Election campaign in 1966, Plaid's first MP knew Carwyn well. Seeing this programme in 1968 would have confirmed what Gwynfor knew he had already seen. Carwyn needed to be a parliamentary candidate. At Gwynfor Evans' request, therefore, Carwyn was asked to stand for Llanelli in the 1970 General Election. His main opponent was a young solicitor from Cynwyl Elfed: Denzil Davies – one of Carwyn's former pupils in Queen Elizabeth School, Carmarthen. Now they were head to head at the hustings. Denzil Davies remembers Plaid's candidate selection:

> The fact that Plaid Cymru chose Carwyn caused quite a stir in the Labour Party, without doubt. He was 'a name', a popular man where it counted most, which was amongst the rugby people of West Wales. This caused a certain nervousness in local Labour ranks at first, as we tried to plan how we would counter his threat. It was very much a case of planning a battle not against Plaid Cymru, but against Carwyn James. There was a real fear that he could attract a significant number of the Stradey faithful to his cause, and that this posed the biggest threat to Labour in the Llanelli constituency since it first won the seat in 1922. And Carwyn's own work ethic was a real challenge too! Whenever I went to canvass in the villages surrounding Llanelli, the message was the same: Carwyn's been here already! There's no denying that he worked very hard on his campaign.

The fear of Carwyn appealing to the rugby faithful was real. It's difficult to overemphasise the strength of such a fraternity in West Wales, even in the days before Carwyn's own major personal rugby successes. This was shown very clearly in a report published the year Carwyn died. Geographer John Bale, from Keele University, showed that the county of Dyfed – the amalgamation of Carmarthenshire, Pembrokeshire and Cardiganshire – had more rugby clubs per head of population than any other area in Britain. There were 82 rugby clubs in Dyfed in 1983, and it's easy to appreciate the sociological and community impact they had. To have a candidate who was from this rugby world, and the coach of one of the leading clubs not only in that area but in the world, was enough to make the Labour Party more than just a little nervous.

Neither Carwyn nor Plaid Cymru themselves, however, made much use of this rugby legacy in the campaign, if Carwyn's official election brochure is anything to go by. The fact that he had such a brochure was in itself an innovative step. It was the result of a change of approach towards marketing and promotion on Plaid's part. Carwyn knew who he wanted to put his brochure together – PR guru David Meredith:

> I received a phone call from Carwyn asking me to meet him in the Angel Hotel, Cardiff, because he wanted ask me to design an election brochure for him. The party had started to realise that it needed to take the marketing side of political campaigning more seriously and that previous election brochures, which had been lifeless and boring with little or no photographs or design work, had to be changed.
>
> I had designed one for Phil Williams in the 1968 election in Caerphilly and I had designed a pamphlet for Gwynfor Evans entitled *The Black Paper on Wales*. A strong influence on my thinking in preparing such publications, and in preparing Carwyn's too, was the approach taken by the Kennedy regime in the early Sixties. One emphasis they had which I liked was the use of red on the front cover. I did this for Carwyn too. He gave me complete freedom to do what I thought was needed, without interfering at all. Meic Stephens wrote most of the words, with Carwyn contributing some of his own.

On the back of the pamphlet are quotes taken from speeches Carwyn made as part of his campaign. Ever aware of the need to touch the subjective side of experience if any communication was to be effective, he would adapt his speech to include issues relevant to the area in which he was speaking. When in Pembrey on the outskirts of Llanelli, for example, he addressed the Ministry of Defence's proposals to buy land there, in order to open a Gunnery Range. Under the heading *Labour's Offer of Jobs – a Gunnery Range!* he makes his point:

> What a vision for the future; what an agenda for a generation. This crude and unecessary intrusion into the lives of a peaceful

community must and will be resisted. Wales has already lost 53,000 acres to military needs, including 2,000 acres of coast; now the Ministry of Defence demands another 15,000 acres and proposes to spend £25 million on moving the range. To teach and learn how to kill. The Ministry of Defence has the money. The Board of Trade hasn't. Was the Ministry of Defence ever concerned with providing jobs? *Gwiredder y broffwydoliaeth: 'Ac ni ddysgant rhyfel mwyach.'* (Let the prophecy be fulfilled: 'And they shall not learn war any more.')

On election day, 18 June, although he came second, Carwyn secured over 8,000 votes – the largest total for his party in the six elections they had fought in the constituency since 1950. As was mentioned time and time again during the days after the

Carwyn James

Gwynfor Evans says

I am proud that the man chosen by Plaid Cymru to contest Llanelli is Carwyn James. His splendid qualities will make him a first-rate Member of Parliament, and you will make history by electing him.
Plaid Cymru is growing swiftly. It will replace the old parties whose policies have wrought such havoc to the national life of Wales and who have stubbornly kept Wales in subjection, without even provincial status.
Before the end of the 'seventies, Wales will have her own Parliament and Government, and everyone will wonder why it did not happen generations ago: because it will appear the most natural thing in the world.
Our programme for 1970 is drafted. If we fulfil it, 1970 will be Plaid Cymru's year. Then we can go on to make the '70s Cymru's Decade.

Meddai Gwynfor:

'Rwy'n teimlo balchder mawr fod Carwyn James wedi ei ddewis i gynrychioli Plaid Cymru yn etholaeth Llanelli. Fe wna Aelod Seneddol ardderchog, a byddwch chwithau'n creu hanes wrth ei ethol.
Mae Plaid Cymru'n tyfu'n gyflym. Mae'n mynd i ddisodli'r hen bleidiau sydd wedi gwanhau cymaint ar fywyd cenedlaethol Cymru ac wedi ei chadw hi'n gaeth heb gymaint a safle talaith.
Cyn diwedd y saith-degau bydd gan Gymru ei Senedd a'i Llywodraeth ei hunan, a phawb yn rhyfeddu na fyddai'r peth wedi digwydd ers cenedlaethau: oherwydd dyna'r peth mwyaf naturiol yn y byd i genedl.
Mae ein rhaglen ar gyfer 1970 yn barod. Os cyflawnwn hi, 1970 fydd Blwyddyn y Blaid. Yna gallwn wneud y saith-degau yn Ddegaid Cymru.

223

result, he had secured about the same number of votes as an average crowd to watch his team play at Stradey.

It is a different matter however, to consider whether Carwyn would have been a successful MP. His political awareness had certainly developed since the student days of the Plaid university group meetings in a coffee shop. But there's little to suggest that he had changed as a person enough to take his place in the cut, thrust and compromise world of politics. Political games were about the only kind he was not very good at. He was too much of an individual.

Carwyn's election fight personified a debate that was to emerge in the discussions about the history of Wales at a later date. The link between rugby and expressions of nationhood is something that historian Kenneth O Morgan mentions when dealing with the Seventies in his book, *The Birth of a Nation*:

> What was… debatable was whether the excitement of international days at Cardiff Arms Park, with their emotional cascades of hymn-singing, did not blunt the passion for a more solid and political form of national self-expression. Beating the English through skill with an oval leather ball appeared to be satisfaction enough.

Grand Slams and Triple Crowns were strong enough expressions of Welshness, a solid enough sign that Wales existed; therefore political expression of the same wasn't so necessary. The decade ended with a 'No' vote in the referendum on devolution for Wales. Carwyn would not have identified himself with such thinking, of course, and oval-shaped nationalism was certainly not enough for him.

CHAPTER 13

Lions and the Long White Cloud

The players have medics these days. We had Elastoplast.
Willie John McBride

DOZENS OF VOLUMES and miles of column inches have been written on the remarkable achievements of the British and Irish Lions on their tour of New Zealand in 1971. Under coach Carwyn and manager Doug Smith's leadership, they secured the first and, at the time of writing, the only Test series victory against the All Blacks. These next pages will only concentrate on aspects of that tour that relate directly to Carwyn.

Carwyn was in the throes of his political campaigning when the process to select the Lions coach began. He was shortlisted, alongside fellow Welshman Roy Bish, the English Rugby Union's candidate Martin Underwood and the Irish Rugby Union man, Roly Meates. It was not possible to select a Scotsman as the tour manager already selected, Doug Smith, was a Scotsman and the coach could not come from the same country as the manager.

Carwyn knew Roy Bish quite well. They had both played for the same Welsh Schoolboys team, Bish from his school in Port Talbot. Like Carwyn, he also divided his time between coaching responsibilities and a job as a lecturer – in his case, at Cardiff Training College. He had more club coaching experience than Carwyn, having coached Cardiff since 1965.

Carwyn had to change his plans in order to go to the interview. He was due to speak at an event as part of his election campaign, but good friend Rita Williams was called upon:

> He was due to open a Plaid Cymru fair in Llanelli somewhere,
> Felinfoel I think. But of course he couldn't go, and I received an
> SOS from him asking me to go instead. It was actually quite a big
> step for him to have to cancel anything in Llanelli at that time,
> for fear of losing momentum or creating a bad impression. But of
> course he had to go to the interview, two weeks before polling day.

He faced his interviewers in a panelled room at the HQ of the East India Company in London, with classic paintings in ornate frames all around. It was no doubt a room that the founder of Llandovery College, Thomas Phillips, would have been familiar with as an employee of the East India Company. Inevitably, Carwyn was asked about the impending election. If he was to be successful, he would not be able to go on the tour. That was of obvious concern to the Lions officials. Carwyn tells us what his reply was:

> I made two points. That I was competing with all my might to win
> the seat, even though the Labour majority was well over 20,000;
> that in the current issue of the *Llanelli Star*, the odds quoted were
> 10,000/1 against, so I politely offered to take the committee's
> pounds back home in the hope that they would all make a quick
> £10,000!

Carwyn was not convinced that he had made a favourable impression on the panel at all. The comments he made weren't out of any sense of false modesty to public enquirers. It was his sister Gwen who heard Carwyn's uncertainties and the reason for them:

> I remember him coming back and saying, 'Well, I'm not going to
> get that job, because of the old politics!' And I told him, 'If you told
> them the truth, doesn't matter what it is, they're sure to see that

you stand firm on what you believe.' About three days after that, I was in the kitchen and Carwyn walked in, in his pyjamas. 'I've been successful!' he said. I think that is the day I saw him at his happiest. So the old politics didn't do him much harm, did it?

Carwyn was the coach for the British and Irish Lions, without ever having coached his country. Judging by the shortlist, the Lions officials cared less for that in those days than they would in more recent years – none of the other candidates on the list had assumed national responsibilities either.

Like Gwen, the Lions officials didn't think that the politics was an issue. Before he could accept the invitation formally, Carwyn's first step was to ask his employers for time off to go on the tour. The management at Trinity College, Carmarthen, agreed to give him time off work for the first month of the tour, but without pay. The last two months of the tour were during the College summer holidays, and therefore not an issue. Llanelli Rugby Club were, needless to say, delighted to allow him the time off.

Luckily for the Lions, Carwyn didn't win the election, even though he gave the Labour Party a good fight. He was then free to begin the process of putting a squad together from the best that British and Irish rugby clubs could offer. He set about his task in his usual meticulous, thorough manner, going to as many club games as he possibly could and studying games that were available to him on film via his extensive network of contacts at the BBC and HTV. But this was a two-way process. Many players didn't know who Carwyn was and they needed to find out about him. He hadn't been an international coach and would therefore not have come across many of the stars in England, Ireland and Scotland. One who knew nothing about Carwyn when his name as coach was announced was Fergus Slattery, the Irish back-row star:

> I'd never heard of him before. There would be no reason why I
> should have come across him, living and playing in Ireland as I

Instructions to Llanelli RFC before leaving for New Zealand

did. The first time I ever saw him was in the training camp we had in Eastbourne before the tour. I was well impressed when I saw him. He was very calm and handled himself very well.

England and Harlequins full back Bob Hiller had a similar experience:

> I didn't know him before we gathered as a Lions squad in Eastbourne. I had seen him before, when I played for Surrey in a county match and he'd come to see the game as part of his Lions scouting mission. I remember that Llanelli were playing the same day and had lost, back in Stradey. I remember pulling his leg about that. It didn't seem to have made a difference!

Some however, did know who Carwyn was. The giant Willie John McBride, for instance – the Lion of Lions and close friend of Scarlets Lions hero, Delme Thomas:

> I had heard the name, from some of the international players I knew in Wales and in England. They spoke very highly of him.

Carwyn had a task of a different nature with some of the players he knew very well. He had to work hard to persuade some stars to go on the tour in the first place, includingWillie John himself.

> I had a call from Carwyn asking me to meet him for lunch one day. The conversation soon turned to the forthcoming tour of course, but not in the way I expected it to. He asked me out of the blue, 'As a senior player, what sort of people playing today would you take with you to New Zealand, to win?' I was astounded. No one had ever asked me such a question before, or any other player as far as I know. After the conversation triggered by that question, he said something else I didn't expect.
> He said that he had heard that I didn't want to go on the tour. I had no idea that he knew that. It was true. I had three Lions tours behind me, '62, '66, and '68. I had decided that the time had come for me to concentrate on my banking career, as that was my pension, after all. So, family discussions had led to me deciding I wasn't available for New Zealand. Carwyn sat back in his chair, pulled on his cigarette, looked at me as he blew the smoke out and said, 'But Willie John, I need you!' Again, no one had ever said that

to me before. I left that lunch ready to tour New Zealand, and as we walked out of the restaurant, Carwyn turned to me and said, 'I promise you this tour will be different.'

With Willie John firmly on board, the Irishman relished the opportunity of working with Carwyn:

I was looking forward to playing with a coach of such reputation. In fact, having been on Lions tours before, I was looking forward to working with a coach. Ronnie Dawson had taken charge of my previous Lions tour, but that was when coaching was in its infancy. Coaching had developed a great deal since then, and the word was that Carwyn was at the forefront of such a development and quite a thinker. That made it even more of an exciting prospect.

Carwyn faced two different situations with his Welsh players, Barry John and Gerald Davies. Gerald faced one particular obstacle that could stop him touring:

Because of my final-year exams in Cambridge, I would not be able to fly out with the Lions and I would lose the first three weeks of the tour. Traditionally, the Lions hierarchy had always insisted that the squad all flew out together, so that was that. On the weekend of selecting the squad, I received a telephone call from Carwyn. He asked if I was able to fly out to New Zealand after my Tripos exams. But there was a condition. If I was prepared to do so, I had to attend the training camp in Eastbourne, which was before my exams. I agreed to fly out late and I accepted the condition. Carwyn had changed a Lions tradition, such was his influence. If he hadn't done so, I would not have been chosen to go.

Match reports from the tour show clearly how beneficial it was for the Lions to have Gerald there. This is how he remembers the time he joined the squad for their first meeting:

The room remained silent for a while. To an unbelieving crowd, unaccustomed to his ways and long used to being second best, Carwyn James had brought his prologue to the tour to a close.

The four nations, each distinctive from the other, shall be one. The challenge ahead shall be met.

'Let me say this,' he said at the Park Lane Hotel. 'Let me simply say this,' with his right hand waving schoolmasterishly in the air, with the inevitable untipped cigarette held between first and second finger. 'I believe that we will win the Test Series in New Zealand.'

There was another vital star that Carwyn had to work hard to get to New Zealand, but for different reasons. Barry John was the Welsh outside half in that famous game against Scotland in the Five Nations which Wales won 19–18 thanks to a conversion kick by John Taylor towards the end of the game. Wales won the Grand Slam that year. This was only a few months before the Lions tour. Barry John remembers:

I scored a try in the game, and as I did so, I had a bang on the back of my head from a Scottish player which pushed my head into the ground. It was a fair enough tackle, but it did some damage. Two weeks later, Wales were in Paris to play against France. Now, it's quite likely that this was the only tackle I ever made, but I tackled a French player hard and suffered another blow to the head and the nose in the process. That was in March and I played very little rugby for Cardiff after that match.

I knew that the Lions tour was approaching and I had said at home many a time that I really didn't feel like going on it, if selected. I'd suffered two knocks to the head in a short space of time. So when the invitation came, I didn't reply to it. Then the phone started to ring. Carwyn. He was clever enough to spend more time talking to Jan, my wife, than to me, so eventually, Jan was working on me with the same arguments as Carwyn was, regularly quoting Carwyn in her chats with me. There was six weeks after leaving Wales before a game would be played, she said, obviously having been told that by Carwyn. Carwyn also promised not to push me too hard in training either. As the deadline to give my answer was approaching, Jan gave me a line that was definitely a wifely one – I should go on the tour as I would be so miserable to have around the house if I didn't! So between the two of them, I went.

The rest, as they say, is history. He left Wales as a reluctant player with two bangs to the head, he came back a King.

The way Carwyn dealt with players on the tour was one of his virtues mentioned by many. He became known as the coach who could deal with people. Llanelli, Wales and Lions star Delme Thomas says that Carwyn instinctively knew whether a player in his care needed an arm around the shoulder or a kick in the backside, whether they needed a longer chat or just a short, sharp word. He would never treat everyone in the same way. Carwyn himself gave us a little insight into the thinking that such an approach came from:

> On tour, as coach, you must happily concentrate every minute of the day. You must be a full person and aware that you are surrounded by different kinds of people. If one person likes soccer, you must know all about his favourite team; or cricket, when the scores are sent over from home. If music, you must have the same ear. Simply, you must know what he likes to drink.

He showed his approach clearly in the way he dealt with Barry John in New Zealand. Delme Thomas remembers one particular story that illustrates this:

> We were in the dressing room before one game and Carwyn was talking about the game ahead. He explained a few moves to us. When Carwyn finished what he had to say, Barry turned to him and said, 'That's all well and good, but if I see a gap, I'm going for it!' Carwyn smiled quietly, turned to me and gave me a little wink, as if to say, 'That's exactly what I expected Barry to say!'

Carwyn knew that he had to give Barry John the freedom to develop his individual flair and instinct, but within a team structure. Fellow British Lion and son of Carmarthenshire Gerald Davies intuitively recognised this:

> Carwyn's confidence in his own ideas seemed to be extrovertly reflected in Barry John's play. Perhaps it's the water they drink in Cefneithin?

232

The way Carwyn used his squad was a testament to his management style. In the four Test matches, he only used 17 players. This compares with 31 used by Syd Millar in the 1974 Lions Test series in South Africa. He knew which player should be used in any particular game and which one should be rested. His use of the two scrum halves, Gareth Edwards and Chico Hopkins, is a clear example of this. Barry John remembers being kept out of one particular game as well:

> The Saturday before the first Test, we were playing against Canterbury. We expected a very hard, physical game and we weren't disappointed! It turned out to be the one of the dirtiest games in Lions history. Carwyn knew beforehand that Canterbury were likely to make me a specific target, and rough me up before the Test the following week. They were likely to make it difficult, if not impossible, for me to play in that match. As a result, Carwyn didn't select me to play against Canterbury.
>
> During the game, I sat on the bench on the touchline. A message came to me from Carwyn, asking me to go and sit next to him in the stand. When I got there he didn't say anything. After a while, he nudged me, pointed at the Canterbury full back and whispered one word in my ear, 'Interesting.' That was it, no explanation or elaboration. But I knew that was the player he wanted me to target in the Test the following week.

Carwyn didn't overtrain Barry John either. He knew that would crush his spirit. But if Carwyn felt that some players were lazy, he would give them extra running sessions. The training wasn't all rugby either. He would often give the squad a chance to play football or cricket, feeling that there was a need for variety on a three-month tour.

Cricket made its first appearance in another ploy by Carwyn to be ahead of the opposition in the mind games. As had been true of some of the Lions themselves, many in New Zealand didn't know who Carwyn was before he arrived there either. So there was a great deal of press interest in that first training session. They wanted to know who he was and what his tactics were. So Carwyn duly brought out cricket gear! The world rugby press and the national and local New Zealand press had to watch the Lions play cricket, gaining no clue at all as to how this new coach approached his rugby.

Willie John McBride was one who was on the receiving end of Carwyn's unusual tactics while out on tour. He received an invitation he didn't expect, as did *Guardian* journalist David Frost, who tells the story:

> One day after lunch in Wellington, he came to me out of the blue – I scarcely knew him at that time – and said he wanted me to come to the theatre that evening with him. He said he had also asked Willie John McBride to come along. I cannot speak for McBride, though I doubt if he was a regular theatregoer in Ballymena, but I had certainly not been inside a theatre for many years. We both felt impelled to accept Carwyn's invitation, and the theatre club's performance of Harold Pinter's *The Birthday Party* remains one of my most vivid memories, not only of Carwyn but of rugby touring. What made the evening was Carwyn's ebullient company. He was in one of those totally relaxed, effervescent, almost irreverent moods as we sat at a table with a bottle of wine and sandwiches.

Carwyn evidently didn't see the need to be with his squad that evening, even though they had a game the following day against Wellington. The result would seem to show that he was right. The Lions won the match 47–9.

It wasn't all success though. Carwyn did seem to fail to deal with one player in particular – ironically, a Welshman. Gerald Davies recalls a rare Carwyn failure:

> If it can be said that Carwyn failed in 1971, it was in the case of John Bevan, our winger. He had an exceptional start to the tour, having scored ten or so tries in the first half dozen matches. But being a raw youngster in 1971, he fell out of form, and form for John meant the art of scoring tries. He could have an otherwise brilliant game but if he did not cross the line, it made no difference what people said to him, John would be dissatisfied. After a few games such as this, John became impulsive and impetuous, and

the more these qualities manifested themselves the worse the game got for him. Carwyn tried all manner of things to get him to snap out of it, but failed.

But for 'Mighty Mouse' Ian McLauchlan, the Scottish forward who enjoyed a very successful tour, Carwyn's management style was a great success:

As a coach, Carwyn had it all put together. One of his ploys was to invite three or four players to his room for a drink and then have dinner together. This was an invitation no one would refuse, not just because it was more of a royal command, but because, as well as being the supreme coach, Carwyn was a very good judge of a bottle of wine. At the first of these little get-togethers I thought he was taking the mickey because he seemed to ask questions about the scrum which were blindingly obvious. 'He's playing the schoolmaster, making me pass a test,' was my conclusion. Then I realised that he was putting out feelers to see the way you thought about things.

What impressed me about him was that he didn't care who got the credit for our success. Always he used the royal 'we'. But his feel for the game was unrivalled and he was a great handler of men. Maybe his biggest quality was spotting when someone had gone over the top and needed a rest. Quietly he would say to them, 'Have a break tomorrow.' And the other players didn't start moaning because they were training while a teammate had a day off. They knew it was Carwyn unobtrusively at work.

A television interlude

As the Lions and Carwyn were playing their way around New Zealand, and into the hearts of the country's rugby fraternity, there were major discussions back home as to how the Welsh rugby faithful could share in the action and the occasion. The Head of News and Current Affairs at HTV, Gwilym Owen, had decided that he wanted a documentary programme made on the tour. These were very early days of sports broadcasting. Sports coverage of matches had begun but programmes about sporting events and documentaries were very rare. This was a forward-thinking initative on HTV's part. Today, looking back on the idea, Gwilym Owen sums it up quite clearly:

> A crazy idea! The kind of idea I wouldn't have pursued if I had thought a little more about it beforehand, as it went against all common sense. But we did it. We sent a crew to the other side of the world, a crew of only three, including presenter Dewi Bebb.

Not only was the crew a very small one, they hadn't even secured the rights to include any clips from the Lions' matches in their programme. The BBC had the rights to show the rugby, and according to them, that included all other aspects of the tour as well. HTV disagreed, but the issue wasn't resolved before the crew left Wales. Gwilym Owen continues:

> Carwyn stepped into the middle of the debate. He wanted to see what was possible for us to film and if he could help in any way to secure that. This is where I must say that I saw his ability and his strengths quite clearly – this is where I saw his true character for the first time. We were allowed to show short clips of matches in news bulletins, *Y Dydd* (The Day) in Welsh and *Report Wales* in English, which were flown back to Cardiff, and Dewi Bebb then doing commentary over the phone. But Carwyn arranged for our crew to travel on the team coach and interview players on the way, for us to film coaching sessions, and he set up specific interviews with players for us. Dewi, as a former Welsh international, had his influence as well, but it was Carwyn that saved the day for us.

His influence and abilities in terms of HTV's programme didn't end in New Zealand. They were called upon once the team arrived back home too. All that had been secured out there was the chance to film. The programme still needed to be broadcast, and rights hadn't been secured. Carwyn had started to work on Welsh-language programmes with HTV soon after starting at Trinity College. He knew the people he was dealing with, including Gwilym Owen:

The BBC had enforced a complete blackout on the showing of the material we had filmed in New Zealand. But we had the footage, and we set about making our programme in the hope that it could be shown one day. In the end, we made a programme an hour and a quarter long. But we couldn't broadcast it.

All discussions with the BBC had failed. They stuck to their guns. There was no shortage of conversations behind the scenes, however. Sir Alun Talfan Davies, vice-Chair of the HTV group, and Carwyn had many discussions to see what could be done.

Carwyn in the end came up with a possible solution, or at least a tactic that could lead to a solution. He suggested that we showed the film in the HTV Clubhouse and that we should invite as many dignitaries as possible to see it. This was to include as many MPs as possible and all HTV managers. Sir Alun Talfan Davies and Lord Harlech [chairman of HTV] agreed to this. The film was shown to a select but influential audience. The story was covered in the newspapers the following Monday and included comments by Members of Parliament that the licensing laws should be relaxed so that HTV could show the film to the public. In the end, that's exactly what happened. Carwyn's plan had worked.

Uniting and conquering

That film would have told a remarkable story. The British and Irish Lions had won a series in New Zealand for the first time ever. They won the first Test 9–3, with McLauchlan scoring a try and Barry John converting two penalties. Many of the Lions players said that this first victory made them too confident, and they subsequently lost the second Test 22–12. This proved to be the wake-up call needed, and the third Test was a comfortable win for the Lions, 13–3. Gerald Davies and Barry John scored a try each, with John converting both and dropping a goal. So the Lions reached the fourth Test 2–1 up and the All Blacks needed a win to level the series. That game in Eden Park, Auckland, was a tight, tense affair. At half time, it was 8–8. A penalty to each team in the second half made it 11–11. Then, 45 m out from the posts, J P R Williams attempted a mammoth drop goal which sailed through the upright, putting the Lions 14–11 ahead. In 55 caps for Wales and 8 for the Lions, that was the only drop goal JPR ever scored. Talk about choosing your moment! New Zealand, through full back Laurie Mains, scored a penalty and it was 14–14. But they failed to score after that and the game ended a draw, handing a momentous series victory to the Lions.

The Lions didn't lose any of their regional or club games on tour either, winning their 20 non-Test games in New Zealand. They did lose to Queensland, Australia, on their way to New Zealand, but then beat New South Wales. The most famous, if not notorious, of these games was the one against Canterbury at Lancaster Park on 19 June. It has become known as the Battle of Lancaster Park. The Lions' two first-choice props, Ray McLoughlin and Sandy Carmichael, had to end their tour after that game because they were so badly injured. There were many fights during the game, with both sides accusing each other of using dirty tactics at set pieces. Carmichael had multiple fractures to his left cheekbone and McLoughlin was left with a chipped bone at the base of his left thumb, when, during one fracas, he swung a punch at Alex Wyllie, who wasn't involved in the fight, and broke his thumb. Fergus Slattery was punched in the face for hanging on to an All Black forward's jersey in a line-out.

John Brooks, remembering the Battle of Lancaster Park in the *New Zealand Herald* in 2005, recalls Carmichael's involvement:

> In the 1966 game between Canterbury and the Lions, violence erupted in the first scrum. It had been rumoured that Howard Norris, a Welsh prop, had backed himself to knock an opposing forward off the pitch. In the event, it was fortunate that it was not he who was carted off.
>
> Fast forward to 1971, and we have Carmichael persistently

boring in on Tane Norton, the Canterbury hooker, blocking his view of the ball entering the tunnel and, therefore, his heel. Carmichael was warned twice by Alister Hopkinson, the opposing prop, but continued to infringe. He was punched more than once for his trouble.

Although the pudgy prop was in pain from his injuries, sources close to the Lions claimed that he was even more aggrieved to be called 'a whinging Pom' by some louts on the embankment. He was proud of being Scottish.

The response to events at Lancaster Park was even more volatile than the altercations on the pitch. One comment in particular incensed the Lions and many in New Zealand itself. Ivan Vodanovich, chairman of selectors and coach of the All Blacks that year, said that the Lions could expect a 'Passchendaele' in the first Test a week after the Canterbury game. His choice of words did not go down well. Lions manager Doug Smith was dismayed at the reference to Passchendaele and reiterated that the Lions would play the type of rugby they had employed successfully on that tour to date. New Zealand were particularly upset by what they saw as the Lions' habit of killing the ball in the rucks, and line-out infringements. Legend Colin Meads was one who said that the Lions 'got away with bloody murder'. John Brooks recalls Carwyn's response:

> On the other hand, coach Carwyn James had insisted that the Lions forwards stay on their feet in rucks to facilitate a clean feed. Aware of the British habit of lying on the ball, he said he set out to insist on creative rucking, so that his talented backs could display their wares.

And display their wares they did, with rugby that was as attractive as the Canterbury game was ugly. Barry John was crowned King, with his fluid running and tactical controlling. He scored in every one of the four Tests, and in every way possible to score – tries, conversions, penalties and drop goals. He scored 30 of the Lions' 47 points in the four Tests. The two little boys who had run around the park in Cefneithin, fetching the ball for various outside halves during kicking practice on damp, dark evenings, had taken New Zealand and world rugby by storm.

Carwyn, Barry and co. did so against a New Zealand team who were the all-conquering presence in world rugby through the Sixties. They had only lost four of the 42 games they had played between 1961 and 1970, which included a run of 17 consecutive victories between 1961 and 1964, and then the same achievement between 1964 and 1970. The British Lions tour of the same country in 1966 had ended in four Test defeats out of four.

The 1971 Lions' success has been attributed to Carwyn's tactical intelligence and his man-management alike. Credit must also be given to the contribution of manager Doug Smith. For all the tactics and training sessions, Carwyn's main achievement was getting his players to the point where they believed they could win. Delme Thomas said that you have to beat New Zealand before you get on the pitch. Gerald Davies said that '...somewhere along the line it became a mental thing, we grew in confidence and we believed it was possible to beat the All Blacks.'

But there were other aspects of Carwyn's character that contributed to the Lions' achievement. One was to do with how he dealt with the media, as he had shown in his interaction with HTV. According to one of the true rugby legends, Colin Meads, Carwyn's way of dealing with the New Zealand media was one of the central factors in the Lions' success:

> Way before the tour ended, and therefore before the result of the Test series was known and the Lions' victory secured, he had the press eating out of his hands. He would sit down for long periods with various members of the press, in groups of differing sizes, and talk to them about rugby in general, rugby in Wales and the future of rugby worldwide. Nobody had done that before and they were taken in by it completely. The psyche at the time was that

New Zealand had their way off the field as well as on it. Carwyn manoeuvred that situation to the Lions' advantage.

Carwyn had faced press questioning of his ability when his selection was announced and when the Lions left on their tour. Doubts were expressed as to whether this prominent Welsh nationalist could unite players from four countries under the British and Irish Lions flag. There were fears that he would even differentiate between the Welsh members of the squad, favouring those who spoke Welsh. Carwyn had to deal with this aspect of press coverage too. This was one of his responses which sums up his approach:

> The day I met my 1971 Lions for the first time, the very first thing I said to them was, 'Look here, be your own man. Express yourself, not as you would at the office, but as you would at home. I don't want Irishmen to pretend to be English, or Englishmen to be Celts, or Scotsmen to be anything less than Scots. You each have an ultimate quality to give to the team and you must know that you are able to express yourself in your own special unique way, both on the field and off it.

Welsh did become an issue for the party on tour, but purely in terms of banter and leg-pulling, with the chief instigator more often than not being Willie John McBride:

> I would enjoy winding the Welsh boys up when they were in a huddle with Carwyn. I would ask them why they were speaking a language no one understood. Carwyn loved the banter and knew exactly where I was coming from. He would give as good as he got as well, and would often deliberately turn to speak Welsh when I approached him and a group of players.

Another Irishman, Fergus Slattery, was aware of the way the Welsh stuck together and did his bit to break the clique:

> I remember going up to a hotel room on the tour, because I knew a certain club was meeting there – the Sunday Drinkers' Club.

It was put together by JPR if I remember, and only Welshmen were allowed into it. I walked right in and declared that I was now an honorary member of the club as well. And to be fair, I was welcomed with open arms.

Carwyn would actively encourage his players to go on social visits while on tour. As far as the Welsh were concerned, this invariably meant visiting the homes of Welsh people who had settled in New Zealand. Once there, they would enjoy the full traditional Sunday lunch, whatever day of the week it was. Delme Thomas states that this was a source of constant amazement for the players from the other countries, as they didn't enjoy such ex-pat hospitality.

Carwyn's tastes didn't change on tour either – in particular, his taste for wine. When the squad had evening meals together, Carwyn and Doug Smith would invite players in turn to sit with them at their table. They also had another custom: Doug would choose the wine one day and Carwyn the next. When it was Carwyn's turn, it was the best wine that he could get hold of. Doug Smith wasn't so particular about vintage. Delme Thomas says that on one occasion, when it was his turn at the table with coach and manager, the wine was Doug's choice. Carwyn took one sip and grimaced, whispering, 'Oh dear! Bloody Tovali!' under his breath – the name of a soft drink made in Carmarthenshire and popular in South Wales.

In an unusual twist, Carwyn had occasion to visit one of the All Black greats at his home. Lions scrum half Chico Hopkins was injured and recovery was proving difficult. Carwyn knew that Maori George Nepia, star of the All Blacks in the 1920s, was familiar with the complementary therapies of his people; therapies that had been passed down to him through successive generations of his family. Following Carwyn's visit, Nepia agreed to go and see Chico Hopkins. Details of Nepia's treatment have not been made public. The Carwyn who was brought up in the spirit of Grandma's remedies and the healing goodness of what nature can offer wouldn't have needed any persuasion to seek out such unusual help for a sporting injury.

His dealings with rugby officialdom in New Zealand were not a factor to be ignored either. Just as he had done with the Lions officials in securing their agreement for Gerald Davies to fly out late, he influenced the procedures of the host nation too, as Colin Meads states:

> I discussed it with the then-Chairman of the New Zealand Rugby Union and he said in no uncertain terms that the same official would not be chosen for the remaining two Tests, because, quite simply, that's what Carwyn wanted. Pring's interpretation of the game suited Carwyn's game plan. However, Carwyn managed to secure just that and Pring was the ref for all four Tests in the end.

But even such historic success didn't mean that there were no detractors. For some, a minority, there was a need to question the success. Anyone, it was said, could have succeeded with such a gifted group of players. Coaching such stars was no job at all. This argument depends on a belief that Carwyn had a greater collection of stars than any previous Lions squad in history. Colin Meads refutes the doubting Thomases:

> Carwyn used the team that he had very well; he dealt with a squad and kept a unity that transferred to the pitch. In-fighting and rifts are common enough in touring teams and the fact that there were none on that tour is an achievement for the management. He did have stars, but no one could have coached the stars he had like Carwyn did. He was judicious and scientific in his approach, in a way we hadn't seen in New Zealand before.

Irish International and '74 Lions coach Syd Millar agrees:

> Carwyn had a mix of players. Some were what's called 'stars', some weren't. He had to raise the game of those who weren't, and make those who were play like stars. And it can be harder to manage a team of experienced players at the top of their game than those who are at the start of their careers.

243

Five-times British Lion Willie John McBride backs him up:

> How do you keep the motivation of a squad of diverse players
> going for three months and more? It's not easy. It takes skill and
> leadership to deal with players of calibre and also to deal with
> them as a collective.

Delme Thomas remembers an incident that gives an insight
into the philosophy needed by Carwyn to hold a squad of
players together for three months.

> He was sitting next to me on a bus on the way to a match
> somewhere, and in the middle of a conversation, he turned to me
> and said, 'You see, anyone can put a saucepan on the fire to boil
> dry. The real achievement is to put the saucepan on the fire and
> keep it simmering for as long as possible and know when to bring
> it to the boil once more.'

Some of those who were happy to accept the magnitude of
the '71 Lions achievement, plus maybe a few of the original
doubters, found further cause to diminish their success
following the 1974 Lions tour of South Africa. Under Syd
Millar's coaching, that Lions squad went through the whole
tour undefeated, thus sparking the debate: which was the
greater Lions team, '71 or '74? Guardian journalist Frank
Keating has no doubt:

> The Springboks were easy meat in 1974 for the world's anti-
> apartheid venom that had been biting deep and painful. In almost
> three years between August 1971 and their first Test against
> Willie John's side in June 1974, South Africa had played just one
> solitary Test, being well-beaten in Johannesburg by an England
> side which had just lost all four matches of the Five Nations
> championship for the first time in a century. No wonder South
> Africa were there for the taking. Three years earlier it had been
> a totally different kettle of fish, as Colin Meads' All Blacks were
> waiting for Dawes' men as bristlingly bellicose as ever, with 18
> wins in their previous 21 Tests.

No doubt it's a wider debate than that, and it is indeed a healthy situation that the merits of two highly successful Lions tours can be debated in such a way. But Keating's words are a very fair assessment of Carwyn's achievement.

Feet back on the ground

Carwyn thoroughly enjoyed his time in New Zealand, and it wasn't just the victory that he savoured. The country itself had made quite an impression on him:

> There was a certain nakedness in the New Zealand countryside. You felt you could taste the earth – almost as if you were back in Wales.

Carwyn's relationship with soil had taken a different turn.

When the squad arrived back at Heathrow Airport, they faced a reception never before witnessed by a returning rugby team. It was more like the welcome pop stars of the preceding decade had begun to experience. This welcome home was a pivotal experience not only for rugby generally, but certainly for Carwyn personally. In the full glare of TV-crew lights, and looking more like a rabbit caught in car headlights, Carwyn very politely answers a reporter's question about the attention they had just received:

> I hope that the players will have about three months' rest now. That is important. And I also hope that the societies – there are so many of them in Wales – will hold back from giving invitations to the players, and me as well. Because one has spoken so much about rugby in the last three months, we need a respite from it so that we can forget about it.

Carwyn was more than aware of the increasing media pressure on his players and on himself. It was a brand new pressure, impossible to ignore, and also proving impossible to resist. This was a turning point for Carwyn, without a doubt.

Lions autographs for a lucky fan

His comments show that he needed a break. They also show that he needed to talk about something other than rugby. Rugby was never everything for Carwyn. The fact that he could make such comments at the height of historic sporting success shows that clearly. From that one interview in Heathrow onwards, things would never be the same for Carwyn. He was always reacting and responding to what happened there at that time, and it was a battle he wouldn't win. Any discussion as to what happened to Carwyn at the end of his life has to go back to this reference point, or it is an incomplete argument. The pressure of such success is a major factor in what happened later.

When Carwyn needed to flee from such attention, he had his refuges. One of these was the home of Llewelyn Williams, his former headmaster at Gwendraeth Grammar School, in Porthyrhyd, near Carmarthen. He would escape there and be left alone in the Williams study, so that he could write, have a cigarette or quietly contemplate life as he looked down on the village around him and the one below him, without anyone being able to see him or even know he was there.

The exact opposite of what Carwyn had wished for at Heathrow happened as soon as he got back to Wales. He was soon speaking at up to five or six engagements a week, throughout Wales and in England also – he could be back and forth to England more than once a week. Delme Thomas and Carwyn cut the ribbon at the opening of a brand new petrol station in Llanelli, a completely new departure for anyone involved with rugby at that time.

Carwyn also went on two Lions-related speaking tours. He toured various locations in Britain with tour manager Doug Smith, sharing stories of their exploits. Max Boyce accompanied them to some of these engagements.

He also did a lot of talks in local village halls throughout Wales, usually on his own, at which he would show the film made by HTV. Carwyn was responsible for choosing where he would go on this tour, and three locations he personally insisted upon visiting were Rhydlewis, Cefneithin and Trinity College. He never forgot where he came from.

Such public occasions would give Carwyn a platform to show his less-often manifested lighter side. In the Welsh-language commemorative volume published less than a year after he died, *Un o Fois y Pentre* (One of the Boys from the Village), David Parry-Jones has a chapter that deals with that lighter side. At such occasions, he had every opportunity to tackle the previously-expressed need to improve his public speaking, and he used humour to do so.

Ever the lover of the classics, he would often turn to Greek mythology and history to explain a particular rugby point. David Parry-Jones recalls a story much savoured by Carwyn:

> The Spartan General Leonidas was debriefing a scout detail to assess the strength of Xerxes's Persian army, which was bent

on forcing through the Pass of Thermopylae and proceeding to conquer the tiny Greek nation. Reported the despairing man, 'So numerous are its bowmen that a volley of their arrows will blot out the sun.' 'Good,' said Leonidas firmly, 'then we shall fight in the shade.'

Carwyn loved that retort of the Spartan general. He would often use the Spartans vs. Athenians analogy in talking of Welsh rugby, with his beloved Scarlets being the Athenians, and teams like Pontypool being the Spartans – however much he admired that team's coach, the infamous Ray Prosser.

The most well-known manifestation of this way of thinking was his phrase before the first British Lions test in 1971, in Dunedin. He told his team, 'Get your retaliation in first.' This is a phrase David Parry-Jones says shows that the mighty All Blacks were 'arch-inheritors of the Spartan tradition.'

The stories he used in his public speaking, according to David Parry-Jones, came from 'the myriad random memories, whiffs of the whimsical in which 50% of Carwyn's life and times were suffused.' He then mentions some of Carwyn's favourite and often-used stories, one of which:

> ...concerned the choir formed in Heaven to compete in a Heavenly Eisteddfod. It consisted of 40 sopranos, 40 altos and 40 tenors, and just one bass who on earth happened to have been Dai Jones from Felinfoel. At the end of the first chorus in rehearsal, the conductor, a very senior angel, complimented the sopranos warmly, 'You are singing like seraphims. Altos, you are in cherubic voice – likewise you tenors. Bass, though – keep it down just a bit.'

Doubtless at the telling of this story, which he loved, he would fill the air with what Parry-Jones calls 'his personal, idiosyncratic rippling giggle, which sounded like a two-stroke engine starting up.'

Some of his oft-remembered comments were private ones, not part of his speeches. An example is his reply to the desire of Merthyr Borough Council to honour him and his achievements by naming a road after him. He said, 'I've told them OK – as long as it's a dual-carriageway!' One street in Dowlais, Merthyr Tydfil was named Bryn Carwyn (Carwyn's Hill), and this in an area which Carwyn had no direct links with. In the Seventies, this was a rare gesture in the name of rugby. It was a further sign of the public response to the dizzy heights that not only Carwyn had reached, but rugby in Wales generally.

In the rugby world, a significant legacy of the 1971 Lions' success was a conference on the coaching principles applied in order to secure it. It was held at the Polytechnic of North London in July 1971. It was a very technical affair, as the book published based on the talks shows. In *The Lions Speak*, every aspect of play is analysed in detail by Ian McLauchlan, Geoff Evans, John Taylor, Ray McLoughlin, Mike Gibson, John Dawes, Bob Hillier, Barry John and Carwyn James.

The Welsh members of the Lions squad were invited to the the Miners' Eisteddfod of 1971 in Porthcawl. They received a rapturous welcome, with the biggest reaction being kept for Carwyn. At one point, he stepped to the front of the stage and recited a large section of a poem: *Y Dyrfa* (The Crowd),

Rugby Books

The Lions Speak

Carwyn James
John Dawes
Mike Gibson
Ray McLoughlin
Ian McLauchlan
John Taylor
Geoff Evans
Bob Hiller
Barry John

written by former Archdruid Cynan (Albert Evans-Jones). Carwyn, ever aware of his literary and cultural heritage, would have known that the work he recited had won the Crown at the National Eisteddfod in Bangor in 1931. It created quite a stir in Welsh circles at that time, with its choice of rugby as the main focus of a major poetic work. It tells the story of a Welsh international rugby player who turns his back on the game in order to be a missionary in China, and therefore deals with the two main religions in Wales. As the main character journeys on his ship to the Far East, he looks into the ocean below him and longingly remembers his rugby-playing days. Gareth Williams and Dai Smith, in their book *Fields of Praise: The Official History of the WRU*, reference this poem:

> It was even more fitting that Cynan's poem should have won at Bangor in 1931. That year, in January at Wrexham, the North Wales Rugby Union had been formed with nine clubs, to seek affiliation to the WRU. In June that affiliation was granted.

Carwyn brought the central aspects of his heritage together on that stage in Porthcawl. It was poetry. It was rugby. It was history. It was Welsh. It was also very new, in that it was, like the opening of a petrol station, a public response to what had happened on the field of play far away.

Back from New Zealand then, Carwyn would enjoy a few weeks of summer respite before resuming his lecturing responsibilities at Trinity College, Carmarthen.

CHAPTER 14

Carwyn the Trinitarian

Di-ddim yw anrhydeddau,
Nid yw bri yn ddim ond brau.
'Honours are as nothing,
Celebrity is fleeting.'
Unknown

TRINITY COLLEGE CARMARTHEN was the second world into which Carwyn stepped from the gates of Llandovery. And like rugby, it too was experiencing new currents of change. In its essence, however, Trinity was an establishment similar enough to Llandovery.

It was a small college when Carwyn arrived there, with around 300 students and 40 staff. But under the leadership of Derrick Childs, its head since 1965, it was expanding and developing. Like the man who brought Carwyn to Llandovery, G O Williams, Derrick Childs would also go on to become Archbishop of Wales. Once again then, Carwyn came under the authority of the Church and traces of old established ways were still to be seen amidst the developments Childs introduced. Specifically, the old-fashioned attitude towards the Welsh language and all things Welsh was still to be seen and heard. The snobbish lack of patience and understanding towards the Welsh-language element of College provision was palpable. The figure leading the stance against such attitudes was Carwyn's Head of Department, and notable Welsh public figure, Norah Isaac. She was a strong-spirited, independent woman who would take no prisoners. She fought her campaign to solidify the Welsh presence in Trinity by headhunting top names in Welsh academic circles. Carwyn was one such acquisition.

Wherever Carwyn travelled in the name of rugby, he would bring a gift back for Norah Isaac. He did so after visiting New Zealand in 1971. He was more than aware that he needed her on board if he was to continue living the life he had chosen to lead. In turn she commented at one time, to Delme Thomas, that Carwyn was the only man who was ever able to tell her what to do. They got on famously.

Two central buildings in Carwyn's Trinity experience were the Church and the Library. There was a service in the Church every morning, between nine and nine fifteen. By the time Carwyn arrived at the College, it was not compulsory for students to attend, but it was often comfortably full for those services. Carwyn was a regular attendee. Under the guidance of John Davies, Tŷ'n Llan, the Library had been developed to be one of the best in any Welsh college. It held all the publications of the Gregynog Press, as well as a copy of the first Welsh Bible, William Morgan's 1588 translation. It also had a copy of William Salesbury's 1567 translation of the New Testament.

Carwyn was appointed to teach on the B.Ed. course, but a few years later this course became a B.Ed. (Hons) degree and was extended by a year. He would open the literary world of Welsh giants such as D J Williams, Kate Roberts, Gwenallt and of course T H Parry-Williams to his students. He was familiar with these people themselves, not just their works. But he would also study the work of poets from the Middle Ages, and hymn writer William Williams Pantycelyn. As Norah Isaac said, the prestige of the playing fields and the fields of books were the same to him:

> He could interpret a poem or a piece of literature with the same precision as he could the play of a rugby team. He would show the same passion, he would lose himself in the thrill and enjoyment of

the moment of both equally. To hear him enthusing about aspects
of Welsh literature the other side of the wall to me was a daily
proof of his deep love for it. Carwyn was a teacher by instinct and
a gifted communicator when he chose to be. But he also insisted
on having the right to be silent.

Echoes of that last sentence of Norah Isaac's can be heard in
many other episodes of his life. Norah Isaac herself developed
that particular thought on one television programme about
Carwyn:

Carwyn lived in his own little spiritual world.

In such a spiritual world, the practicalities of the day-to-day
were to prove unimportant. Carwyn was not good at running
his life. Carmarthen and Llandovery colleagues stand as one to
testify that there was no order to his affairs, no diary, no filing
systems, no banking of cheques, no putting away of gifts he'd
received for his speaking engagements. The usual depository
for such things was his car. One shoe from a pair, a tie, a shirt,
cheques too old to cash, newspapers, documents, books – they
were all there on the back seat or in the boot. Norah Isaac,
and others, understood the spirit, the attitude behind such
outward, practical evidence.

Not that this untidiness and disorder ever cast a shadow
over people's view of Carwyn in any way. It was seen as an
endearing aspect of his personality, however much it sometimes
tested the patience of those close to him.

One of Carwyn's fellow lecturers at the time, Malcolm Jones,
remembers the impact his arrival had on the College.

There was a definite charm about him when he arrived. You felt as
if you were under some kind of spell. Everyone wanted to talk to
him. But, more often than not, Carwyn wanted to flee. I remember
him telling me that he used to love going to a church when he
was away from home. The reason for that, he said, was that he
could then be anonymous, a stranger. He could be himself and

experience a little of the peace he sought for himself. There was something about Carwyn; he was so close to you, a friend, but yet so distant. That strange duality was always there in him, but yet, no one would ever tire of being in his company. We couldn't get enough of him.

This need to be apart would be seen in his insistence on staying away from the staffroom at Trinity whenever he could, but most definitely on Monday mornings. They would be the Mondays after rugby games the Saturday before. Win or lose, he didn't want the post-mortems. He had very little patience with armchair critics and touchline experts who knew exactly how they would have managed any particular game. Carwyn would have specific company on those Monday morning escapes, and they happened in one specific place. Outside the shop on the campus there was a yellow rubbish bin with a silver lid, nicknamed the Dalek. Next to the Dalek, he would meet fellow lecturer Dafydd Rowlands, who was also a poet. The two would become very good friends. A chat and a fag amongst the rubbish and the stubs was far better for Carwyn than pompous staffroom pontificating. In the company of Dafydd Rowlands, a man of independent thought and sharp literary mind, those discussions would hardly have been idle chat about nothing in particular. The two would also meet regularly for lunch, usually in the Chestnut Tree on the main road out of Carmarthen towards Swansea.

Carwyn would often be called away from Trinity, on those speaking engagements that accumulated incessantly after the Lions tour, and so many other responsibilities. His Head of Department was aware of the reason for such demands, and was wise in her response to them:

> Between the election activity, the teacher training, addressing societies and organisations galore – some of national importance, others of local significance – and writing references, there was hardly time for respite in his overflowing life. But he could use his sharp mind to concentrate on what was in front of him, and he

was fortunate that he could dart skilfully from one discipline to another.

All that was evidently true. But Norah Isaac seems to ignore the very real fact that Carwyn also applied his sharp mind to asking other people to do things for him, including writing articles and speeches that he had no time to write.

This new activity provided Carwyn with an ideal escape route as well, an escape into his own world that colleagues had noticed he needed. They knew that if Carwyn said he had to leave the company he was in in order to go somewhere, that could quite often mean that he wanted to be just anywhere other than where he was. His aim was to leave, not to arrive. In Trinity days, the demands on his time increased and so did the need to be somewhere else.

Chekhov and Dr Finlay

In addition to teaching Welsh Literature, Carwyn lectured in two other fields as well, as Welsh came under the wing of the Drama Department. He dealt with Television and Radio drama, and Russian plays. The first of these two disciplines was a relatively new area of academic study, not offered by many higher educational institutions. It was an innovative inclusion on a degree course. It was studied by the Drama Department, as Media Studies did not exist at that time. Carwyn was once again involved in something new.

Within this new field, Carwyn had one prominent hero. Cedric Messina had transformed television and radio drama in the 1960s and in the early 1970s. He had been born in South Africa to Welsh and Italian parents, and had received very little formal education. In 1962 he created the ground-breaking TV drama, *Dr Finlay's Casebook*, a series based on the exploits of a GP in a small Scottish village. Four years later, he produced another series, *Play of the Month*. This was another popular but also influential series, bringing contemporary plays into people's living rooms. His achievement in the Seventies was to adapt the plays of Shakespeare for television, following his first attempt at televising the Bard's work, *The Merchant of Venice*, in 1972. This was one of the TV plays Carwyn taught at Trinity.

It was natural enough for him to lead the study of Russian plays. He had come across many Russian playwrights during his National Service and had stayed with them after leaving. Chekhov was his favourite, and *The Seagull* the work that he warmed to most. He could see his own relationship with a long-sought-after place – an Oz, a nirvana, an idyllic respite the other side of the here and now – reflected in the point his hero Chekhov made about the Moscow of his mind.

> Chekhov's characters always wanted to escape. Their nirvana was Moscow. Little did they realise until they had been there how much more important their own little patch of earth was. I believe strongly that we each belong to a patch somewhere and that the real nirvana of life is to contribute to that patch.

Carwyn here returns to the theme of escape and the importance of one's home patch. In doing this, he touches on a popular theme in the film world generally, but in *The Wizard of Oz* specifically. The Gwendraeth Valley was his Kansas. He needed neither Oz nor Moscow, because he had his return in the soil from whence he came. But like Chekhov and Dorothy, he was always aware of the pull of that other place. He would regularly stumble and trip over those uneven yellow bricks as he faltered on the road between Moscow and Cefneithin, Oz and Rhydlewis. In those Trinity days, his ability to keep a clear focus on the square mile that defined him would wax and wane to a dramatic degree.

As he shared the riches of Russian literature with students in Carmarthen, he extended his involvement with the language and literature of that country into a third decade. This is the period in which he appeared on TV with Melvyn Bragg, singing the '*Stanochek*' song with the JSSL choir. Carwyn might well have kept the nature of his work during his National Service extremely quiet and private, but he definitely didn't do so with the Russian language, and especially not its literature.

A packet of fags and the Pied Piper

Whatever aspect of the curriculum he was teaching, there was a definite pattern to his classroom delivery. He would usually arrive punctually in his lecture room. He'd take a packet of 40 cigarettes out of his pocket, along with his lighter, and lay them on the desk. The first fag would be lit. He'd sit back in his chair, close his eyes, and begin.

Student stories show that Carwyn had the same approach in the lecture theatre as he did in the changing rooms of world rugby stadia, the unifying factor being the way in which he dealt with individuals. One of his students, Cleif Harpwood, lead singer of innovative band Edward H Dafis and a prominent figure in the developing Welsh rock scene while he was at Trinity at the start of the Seventies, remembers his approach:

> He had the ability to take the students with him wherever he wanted to go. He would inspire us with the way he would present us with ways to open up whichever subject we were studying at the time. There's no denying that he had the gift of addressing and admonishing students. Listening to him reciting various forms of poetry from memory was nothing short of thrilling.

Cleif Harpwood, like many other students thoughout Wales in that period of Welsh history, was actively involved in the protests of the Welsh Language Society, calling for increased status for the Welsh language. The late Sixties and Seventies saw a concerted campaign to achieve this end, with protestors daubing English road signs with green paint and climbing television masts. Many Trinity students would take part in such protests, taking Carwyn back to his own student protest days. Cleif Harpwood remembers this bringing together of lecturer and student protestation:

When we went to protests in various parts of Wales, we would obviously miss lectures. Carwyn was astute in the way he would deal with this. He would make it clear to us that he was aware that we had not fulfilled our obligations to attend lectures. In this way he fulfilled his College duties. But once official responsibilities were met, he would then ask us if the protest had gone well and he would let us know what we had missed and which texts we needed to study in order to catch up.

Norah Isaac's previous comment about Carwyn's relentless activity included a reference to his teacher training. This included of course the need to visit various Carmarthenshire schools in order to observe student teachers at work. His head of department remembers the impact his vists had on Carmarthenshire schools:

The experience of seeing him crossing the yards of primary schools was like picturing the Pied Piper of Hamelin in action. The children would flock towards him. They had to have his autograph. He would speak to each individual and would include a personal message with each signature. The student's lesson in the classroom was also more inspired because of the euphoria surrounding their lecturer. But Carwyn would be harsh in his criticism of any educational process he thought was betraying the Welsh language, and when he perceived the communities of his own square mile to be diluting their Welshness.

Many of Carwyn's students testify that he really appreciated their use of audio-visual resources in their lessons, and he warmed to its use in their communication. This use of word and image together resonated with Carwyn's pedagogy.

Trinity head Derrick Childs introduced a new system within the college which meant that every lecturer became a personal tutor for a dozen or so students, on an inter-disciplinary basis, and across more than one degree year. Huw Williams, now a staff member of Tinopolis TV production company, was a member of Carwyn's tutorial group:

The tutorial group would almost never meet on campus, Carwyn made sure of that. He could drive, as could one of our tutorial group, and as a result two car-loads would leave Carmarthen and head for a small pub in the village of Alltwalis, The Mason's Arms. That's where we would have a pub meal and a pint. Carwyn would always pay, but he would very rarely eat as much as we did. At those social tutorials, we would discuss everything under the sun – everything that is, other than actual college work.

How significant that Carwyn would choose to flee from the centre to the fringes with his tutorial group.

During his Trinity days he fulfilled the same role as he did in Llandovery. He brought the Welsh-speaking and the non-Welsh-speaking fraternities together. Usually that was in the name of rugby. Officially, he had very little to do with the College rugby team in Carmarthen, but of course, how could they ignore the man who who had achieved so much in world rugby? He did get involved – an involvement which brought the two perceptions of what it is to be Welsh together. In the Trinity rugby scene, it was a source of constant consternation that the man in their midst was actually a lecturer in Welsh literature. One student who crossed both camps was Steff Jenkins. He was a student of Carwyn's and also a rugby player. Steff played for the College as well as his home village team, Crynant. Later in life, Steff Jenkins would be the Leader of the Urdd Camp in Llangrannog. At the beginning of any week, Carwyn would ask Steff how the game had gone the previous weekend, showing that he had already checked the score beforehand.

That meant so much to me, I must say. It was a very difficult time at Trinity in that period because it was a time of protesting in the name of the Welsh Language Society, but there was a very strong anti-Welsh element there too. Many from that group didn't understand me at all because I played rugby, spoke Welsh and protested in the name of my language as well. I remember one conversation between myself and some of the rugby boys which shows this clearly.

'I've never worked you out.'
'What do you mean?'
'You play rugby.'
'Yes?'
'From Crynant… Seven Sisters?'
'Yes!'
'But you're a gog!'

In Welsh, *gog* is the usual term for someone from North Wales, but at Trinity it was the term for any Welsh speaker, wherever they came from. It was always a derogatory term. Carwyn was a complete enigma to such people. He challenged their preconceptions. His presence, as well as his attitude, challenged their mindset.

On a wing and a prayer

One of the traditions at Trinity was to take new students on a coach trip around Carmarthenshire so that they could get to know their new surroundings better. On one occasion, when Carwyn was asked to lead one of the trips, they had arrived at the village of Llanarthney in the Tywi Valley. Norah Isaac had asked him to speak about the history of the village and also about the life and work of David G Jones, a prominent Welsh hymn writer, who is buried there. When the coachload arrived at Llanarthney, Carwyn had no idea where the hymn writer was buried. The students were supposed to stand around his grave and sing one of his hymns, so Carwyn's lack of knowledge was a problem and Norah Isaac would not be happy. Ever resourceful, Carwyn had an idea. He addressed the students in front of him, promising the princely sum of half a crown to the first student who found the grave. That was more than enough incentive for cash-strapped students – enough also to overcome the fact that they probably had no interest in this Welsh hymn writer anyway. In no time, the grave was found, the hymn was sung and two individuals were more than happy: Carwyn for getting out of the hole he'd been in, and the student now holding the half-crown coin.

Carwyn used his contacts at HTV in order to create a TV series based on one particular course at the College. Malcolm Jones and Cyril Jones had created history packs for schools and Carwyn approached Malcolm Jones one day with a specific request:

The title of our schools' package was *Hel Hanes* (Hunting History) and the first pack we did was the story of the Rebecca Riots. Our aim was to teach history by telling stories in an interesting way, and using primary sources whenever we could. Carwyn asked us if we would like to make a television series for HTV based on these packs. 'Come to Pontcanna,' he said, 'and we'll make the programme.' It was as easy as that!

Carwyn met Malcolm and Cyril Jones in the reception area of HTV Studios, Pontcanna, having just driven down from the North of England after speaking at a dinner there. The three discussed the programme content and order over a coffee before going into the studio.

Carwyn wrote four words on the back of a cigarette packet. That was the structure of the programme, and in we went to the studio! It flowed smoothly, with Carwyn leading the discussion expertly. When we forgot some point or other, Carwyn would pick it up and weave it back into the flow of the programme.

The recording over, the three stood in Pontcanna car park. Carwyn was obviously tired after his trip to the North and recording the programme.

'You can drive, can't you?' he asked me, as he threw his car keys at me. He went straight to the back seat so that he could have a lie down, and I went to the driver's seat. Well, what a state that car was! It was an absolute mess. Cyril had to move a lot of papers from the passenger seat before he could sit down and Carwyn had to move a lot more so that he could lie in the back seat. The minute we arrived at Cefneithin, he asked us into Hawen, so that we could have a cup of tea and a cake, prepared by his sister Gwen. And that's how it was.

Life was good for Carwyn. He warmed to the contribution he was making to the life of students from all over Wales who wanted to study the literature of their country. He'd made his mark with the secondary pupils in Llandovery, and now he was educating older young people – adults even. He was developing a good relationship with HTV as well as an understanding friendship with literary man Dafydd Rowlands. He was coaching Llanelli and enjoying success. All was well in Carwyn's world.

CHAPTER 15

The year of four milestones

…now was the time for bigger guns.
Jilly Cooper, *The Sunday Times*

WITHOUT A DOUBT, Carwyn had many years that he himself could regard as seminal in his life, in whichever one of his areas of expertise. There might well have been years with greater singular successes – the Lions in 1971 being an obvious example – but 1972 was a year which included many varied milestones in the same 12-month period. They came from the diverse worlds of broadcasting, rugby, Welsh language culture and politics – the strands that made Carwyn's rainbow.

A pioneering series

With 1972 barely two months old, Carwyn was involved in a pioneering television series which broke new ground in sports broadcasting worldwide, not just in Wales. When HTV launched the series *Rugby Skills*, it was branded as 'the first of its kind'. It was a series that grew directly from the emerging coaching scene in Welsh rugby. The WRU's first director of coaching, Ray Williams, was involved. He was the one responsible for the coaching sessions in the series, which would explain the technicalities of various moves to the viewer. Carwyn presented the programme, explaining what was happening on the pitch, and Welsh coach Clive Rowlands supplied his observations. These were the three at the very top of rugby coaching in Wales, which was in itself at the forefront of coaching in the world. Subsequently, the series had an air of authority that resonated worldwide. Carwyn's success in New Zealand less than a year before this gave additional international gravitas to the venture. The series was produced and directed by Euryn Ogwen Williams:

> The series broke new ground in terms of both rugby and broadcasting. We would not have been able to make such a series without the cooperation of Ray Williams, and it was on his insistence that Carwyn presented the programme. This came directly from what was happening in the rugby world at the time. In terms of broadcasting, HTV at the time was developing a reputation for its educational programming. So we had the idea of making a rugby coaching programme under the auspices of our education department.

This was further evidence that Wales was leading the world in terms of rugby coaching. Part of such a development was nurturing Cyncoed College in Cardiff as a centre of excellence for developing rugby players. Students from this college were the ones used for the routines in *Rugby Skills*, as Williams discusses:

> The students from Cyncoed were used for all the individual moves that Ray demonstrated in the series. These sessions were shot in Cardiff Arms Park, on film, as using an Outside Broadcast unit would have been too expensive. It was also a far easier way to work.

Every individual move – for backs and forwards – was recreated, filmed and analysed. They looked at the technicalities of scrum, line-out, ruck, maul, back play, team training and team practices. The target audience was players, coaches and supporters alike, each being able to appreciate the moves shown from their own perspective. These were extremely technical programmes, keen to reflect the broader culture of increased emphasis on the coaching of rugby. The whole concept of coach was new and there was an aim through *Rugby Skills* to explain exactly what this new sporting animal was doing.

It was a big risk for HTV to embark on such a project. It was broadcast on the ITV network throughout Britain and also in New Zealand, South Africa, Canada and Australia. A video was made of the series that proved to be a commercial success, as it was still for sale six years after the series was broadcast. It was without doubt a successful means of keeping Welsh rugby coaching in the world shop window, but also, through that, it would secure a high profile for Carwyn in every country in the world where rugby was played. It was also another example of Carwyn being at the forefront of a new idea.

The Jubilee Game

A few months after the broadcast of that series, Carwyn put his name to a one-off celebrity rugby match that was held in the name of an organisation he had been involved with since he was a schoolboy. Urdd Gobaith Cymru, the Welsh League of Youth, was celebrating its fiftieth anniversary. Many events were arranged to mark that achievement, including the Jubilee Game, which was a rugby XV chosen by Carwyn James to play against a rugby XV chosen by another who had been an active Urdd member, Barry John. In effect, it was a British Lions XV to play against a Welsh XV. Arranging such a match was a clear indication of the Urdd's ambition, as it was an obvious mark of Carwyn and Barry John's respect for the organisation.

On a Wednesday evening in April therefore, giants from the world of rugby walked out on to the National Stadium turf under the banner of the Urdd. The match programme includes contributions by rugby giants of the era such as Cliff Morgan, who wasn't usually associated with Urdd activities or events held in the name of Welsh-language organisations. He mentions his attempts to learn Welsh in Tonyrefail Grammar School, and that he had worn a Welsh learner's badge for long periods of his time there. He says that he still had the

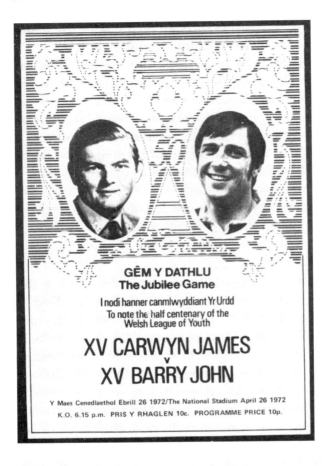

GÊM Y DATHLU
The Jubilee Game

I nodi hanner canmlwyddiant Yr Urdd
To note the half centenary of the
Welsh League of Youth

XV CARWYN JAMES
v
XV BARRY JOHN

Y Maes Cenedlaethol Ebrill 26 1972/The National Stadium April 26 1972
K.O. 6.15 p.m. PRIS Y RHAGLEN 10c. PROGRAMME PRICE 10p.

XV Carwyn James
v
XV Barry John

GÊM Y DATHLU-THE JUBILEE GAME

I nodi hanner canmlwyddiant Urdd Gobaith Cymru
To celebrate the half centenary of the
Welsh League of Youth

26 Ebrill 1972   K.O. 6.15   26 April 1972
Y MAES CENEDLAETHOL
THE NATIONAL STADIUM

EISTEDDLE   GOGLEDDOL
NORTH   STAND

Bloc **Block**	**E**
Rhes **Row**	**14**
Sedd **Seat**	13
Pris **Price**	75p

badge, but that his efforts to learn the language hadn't been successful. There was a very active branch of the Urdd at his school and many activities were held there in its name, from entertainment evenings to Sports Days, and guest speakers such as Iorwerth Peate, founder of St Fagans National History Museum, and rugby star Cliff Jones. At the end of the Second World War, Morgan went to his first Urdd camp:

> Years after my visits to Urdd camps, I played rugby with Carwyn James. We were responsible – though not us really but the Welsh selectors – for splitting South Wales in two. The West wanted Carwyn in the red jersey, the East wanted me. I promise you that we never thought in that way, and in fact were the best of friends. We played together for Wales against the rest of the Lions in 1955 and at half-time I asked Carwyn if he'd like to move into fly half rather than stay in the centre. It was the biggest mistake of my life, for he immediately dropped a goal and scored a glorious try! 'Back into the centre,' I said!

He then acknowledges the contribution the Urdd made generally to his life:

> It's the togetherness, determination and sense of values the Urdd teaches that makes individuals, in a Welsh Rugby team for instance, play for each other... I am longing to see Tommy Scourfield, 'Tommy Tumble', the man I copied when I first introduced a *Noson Lawen*. Come to think of it, Tommy and the Urdd have a lot to answer for. If I'd never gone to the Urdd camp and tried to copy Tommy, I would never have joined the BBC.

In the same programme, another former Welsh international takes a different approach. He addresses the hot topic of the time: whether the rugby union game should turn professional. Dewi Bebb states that such a move would not benefit rugby union, as it was a game played to a very high standard already. He does, however, admit that at some point in the future, union players would have to receive some form of financial incentive.

That wouldn't happen, officially at least, for another 25 years.

On the pitch that early evening in April, there was a real feast of rugby for those attending, including a great solo try from Barry John. The tens of thousands of fans present at the game however, didn't realise that it would be the last time Barry John would play rugby. Following that game, the 27-year-old king declared that he was to hang up his boots for good. There's a heavy significance in Barry John's act of putting his boots on the hook for the last time, because in that all-too-premature act was an early sounding of what was to follow in Carwyn's own life. The accolades and expectations of the 1971 success proved to be a burden too heavy for Barry. Success would also prove to be an uncomfortable and unbearable burden for the other boy from Cefneithin, Carwyn James. The seeds of his demise were also sown in the heady pastures of historic Lions success.

A refusal to travel

A few weeks later, Carwyn walked back into the troubled arena of sport and politics, 18 months after his refusal to watch Llanelli Rugby Club play against South Africa at Stradey Park. That same club had arranged to go on a tour of South Africa, a few months before they were to play the All Blacks at Stradey. Carwyn maintained his stance and refused to go with his club. Phil Bennett was chosen as captain and it was he who was given the responsibility of preparing the team for their tour matches, reverting temporarily to the old pre-coach days. It would be a complete fallacy, however, to think that Carwyn had no influence on what happened on tour just because he wasn't there.

One major decision affecting the club was anounced on that tour. Delme Thomas, three-times British Lion and member of the conquering 1971 team, had decided that he was not going to play first-class rugby any longer. His first child had just been born, and he thought that it was time he gave up in order to spend more time at home. Carwyn had other plans. He was insistent that Delme should be Llanelli RFC's captain for the forthcoming season, when they would play the All Blacks. Delme knew that they would be coming to Stradey, as Carwyn had told him out in New Zealand the year before, but had still decided that he would not be a part of it.

On the plane back from South Africa, however, the club Chairman had a conversation with Delme and said that Carwyn wanted him to be captain of the club for the forthcoming season. A certain enthusiastic young player overheard this, and bellowed his unequivocal approval for all to hear. Ray Gravell fully supported the choice of new captain. Carwyn had his way even though he was absent and his team were tens of thousands of miles in the air!

President of the Day

That year, Carwyn received a letter from Buckingham Palace offering him an MBE for his services to rugby following the Lions success the year before. He also received the highest honour the National Eisteddfod, the annual flagship Welsh-language cultural event, could offer, by being nominated as a member of the Gorsedd of Bards – the prestigious Eisteddfod committee which awards honours and stands as gatekeeper of Welsh cultural values. Carwyn turned down the honour from the Queen and accepted the one offered by the Eisteddfod.

The National Eisteddfod is a cultural gathering that meets for a week every year, alternating its festival site between North and South Wales. It's a significant occasion in the Welsh calendar and one of the largest events of its kind in Europe. An ancient, week-long annual festival, with a strict Welsh-language-only rule, it draws tens of thousands to its site every year. In 1972, the event was held in Haverfordwest, Pembrokeshire, and Carwyn was asked to be the President of the Day on the Tuesday. This was the day on which the winner of one of the two main poetry competitions, one of the highest honours at

Honours – In Confidence   10 Downing Street
                                       Whitehall

Please quote this·   17 November 1971
reference in your reply
    M.B.E.

        Sir,

            The Prime Minister has asked me to inform you,
        in strict confidence, that he has it in mind, on the
        occasion of the forthcoming list of New Year Honours,
        to submit your name to The Queen with a recommendation
        that Her Majesty may be graciously pleased to approve
        that you be appointed a Member of the Order of the
        British Empire (M.B.E.).

            Before doing so, the Prime Minister would be
        glad to be assured that this would be agreeable to you.
        I should be grateful if you would let me know by
        completing the enclosed form and sending it to me by
        return of post.

                            I am, Sir,
                            Your obedient Servant,

                            RtArmstrong

        Carwyn James, Esq.

The offer from the Palace

the festival, would be crowned, and the one set aside in those
days as the day for young people.

As President of the Day, he would officially address the
crowd in the main pavilion at the beginning of the day's
proceedings. He prepared his speech meticulously. His friend
Rita Williams says that he would spend time in her cottage

in Cilycwm, near Llandovery, working on what he was going to say. His fellow lecturer at Trinity, Dafydd Rowlands, tells of Carwyn doing preparatory work for the speech when they went to see a cricket Test match at Edgbaston together. Carwyn took with him a copy of *Gyda Gwawr y Bore* (With the Morning Dawn), written by Aneirin Talfan Davies, a poet, broadcaster and literary critic. It was this book that Carwyn would read in bed when they returned from their cricket. The fruit of his nocturnal reading would be heard in his Haverfordwest Eisteddfod speech.

When Carwyn opened his speech, it was obvious that he was aware of the reorganisation of local government that was about to be introduced in Wales. He knew that the county they were in, Pembrokeshire, would soon no longer exist, as Dyfed, the bigger, newer county established in 1974, would encompass Pembrokeshire, Carmarthenshire and Cardiganshire. He then asked the question: in the light of local government reorganisation, what is the future of the Eisteddfod? A burning issue then, and still to this day, was whether the Festival should have one permanent home or continue with the traditional arrangement of alternating between North and South Wales. Carwyn gave his own alternative:

> In light of the fact that we will soon have Dyfed, Clwyd, Gwynedd, Powys, Glamorgan and Gwent, I think it's about time that we start thinking in terms of having a permanent home in more than one place in Wales, so that we will be able to hold cultural events there that will be of benefit to those areas all year round. This will, I believe, be a creative opportunity for us to draw closer to our fellow Welshmen who are not able to speak Welsh, and they can then hold festivals in these homes and on these hearths whenever they wish to do so… I would like to see such centres established, so that we may feel unity as a nation again, and dialogue between the Welsh-speaking and the non-Welsh-speaking people of Wales, because I believe that those who don't speak Welsh have a great deal to contribute to those of us who do.

His speech shows clearly, in other passages as well, that he identifies strongly with the Anglo-Welsh culture. He sees the need for the two cultures to increase their awareness of each other and to understand each other better. He quotes two lesser-known Welsh poets, Bryn Griffiths from Swansea and T S Jones, who died in Australia. The latter is mentioned in that bedtime reading book Carwyn took with him to the cricket in Edgbaston. Author Aneirin Talfan Davies records a conversation he had with T S Jones, who uses the phrase, 'you are destined to live on your grandmothers' memories,' in the context of living a past heritage which isn't a present reality. Carwyn adds his response: 'That is a significant statement, as far as I can see.'

Talfan Davies outlines the contribution made to Welsh culture by those who didn't speak the language, a contribution that came from a strong sense of Welshness and nationhood.

In his speech, delivered in Welsh, Carwyn then asks, 'To whom do we belong?' He sets his answer in the context of the old Welsh Mabinogion myths and legends, written in the twelfth and thirteenth centuries but based on oral stories that date much further back. They are the oldest prose literature of Britain. He refers specifically to the story of Pwyll, the Ruler of Dyfed, who traded places with the leader of Annwn, Arawn, each then ruling the kingdom of the other for a whole year. Pwyll nurtured a close relationship with the people in his new kingdom of Annwn. Arawn, however, was a meticulous organiser and administrator, but with less of the warm appeal. Arawn also had no memories of his own kingdom, whereas Pwyll had fond memories of his Dyfed:

> With no memory, there is no nation. The memory of a nation is its history, and a nation keeps its memory alive by ensuring that its history is a part of the education system. This, for me, is the great sadness of things in Wales during the last century. You, who belong to Education Authorities, will you listen? Directors of Education in our counties, headmasters of our schools – especially secondary

Carwyn Rees James

Michael and Annie James and their four children: Eilonwy, Dewi, Carwyn and Gwen

James family collection

Rose Villa on the far right, Cefneithin primary school on the left
Alun Gibbard

The house in Rhydlewis that Michael and Annie left when they moved to Cefneithin
James family collection

Welsh Schoolboy honours finally achieved

James family collection

Carwyn's caps in a cabinet at Cefneithin RFC

Cefneithin RFC

The poise and balance of the schoolboy player
James family collection

Eight Gwendraeth Grammar School internationals. L–R Peter Rees (1947–48), Barry John (1966–72), Handel Greville (1947–48), Clive John (Wales B 1971–72), Fred Morgan (1938–39), Desmond Jones (1947–48), Robert Morgan (1962–64), Carwyn James (1958–59). Lion D Ken Jones (1962–66) was absent the day this photograph was taken. Gareth Davies and Jonathan Davies would follow these men into Welsh shirts
Gwendraeth Commemorative Volume 1925–1975

The student player, Aberystwyth
James family collection

The PE class on Carwyn's degree course (Carwyn fourth from left, second row from the back)
Geraint Griffith

Close friends Dafydd Bowen and Carwyn on holiday together, probably in Dublin
James family collection

Carwyn (back, right) and fellow Welsh students with their professors, including T H Parry-Williams (front, centre) and Gwenallt (front, second from right)
Dr Brynley F Roberts

Carwyn on Aberystwyth
University Students'
Representative Council (third
from right, front row)
James family collection

The first James family graduate
James family collection

Musker, RN, Coulsdon, October 1952 intake

JSSL days – outside the classroom huts during a grammar lesson (Carwyn sixth from left, back row)

Dennis Mills collection

J. S. S. L.
SEASON

R. U. F. C.
1952 - 53.

A.C. G. Caygill, Cdr. C. Clubb, Pte. K. Bonser, Gnr. D. Stewart, Pte. F. Bonser
Cdr. A. Clark, A.C. R. Lester, A.C. J. Leeming, Cpl. R. Berrett, A.C. B. Warren, Cdr. P. Barley, Cdr. G. Andrews, Cdr. A. Fletcher
Cdr. E. Copson, Sgt. G. Rosser, Flt.Lt. P. Field, Lt.Cmdr. D. Inglis, Cdr. C. James, Cdr. M. Stone, Cdr. A. Balch

Joint Forces rugby (Carwyn holding the ball)

James family collection

Proud recipient of the Middlesex Sevens trophy at Twickenham
Parc Y Scarlets collection

Carwyn the chapel deacon leads the Llandovery College choir boys to the church service
Alcwyn Deiniol Evans

Llandovery College staff (Warden and future Archbishop of Wales G O Williams is fourth from right in the front row, and T P 'Pope' Williams to his right. The College's next Warden, Des Tree, is fourth from left in the back row, and Carwyn on the extreme right)

Llandovery College

The ambitious College teacher

Llandovery College

Carwyn's room to the left and the dormitory corridor of the boys in his care to the right
Alun Gibbard

The popular Welsh international player at the Urdd (Welsh League of Youth) Camp, Llangrannog
James family collection

With Swansea RFC, leaving for Romania (Carwyn fifth from left in the back row)
Swansea RFC

His country calls. Wales vs. Australia 1958 (Carwyn front row, second from right)
Parc Y Scarlets collection

Country and community – at Cefneithin RFC after winning his first cap for Wales

Six Llanelli players turning out for Wales in the same game in 1958: R H Williams, Terry Davies, Carwyn, Wynne Evans, Ray Williams and Cyril Davies

David Rogers collection

R H Williams needs all the help he can get to light his cigarette – Carwyn and Wynne Evans are at hand

David Rogers collection

Llanelli Station – Moscow-bound (Carwyn third from left in the front row)

David Rogers collection

A warm welcome and flowers at Moscow Station
David Rogers collection

Carwyn the athlete in training at Moscow University
David Rogers collection

The squad in Moscow (Carwyn on the right in the front row)
Parc Y Scarlets collection

Llanelli RFC and Sables RFC (a combined Universities team from South Africa) February 1957, Stradey Park (Carwyn on the floor to the left of the ball)
Les Williams collection

schools, college lecturers and school teachers: listen. Listen to the satire in the words of this poet, and he is so right:

Yn gynnar yr eisteddem i lafarganu siâp hanes,
Dysgu am Leisa drws nesa
Ond gwybod dim am Mam.

('From early days we chanted the shape of history,
Learning about Lizzie next door,
But knowing nothing about Mam.')

I know this poet. He has nothing against the Queen, no more than I have, apart from in this context. Learning about Lizzie next door, but knowing nothing about Mam. 1066. 1066.

He refers here to the poet who would be honoured in the Eisteddfod that afternoon in one of the main events of the week, the crowning of the bard. The winners of both main poetry competitions, one awarded the Eisteddfod Crown and the other the Eisteddfod Chair, are always a closely-guarded secret and not announced until the ceremony itself, amongst great pageantry and pomp. In quoting from this poem, Carwyn had shown that he had clearly read it. That is no great surprise. It was written by his colleague amongst the cigarette stubs by the Dalek at Trinity, Dafydd Rowlands. Carwyn was careful not to break a time-honoured tradition by announcing the name of the winner, but he did quote from the winning work before it was announced. Carwyn did know that his friend had won. The night before, on the Monday, Dafydd Rowlands, his wife Margaret and brother Gerwyn, Carwyn and his brother Dewi had been for a meal in The Salutation in Felindre Farchog, not far from Haverfordwest. They were celebrating Dafydd winning the Eisteddfod Crown.

Carwyn makes his point about the lack of teaching of Welsh history in schools very forcefully. This part of his speech has been quoted often since then by those wishing to make the same point. But Carwyn made far more of an issue in that speech of the relationship between the Welsh who speak the language and those who don't. He is as critical of some attitudes shown by Welsh speakers towards those who don't speak the language as he is of the lack of teaching of Welsh history.

He brings the two issues together then, with emphasis again on the education system:

> Teaching a language is important, but if we give them memory, if we teach history, more than likely there will be a passionate desire then to learn the language... in order that the children can know about the glory of our little nation and in that same way we will arrive at what I referred to earlier: the unity of our nation.

He refers to the subject of the main poetry competition, Renaissance, and he links this to the fact that the Tuesday was also Young People's day at that Eisteddfod. He was aware, he said, of a renaissance amongst the young people of Wales. It was different to the same kind of renaissance amongst young people in other parts of the world, in that it was cultural and pacifist. 'Our young people know what they are fighting for,' he says, and continues:

> Who is responsible for igniting the spark in the hearts of these young people? Is it you? Is it me? I'm sure that those of us who are middle aged have room somewhere in the bigger picture. Maybe there's room for bridge building – there's certainly a need for bridge building. But we must also take sides. We cannot sit on the fence any longer. Do we belong to Pwyll? Do we belong to Arawn? Do we belong to the Archbishop of Wales or to the Lord Chancellor? We have to make our minds up one way or another.

This was a speech that had no shortage of gravitas. It outlined Carwyn's cultural nationalism but also stated firmly the need for unity and the role that those who spoke Welsh should take in that process.

One visitor to the Eisteddfod field that week was Jilly Cooper. She was then a *Sunday Times* journalist, sent by the paper to write a piece on the Eisteddfod and what it entailed.

THE SUNDAY TIMES, AUGUST 13 1972

A great tribal conjunction in the mud

EACH year, on the first week in August, the Welsh stream into one spot for their annual Eisteddfod, a sort of cultural Ganges where they immerse themselves for a week in a lovely bath of verse, song, and gossip.

Last week the holy spot was a boggy field just outside Haverfordwest in Pembrokeshire and despite the mandatory downpours of rain (without which no Eisteddfod would be complete) they again showed up in force for this great tribal conjunction in the mud.

Shaggy-haired poets and harpists, bards and beatniks, teachers and stooped grandmothers, they all came in over the hills on Monday for the gathering of the clans and yesterday they all trooped home refreshed and replete with tricky verses and all the latest scandal from all corners of the province.

For the Welsh don't just send Christmas cards to old friends and forget it; they hug one another at Eisteddfods and forget it. Through the circular walks you can hatch a plot, discuss rugby, bury old quarrels, learn who has got in the family way lately, stop to buy an organ or love spoon, and, even get a car sticker saying "Keep Wales Tidy: Dump Your Rubbish in England."

The Eisteddfod is about the only place where you can find a huddle of men standing knee deep in mud reciting poems to one another. Beer is drunk by the gallon but the abiding joy is to walk from group to group on the field with arms open wide ready to give the next old friend a gorilla-like embrace.

Last week Huw Wheldon was bobbing around amidst the music making; Sir Geraint Evans, the opera singer, was there; so, too, was Barry John the greatest rugby player ever (or so they say here). There was Robin Griffith, an actor who is trying to make a film of himself as a KGB agent in the field. The trouble was every time he stood around looking furtive for the cameras, one of his aunts fell on him and gave him a bone-crushing hug.

Oooh, look you—over there's Carwyn James, the British Lions coach on the all conquering 1971 rugby tour. Carwyn received a special ovation when he was admitted to the white-robed order of Bards at the Gorsedd ceremony on Thursday.

The ceremony was held in bristling sunlight on the ground next to Haverfordwest Football Club and the procession led in by the Bard Herald, Dillwyn Miles, together with the Horn of Plenty used to give the Arch-druid a symbolic sip to keep him going. It is, of course, the elaborate and changeless ritual which is at the centre of an Eisteddfod. Throughout the week bards walk around in coloured nightshirts and red faced trumpeters tootle away as if advancing on the walls of Jericho. Swords are flashed and horns held aloft and while the ritual means different things to different Welshmen, all eyes swell up with tears when the various winners are announced.

The way the chubby author Gwyn Thomas puts it: " Each and every one of us, from the time he got the shawl out of his mouth and could shout ' Yma! ' (' here! ') when the Eisteddfod conductor called out the name under which he had entered, was an Eisteddfodwr, a real gone guy behind the banner of the festival."

All entries are, of course, in Welsh and the old Welsh rule is still wielded with the ferocity of a tomahawk. For words and their usage in the language are dear to the Welsh and last week we heard enough polemics to keep all of us going for another year. The Welsh are nothing if not masters of rolling polemic.

In the pavilion one president of the day, Gwilym Jones, said that the placard-carrying youths of the Welsh Language Society who went to jail were like the Jews bearing the insignia of their faith to the gas chamber. The time for small arms was at an end. Now was the time for bigger guns.

Druid ceremony at the Eisteddfod: Archdderwydd Brinli with his attendants prepare for the elaborate and changeless ritual

Oooh! Look you – over there's Carwyn James, the British Lions coach on the all-conquering 1971 rugby tour. Carwyn received a special ovation when he was admitted to the white-robed order of Bards at the Gorsedd ceremony on Thursday.

Jilly Cooper evidently wasn't in Haverfordwest long enough to pick up any actual Welsh idioms in the English language and fell back on the old, hackneyed ones. She did, however, meet Carwyn and Dafydd Rowlands for a coffee during her visit, and write an article that introduced the *Sunday Times* readers to the whole idea of an Eisteddfod.

275

The Eisteddfod is about the only place where you can find a huddle of men standing knee-deep in mud reciting poems to one another. Beer is drunk by the gallon but the abiding joy is to walk from group to group on the field with arms open wide ready to give the next old friend a gorilla-like embrace.

She also caught the political mood of the week-long event, through being present in the Main Pavilion during the speech of one of the Presidents for the day, even though she unfortunately missed Carwyn's speech on the Tuesday:

In the Pavilion one President of the Day, Gwilym Jones, said that the placard-carrying youths of the Welsh Language Society who went to jail were like the Jews bearing the insignia of their faith to the gas chamber. The time for small arms was at an end. Now was the time for bigger guns.

Those words serve to give a glimpse as to why Labour-dominated rugby committees across the length and breadth of the Valleys might have struggled with Carwyn's association with all they perceived to fall under the banner of the nationalists' cause.

February, July and August 1972 saw four significant milestones for Carwyn. There was to be a fifth, bigger than the others, and one that deserves a chapter all of its own.

CHAPTER 16

The day the pubs ran dry

Oh the beer flowed at Stradey, piped down from Felinfoel,
And the hands that held the glasses high
were strong from steel and coal,
The air was filled with singing and I heard a grown man cry,
Not because we'd won but because the pubs ran dry.

Max Boyce, '9–3'

CARWYN'S LAST SIGNIFICANT milestone of 1972 was in the October of that year. It's a date that has its place in Llanelli folklore, certainly, but also in Welsh and world rugby history. 31 October 1972: the day Llanelli beat the All Blacks; the day the celebrating fans drank Llanelli pubs dry.

The visit of the All Blacks to Britain in 1972 was their seventh, the first having been back in 1905. Every visit by such a mighty team had a significance. In those days, seeing the All Blacks on British soil was a rare occurrence, as only seven visits in over 60 years shows. They were, therefore, special occasions. Individual tours became significant for varying reasons as each one unfolded, but the '72 tour had a special significance before the touring team had left New Zealand soil. They were to face the man who had masterminded the series defeat for the All Blacks at the hands of the Lions. Carwyn was now to pit his club Llanelli against them. It would be rather naïve to think that the All Blacks didn't have revenge on their minds as they headed West towards Stradey Park.

Carwyn had begun his preparation for this game back as far as the Lions tour in 1971. He knew then that the All Blacks

277

would be in his club's home town the following year and he'd shared that information with the Llanelli boys on the Lions tour, Derek Quinnell and Delme Thomas. He later established Delme as the captain for the season. He also knew that he needed to prepare for this game in a way that was different to preparation for any other game, and that meant far more than working tactics out on the pitch. Famously, he told his players before the match that rugby was a thinking game. He'd started his over a year before the actual fixture.

Board room and ballot box rugby

Carwyn's first moves were in the Llanelli RFC committee rooms. He knew that he had to win there to stand any chance of winning on the field. He called for a meeting with the Committee, which Marlston Morgan, a committee member then and more recently the President of Llanelli RFC, remembers:

> There's no doubt that a major emphasis of the committee at that time was making sure that we were always attractive enough a side to secure a fixture against a touring team... Carwyn and Norman Gale were both on the committee, but having separated the administrative matters from the rugby itself in the run up to the 1972–73 season, they concentrated just on rugby matters.

In *Scarlet Fever*, the booklet published to commemorate the match, Carwyn refers to the structural changes that were made to the way the club was run:

> May I thank Mr Handel Greville and his committee for leading Great Britain in the matter of selection, by asking the coach to be Chairman of the selectors and to be responsible for picking his own committee. I immediately accepted and asked Norman Gale to be assistant coach and team manager, and invited Delme Thomas as captain to make up a selection committee of three.

Carwyn here gives the impression that he was invited to implement this new structure. But such a change was without question the result of months of suggesting and influencing by Carwyn. This was the result he wanted and it's a clear example of the old management adage: 'let them think it's their idea'. The Llanelli Committee were happy to go along with Carwyn's strategy. Llanelli committee members, as Carwyn said, were leading British rugby in their demonstrative development of the game. In the edition of *Welsh Rugby* magazine at the end of the successful 1972–73 season, Carwyn gives his view on the game and how it was run very clearly:

> Gone are the days when a full committee of a dozen or more people get together for a couple of hours to select a side. I feel quite strongly in these days of squad systems that selection committees are quite superfluous, and I'm sure that you don't need five men to pick the Welsh team.

The committee's outlook meant that he was able to implement new systems at the club, based on a definite philosophy:

> Rugby football is at its best when the two sides are intent on playing the attacking creative game.

Carwyn objected quite vocally to an obvious trend in Welsh rugby at the time: the tendency for clubs to have two squads – the weekday games squad and the Saturday game squad. At Llanelli, for example, they used 100 players in one season in order to implement this system. The main players would play on a Saturday and the others would play midweek. In order to maintain such a structure, Llanelli would draw heavily on the local village teams to bulk up the numbers. But this was more than a making-up-the-numbers exercise – it was also a social exercise of some significance. It established a strong bond between club and community; between town and hinterland. It also played a part in affirming the long-established links between the small local clubs of the Llanelli area and the prestige side they played a part in developing.

Carwyn would no doubt have been aware of that heritage link between club and feeder clubs. But awareness and appreciation of heritage is no guarantee of future success and Carwyn knew that. He introduced sweeping changes to the club's fixture strategy as a result:

> Most leading clubs in Wales are guilty of over-burdening their fixture lists with the result that by the end of an eight-month season, players feel a little jaded and stale. For this reason, selection committees have to adopt the squad system and rest their key players in some matches to make sure that they have an edge for the important competitive games. In this context, we at Llanelli – and I take full responsibility within the system for this – owe an apology to some clubs for not turning out a full-strength side. One or two of the Monmouthshire clubs have cause for complaint and I sincerely hope that this can be borne in mind in future, otherwise the clubs concerned may lose much of their support.

Carwyn could see fans voting with their feet by staying away from games against teams that didn't field their full-strength squad. He knew that not playing a first choice team would give opposing clubs the impression that they didn't treat them seriously and indeed, disrespected them. He knew that was not good for the development of the game as a whole. As ever, his mind was on tomorrow, not today.

The big day gets closer

Once the structures Carwyn wanted were in place at Llanelli Rugby Club, he could move on to matters concerning rugby training and match preparation – particularly for the forthcoming game against the All Blacks. None of what follows would have happened without the boardroom changes Carwyn secured in the year or so before the big game. The issue of team selection was of paramount importance, and not surprisingly, Carwyn had his own inimitable way of approaching such an issue, as Carwyn's choice of captain, Delme Thomas, recalls:

We met in Carwyn's house in Cefneithin and the whole discussion was over in about an hour. It was fairly straightforward. That is apart from three positions. There was a little talk about the full back position, with Bernard Thomas' name mentioned. But that wasn't too serious a suggestion, more mentioned in passing. Roger Davies was the obvious first choice for us all. But the other two were a little bit more difficult.

Alan James and Selwyn Williams had been faithful servants to Llanelli and it was very difficult for me personally to even discuss the possibility of them not playing. Don't get me wrong, it wasn't a case of having any problem with Tom David or Chico Hopkins, they were obviously talented players. But I felt bad that we were talking of Alan and Selwyn maybe not playing.

Tom and Chico were brought into the club by Carwyn specifically for the All Blacks game. Following that meeting between Carwyn, Norman Gale and Delme Thomas in the Hawen bungalow, the three were joined by Phil Bennett. As a senior player – one who had led his club on their tour of South Africa – Carwyn respected him highly. Carwyn was also not one to bear grudges because Phil had gone on that controversial tour. The four then went for a meal at The Angel Inn in Salem, near Llandeilo. Over a meal and a bottle of wine, undoubtedly chosen by Carwyn, they discussed the impending game and put the world to rights.

As Carwyn put his team in place and then prepared that team for the match, the world's rugby journalists turned their attention to West Wales. In their midst was veteran New Zealand rugby journalist, Terry McLean. His visit to cover the All Blacks' seventh tour of the UK was the twenty-third tour he had reported on in 22 years. He arrived in Carmarthenshire a good few days before the match.

It was a pleasure for me, this first night in Wales, to go with Carwyn James to his home in Cefneithin, a small village of 800 residents about 12 miles from Llanelli. I spent the night in talk with Carwyn, his older sister Gwen and their mother, an elderly lady in her seventies who is so very Welsh that to this day she prefers the Welsh rather than the English for her conversation.

The following day he went to Carmarthen with Carwyn. While Carwyn was at Trinity College, he wandered around the town on his own before having lunch with Carwyn and some of his fellow lecturers:

This was for me, as a citified New Zealander, a dip into another world of strangely-rural sweetness.

He then returned to Cefneithin and had tea with Barry John's family before returning to Hawen to spend time with Gwen and her mother. These conversations made a definite impression on him:

The one thing which remained salient in my mind was the talk by Gwen and Carwyn of how they remembered, as children, seeing their father come home daily from the pit, black from the coal he had worked in, and changing, with scrubbing, into near normality. They remembered too the first signs of the silicosis which was to eat through his lungs and his life, lingeringly, painfully... Who could doubt that a people living in intangible but constant fear that a beam might give, a rock face fall or, perhaps worst of all, dust creep into his lungs, would acquire some special qualities of determination and resolution?

These visits gave Terry McLean an insight into Carwyn's background and through that, his personality. He saw him in his own environment, not just as the coach on a Lions tour:

That was, that is, the inherent quality of Carwyn James as a man, a scholar and, not least, a coach. He is, to meet, amusing, charming. He loves to talk. He loves even more to sing – which he does extremely well. There is laughter in his eyes and in his voice and when he is especially amused his face crinkles in wrinkles of delight... But underneath, he is steel. How could the true Welsh be anything else, growing up in the Valleys...?

As much as Carwyn was rigidly controlling every aspect of preparation for the game, he didn't have it all his own way. At a crucial time in the team preparation, weeks before the game, Carwyn lost four of his best players. The four were chosen to play in a match in Edinburgh, between a combined England/Wales team against a combined Scotland/Ireland team. Phil Bennett, Derek Quinnell, Chico Hopkins and Roy Bergiers were taken from Carwyn and he wasn't happy. He described the decision as 'a bit rough'.

When Carwyn worked with his Llanelli team, he was nowhere near being in the same situation as he had been when preparing the Lions to face the same opposition. If on that tour he had a squad full of quality international players, the Stradey team were completely different. Ten of the XV on the pitch hadn't played for their country at all at this point, though many of those would go on to shine for Wales after 31 October 1972. Carwyn's man-management, team-building and motivational skills were to be tested in a new way. On the match day itself, that included starting the day in a way not common amongst rugby teams at the time. They met in a local hotel in order to travel to the match together, a practice more usually associated with FA Cup Finals than rugby games.

All players were instructed to go the the main local hotel at the time, the Ashburnham in Burry Port. There, they were to relax together, have a meal and listen to motivational speeches by invited guests including Ray Williams, the WRU's Head of Coaching. Having been there a while, Carwyn noticed that the players were too fired up too long before kick-off, and decided he needed to deal with this. Phil Bennett remembers:

> Carwyn noticed, I think, that we were heading to go through the roof a little too soon, especially after Norman Gale shared a few of his not-so-choice, direct, words with us. So he took us all out for a walk, to ease the tension a little bit. He took us over to the Ashburnham Golf Club, and we went for a short walk there to get some fresh air.

When Carwyn thought the break had served its purpose, he took them back to the Ashburnham. Then it was time for them to get on the bus and journey the four or five miles into Stradey, along the main road from Llanelli to Carmarthen. This bus journey had quite an impact on the players. It was a new experience for them, and one which gave them a definite sense of occasion, as Tom David recalls:

> It looked like there were millions of people everywhere. I could tell what this meant to the people of this area. That was so obvious on that coach journey down. There's no doubt at all in my mind, Carwyn had that in his mind too when he decided we would arrive at Stradey together by coach.

Tom David, Chico Hopkins and J J Williams were the 'imports' brought into the team to strengthen the squad for this one game. They came from Pontypridd, Maesteg and Bridgend. They needed to gel with the others and buy into the wider community significance of Llanelli facing the All Blacks. The bus journey achieved just that.

One of those on the bus was more nervous than the rest. He was the youngest player, which was one reason for his nervousness. But he was also Ray Gravell: excitable, hyper, passionate, emotional Ray Gravell. Delme Thomas was asked to sit next to him:

> Ray was on pins more than usual that day and that's why Carwyn asked me to sit next to him. I don't think he sat still for a second on the whole journey. The best I could do was to keep on with the small talk in order to try and quieten him.

When the bus arrived at Stradey, the crowds had already gathered and gave them a rapturous welcome. With the players in the dressing room, word got out that the All Blacks had arrived. Many of the players stood on the fixed benches they had been sitting on, in order to peep out through the narrow windows high in the wall above. Carwyn was not happy with this at all. He told them to sit back down, saying that there was no cause to pay the All Blacks such respect by giving the appearance that the Llanelli players admired them.

In the dressing room, he shared a story from his Lions tour the previous year: the one relating to his visit to George Nepia's house. In his match-day programme article, he says that while he was at Nepia's house, the All Black took out a scrapbook of the New Zealand tour to Britain in 1924. He mentioned the game against Llanelli in that year particularly:

> George remembered it vividly and recalled with enthusiasm the excitement of the match. Many here today will also relive some of those thrilling moments; will think of George Nepia and Ernie Finch, and in time-honoured Llanelli style will say that the Scarlets deserved to win. But the records say that they lost, and the records will also tell us that every confrontation between the Scarlets and the All Blacks has had a similar sad ending.
>
> In the dressing room today the Llanelli players will be reminded of those sad endings, they will be told that the world, and more particularly the staunch Scarlets supporters, don't want to know a loser, but they will also be told that we have probably one of the finest sides ever to represent Llanelli – of this I personally have no doubt.

Leading that fine side was three-times British Lion Delme Thomas. But however much experience he had, Carwyn knew that he needed to be encouraged and supported as much as the others. The way he chose to do so was to take Delme out on to the pitch about half an hour before kick-off. He wanted Delme to see the expectant crowd, to savour the atmosphere and in doing so, to appreciate the significance of the event.

Much has been written of the game itself and the match has been replayed time and time again over the last 40 years or so. The score, 9–3, has become a magical, legendary number. The real significance of that game hit home at the blowing of the final whistle, Llanelli having secured a famous victory.

The headlines spoke of 'Scarlet Fever' 'The Day the Pubs Ran Dry!' and 'Magnificent Scarlets!' The victory had an impact on popular culture outside the world of rugby. Within days, Max Boyce was singing live on Radio Wales, celebrating the victory in a song written for the occasion. These were early days of sports broadcasting and the match was televised, with commentary by David Parry-Jones. This also helped to enhance the impact of the event. The world famous Groggs creator, John Hughes, was inspired by the victory and the impact it had to develop rugby characters instead of the mythical characters he had created previously. An early one was one of Delme Thomas in his famous celebratory pose: both arms in the air, bent at the elbows.

That pose of Delme's, when he was lifted high on the shoulders of the fans, was criticised by some in New Zealand as being derogatory and demeaning the opposition. One prominent New Zealander jumped to Delme's defence. Terry McLean understood the gesture perfectly:

> But did they not understand, these critics, that Delme and Carwyn and all of the Welsh were brothers under the skin? That having lived so much in the misery of mining and associated crafts, they had come to believe they could, if they tried, conquer the world? Which, right now, they had done. Delme Thomas was not a man riding on shoulders, he was Archangel of Cambria.

If McLean describes Delme as the Archangel of Cambria, it would be interesting to know how he would describe Carwyn. No doubt he was a major factor in maximising the victory's impact. Winning the Test series gave him an exalted status. Beating the same opposition with his club team took him into the realms of legend. The fact that he did all this with little more than a quiet smile of joy gave him an aura that added to the mystique.

For the players, as for Carwyn, this was a victory that grew from an overwhelming and deep-rooted sense of community.

Delme's 'provocative'
gesture captured in
Grogg form
Alun Gibbard

One celebration of
success
E Meirion Roberts

What meant the most to the whole club was that they achieved what they achieved on their own home turf. Delme Thomas' speech to the players before the game is one of those pre-match speeches noted as amongst the most memorable. It had Phil Bennett in tears. In it, Thomas sums up that link between community and rugby team succinctly. It powerfully sums up what 'in front of my own people' means. Carwyn could have said the same:

> I said I had been lucky to have been capped for Wales and been on three Lions tours. But none of that meant anything to me. This was the day I wanted more than anything else. It wasn't in a foreign country, it was in front of our own crowd. We knew Stradey would be packed with supporters who showed passion like no one else. I said that you could keep all the Welsh caps and the Lions jerseys. This is what I want – to beat the All Blacks at Stradey. That would mean more to me than anything else I had achieved in the game.

Gareth Jenkins and Phil Bennett were steelworkers at work in their foundry the day before they played the All Blacks. They both summed up the victory in the same spirit as Delme. Phil Bennett had caught Carwyn's attention years earlier:

> I was offered a scholarship at Llandovery College when I was about 15, by Carwyn James. At the same time, some football clubs were interested in me as well. But my father had a nasty accident in the steelworks so all those offers meant nothing to me. At 15 I went into the steel industry myself, so that I could help to support the family. That was a massive culture shock. I went from being in school, playing for the school team and for Wales Schoolboys to the heavy working world of steel. But once I got used to it, it was without doubt the greatest university I could possibly have gone to. I mixed with all sorts of men, with all sorts of interests, backgrounds and intelligence.

For Phil Bennett and the others, it was more than a rugby achievement. Its resonance was the fact that victory had been achieved by men from a small working-class town whose roots were in the traditional heavy industries from which the club was formed, and which were integral to the shaping of Wales itself. 80 minutes on a rectangular patch of grass was both history and heritage.

This awareness of history would have informed Carwyn's appreciation of his rugby generally and individual matches specifically as much as it informed his politics and his sense of Welsh identity. In this the rest of his team were as one with him. Rugby gives Wales an identity it doesn't enjoy in so many other areas.

CHAPTER 17

After October:
Barbarians and wives

Yes, they're sharing a drink they call loneliness
But it's better than drinkin' alone.

Billy Joel, 'Piano Man'

THE FIRST DAY of November 1972 was the first day of the rest of their season. Things would never be the same again, but life had to go on – there were matches to be played in cup and league. Not much was actually done on that day though, with many suffering the effects of celebrating long into the night. Delme Thomas, however, was in work at eight o'clock that morning, back doing his job as a linesman with the Electricity Board.

The difficulties in dealing with success following the Lions tour were now compounded by a new success. The demands on Carwyn's time increased significantly. Not only the speaking engagements and public appearances, but the dinners held in honour of Llanelli's victory. There was no shortage of dinners. Trinity College arranged a victory celebration dinner in the Ivy Bush Royal Hotel, Carmarthen, for example.

Added to this were the events held to mark the centenary of Llanelli Rugby Club that year, which meant even more dinners and speeches. Ironically, this particular increased pressure was unnecessary as it actually wasn't the club's centenary year. It had been decided, no one is sure why or

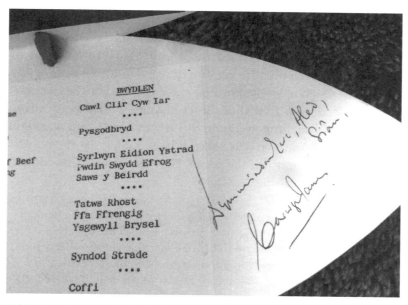

BWYDLEN
Cawl Clir Cyw Iar
••••
Pysgodbryd
••••
Syrlwyn Eidion Ystrad
Fwdin Swydd Efrog
Saws y Beirdd
••••
Tatws Rhost
Ffa Ffrengig
Ysgewyll Brysel
••••
Syndod Strade
••••
Coffi

Celebratory banquet, Ivy Bush Hotel, Carmarthen

by whom, that 1872 was the year in which the club was formed. The meeting that decided to start a team in Llanelli was actually held in 1875 and the first game in 1876, but, in the true spirit of not letting the facts spoil a good story, Llanelli's victory against the All Blacks was heralded by the club as all the more special because it happened in their centenary year. If the facts had been checked, Carwyn would have avoided one layer of demands on his time. He didn't, and victory extended the period in which he was stretched beyond capacity. If that period started at Heathrow in August 1971 and continued through 1972, victory for Llanelli extended that period through 1973 and into 1974. If indeed it ever fully stopped before Carwyn died.

Back on the field of play, Llanelli had to carry on with their fixtures. Not surprisingly, they lost the Saturday after beating the All Blacks, to Richmond. Not all of the players had recovered from the Tuesday before! The following January the All Blacks were back in Wales again, this time to face the Barbarians. This was the match that saw one of the greatest tries ever scored, Gareth Edwards ending a move begun by Phil Bennett. It's still a hit on YouTube even now!

The Barbarians' longstanding tradition is that they weren't ever coached, and that that didn't change with the advent of coaches and coaching systems. But it was a rule that was bent a little in 1973. Carwyn was asked if he would assist the players in their preparations for the game. He was asked by his captain on the 1971 tour, John Dawes:

> I saw Carwyn in the Angel Hotel a few nights before the game. I asked him if he would help in our preparation for the clash with the All Blacks. He said he would. He met the squad twice before the game. He came to run a training session on the Friday, in Penarth, and then he saw us on the day of the match when he went through some moves and gave us his usual inspirational pep-talk.

This involvement with the Barbarians had been called for by at least one rugby journalist. John Reason mentions this in a *Daily Telegraph* article looking forward to the arrival of the All Blacks touring party:

> Sadly, Carwyn's involvement in the All Blacks' coming tour is only minimal. Because the British Lions still do not play matches at home against the touring sides, the chances are that the only contribution he will make will be the one he makes today as Llanelli's coach. That is not enough. What a nice gesture it would be if the Barbarians were to come to Carwyn James and to say to him, 'You take over the team for the last match of the All Blacks' tour.' It is a tribute he well deserves, because he has done British rugby proud.

No one objected to the fact that Carwyn coached the Barbarians. And in doing so, that made a third occasion when a team under his care had beaten the All Blacks. The former

Official recognition of his unofficial role

head of rugby at Llandovery was now at the top of rugby coaching throughout the world.

Somehow, in between these successes and celebrations, he had to fit in what could loosely be called normal days at the office. He had poets and books to talk about with students and training sessions to run with his club, preparing for games against clubs across the length and breadth of the South Wales Valleys and the other side of Offa's Dyke as well. A new innovation in 1972 was the introduction of the Welsh Rugby Union Challenge Cup. Llanelli reached the final of the inaugural competition, but lost to Neath. They reached the final at the end of the 1972–73 season, and comfortably beat Cardiff. That was the beginning of a run that saw them win another three Cups in succession, all under Carwyn James. This was another part of the process that led to Llanelli being called the Man U of the rugby world.

A change of epic proportions was implemented by Carwyn as 1973 moved on. It had already been decided that the club were to tour Canada at the end of the season. Carwyn wanted to implement one change for that tour – wives and girlfriends should be allowed to go as well. It would have been easier to accept before the game that Llanelli were going to beat the All Blacks than it was for many to accept that the women would be allowed on tour. Carwyn's thinking was that the wives and girlfriends had been as much a part of the success that Llanelli had enjoyed that season as the players on the pitch had been. Not only had they supported their men at home, but many were also involved in a very practical way with running the club. After-match sandwiches were made by many of these wives, for instance. Gender division was very clear then: women did what were deemed to be women's things, usually revolving around catering; men played the rugby, and that's it. Putting the two together was unheard of. The wives and girlfriends were, of course, delighted with Carwyn's decision. Many of the men weren't too sure. Touring was an especially macho and drink-fuelled rite of passage in a club's life. The phrase 'what goes on tour, stays on tour' is a rugby mantra for a specific reason. Now, 'what goes on tour' would be shared with the women. But it happened, and it went very well. Some of the players who were single struggled a little with the whole idea because they were put in a position they hadn't been in before as well, one of being more isolated in mixed company. Other clubs in Wales gave Llanelli the best of their ribbing banter on the issue, with comments using words like 'cissy' and 'powder puff' flying across to the West. The more serious criticisms of Carwyn's decision said that he was going against the very spirit of the game in allowing women to tour. For Carwyn, though, it was the right thing to do and that was that.

Caring and leaving

Taking the wives on tour showed one particular side of Carwyn that the players were more than familiar with. They knew that this highly successful coach had a more vulnerable side, a softer side, a caring side. He could also be a very private man, as his fleeing from the Trinity staff room showed. The thread that regularly linked these traits was a sad loneliness. It was common for Carwyn to call late at night at the homes of some of his players – more often than not, the recently-married Phil Bennett's home.

> There would be a knock on the door at about nine o clock at night. It was Carwyn. Sometimes he had a bottle of red wine in his hands, sometimes not. He would come in and chat for hours. The bottle of red would be emptied. Quite often he would fall asleep and we would have to wake him so that he could go home. It was as if he didn't want to go home. Seeing him at those times made me feel sad for him. It was his golden era, the world knew about him – and yet there he was late at night fast asleep in our armchair in Felinfoel, an empty bottle by his side, or an empty coffee cup resting on his hand.

But Carwyn could never be called indulgent in his loneliness and it was never a barrier between him and other people if help was needed. Phil Bennett again experienced this side of him, the caring Carwyn, in a very real and practical way.

> On one of his visits, we shared with Carwyn that we had gone through a personal tragedy when we lost a child. It was a huge blow to Pat and myself. Not long after there was a knock on the door. It was Carwyn again. He asked us if we had any plans for the weeks ahead. We said that our loss meant that all plans were on hold. He put his hand in his pocket and handed us an envelope. Inside were air tickets for us to go abroad on holiday, and the hotel was sorted too. He said that we needed time to escape and to rest and that we had to go. I was to forget about rugby and training, he said, because there were far more important things in life.

Scrum half Chico Hopkins experienced the caring Carwyn as well in a different way, when his father passed away.

> I had joined Llanelli and there were only a few weeks to go to the All Blacks game. We were playing up at Cross Keys. Half time arrived and I could see Carwyn walking over to us players on the pitch. That was rather unusual and then he asked me to go off the field. I didn't think I had played that badly! Anyway, subs weren't allowed then except for injury and I knew I wasn't injured. He could see I didn't quite get what was going on, and he said that my father had been taken ill. I had gone to the game in the car with my father and brother from Maesteg.
>
> I went with Carwyn, and when we got to the touchline, Carwyn had to break the news to me that my father had actually passed away. He just fell down dead, watching the game, standing next to my 14-year-old brother. You can imagine the effect that had on me and him. Going home from Cross Keys without our father, to tell our mother what had happened, was awful.'

That tragedy hit the Hopkins family hard. Chico has no doubt that it affected his play for Llanelli after that.

> I had tremendous support from Carwyn – he was very patient and understanding. Personally, I didn't think that I would be up for playing the All Blacks at all, because my head was all over the place. But Carwyn used what had happened as a motivation instead of an obstacle. He persevered with me and I obviously did play and had a fairly good game.

Only a few weeks after the October victory, Chico was to leave Llanelli and go North to play Rugby League, joining Swinton for £8,000. In his mind, that was a move with a direct link to the passing of his father.

> My father would always encourage me, throughout my career. I'd had an offer to go North the previous season and my dad was all for it. When the offer came after he died, I grabbed it with both hands, thinking I was doing something that my father wanted and

would be proud of. I probably wouldn't have gone otherwise and would have stayed with Llanelli. That's probably what I should have done.

Years later, Chico was to suffer a nervous breakdown, which he put down as the reaction to the tragedy that shook his family in '72. He says that things would have been a lot worse if Carwyn hadn't shown the support he did while he was in the eye of the storm.

Carwyn fought for his own family at this time too. After suffering from respiratory problems for years, his father had passed away, living just long enough to experience his son's success in New Zealand in 1971. As the widow of a coal miner, Annie was entitled to free coal after the death of her husband. The National Coal Board, however, had other ideas. They argued that as pneumoconiosis was not the official cause of death on the certificate, they were under no obligation to give her free coal. Carwyn wouldn't have it and he sought the support of The National Union of Miners in South Wales, but they proved to be very unsupportive as well. He employed a solicitor to challenge the decision and took the case to court. He won, and his mother was given her free coal. He was disappointed by the attitude taken by the Coal Board in South Wales, that they had been so obstinate in their refusal of the coal, even though Michael James had been a collier for nearly 30 years.

When the 1973–74 season began, life was settling back into a certain degree of normality for Llanelli RFC, if not for Carwyn. It was to be a more usual season. Carwyn, however, had some plans of his own. He decided to bring his association with Trinity College to an end in order to pursue a career in broadcasting and journalism.

In the broader picture, they were uncertain times for training colleges like Trinity. There was talk that their funding was under threat of being cut altogether in some cases, and there was a feeling of insecurity amongst the staff of such educational establishments. Quite a few left Trinity at this time because of this uncertainty, unsure if they would have jobs in a year or two's time. There's no direct evidence that this played on Carwyn's mind in his decision making, but it would certainly have been the talk of his fellow lecturers in 1973–74. As it happened, cuts were made at Trinity a few years later. Carwyn leaving was felt deeply by Trinity staff. Norah Isaac said that 'the loss to education was massive'.

Rugby journalist Clem Thomas went much further in his reaction to Carwyn leaving Trinity, seeing in it a deliberate tactic on Carwyn's part:

> I often felt it was a mistake when he forsook the academic life to join the hurly-burly of the sports media. Sometimes I felt that it was a form of revenge for the neglect of his talent by Welsh rugby.

In his new job, Carwyn was indeed in a position to analyse and comment on all sorts of aspects within the game of rugby in Wales. If this was a form of revenge, either conscious or unconscious, did he fully appreciate that he was in effect walking into another world that would neglect his talents and not use them to their full potential? He was drawing closer to a new hearth without appreciating that flames can burn as well as warm.

For Carwyn personally, it drew down the curtain on a significant period of his life and career. It had been five years or so of stark and dramatic contrast to the halcyon days of public school life in Llandovery. He had been catapulted to the world's attention when he not only contributed to the development of the game he loved, but picked it up by the scruff of its neck and gave it a good shaking, to the very marrow of its bones. He experienced unique success in doing so. At the same time, he had fed dozens of students with the gems of Welsh literature and also furthered his broadcasting career. They were indeed the years of the fatted calf. The years ahead, however – the eight he had left in this world – would prove to be far more sparse and difficult.

CHAPTER 18

The rejected coach?

There is no gainsaying the romantic view as to who is the most admired coach in rugby – Carwyn James of Wales.
Mick Cleary, *The Daily Telegraph* (2007)

ANOTHER JOB HAD been vacated not long before Carwyn made his decision to leave Trinity and academia. Wales coach Clive Rowlands had decided to call it a day, and the search was on for his successor. He had taken his Welsh team to great heights, winning the Grand Slam in 1971, the first time the Welsh had done so since 1952, thus marking the start of another Golden Era for Welsh rugby. During the same period, Carwyn had achieved his successes with the Lions and Llanelli. In addition to conquering the All Blacks, Llanelli had won two Welsh cups in a row by that year as well.

But it was not only the results that made Carwyn a world-renowned coach. It was also the style of play he developed in achieving those results. It was free, open rugby, full of style and grace – although it must be said that his club's victory against the All Blacks wasn't secured by such flowing rugby. That was a victory more grafted than crafted, and shows the core Carwyn trait of knowing how to win. Carwyn's overall approach drew admiration and reverence from those who played for him, and respect and recognition from those who ran the game of rugby in every country where the game was played in the world. It was a personal, emotive, approach that resonated with the worlds of opera, ballet and poetry that also were a major delight to this rugby genius. His rugby writings often included references from these art forms as he saw the rough and tumble of the oval-shaped ball game through the same eyes that would watch opera or read poetry. He said:

> I see rugby football as a piece of opera, a piece of music. It is something that can flow like music and opera and can be beautiful to watch.

He was, then, according to many in the Welsh rugby world, a natural, obvious choice to be the coach of the Welsh rugby team. But there was more unity in the wider rugby world in backing Carwyn as coach of Wales than there was in Wales itself. This chapel man was no prophet, but he suffered more than his fair share of dishonour in his own country.

Prior to 1974, Carwyn had put his name forward to be one of five Vice-presidents of the WRU. The decision was to be made through voting, and it was the member clubs, mainly across South Wales, who had the right to vote. Carwyn failed to secure enough votes from these clubs. It's hard to imagine how Carwyn would have taken that rejection, and even harder today to understand why so many clubs decided they didn't want to vote for Carwyn and chose others in his place.

Something similar had happened before he left Llandovery. Towards the end of his time there he stood for election to one of the WRU regional committees. David Gealy, his deputy in the Welsh department at the College remembers a phone conversation relating to that application:

> Carwyn and Gwynne Walters had tried for the same kind of position, and the talk was that both stood a very good chance of succeeding – in fact as sure as anyone could be that they would succeed. But that's not how it turned out. I remember being in Carwyn's room after he'd heard that he had not been successful. He said that he had to make a phone call. I gathered soon enough that the man on the other end of the phone was Cliff Jones, a leading WRU official at the time. Carwyn told him exactly what he thought of him, in no uncertain terms. He was very annoyed and

very disappointed at the same time and it transpired that this was because Cliff Jones had not supported Carwyn in his attempt to get on to the committee. And then Carwyn said, in full rage, 'The worst thing about all this is the fact that you don't want change! You just don't want change!' Carwyn was really agitated and there's no doubt that's the worst I ever saw him.

The phrase that showed his anger had cranked up a notch or two, 'You don't want change!', is particularly telling. On one hand it says a great deal about the WRU: as innovative as they had been in developing the whole idea of coaching in the first place, internal, structural changes to the way things were done were obviously a totally different ball game. Parochial prejudices would conquer all else. On the other hand, it shows us a great deal about Carwyn. He wanted change and the fact that others resisted it angered him. That's the forward-thinking Carwyn. But he could only show such a confident attitude when he himself had both feet on a comfortable terra firma. He needed security to make him feel free; he needed the roots to help him fly.

There is yet another example of Carwyn being rebuffed by the WRU which happened just before the above incident. In 1968, a tour was arranged for the Welsh team to Argentina. The Welsh coach, Dai Nash, was not chosen to take his team on the tour – the whole idea of coaching was that new. John Robbins, Clive Rowlands and Carwyn were considered. The previous year, Carwyn had been asked to coach a West Wales XV against the All Blacks. He did therefore have some experience of coaching a representative team against a touring international team. John Robbins, a former Welsh international and British Lion, at that stage had more experience of coaching adults, having had some coaching experience with the 1966 British Lions. But newly-appointed WRU member Clive Rowlands was the one who was chosen to take Wales to Argentina.

A picture was forming. The Head of Rugby at Llandovery

had been twice rejected, and the successful coach of the '71 Lions was also subsequently rejected. It is quite surprising that the man who had achieved so much had failed in his attempts to be a part of the organisation that was responsible for developing the game in Wales, when he had played an integral part in that development. In a four-year period, he failed four times to become a part of the WRU, either as committee man or as coach. There was more to come.

Why Carwyn was rejected so consistently by WRU officialdom at this time is another matter. There was a definite political culture within South Wales that divided an already small region. South Wales was a region of two halves – east and west, and never the twain shall meet. There was a conviction amongst players from the west that they had to play twice as well as their counterparts in the east in order to play for Wales, the selectors having a natural East Wales bias, it was believed. This was cemented by the daily Cardiff-based newspaper, the *Western Mail*, and in particular their influential rugby correspondent, J B G Thomas, who, as mentioned earlier, was considered the de facto selector of the Wales team. He strongly favoured the eastern clubs, it was said.

Carwyn's close friend and fellow *Guardian* journalist Frank Keating was more than aware of this tendency.

> In [Carwyn's] beloved Welsh-speaking West he has long been canonised; eastwards, nearer the capital with its charcoal suits and Rotary Clubs and envious, careful middle-class, he is regarded with suspicion.

Another *Guardian* journalist, David Foot, also saw the situation very clearly from afar.

> In many ways, Carwyn was very much a part of Wales' inner establishment: Welsh-speaking, white-robed, steeped in the cultures of his native heath, erudite. Yet when it came to rugby, at the highest level in his own country, he was critical and despaired

of entrenched attitudes. Maybe his popularity and his strongly-held views worked against him. Some of the game's hierarchy were certainly exceedingly wary of him. He was too much of an individualist, not receptive to a second point of view, they said. They bristled at his implied criticism of WRU policy and had no wish to see him up-tip the apple cart with his strong, singular presence. All right, he wanted to run the whole show and he knew he could do it better than they could.

With these thoughts in mind, it didn't help Carwyn's cause that he not only came from West Wales, but had also stood for Plaid Cymru in a General Election at the start of the Seventies. For the Labour-dominated regional committees up and down the industrial Valleys, the thought of a nationalist in charge of the Welsh rugby team was simply too much to stomach.

There was also another issue, a brand new and challenging one for those within the macho world of Welsh rugby. Apparently rumours abounded about Carwyn's sexuality, and this stopped a lot of people from voting for him. There was no room for such a person on WRU committees, they believed. If this is true, and there's no reason to doubt that it is, then it's a very early indication of the rumours about Carwyn being gay, rumours that would cause inner torment for him in the last years of his life.

Despite a lack of unanimous backing, and despite previous rebuffs, Carwyn did write to the Welsh Rugby Union with reference to the vacant coaching position. His letter of application is very illuminating. As he applies for the post, he also withdraws his application.

Hawen
Cefneithin
28.1.74

Dear Sirs,
    Many thanks for the opportunity to allow one's name to go forward to be considered for the position of the Welsh National Team Coach. By implication only I gather that the terms of

reference are as ever; that is, that the present system will continue.

Am I to understand that the appointment is a three-year one? Will the Big Five continue in its present form as a permanent institution? Will they be appointed annually – as at present – and the coach for three-year periods?

Since the present Big Five have already nominated the Coach of their choice is it your honest assumption that any other nomination will be acceptable? Will there be an interview for the post, and will the other applicants be told who is in contention?

I feel I have to ask all these questions, otherwise one is obviously compromising himself totally. Any National Team Coach must surely have his own views on Coaching, Selection, Team Management etc., and these may not necessarily tie up with the present system. To be appointed and then to disagree leaves one in an invidious position.

The present Big Five obviously work happily together. They are a team, as they should be, and I respect them for it, and their nomination for the next Coach suggests, rightly, that they want to remain as a team.

I personally feel that changes are now necessary. I will put my views very briefly because certain journalists, without reference to me, have 'jazzed up' a lengthy interview I gave to the *Swansea Evening Post* some time ago. These are my main points:

1. That the National Team Coach, as in some other countries, should always be the Chairman of Selectors.

2. That the Chairman of Selectors be allowed to chose two, three, or even four Advisers to help him – preferably three.

3. That preferably these would be Coaches now active within their Clubs.

4. That they would be chosen for their experience as players (forwards/backs), as coaches, and with reference to geography.

5. That the National Team Coach and his Advisers should seek the assistance of all club coaches in Wales and attend club coaching sessions as from September. Wales, from a Rugby point of view, is sufficiently small to put these ideas into practice. Elsewhere, they would be impracticable.

Wales has been at the forefront in its thinking in recent years. It is of no use at the present moment for the WRU members to bemoan the fact that other countries are catching up with us. The answer surely is that we must always try and out-think them.

Having considered my position over and over again I have
reluctantly come to the conclusion that I mustn't allow my name to
go forward. I know that I am asking too much of the Union – that
change takes time. But I felt, however, that it was only fair to make
my views known for the sake of the appointment – we all want
the new man to be successful. He must be given the freedom to
express himself.

A Coach, like a teacher, is an expression of personality, and
he has to dominate if he has to succeed. This he can't possibly do
with a small committee who are responsible for his appointment.
Whatever the future policy, it is important as a matter of principle
that he is appointed by the full Executive Committee of the Union
and he should always be answerable to them. The dictator must
observe humility!

My questions are rhetorical and I don't expect a reply.

Yours faithfully,

Carwyn James

This letter clears one technicality that has lingered in Wales
since Carwyn left this world. Throughout those years, the story
has been told that the WRU rejected Carwyn's application.
They didn't. He withdrew it himself: 'I mustn't allow my name
to go forward.' The WRU couldn't consider an application that
wasn't presented.

But this in no way exonerates the WRU. There were things
they could have done to secure the services of one the greatest
coaches the world has seen, if not the greatest. They could
have tried to persuade him to change his mind. They could
have discussed his objections with him in the name of finding
some middle ground, a workable alternative. Carwyn's letter
states that he had previously made his point of view public,
so his thoughts would not have been unknown to the WRU. A
series of articles in the Cardiff-based *Evening Post* a year or so
prior to the letter, for example, saw Carwyn develop the same
rugby philosophy. The WRU were aware of this and still saw
fit to invite him to try for the Welsh coach job – a suggestion
that they might well have been willing to discuss issues with

him. But in the end, they didn't approach him at all, taking his withdrawal of his own application seriously.

Clive Rowlands' response

The outgoing Welsh coach, Clive Rowlands, was on the WRU selection committee – the Big Five, as they were called – at the time of choosing his successor. In a conversation with the author for this biography, Carwyn's letter was mentioned. Clive Rowlands stated that he had no recollection of its contents over 40 years later. He was asked if he would like it read out to him and he agreed. He responded to each point as it was read out, but not before making it clear what the relationship between the two individuals was.

> People say that the two of us didn't get along at all. I don't understand that. We would meet regularly outside the official rugby circles, and he would also come to stay with us fairly often in our home in Cwmtwrch.Many believe that I stood against Carwyn and that's why he didn't get the job. That is pure nonsense. When I coached Wales, people would say that Carwyn should be the Welsh coach. What was I supposed to do? Train Wales to lose so that they could bring in the new coach?

When Carwyn's thoughts as expressed in his letter were mentioned, he says that it was quite likely that he had deliberately forgotten them. He was, however, happy to hear them again.

AG: The first point, Clive. He says that the coach of the national team should be the chairman of the selectors, as happens in some other countries.

CR: Within the Big Five in my day, I would always have the last word if there was any disagreement about having to choose between two players. For example, if we had to choose between Charlie Faulkner or Glyn Shaw as props, or Bennett or John as outside halves. One player would suite a particular game better than the other, and I would choose, according to how I would see the game. He mentions having the coach as the chairman of a group of people, which shows clearly that Carwyn didn't want to run everything in his own way, which has been the popular perception over the years. He wanted a team around him, as he had in Llanelli and with the Lions. That's exactly what he would have had with Wales as well.

AG: He mentions the need for the coach to have two, three or four others to advise him, three ideally he then says.

CR: How does that differ from the Big Five, then?

AG: These men who advise should be active coaches within their clubs, he says.

CR: All of the Big Five at the time were active within clubs across South Wales, and had been for years before any involvement with the Big Five. Many were active in developing a coaching system when such a thing didn't exist.

AG: These men, he says, should be chosen according to their experience as players, as backs and forwards, their experience as coaches and that there was a need to be aware of geography as well.

CR: The Big Five were either Welsh international players or British Lions. I think Carwyn might be referring there to the rift between East and West Wales that existed in the rugby world. He is right to say that because such a rivalry did exist. But as far as the Welsh selectors of the time were concerned, the boys from the East were in a minority. [Harry] Bowcott and Cliff Jones played for Cardiff, but [Rees] Stephens had played for Neath and I played for Llanelli and Swansea. Alun Thomas had played for Cardiff, Swansea and Llanelli. But Carwyn was right to note that point.

AG: And finally, the Welsh Coach and his advisers should look for the support of the coach of every club coach in Wales, by asking them to be a part of national coaching sessions at the start of each season. Wales, he says, is a small enough country to allow this to happen.

CR: I held regular coaching sessions with the coach of every club in Wales, concentrating on individual needs within the game as I saw them at the time: for example, the scrum or the back row. But, despite the fact that this was happening and wasn't something new that Carwyn was asking for, how the coaches reacted to what I had to say was a completely different matter. Some would listen, but others would ignore me. What I then had was a mixture of players, some of whom had been coached as I wanted them to be and others who hadn't received such coaching. Therefore, that sounds like a completely acceptable suggestion, but not of necessity one that would work.

In response to questions as to why the WRU decided to chose John Dawes as the new Welsh coach, he offers one specific suggestion.

I haven't thought of this before, but it's quite likely that the Union favoured stability and continuity in choosing Dawes. When I captained Wales, Dawes was a player. When I was coach, Dawes was captain and when I was manager, Dawes was coach. The Union most certainly favoured building on such foundations. Things were going well for the Welsh team, so why take the risk of changing a system that had given continued success? The choice at the time was between Carwyn and John Dawes. That's it. Carwyn pulled out and John walked in through the door.

This interpretation, however, is taking the story on one level only. But it is far more complex than the WRU refusing one man for the top job in Welsh rugby. It is perhaps more insightful to ask, what does this particular episode say about Carwyn himself? This approach to Carwyn's relationship with the WRU in the context of the Welsh Coaching vacancy is far more telling with regard to Carwyn the man than it is in terms of how he was treated by the Union that ran the game he loved in his own country.

A tired man

The circumstances surrounding the fact that Carwyn James never coached Wales, despite the fact that so many thought that he should, give us a clear insight into many aspects of Carwyn's life. Events that put him in a position where he could be considered, and then subsequently rejected, as coach of Wales tell us a great deal about the inner Carwyn, and also the way his fellow Welshmen reacted to him. This one incident then, in 1974, when he was in his mid-forties, opens a significant window on Carwyn James' life as a whole.

The letter doesn't resonate with the confidence and focus of a man who had achieved so much in rugby that most in that sporting world thought that coaching Wales was his divine right. Hadn't Alun Richards called him one of the most confident Welshmen of his generation? Carwyn doesn't exude the same belief that so many others did on his behalf. There are many complex and personal reasons for this apparent insecurity, however, which lie embedded in Carwyn's upbringing and subsequent life experiences. They are political, emotional and psycho-geographical forces that drove Carwyn James in all that he did.

Psychologically, confidence and ambition were usually part of Carwyn's DNA. As a teacher and head of rugby in Llandovery College, he began to think of coaching the British and Irish Lions. Not only had he not coached his country at that time, he hadn't coached a first-class rugby club in Wales either. But Carwyn didn't allow such things to prohibit him from thinking about far greater things, which would indeed have looked impossible at the time to most in the game. So why then did he deem the obstacles to being coach of Wales insurmountable? He had far more success and experience by that time. He was known throughout the world for his achievements and his pioneering rugby philosophy. But such support was seemingly insufficient.

Counter-intuitively, the success he had enjoyed could well have been an obstacle to his Welsh coaching ambition, rather than the fuel for those ambitions in the first place. The problem with success is having to follow it up. Where could he go next? He'd beaten the All Blacks with the Lions and his club. Wales, at the same time, were in a Golden Era of sparkling rugby and star players. How could he improve on his own achievements and the success of the Welsh team? It is credible to argue that he could have worked to ensure continuing success, but with such a task comes the very real possibility of failure. Carwyn wasn't ready for that.

He'd already shown that success didn't sit comfortably on his shoulders, or rather, that the trappings of success didn't. There's no doubt that he was overwhelmed with the attention the British and Irish Lions received when they returned from New Zealand in 1971. At Heathrow Airport, in the full glare of lights, cameras and thousands of welcoming fans, he asked that his players be left alone and given time to rest in the months following their return to their domestic worlds. It didn't happen, and he more than anyone else, was thrown into the full public spotlight for a long time after. He didn't like to refuse the invitations which followed to perform five or six speaking engagements a week throughout Wales and England, but his politeness cost him personally.

By 1974 Carwyn James was a tired man. He wrote his letter to the WRU in January of that year, when he was still a lecturer at Trinity College, Carmarthen, but he had already decided to leave at the end of that academic year. He had been persuaded to stay on as coach of Llanelli, but changes were afoot. He would be moving to live in a bedsit in Cardiff – moving out of the family home in Cefneithin, where he lived while at Trinity, and breaking the structured security he had enjoyed at home and previously during the 12 years at Llandovery College. In doing so, this man – who was at the pinnacle of world rugby having achieved the seemingly unachievable – moved to a bedsit in a friend's house.

The letter was written on Monday 28 January. Less than two weeks prior to that, on Thursday 13 January, his mother had passed away. She had only just been buried, therefore. Carwyn had an innate need to feel a strength underneath him and all around him through every independence of thought.

By the time he wrote the letter, the greatest strength of his life thus far had gone. He was only beginning to contemplate the emptiness left behind by the passing of such a formative, dominant influence. It might not have been enough on its own for him to change his mind, but it certainly was a central factor in a process that had started sometime earlier, and would have weighed down on him when he put pen to paper.

His friend, author Alun Richards, understood the wider implication of Carwyn not coaching Wales.

> Merlin waited for the nation to call him, but the nation never did.

Whatever the facts of the situation, there's no doubting the perception of them, and Alun Richards succinctly encapsulates the weight of those expectations. Such a weight precluded any hope of their realisation.

Carwyn's involvement with the WRU brings to mind the words of Professor Gwyn Alf Williams:

> What people believe to be true is as significant for history as what actually was true. Myth itself can become an operative historical reality.

In this story, the operative historical reality is that Carwyn was rejected because he couldn't have his own way. This chapter in the life of Carwyn, the Merlin of our rugby world, has an integral part in the rugby folklore of Wales, whatever the facts relating to it may be. The truth remains – Carwyn did not coach his country and Wales lost the opportunity to be led on to the field of play by perhaps the greatest coach the world has seen. Carwyn himself, however, had more of a role to play in this decision than has been accepted to date.

CHAPTER 19

At the city gates

And indeed there will be time
To wonder, 'Do I dare?' and, 'Do I dare?'
T S Eliot, 'The Love Song of J Alfred Prufrock'

A NEW LIFE meant a new home for Carwyn. He left the Hawen
bungalow and moved into a bedsit in the Penylan area of
Cardiff. Once he settled there, his new world almost entirely
revolved around rugby. There was no teaching, no lecturing.
It's an easy headline that says Carwyn's world disintegrated the
minute he moved to the city. That wasn't the biggest change for
him. The greater change was the increased importance rugby
took on in his life because of that move. For the first time, rugby
was everything. There was nothing to offer the balance that he
had previously enjoyed. He was, more than he'd ever been, face
to face with the beast that had shown him disappointment,
disillusionment and rebuttal on many an occasion. The eye
contact was more immediate and direct.

This would have been the seminal change had he not
moved to the city. But choosing to move home at such a time
proved to be an additional challenge. He could face anything
if his feet were on solid ground, but now he faced his biggest
change at a time when his terra firma wasn't there. It was a
double blow.

He didn't know for sure, but he probably had more than an
inkling that his main successes were behind him by that point,
as his response to the Welsh coaching vacancy suggests. He
was in effect moving from his house on the rock and building

a new one on sand. That was in Llwyn-Y-Grant Place, Penylan, Cardiff. His landlord was Derrick Jones, a pharmaceutical rep known to all and sundry as Doc. He came from Pen-y-groes in the Amman Valley, the one next to Carwyn's Gwendraeth Valley, and his father had worked in the same pit as Carwyn's. Because of Doc's work, his home was known as Voltarol Towers by its residents and their friends. Doc was recently divorced, which was why he was renting out rooms in his home. *Western Mail* journalist Bruce Morris also lived there. Not long after Carwyn settled there, another tenant moved in: John Dawes – the man who was given the Welsh coaching job Carwyn didn't get. The official coach and the people's choice lived under the same roof. As Dawes explains, this didn't seem to be a problem:

> Carwyn was far too much a professional and too much of a gentleman to let that interfere in our friendship. It was Carwyn that suggested I went to stay there, as getting the Welsh coach job meant me leaving London Welsh to come back to Cardiff. We would have chats about the game, of course, and about specific forthcoming games, but he never ever imposed his views on me.

Once John Dawes was there, Voltarol Towers became Coach Towers!

A further implication of Carwyn living in Coach Towers was the absence of the familiar reassurance of family members. Not one of his three mothers was there to look after him. At the times when he had left their care previously, he had been within institutions that gave him the support network previously provided by his family. The Navy and Llandovery were his surrogate mothers. 1974 reality however, was a rented room in a house full of bachelors.

Structure and discipline wouldn't have been obvious organising principles. His was the bachelor life of a famous person in Wales, where he would also be increasingly exposed to what Dylan Thomas called 'the eternal ugliness of the Welsh people'. This ugliness came from what Freud described as the

Carwyn in his bachelor digs

narcissism of small differences; a judgmental attitude that comes from an oversensitivity to small differences in those close by. This can lead to ridicule and bickering between individuals, to more serious conflict when it's between small nations. In Carwyn's small nation, small differences were greatly exaggerated and cause enough for schism.

Up until that point the one obvious indication of the untidiness of Carwyn's life, and his inability to keep his possessions in any kind of order, would have been the interior of his car. As mentioned previously, on the back seat, the front seat and the floors, there were papers, newspapers, unpaid cheques, parking fines, documents, a coat, a single shoe, ties given to him by rugby clubs, magazines, notes on a multitude of rugby matches and so much more. Now the room in which he lived turned out to be just as messy. Through all of this, however, he still presented himself immaculately.

Carwyn's inability to do the simple things in life is shown in two stories told by Doc and BBC colleague Martyn Williams. This is Doc's story:

> About two o clock one morning, I was away from home and I remembered that I had put a casserole in the oven about midday the day before. I phoned Carwyn and asked him to turn the oven off. I got home about nine that morning to see that the oven was still piping hot, though the casserole was on the table nearby. 'What happened, Carwyn?' I asked. The answer came back – he didn't know how to turn the oven off.

Martyn Williams remembers a story involving another Coach Towers resident, Angharad Trenchard-Jones, the cat.

> Doc was once more away from home because of his work. Carwyn was given the responsibility of looking after the cat in his absence. When Doc returned home, he went to feed the cat as he usually did. But she didn't want to know, and refused the food he offered. He opened a second tin to see if that would work. Angharad Trenchard-Jones still didn't want to know. He asked Carwyn if there had been any problems with feeding her while he was away. 'No,' said Carwyn, 'I gave her the lamb that was in the kitchen every day.' That was the lamb that Gwen had sent Carwyn for his Sunday lunch. Doc still didn't understand why the usual cat food hadn't been given, until Carwyn eventually confessed that he didn't know how to use the tin-opener!

Fortunately, there was less need to cook in Cardiff, as there were plenty of restaurants close by. Carwyn's favourites were the Riverside Chinese of an evening, and Gibsons during the day. Both were popular BBC haunts.

As far as his work was concerned, he set about developing his broadcasting. In the February of 1974, before leaving Trinity, he made a programme for the BBC called *Dilyn Afon* (Following a River). He went on a journey through the Gwendraeth, presenting the fables and virtues of the two Gwendraeth Rivers, the rivers that irrigated his home turf. It was a year when he made programmes for both the BBC and HTV, which was unusual. Both channels usually preferred to stick to their own, and not to use someone who worked for the other side.

In Conversation

As 1974 drew to a close, he recorded a series in English for HTV called *In Conversation*. It was broadcast in January 1975. There were four programmes in the series, in which Carwyn interviewed four leading figures who had varying ties with the sporting world. His guests were Irish international and five-times British Lion, Willie John McBride; influential sports journalist from New Zealand, Terry McLean; Englishman and music and cricket correspondent for *The Guardian*, Neville Cardus; and South African rugby administrator Danie Craven. Carwyn was at his best in these programmes, showing his ability and understanding. The fact that he drew four big names from outside Wales to the studios in Pontcanna says a great deal about him. This was the best use of Carwyn in a television studio, as he was given the freedom to play to his strengths.

The author has obtained transcripts of three of those programmes, and one instant impression they make is how little need there was for retakes and the re-asking of questions. Carwyn had a clear philosophy about interviewing. He believed that the only question that should be prepared beforehand was the first one. The next question would come from the answer to the first, and so on. Consequently, that first question had to be a good one, not a soft way in, but a direct beginning. His interview with Danie Craven is a good example of this.

> Now, Dr Danie, I have no doubt that you are the world's no.1 rugby figure. Would this be easier for you if you were not a South African?

Danie Craven's reply is to ask Carwyn what he means by such a question. Carwyn responds by asking the exact same question but in a different way. The resultant conversation is then about apartheid and rugby in South Africa. That conversation had a significance at the time because of the row in the sporting world about the reaction to apartheid. It also had a further significance because of Carwyn's own two previous personal encounters with that international row – refusing to watch Llanelli play South Africa in Llanelli, or to tour the same country with his club. The programme played a significant role in Carwyn's shift of attitude on apartheid. His questioning in it more than suggests that he wants to understand the situation, from a man he evidently respects. Craven explains his standpoint:

> Everybody in our country realises that we are facing a problem and a very big problem at that. Everybody is doing a lot of thinking in this connection and a lot has been done in the past, but I think where people disagree with us is that they want to have a revolutionary way to solve our problems, whereas we say, 'No, we are dealing with it in the evolutionary way.' The fact of the matter is that I feel it's our problem and only we can solve it. People are criticising us all the time – that doesn't help.

Carwyn follows up by asking what the next step is in the process that Craven has just outlined. They then discuss where rugby coaching is at in South Africa. It's made clear that there was no Coaching Organiser in that country as there was in Wales, and that Danie Craven wasn't convinced that there was a need for such a role – even though he admitted that there was a need for a more formal coaching structure.

And then when the conversation returns to apartheid, in the context of coaching, Craven says that there was no black player who could play to a high enough standard to be considered for selection as an international Springbok. Developing a coaching system in order to make sure that black players would reach international standard was a part of the evolutionary process Craven referred to. The programme draws to a close with Carwyn making his own position clear:

CJ: Now, you will appreciate that during the last few seasons
       I have been an opponent of what has been happening
       in rugby football in South Africa. Recently I was asked
       whether I would like to come out to coach to South Africa.
       Could you give me some reasons why I should come along?
DC: Well, Carwyn, it's obvious. We form a brotherhood of sport,
       of rugby. Wherever the game is played, we have our friends,
       and to me a rugby player in one country belongs to all of us
       because of this world of ours which is our own. If we have
       a friend and he is in hospital, we go to see him. If we have a
       friend who gets into trouble, we support him. We stand by
       him. Now, South Africa is in trouble but we are still rugby
       players, we are still respected wherever the game is played,
       so I hope, and I think it is so. That being the case, even
       if you have something against us, you will still be on our
       side. I think the more you would come to South Africa, the
       more you could help South Africa with its problems. But
       by staying away, I don't think you will help us. So you must
       come to us.

In the years following this programme, Carwyn went to South Africa more than once. The overall impression throughout the programme is that Carwyn is asking his questions in order to understand Craven's viewpoint, not to catch him out. But that doesn't mean he is not direct in his questioning.

In the years after the broadcast of the programme there were significant developments on the battlefield of sport and apartheid. In 1977 there was a Summit of Commonwealth Leaders at Gleneagles, which resulted in a declaration that Commonwealth countries would not develop sporting ties of any kind with South Africa. The following year, the Scottish rugby team cancelled their proposed tour to South Africa, and the Spingboks didn't tour Britain as planned. In 1979, Australia cancelled a tour of South Africa. But it wasn't a straightforward situation. In that same year, many clubs went to the country on rugby tours, including Llanelli, Cardiff and Newport.

In the last years of his life, Carwyn wrote a book with former 1971 British Lion Chris Rea, called *Injured Pride*. It was an account of the British and Irish Lions tour of South Africa in 1980, a tour which Carwyn covered as a reporter for the BBC. The first chapter of the book is entitled 'Sport and Politics', and the last chapter discusses what future there is for rugby in South Africa. They refer to the reaction of the Welsh clubs to their visit to South Africa:

> They all said the same thing. South Africa had gone a long way towards fulfilling the demands of the politically-minded. These reports, and their own observations, made a great impression on the four home unions' committee.

The response to this favourable feedback from the clubs was that the four home unions invited a South African Barbarian team to tour the UK. The British government, under the leadership of Margaret Thatcher, was not happy at all. She reiterated the Gleneagles agreement as the basis of her objection. She was not placated by the condition the Unions imposed on their South African counterpart, which stated that the squad should include eight white players, eight black and eight of mixed race. That condition was accepted and the tour went ahead:

> Most important of all, though, the tour was a success from every point of view. The players were good tourists, and the integration of colours was perfect.

The tour was seen as a success, one which managed to integrate players from various ethnic origins in the same squad. To apartheid's opponents, however, this was a superficial exercise which concealed the reality of the situation. Carwyn's viewpoint in the book *Injured Pride* is that he saw the value of the South African Barbarian tour. It was a sign of the progress made, a step on the evolutionary path Craven had outlined in the programme for HTV.

Plans to send the Lions to South Africa were already underway when the Barbarians came to the UK, but it was still not a clear-cut decision. All four unions were contacted by the Minister of Sport, reiterating the government's position of standing by the Gleneagles agreement. The Irish and Scottish Unions voted first, and came down in favour of the Lions tour by a large majority. Wales were next and they decided to back the tour as well, but with the smallest of margins: 13 votes to 12. England backed the tour with a large majority.

In *Injured Pride* Carwyn makes his point clear:

> Few people care for the policy of apartheid which has prevailed in South Africa, but most ordinary level-headed sportsmen, and women, are too engrossed in their particular pastime to bother about the political thinking of their opponents... Until Russia invaded Afghanistan, it could be said that because an Englishman wanted to run in the Olympics in Moscow it did not mean that he agreed with or condoned the type of government under which the people in the Union of Soviet Socialist Republics have to live. Neither did it mean that because a man played rugby against South Africa that he agreed with or condoned apartheid.

The Carwyn preparing Llanelli to play South Africa in January 1970 wouldn't have expressed such views. But he wasn't a man to close his mind on an issue once and for all. He was open to persuasion, a man who would hold to a standpoint until reasoned argument persuaded him otherwise. At the end of the book, as he looks ahead, his comments are more political:

Time is not on the side of the white minority. They must, as soon as possible, legislate more in favour of their second-class citizens, educate them better, and give them far more responsibility in the running of the country. The voice of Bishop Desmond Tutu is an important one to which South Africa's Prime Minister must listen.

An over and an octave

In that same series, on the programme broadcast on 29 January 1975, Neville Cardus was his guest. Without doubt this was the man who was more of an inspiration for Carwyn than anyone else. Carwyn himself described him as his *maestro di vita*: his master of life.

They were both united by a simple, working-class and not-privileged upbringing, a passion for the arts and a deep love for sport, and the way they both combined art and sport in their work.

Cardus was 77 years old when he recorded the programme and Carwyn 30 years younger than him. There's an air of master and disciple to this programme, although Carwyn more than holds his own as he faces his hero. In a warm, personal moment, the two share memories of their common childhood ritual of having a bath in front of the coal fire, singing the modulator and playing on the streets:

CJ: I love this sentence which you wrote, Sir Neville: 'Snow glistens in all the memories of one's boyhood.' You know, this sense of wonderful fairyland amongst cricket and music for you?

NC: I don't think we talked about 'escape' in those days. That was a thing... a lot of words have been invented that I never used to hear. I lived in a very poor place where we never knew where the next week's meal was coming from but I never heard the word 'frustration' and I never heard the word 'escape'. I went out in those days to enjoy myself... I decided that I was going to make my living from the things I loved and I was very fond of cricket.

Cardus learned his cricket on the streets of Rusholme in Manchester and at the ground at Old Trafford. He learned his music from books in the Manchester Free Library and the Hallé Hall (Free Trade Hall) in the city. He taught himself German so that he could better understand the classical music world. Carwyn, for his part, initially familiarised himself with opera and theatre in the Cross Hands Hall before going on to understand Welsh, Russian, Italian and English drama and literature. He indulged in cricket in his home village and on holiday in Rhydlewis, as well as in Llandovery. He too appreciated his culture through more than one language. Like Cardus, he saw sport as an expression of the society into which he was born:

> CJ: With reference to McLaren, you write somewhere about him and say, 'In those days there was aristocratic leisure.' Were there such days?
>
> NC: ...Now, you've got the Welfare State today, which has been a marvellous thing, but you have an average now. There's no working class and there's no aristocracy, and things are very average and the individuality is going. Certainly going out of cricket. The curious thing is the individuals remaining in first class cricket today are the overseas players...

The basis for their mutual admiration was the fact that they shared the same values and spirit.

Cardus wrote two autobiographies, but both were then edited into one volume called *My Life*. The last chapter is called 'Fulfilment':

> I became a *Manchester Guardian* writer and I travelled as far from my Manchester slum as Australia. I heard music in Vienna and I saw cricket played in Sydney. These were not so much ambitions as the dreams of a waif and stray... The chances were a thousand to one against any considerable development of whatever gifts were inherited by me...

Carwyn was as fortunate. He too came from an unassuming, ordinary background. It wasn't as impoverished as Cardus', but it was no more privileged. Carwyn also had a language and a culture to lift him from the simplicity of his beginnings and to open a window on the world that Cardus hadn't had. But both saw the world in the same way and were united by a philosophy that Cardus sums up in one sentence:

> Without creative urge and imagination, man would be less than the animals.

Cardus and Carwyn were unusual in that they expressed such a philosophy in both the sporting and cultural worlds.

Amongst the hundreds of invitations Carwyn received to speak to organisations and societies, following his Lions success in particular, was one to speak at the Mount Sorrel Hotel in Barry. He was invited there by the businessmen of the town. One of their number, a member of the family who owned the Dan Evans department store in the town, Alcwyn Deiniol Evans, remembers the evening well. The audience invitation had been thrown open to the rugby clubs of the area as well, because of who the speaker was. Subsequently, the room was full to bursting on the evening Carwyn was to speak there. Everyone wanted to hear what the successful coach of the British Lions had to say. Carwyn got to his feet to address the expectant crowd, and announced his topic for the evening – Neville Cardus and his love of music! That's what Carwyn wanted to share, and it mattered not one whit to him what the audience wanted to hear. There is no official record of how the Barry rugby boys responded.

Coach Towers

Carwyn's writing would usually take place at the kitchen table in Llwyn-y-Grant Place and would go on into the early hours of the morning. The demands on his time showed no sign of abating, either. His landlord, Doc, noted that at this time in

Carwyn's life, it was not unusual for him to be out speaking to groups six evenings a week, which could often include going back and forth to different parts of England in the same week. There were occasions when every speaking engagement in one week was in England. On such occasions, Carwyn would often ask friends to drive him to his destinations. One of these was BBC colleague Martyn Williams:

> Every time I took him somewhere, he would more often than not want me to take the more indirect route. If we left Cardiff, for example, in order to go to somewhere in Monmouthshire, he would ask to go towards Merthyr and the Heads of the Valleys route as opposed to the more direct route eastwards. Whenever there was an opportunity to do so, he would turn towards the hills and the mountains, even if that made the journey longer. I think that said quite a lot about Carwyn at that time.

This need to lift up his eyes to the hills, from whence he would evidently receive some help, was a very biblical habit for Carwyn, resonating with his Sunday School upbringing. But, in another manifestation of his inherent dualities, he would also seek excellence wherever he could, and chose to spend time with the most high profile of people. An example of this surfaces in another story told by Martyn Williams:

> I arrived at the house in Penylan one day. As I walked into the living room, I could see that someone was sitting in one of the armchairs. Carwyn introduced me to him, but there really was no need for such an introduction. I knew it was successful football manager Dave Sexton. I sat there quietly listening to two sporting geniuses discuss their craft. I could see that both were learning from each other.

A central tenet of Carwyn's philosophy was to learn from the best. Sexton was a particularly good example of this desire. Carwyn befriended him while Sexton was at Chelsea, experiencing both FA Cup and European Cup Winners' Cup success with the London side. They were still good friends when Sexton joined Man U the year Carwyn left for Rovigo. The former coach of the Man U of the rugby world kept his alliance with the coach of the actual Man U.

Theomemphus and the Cup

In 1976, however, he decided to end his links with coaching at Llanelli. He had said that he was going to do so previously but this time it was for real, bringing seven very successful seasons with the club to an end. It was another move that lifted one of the secure anchors of his life. He would soon resume coaching with another club, but before he did so, a book was published that revealed a great deal about Carwyn.

The book was a Welsh-language novel, called *Mae Theomemphus yn Hen* (Theomemphus is Old) and it was written by his friend, poet and fellow lecturer, Dafydd Rowlands. Carwyn played a part in the story of that novel. The title comes from a 1764 work by prolific Welsh hymn writer, William Williams, Pantycelyn, *Bywyd a Marwolaeth Theomemphus* (The Life and Death of Theomemphus) which is a work looking at the emotions and temptations that Christian conversion addresses and deals with. For Dafydd Rowlands, a former Presbyterian minister, it was a work based on a very personal psychological journey to find out more about his father, who had left the family home when Dafydd was a child. From that point onwards, there was no contact at all between father and child, even though, remarkably, they still went to the same chapel for a short period of time. Following the father's death, however, Dafydd the son wanted to know more about the man who had given him life, but whom he had grown to hate and despise. As the words on the back cover of the book say, in relation to the novel's main character, John Rawlins:

> John Rawlins was brought up on hatred and bitterness towards
> his father. He hated him with all his soul through the difficult and

325

lonely years of his childhood, a hatred that became an integral part of his constitution and personality.

Dafydd the son set out on a journey to know more about his father's roots in Ireland. He had a travelling companion on that search, Carwyn James. The other main character in the novel is called Llwyd. He is Carwyn. The two travelled to Ireland together in 1973, although the book wasn't published until 1977. It was hailed as an innovative work, a self-exploratory novel which was a combination of descriptive, lyrical and stream-of-consciousness prose as well as reflective, analytical free-verse poetry.

Descriptive passages in the novel more than suggest that Llwyd is Carwyn: there's the untidy car full of papers, books, unopened letters, unpaid cheques and, particularly, the one shoe. There's also the habit of falling asleep while travelling in the car, his delight in stopping for meals at every opportunity, as well as his fondness for red wine and Solzhenitsyn. There's the rugby link and the fact that Llwyd has many female friends.

It's also easy to recognise Carwyn's character in the character Llwyd in the novel. The mannerisms, the sayings, the attitudes are all Carwyn's. In fact, it's difficult not to think that the work is a factual account of Carwyn James. This feeling takes a surreal turn in the second half of the novel, when the character Llwyd is sitting in a pub in Ireland deep in conversation with some locals as to the rugby merits of a certain Carwyn James! This amusing snapshot gives us a picture of Carwyn's own personality. He is in a group of people talking about himself, but under another guise. He himself knows who the real Carwyn is, but he's talking with others as if he's someone else, in an echo of the yearning for privacy and reluctance towards disclosure that was inherently Carwyn. Significantly, the novel shows that not even Llwyd's friends know him properly.

In an experimental novel such as this, which is as much of a psychological journey as a geographical one, questions are asked about identity, belonging, relationships and loss.

More complex questions about existence are also asked, not surprisingly for a man who was both a minister and a poet. The darker side is visited and explored. As the character John Rawlins faces such issues, it's difficult to separate Llwyd and Carwyn in the novel.

As much as this is the story of Dafydd Rowlands' personal quest, it would be misleading to think that Llwyd was a secondary character, however. Self-exploratory passages interject with the storytelling narrative, and Dafydd Rowlands' journey to find his father's roots turns into a metaphor for Carwyn's journey to find himself. Carwyn's role in the narrative is something that has impressed Catrin Heledd Richards, who is writing her PhD thesis on Dafydd Rowlands and *Mae Theomemphus yn Hen*.

> At the beginning of my research, I thought that Llwyd was a secondary figure, almost incidental, there to prop up the main story. But now, having studied more of the novel and Carwyn's own life, it's evident that the novel is dependent on the character based on Carwyn. He is there to give a certain lightness to the narrative, an essential counterpoint to the psychological and emotional exploration. It's as if Llwyd embodies many of the characteristics that would have been Rawlins' if his father hadn't disappeared, the Rawlins without the bitterness and resentment. Further, as Rowland's search for his father develops it becomes evident that Llwyd's chracteristics are similar to John Rawlins' father's traits. This emphasis on the relationship that father and son could have had develops a further significance when seen through the eyes of a childless Llwyd.
>
> Rawlins' psychological exploration is a mirror on Carwyn's own life. It's possible that Rawlins' meditations are based on a great deal that Dafydd Rowlands knew about Carwyn himself. There's a heavy irony in the fact that the journey Rowlands and Rawlins embark on is what Carwyn experienced himself: the journeys to the dark side, the asking of questions relating to identity and belonging. This is especially true of the section that deals with his thoughts on children. Rowlands knew that Carwyn loved the company of children even though he had none of his own.

In another work of Dafydd Rowlands, 'Archipelago', a poem written for one of his sons, he says:

Nid bywyd yn unig sy'n daith;
Mordaith yw'r hunan hefyd
Mae gwybod hynny'n bwysig;
Mor bwysig â dysgu nofio
Rhwng ynysoedd dy feddwl.
Nofio sy'n cadw rhywun rhag boddi.
Nofio, ac adnabod y môr.

'It's not only life that's a journey
Self is a sea journey too.
Knowing that is important,
As important as learning to swim
Between the islands of your mind.
Swimming is what keeps one from drowning,
Swimming, and knowing the sea.'

Reading this novel certainly gives us an intimate view of Carwyn that is not to be found, for example, in the personal memoir of his friend Alun Richards. There's a phrase in the original eighteenth-century Theomemphus work that resonates with Carwyn's own life. Williams the hymn writer implores the reader to pay heed to Theomemphus' plight:

Ond cymmerwch Theomemphus ar ei ffyn baglau, a charwch ef,
canys y mae yn tynnu tua'r bywyd.

'But accept Theomemphus on his crutches, and love him, because he is pulling himself towards life.'

It would be a long haul for Carwyn on his own particular crutches, supporting his own particular failing limbs. But he was always pulling towards life.

CHAPTER 20

Ti voglio bene

*Dissi, a quelle parole, che gli uomini che volevan fare
a lor modo, bisognava che si facessino un mondo a
lor modo, perché in questo non si usava così.*

'I said, in response to his words, that men who wanted to do
things in their own way had better make a world in their own
way, because in this one things were not done like that.'

Benvenuto Cellini, *Autobiography*

TO ALL OUTWARD appearances, Carwyn was a busy and
productive man during these years. Journalism and
broadcasting kept the wolf from the door. He was a rugby
correspondent for BBC Wales, who would also contribute to
BBC Network sports programmes. In 1976, for example, he was
reporting on events in the Commonwealth Games in Canada.
He had started to contribute to *The Guardian* as well.

But a new voice began to call on Carwyn, one with an Italian
accent. Rovigo Rugby Club in Italy needed a new coach and
they wanted someone of excellence. Carwyn was approached,
and his answer was almost immediate: he would accept the
position. The news spread like wildfire through the rugby
world, accelerated by the fact that the British and Irish Lions
were on tour in New Zealand when the news was announced.
Just before the beginning of the 1977–78 season, Carwyn
moved to live in Italy.

Rovigo lies on low fertile flatlands between the two rivers,
the Adige and the Po, in the Veneto region of Italy, the same

region as Venice. The plains reach out for miles around the town, towards the foothills in the distance, giving the warm light of north-eastern Italy plenty of room to play. Carwyn had never before experienced such expanse around him. There were no black pyramids here, no narrow valley slopes, no city concrete all around nor darkened corridors of learning. Rovigo certainly gave him a new vista. The hope was that it would also prove to be the balm that would change his outlook.

Via I Monti

Carwyn's new home was number 5 Via I Monti in Rovigo town. He had a first-floor three-bedroomed flat there. Carwyn would have wanted to learn Italian as a mark of respect for the people and culture he was now a part of. The club were just as keen for him to do so and contacted an English teacher at a local state grammar school, the Liceo Scientifico, who also taught in a private grammar school, the Liceo Linguistico. This was called the Collegio Vescovile, in light of the fact that it was a college run by the Rovigo diocese. The rugby club asked Angelo Morello to be Carwyn's tutor. He agreed, and the two became lifelong friends. Angelo shared his recollections with me:

> I had no particular interest in rugby, although living in Rovigo it was impossible to ignore it. Rugby was everything here; it was and still is a rugby town, like no other in Italy. I'm sure that helped Carwyn settle more quickly than he might have done otherwise. Franco Olivieri, the main man at Sanson Rovigo, flew to the UK to ask Carwyn to be coach at his club. There was a clear sense at the time that things weren't going that well for Carwyn in Wales. His relationship with the rugby authorities there was not good and he was not popular in all rugby circles. Olivieri asked if I could help by being an interpreter for the new coach. That's how we met.

Angelo soon realised that Carwyn had felt a strong need

to turn his back on the situation in Wales. Two words Angelo says he often heard Carwyn use in relation to the Welsh rugby world were 'judgmental' and 'philistine'.

Within the first two months of Carwyn moving to his flat, *Sunday Times* rugby writer John Hopkins went to stay with him. Author and friend Alun Richards was already there. The three went out for a meal one evening and Hopkins asked Carwyn why he had moved to Italy:

> He was tired, he said. His success with the 1971 Lions had cast him on to a carousel that was spinning faster and faster. While his bank balance increased, his health deteriorated. The prospect of a sabbatical, as he called it, of learning a new language, of getting back to coaching and having the time to finish a book on rugby, were irresistible.

He had thrown in his lot with rugby when he left Trinity, despite the disappointments he had experienced in the name of the sport. He was stubborn enough to do so – he also knew what he had achieved, and that spurred him on. He didn't persevere with his rugby ambitions just to prove a point to his detractors, but that kind of motivation wouldn't have been too far below the surface.

Carwyn got to grips with day-to-day life in Italy. The man who couldn't turn the oven off in Cardiff had to go shopping for food in Italy, and in Italian. The man who wouldn't bother to cash cheques and who turned to bank manager brother Dewi to ask what his bank balance was, had to use Italian *lire* to buy his goods. The club, thankfully, had aranged for someone to clean the flat for him three times a week, and she would wash his clothes too. He was also given a car, a red mini.

Language and bulls

Carwyn took to the task of learning Italian with ease. As with Russian, he then started to read literature in his new language. A particular favourite of his was an Italian translation of

Ernest Hemingway's *Death in the Afternoon*, as Angelo Morello remembers:

> I would go to his flat and we would sit at the table and read through the book. It was remarkable really that Carwyn could learn the language by reading the novel in Italian, but he enjoyed it so much. I would often take my daughter with me to these lessons and she would sit and listen to Carwyn reading.

BBC Wales filmed one of these Italian lessons, during which Carwyn read from Hemingway. The programme was made by Onllwyn Brace and called *Llanelli Bolognese*. Angelo and daughter Marcia listen as he reads one of Hemingway's famous sentences, in Italian:

> ...without the sun, the best bullfighter is not there. He is like a man without a shadow.

In an article for an Italian newspaper, Carwyn uses this sentence as he reflects on a game his team have just played in inhospitable weather:

> There was no sun, no light. It was a bleak, damp day; the breeze blew across the field into the stand, and it was cold, miserably cold.
>
> During the match my mind wandered and I thought of Spain and the sun and Hemingway's *Death in the Afternoon*. He contends, rightly I think, that the theory, practice and spectacle of bullfighting have all been built on the assumption that the sun must shine; and when it doesn't shine, over a third of the bullfight is missing. The sun is the best bullfighter, and without the sun the best bullfighter is not there. He is like a man without a shadow.

Like Carwyn, Hemingway moved to live in a strange land, and this work of his that Carwyn loved was as much about the author's impressions of his new land, Spain, as it was about bullfighting. Carwyn would have warmed to Hemingway's concise, understated style as well, a style he himself used orally and in the written word. As a person, Hemingway was a complex man. War, love, loss and barrenness are regular themes in his work.

Carwyn also used records to help him with his Italian, ones he would play in his flat regularly. Referring to this way of learning, Carwyn said once:

> Quite often, that's the only voice that could be heard in the flat.

A throwaway line almost, but one which shows that not every minute was one of excitement. Having said that, he made a conscious decision not to install a phone in the flat. Another duality.

Mediterranean blood

Angelo Morello impressed on Carwyn very early on that he needed to understand the Italian temperament as well as the language and culture.

> I told him that he needed to be a lot less North European in his attitude and in his way of dealing with people, and a lot more Mediterranean. There was no point in him expecting people to turn up ready and fit and knowing what to do. He needed to be more like a father telling the child 'this is what you must do: do this, do that...' Carwyn didn't win the title in his first season because he didn't grasp this clearly enough.

This was evidently a topic for broader discussion for Carwyn, as John Hopkins remembers a similar conversation:

> 'Italian players are serious, but only up to a point,' James said one night as we sat and talked after dinner. 'There is something of the amateur spirit about them that reminds me of the pre-coaching days at home.' His biggest problem he said, had been to blend his own Celtic approach with the less-disciplined, more bravura Italian temperament.

Carwyn imposed one match-day discipline which would have challenged the bravura Italian temperament. He put a stop to their habit of having a full meal, with wine, an hour or so before a game. A brave step indeed for a man in Bacchus' own country. He did know how to give back if he had to take away though. He began the tradition of both teams sitting down for a meal together after the match, something which was well-established back in Wales. Prior to this, both teams would leave the stadium as soon as the game was over.

On the speaking circuit in Britain, one of Carwyn's popular talks was the one in which he described the national characteristics of a people according to the way they played their rugby. He wrote an article along these lines about the Italians:

> They are gentle people who burst into emotion much more easily than our players back home. They love the instant comment, the shrug of the shoulders, the volley of words. Their volatile temperament has to be curbed. Perhaps I am doing them an injustice by not allowing them to talk, but I feel that discipline is far more important. In training I am deliberately quiet because I want them to be quiet as well.

A few years before this, he wrote a very similar piece for the *Western Mail* back home in Wales, but with reference to cricket, not rugby. In an article entitled 'Bradman... lbw James', an echo of his childhood reminiscences for the same paper, after describing his own cricketing experience of going to see Glamorgan as a child, he then comments on the relationship between cricket and the Welsh:

> I have heard it said, too often, that cricket is not a game for Welshmen. They may be alluding to the birth of the game and its history, but the pedigree of rugby football is equally suspect, and we seem to be doing all right at that.
> Is it temperament, then, that the game of cricket is too slow and ponderous for us? There is, I suppose, some truth in the

belief that we lack stamina, that we start well and finish badly and maintain our enthusiasm for short periods only. And then we think of Emrys Davies and Allan Jones: stayers, grafters, with the guts, the durability and the hardness of purpose to match even the Australians.

Craftsmen doing an honest day's work. Untypical, it could be said, the triumph of self-discipline over the Celtic temperament, in which unquestionably there is poetry, style and the spirit of adventure, but dampened too often by a climate too cold and wet to breed the cavalier-type batsmen who thrive on hard wickets on which shots can be played because the ball comes through true and fast.

With such an acute understanding of the way national characteristics guide the spirit and execution of any particular sport, it's little wonder that this was a part of his settling in Rovigo. Before his first season ended, he reflected on his arrival in Rovigo.

Naturally, in my first few weeks as coach of Sanson, I made many mistakes. I didn't understand Italian rugby. Now, having seen every team in the Championship, my understanding is better. It is likely that from now on I shall make fewer mistakes.

Carwyn was a part of a broader Welsh rugby presence in Italy. Also there was former candidate for British Lions coach, Roy Bish, who was coach of the Roma rugby team, known as Algida after an ice cream brand. Before that he had been coach of the Italian national team and he would go on to coach Treviso. Gwyn Evans was now in charge of the Italian national side, and Bernard Thomas, one of Carwyn's prodigies from Llanelli, played for Rovigo. The Welsh made a significant contribution to the development of Italian rugby in the Seventies. Carwyn was asked to be the coach of the Italian national side. But he knew that would involve a lot of behind-the-scenes politics which came far too close to the situation back home in Wales for him. He therefore gave them a wise answer. He said he would coach the Italian team on the condition that he was assisted by former French international Pierre Villepreux, working in Italy at the time, and one other coach. This was a first-class way for him to say no without saying no.

Visitors

Carwyn's sister Gwen went to stay with her brother more than once, but Alun Richards was the first of Carwyn's friends to be invited to stay with him in Rovigo – a clear sign of their friendship. That's what we might conclude, at least. The reality was different, as Richards says in his book, *Carwyn: A Personal Memoir*.

> At this time in 1977, although I had met him previously and known of him for most of my adult life, I did not really know him… and as I was fond of telling him, we were as different as chalk and cheese… I was known in Wales for my critical views on the Welsh establishment. He on the other hand, apart from his differences with the Welsh Rugby Union, was one of the most confident Welshmen of his generation and moved easily in those Welsh-speaking areas of Establishment Wales which, in my view, stubbornly refuse to admit that there is no greater dividing line than that formed by language.

Alun Richards came to understand that many had been invited, and as he says,

> He needed them all. But only a few came.

Carwyn might well have wanted to flee from Wales, but he didn't want the Welsh to flee from him.

His loneliness was often that experienced within a crowd. His flat was often full of visitors, players, officials, friends and the guests who did turn up. Two regular callers were Dirk Naudè and Dries Coetzer, two South African players in the Rovigo team. Dirk Naudè was the jumper in the line-out. Dries was very clever, and a little shorter than Dirk. Naudè was incredibly strong and very difficult to stop or tackle – it often took two or more players to stop him. Visitors rarely arrived empty-handed. When these social gatherings were over, the cleaning lady faced a significant challenge!

When Alun Richards got to know Carwyn better, he came to see that many took advantage of Carwyn's kind nature:

> For there was in him a sensitivity that made him the prey of other people, a gentleness of nature that did not want to offend, the capacity for which he secretly admired in other people.

In *Llanelli Bolognese*, Carwyn shows that he warmed to the people and town of Rovigo.

> The word to describe them [from a fourteenth-century poem by Cino da Pistioa] is *'gentilía'*, I think; a warm people, close to you, they like a chat and their interests are wide-ranging. I think that they are very fortunate that they have a splendid theatre, a glorious art gallery, beautiful churches and most of the residents live in a villa or a flat.

Carwyn is back in the rhythm and swing of life in Cefneithin and Cross Hands, with an art gallery thrown in for good measure. He would have heard echoes of the conversations in the shop, the Post Office or on the street corner; holding Dafydd Morris' hand to go to chapel and rugby as a backdrop to it all. In that same programme, Carwyn delivers a fairly long piece to camera, walking from the back of the stage in the Teatro Sociale to its front:

> A snippet of *'Sosban Fach'*, a hymn or two, says (Welsh poet) Crwys, and that's the thrill that faces any player as they come out in the Arms Park. But in walking on this stage, this is the wonderful sight that Gigli would have seen when he sang here. For me, he is one of the best tenors in the world, better even than

Caruso. This theatre reminds me of the Bolshoi in Moscow. It's a theatre typical of so many in so many Italian towns, where it gives prominence to culture, especially singing and especially opera. I am so pleased that I've had the opportunity to listen to so many wonderful voices singing in such a wonderful theatre as this.

He would also travel to Padua to see operas and, of course, to Venice. He was a regular visitor to the Accademia dei Concordi, the art gallery in Rovigo, and he had his favourite paintings there. He was particularly drawn to *Madonna Col Bambino* and *Cristo Portacroce*. The former is a painting of Mary and the baby Jesus, the latter an emotive painting of the crucifixion. He was also a regular visitor to their weekday talks on various cultural subjects.

Between the theatre and the Accademia was one of Carwyn's favourite wine bar and coffee haunts. Others lie behind the Accademia on the town's second piazza. The church overlooks both. Daily, the townsfolk would congregate on these piazzas for a chat and a coffee, Carwyn regularly in their midst. By the end of his first season in Rovigo, Carwyn could count many of these people as his friends.

Carwyn had started to teach in the grammar school where Angelo taught, taking classes every Wednesday from eight in the morning until one o'clock. He taught young

Carwyn and the *Madonna Col Bambino*, Rovigo Rugby Stadium
Paolo Giolli

338

people between 14 and 18 years old and shared his knowledge of English Literature with them, in particular Shakespeare and Milton. Lessons over, each student in turn invited Carwyn to have lunch with them. He did his utmost to accommodate them all. Angelo Morello remembers one lesson in particular:

> He was sharing his love of Milton with them and discussing specifically that day the sonnet he wrote on his blindness, 'When I Consider How My Light Is Spent'. His interpretation of that work and his storytelling had a major effect on one student. I can remember her sitting there, in some kind of hypnotic trance as Carwyn spoke.

Carwyn was also teaching at the private grammar school there, Collegio Vescovile. Once again he was in an ecclesiastical educational establishment. Another who made the journey to visit him was his former Head of Department at Trinity, Norah Isaac. Carwyn wasted no time in involving her in some lessons when she was in Rovigo just before Christmas 1977. She taught the students how to perform *Hamlet* but she also shared some of her Welsh heritage with them. She took a drama class there, working with a group of girls on the Welsh fable of Blodeuwedd. She wrote to these girls after returning to Wales:

> You, the eight ladies who enacted the dialogues yesterday, displayed both interest and talent. I would have loved to stay with you to see the steady development in dramatic technique. You showed versatility in the way you were able to change mood and character, while in the crowd-scene situation there was real drama. All this, to me, was a thrill and more than compensated for the misery of the weather!

She ends the letter, 'My privilege was to meet you; my pride to have "taught" you, All my *cariad* (love), Norah Isaac.'

Carwyn also taught fairly often in the school. There are stories of him teaching Italian children to say the Welsh place name Llanfairpwllgwyngyllgogerychwyrndrobwllllanty siliogogoch. Ever the educator, in one instance he picked the word 'candle' and discussed what that word was in different languages, including Welsh. He also shared some Welsh hymn and folk tunes with them.

Norah Isaac enjoyed Rovigo social life with Carwyn. She went to the Teatro Sociale, for example:

> How many towns in Britain, of similar population to that of Rovigo, could boast of such a performance in such a theatre on this particular Saturday evening?

She enjoyed the café culture very much, but there was one major reservation:

> The story is the same everywhere. These places exist mainly for menfolk! Where are the womenfolk? Are they not like us in Britain, turning in and out of cafés for chats and scandals daily?

The All Blacks once more

Carwyn and All Blacks history came face to face once more in 1977. That was the year in which the rugby giants from New Zealand went to Italy for the very first time. They were on their way to France and a stop-off in Italy was arranged en route. Carwyn was asked to prepare a President's XV team to face the All Blacks. The match was in Padua, and Alun Richards and John Hopkins went with Carwyn to see the game.

New Zealand won 17–9, a very respectable score indeed for the first Italian attempt to challenge the All Blacks. Carwyn was happy with that result. He declared, like a proud parent:

> Italian rugby came of age.

Two years later, the full national Italian side would face the All Blacks for the first time. Carwyn was again involved in an innovative development.

Carwyn in print

Carwyn contributed regularly to two Italian newspapers while he was there. During his first year, he wrote for *Il Resto del Carlino*, a Bologna daily which was also distributed in the regions of Le Marche and Emilia-Romagna. In his second year, he wrote for *Il Gazzettino*, a Venice newspaper that was distributed widely through a large area of north-eastern Italy. He chose to write for both in order not to be seen to favour one over the other.

As regards rugby, *Il Gazzettino* was much more important because this sport was, and still is, highly popular in the Veneto region. Having said this, Emilia Romagna has had some good rugby clubs; for example Parma, now the home of Italian regional team Zebre. On both papers, Carwyn was paid much more than the best-paid local freelance journalists – on *Il Resto del Carlino* he was paid L.30,000 an article and the following year *Il Gazzettino* paid him L.80,000. Alun Richards' and Norah Isaac's articles were paid the same, the cheque made payable to Carwyn in both cases. But money wasn't the issue for Carwyn, and he didn't care about any payment.

30 articles that he wrote for these papers came to light during the research for this work. The articles are all the originals in Carwyn's handwriting which were sent to Angelo Morello for translation. Many articles include instructional notes from Carwyn to Angelo. One article is in Alun Richards' handwriting, no doubt a further example of Carwyn asking a friend to bail him out of a deadline he knew he wasn't going to meet. He did the same with his articles for *The Guardian* – with BBC colleagues Martyn Williams and Emrys Jones stepping in – and Welsh-language cultural magazine *Barn* (Opinion), with Rita Williams helping out in this instance.

Carwyn's writing says a great deal about him. Every article follows the same basic structure. Firstly they are all match reports. The opening invariably includes a literary or historical reference, or a philosophical comment. Then the report on

3/1

Dear Angelo,

Ciao.

①. Il Resto — articolo — enclosed which I leave with *Sandro* + photograph, which he will deal with.

②. Can you please translate the article, " Impact of the counter-attack ", for the Italian Federation + please send it to Bryn Evans at Genova. Many thanks.

③. I have been given a lovely book by the Director of my Bank — multi bello libro (Opera grafica — Cagli) — + I wonder if you would send him a letter of thanks on my behalf. His address is on the enclosed envelope.

④. Also, please a letter of thanks to the President of Sansa Rugby, Possetti (+ thanks to the Dirigenti), including the following points:
  ⓐ Many thanks for the Xmas gift of paintings / drawings by Navarrini G. — ex-player of Sansa.

Note to Angelo Morello about translations

342

the game in hand, often including a technical analysis, before bringing the article to a close by applying the comments made in the opening paragraph. He regularly refers to Wales.

In one article, entitled 'Between the bulging Po and the tearful Adige', he describes a game against Piacenza which Rovigo won. But despite the victory, he had seen things in the game that displeased him. In order to make his point, he turns to the ballet world:

> We live in a world and in an age of indiscipline. But excellence only comes through discipline. I saw evidence of this in the Teatro Sociale Rovigo on Saturday night in a demanding, physically-hard presentation of *spettacolo di balletto* by Carla Fracci, Lawrence Rhodes and James Urbain. I had more pleasure there in 10 minutes than in the whole 80 minutes in Piacenza.

A win wasn't enough for the Maestro. That same article shows that Carwyn had just received an invitation to coach in Australia:

> On Friday I received an invitation to conduct a three-day coaching seminar in Sydney to prepare the Australian team for the visit of Wales and their tour of New Zealand. Unless they can change the dates from the first week of December until Sanson have played Petrarca, the answer has to be a firm 'no'.

Carwyn's priorities were crystal clear. A less-important league game for Rovigo was his commitment, and the Australians had to be turned down.

He dealt with the psychology of sport in many of these articles. In one example, he rejoiced in the fact that two key games would be televised, so that he could watch them and analyse both the methods of play and the attitude of the players. These games were Italy vs. England in football and the All Blacks vs. France in rugby.

As an echo of his mantra in the Stradey dressing room before the Llanelli game against the All Blacks, when he repeated that it was a thinking man's game, Carwyn also has his set phrases in these articles: Unquestionably, matches are won and lost in the dressing room. The name of the game is pressure. A good team believes in itself. Winning isn't everything, but wanting to win is. He was ever the master of *le mot juste*.

Carwyn wasn't a man without humour, even if he might not be a constant source of gags and jokes. In one article, he retells a legendary Llanelli story. Llanelli were playing against the Barbarians, the first match under floodlights at the ground. One fan was getting increasingly annoyed by the attitude of one of the Barbarian players. After another perceived transgression on the player's part, the fan had had enough. He shouted out at the top of his voice, 'Go back to Barbaria, you dirty swine!' Carwyn also writes about another contribution from the terraces from that same game. Llanelli were ahead against the Barbarians by two points, but gave away a penalty towards the end. If that was converted by the Baa-Baas, they would win. As their kicker took the penalty, a Llanelli wag shouted out, 'Turn the lights off, boys!'

Carwyn does make an attempt at joke-telling in another article:

> The breathalyser had just been introduced, and on the Saturday Wales were playing England at the Arms Park, Dai was explaining to his friends that the police had a fiendish new device in their patrol cars. 'It smells your breath,' he said indignantly, 'and it can tell immediately if you've had too much to drink.' 'That's nothing new,' came a voice from beside him, 'I've been married to one of those for 20 years!'

Carwyn could not have written so many articles without ever referring to the myths and legends of his motherland. He mentions the story of Pwyll, the subject matter of his speech at the Haverfordwest Eisteddfod. He also refers to the Bard of Stratford. After one match in which the referee had made himself far too prominent, Carwyn writes:

Despite his obvious ambition, many more equally reluctant suns will have peered at him before he is ready to play Hamlet.

Julius Caesar is referenced in another review, one following a match against the Algida team from Rome. Carwyn's cultural priorities are prominent once again.

The miracle of another spring, with a burst of new life, is upon us again. Defying the hard, snowy winter, the proud yellow daffodils have surfaced in my garden in Wales, as have the sweet-smelling violets in Rovigo.

The main character of one of my favourite Welsh novels was a sick man but he always comforted himself with the words, 'I shall get better in the coming of spring'. But he never did. The vitality of the rejuvenation of nature was too much for him.

Carwyn was in Rovigo on St David's Day 1978, and he made the most of the opportunity to share that with the people of Rovigo.

Somehow I had a feeling that things would go right in the week when Welshmen celebrate the birth of their patron saint, Saint David. At home, we attend concerts, we hold 'eisteddfodau' (competitive concerts) and some of us have to speak at a number of dinners, held over a period of a fortnight; joyous and wet occasions when we talk with reverence about our saint, who was a teetotaller. I shall remember this St David's Day in Rovigo for three reasons: a recital in the Teatro; Wales' close victory over Ireland and Sanson's fine display against Piacenza.

He kept a close eye on the fortunes of the Welsh national team. One article refers to the Welsh victory against Ireland, 20–16, securing the third Triple Crown in succession. Carwyn says that he flew back to Wales to see that game. Needless to say, he was probably in a very small minority who thought that such a victory, as welcome as it was, was no guarantee of continued success and development. There would not be another Grand Slam for nearly 30 years.

In his second season in Rovigo, he kept to the same basic structure for his articles, but the content emphasis had shifted. He is more reflective, more personal even. There are more references to Wales, less technical rugby analysis and more general observations from outside the world of rugby.

His author friend Alun Richards contributed at least one article to one of these papers, although it is not clear which paper. His article, in his own handwriting, deals with the last game he saw on his holiday before returning to Wales.

> In Portugal there is a saying that the wind from Spain blows nobody any good. On Sunday, at Rovigo's splendid stadium, the wind from Trieste brought us a regatta of rugby football rather than a game, with 60 points on the scoreboard. The wind ruffled the kickers but the sunshine blessed them. It was a holiday affair and yet, to the purist, strangely disappointing.

He ends the letter by thanking 'all those in Sanson who have made my visits so enjoyable.' These words show that he visited Carwyn more than once in Italy. His next sentence after this one also shows that he was there at the end of Carwyn's first season, when they just failed to win the championship, coming second to Treviso by two points:

> And apologies...

Ti voglio bene

In his second season, Carwyn led Rovigo to the Italian Championship. His aim had been to do so at the end of his first season and then return to Wales. As that didn't happen, Carwyn would not return to Wales without achieving his goal. He successfully negotiated with the BBC that he would stay put in Italy for another year. He had unfinished business.

There's a story about him visiting a Treviso player who was in hospital because of a serious injury he had suffered during a game. This caused some considerable commotion and consternation amongst the Rovigo fans. Why was their coach going to see one of the enemy? The situation was resolved eventually, with the fans understanding that Carwyn had good reason for his visit, and accepting that.

When they won the Championship in 1979, in addition to the honour and the trophy, and yet another notch on Carwyn's rugby bedpost, they had the additional honour of being invited to meet the Pope. Pope John Paul II, Karol Wojtyła from Poland, wanted to meet the victorious club at the Vatican. Chapel deacon Carwyn spoke to the Pope, who as the story goes, told Carwyn that he had heard that rugby was a dirty game. Carwyn's reply was the succinct, 'Not if it's played properly.'

Championship victory secured, it was time for Carwyn to head back to Wales. The time had come to bid *arrivederci* to those who had become his colleagues, acquaintances and, in some cases, his friends.

The books on the shelf

It was Auden who said that a good book is one that reads us. The books on our shelves say a great deal about us. We therefore need to consider the books that Carwyn left on the shelf of the flat in Via I Monti. The list of the books that were on those shelves is revealed here for the first time.

It is to be expected that there were sporting books there. They were *The Autobiography of a Cricketer* by Colin Cowdrey; *Political Football – The Springbok Tour of Australia 1971* by Stewart Harries, which was an attempt to outline the link between rugby and apartheid that Carwyn had grappled so hard to understand; and not surprisingly, *My Life* by Neville Cardus.

Equally unsurprising was the fact that there were Welsh books on those shelves. *Cyfle i Nabod* (Chance to Get to Know) by T J Davies; *Tro yn yr Eidal* (Tour in Italy) by O M Edwards, which was an account of the author's journey to Italy in the early 1920s; and a copy of *Y Caniedydd* (The Singer) hymn book. It's easy to picture Carwyn sitting in his flat or walking around doing household chores, singing his favourite hymns.

There are two more political volumes in the collection. *Inside Number 10* by Marcia Williams and *Kontinent 2 – The Alternative Voice of Russia & Eastern Europe*. Marcia Williams' book talks about the world that she was a part of as Secretary to Prime Minister Harold Wilson. *Kontinent 2* takes Carwyn back to his JSSL days, when he would have been part of a system that opposed the USSR administraion. This is Tony Cash's response to the fact that this book was in Carwyn's possession in 1979:

> It's no surprise at all that Carwyn would have a dissident Russian publication in his possession. That's where his normal inclination would lie. It is interesting, however, that he should still be actively involved in keeping up with that scene over 20 years after he left the JSSL. It was obviously still very real to him.

He evidently read books in four different languages when in Italy. The more literary books he left in Italy were: *Memoirs* by Benvenuto Cellini; *English Romantic Poets* edited by M H Abrams; *A Hemingway Selection*; *A Writer's Notebook* by W Somerset Maugham; *The Pocket Oxford Dictionary* and a *Dictionary of English Quotations*.

There are also books there that are rather more surprising, and ones that raise a few questions: *Crowd of Lovers* by Laddie Marshack; *More Sex Life Letters*, edited by Anne Hooper; *Delta of Venus* by Anais Nin; *The Venetian Affair* by Helen MacInnes. These are a mix of romantic, feminine and erotic literature.

Anais Nin's volume is particularly significant. It was a publication that created quite a stir, if not a scandal, when it appeared – similar to the *Fifty Shades of Grey* effect in recent years. It was published at the time that Carwyn arrived in Italy. It's a collection of erotic short stories which deal with the essence of sexual identity, being gay and sexual abstinence. These were issues that were evidently relevant to Carwyn, and ones he felt safe to explore far away from home, with no eyes prying over his shoulder. It's a reading list that indicates sexual exploration and self-analysis. Two other books, to be found on the shelf of his home in Cefneithin, would take this exploration a lot further. But that's later. Rovigo gave him a safe distance in which to read such books.

This self-exploration would shed both light and darkness across Carwyn's soul, as he tried to work out which was which. Angelo Morello saw these conflicting periods in Carwyn. He says that he was very concerned for Carwyn at moments when it was time to say farewell to any company he was in. He feared for Carwyn when everyone else was gone. Back in Wales, this is when Carwyn would knock on Phil Bennett or Derek Quinnell's door, but they weren't around in Italy. There, Angelo fulfilled that role, as much as his own family commitments allowed.

Angelo will never forget an evening spent in Carwyn's flat. Carwyn turned to him, knowing that he was going back to Wales, and held out his copy of Cardus' *My Life* to Angelo.

> Why would he do that? It was one of the most influential books in his life. Why did he give it to me? Cardus was his *maestro di vita*, as he told me many times. That has played on my mind ever since.

A rugby festival

After Carwyn had long left Rovigo, there was a strong desire in the town to honour his contribution to their rugby development. The result was the formation of the Carwyn James Rugby School. Carwyn's nephew, Llyr James, played a central role in the development of the School.

> My father, Dewi, his cousin Gwilym Thomas, Gerallt Davies and myself went out to Rovigo in 1996. We met the Angelo that we had heard so much about. The following year, Llanelli were playing in Treviso in the Heineken Cup, and over lunch on that trip, Angelo suggested that we hold a rugby competition in Carwyn's name, with teams from Italy and Wales to compete. In June 1999, Angelo

349

brought 25 players over from Italy to Wales. I organised three games for them, one in Llandovery and two on the playing fields of Gwendraeth Grammar School. From the year 2000 onwards we formulated the Easter Trophy for such visits, and it's still going.

The following year, at Easter in 2000, a rugby team from Tumble, near to Carwyn's Cefneithin, represented Wales in the first compettion in Italy. 20 players went from Tumble, plus five of the players' fathers, Llyr and Gerallt Davies. Two teams from Argentina were also there, as well as the Italian Carwyn James team. Twelve Easter Trophy competitions have been held to date, and Welsh teams have competed in eight of them. The remaining four were fought out between Italian teams. The best year for Welsh involvement was 2001, Llyr describing how the competition produced top-quality rugby.

> We travelled down to the mountains east of Rome, to L'Aquila. There were teams there from seven or eight different countries, including a team that was made up from the best of the Welsh boys out there and the best from the Carwyn James School team. A special rugby shirt was designed for the school team, based on the fact that Wales and Italy's flags share the same three colours of red, white and green. That team won the competition that year.

In 2004, a seven-a-side competition was started for young players, in the hope that only needing to recruit seven boys at a time would make things easier and spread the game further. That Easter, a full XV competition was held as well as the seven-a-side one. In addition, individual teams went out as a result of Angelo's arrangements. They were Dolgellau and Nant Conwy from North Wales and Tumble from the South. From this, another development grew, as Llyr continues:

> As the years went by, it became clearer that the Welsh influence on rugby development in Italy needed to be deepened. The way we decided that could be done was to pay for coaches from Wales to go to Italy. The first to go was Gareth Williams from Tumble, a

specialist in the seven-a-side game. Since then former Scarlets and Wales coach Gareth Jenkins and former Scarlets and Leeds coach Phil Davies have been out there. As the saying emphasises, it was far better to teach the Italians how to fish instead of just throwing fish at them all the time.

In 2015, Wales was represented by two teams, one from Meirionethshire and the other from Radnorshire.

The Carwyn James Rugby School received a significant boost when Welsh-Italian artist Andrew Vicari donated a substantial number of copies of the portrait he had done of Carwyn for the 2000 National Eisteddfod in Llanelli to the School so that they could be sold to raise funds. They sold very well and raised a considerable sum of money. Vicari's parents had left the Parma region of Italy in the 1930s to move to South Wales, and he was born in Port Talbot. Going on to become the highest paid-living artist, he was the perfect ambassador for such a Welsh-Italian venture, and was president of the Carwyn James Rugby School for nearly ten years. Other than this financial support, some Rovigo banks contributed sponsorship and Angelo Morello's own travel company donated funds, as have various individuals. As things are at present, there is some doubt if the competition can continue unless funding difficulties are overcome.

Carwyn's nephew, Llyr James, sponsors one specific aspect of these tours by Welsh teams in the name of his uncle. It's a gesture his uncle would undoubtedly be proud of and it shows clearly that they share the same DNA:

> Every team from Wales that travels to Italy under the banner of the Carwyn James School of Rugby goes on a day trip to Venice. Understanding and appreciating a little of the culture of the country is central to the whole experience. A line of poetry, written by Ceri Wyn Jones and seen on the rugby shirts Carmarthen Quins players wore in the competiton once, sums it up: '*am mai mwy na gêm yw hi.*' – 'because it is more than a game'.

Progetto Galles Celtico

Welsh-Italian links in the name of Carwyn James haven't only been on the rugby field. As insistent as the people of Rovigo were that they wanted to remember his rugby legacy, they were also keen to celebrate the cultural spirit that Carwyn showed. Former BBC television and radio producer Wynne Lloyd, who had contributed so much to the development of BBC Wales schools and music programming, went out to Italy a month after Carwyn had died. He loved all things Italian anyway, and in February 1983 went on a pilgrimage to Rovigo. He met many of Carwyn's rugby club colleagues on that trip:

> The president of the club was hosting a big party on his farm on the outskirts of the town – a *festa*, during the week of the *carnevale*, before the cloud of Lent. Everyone there was linked in some way or other to the world of the oval ball. As the evening wore on and warmed up, the floodgates of memories of Carwyn opened. Many shared their own particular story. A doctor, who had previously played for another team, told how he had once approached Carwyn, asking him for careers guidance. Which should it be, he asked, rugby or medicine? He reported that Carwyn's answer was, 'Which one is most important to you?'
>
> Another came up to me and asked if I knew the tune that Carwyn would often sing, the one with the long name, he said. He hummed a few bars to me and I recognised the tune as the one we refer to in Welsh as '*Tôn y Botel*', the 'Bottle Tune' [a hymn tune more formally known as 'Ebenezer']. I joined in with his accompaniment, singing the Welsh words, and he started to remember some words himself as well. Others joined in and in the end, we nearly had a Male Voice Choir of Italian men singing in Welsh.

Wynne Lloyd also became a friend of Angelo Morello's after this. Years later, they organised a series of cultural events in Rovigo in memory of Carwyn. *Progetto Galles Celtico* would have events in Welsh and English by people brought over from Wales. It was held between 29 November and 14 December

The pioneering coaching course for Welsh Schoolboys and Youth Internationals, Aberystwyth 1966 (Carwyn fourth from right, front row)

The singer and his Lions

The master coach

Proud parents welcome their victorious son back from New Zealand.

Cefneithin RFC

The ties Carwyn brought back from New Zealand from each province the Lions played against, proudly presented to Cefneithin Rugby Club

Cefneithin RFC

The rugby and mining heritage of Wales under discussion – Barry John, Carwyn and NUM leader in South Wales, Dai Francis

Cefneithin RFC

Cliff Morgan and Carwyn, two legendary rugby broadcasters and thinkers

Three thinkers in world rugby: Fred Allen from New Zealand, Dr Dannie Craven from South Africa and Carwyn

The unofficial Welsh selector, the *Western Mail*'s rugby correspondent J B G Thomas, looking through copies of the paper with Gerald Davies, Gareth Edwards and Carwyn

The star-studded Urdd Jubilee Game and Barry John's last ever match – Carwyn's team in white, Barry John's team in green

James family collection

New roots in Italy – Carwyn's
flat in Rovigo
Alun Gibbard

A regular Rovigo haunt
– the Accademia
Alun Gibbard

Another arena
where he spent a
great deal of his time
in Rovigo: the Teatro
Alun Gibbard

In Rovigo, author Alun Richards shares his thoughts on handling a rugby ball with Carwyn. The club's two South African players, Dries Coetze and Dirk Naudè, are evidently amused

Carwyn was a coach who would connect with his people in Rovigo

A Papal recognition of Rovigo's championship success

Lonelier times for reflection and
contemplation away from home
Luciano Pavanello

Reading back home in Cardiff

Carwyn's interest
in cricket was as
passionate as his
interest in rugby
James family collection

...and his ability as a
snooker player was
also masterful

The trappings of success – an incessant round of dinners and speeches…
James family collection

…and invitations to functions unknown before then for rugby players. Here he declares a petrol station in Llanelli open, along with Lion Delme Thomas
Delme Thomas collection

Carwyn and Plaid Cymru's first MP, Gwynfor Evans, delight in a new expression of rugby commercialism

Arwel Davies

The proudly-accepted Eisteddfod honour: becoming a member of the Gorsedd of Bards

James family collection

Carwyn the community entertainer. Tumble Village Hall celebrates Christmas, miners' library books lining the back wall

James family collection

Not the dual carriageway he joked about, but a 1970s recognition in Dowlais, Merthyr Tydfil of Carwyn's success and influence

Where it all ended

Sisters Gwen and Eilonwy and brother Dewi (in the middle) at the unveiling of a bronze bust of Carwyn in BBC Wales' Broadcasting House

James family collection

The première of the BBC documentaries on Carwyn's life after he died – one in Welsh, the other in English. Ray Gravell, Jonathan Davies, Gerald Davies, Max Boyce and Barry John in Cefneithin Rugby Club

Dewi James with Andrew Vicari's portrait of his brother Carwyn
James family collection

Aled, Carwyn's great nephew, representing the family at the ceremony to accept Carwyn into World Rugby's Hall of Fame, over 30 years after he died
James family collection

Cefneithin remembers one of their own. The memorial service in Tabernacl Chapel in 1983

Some of the Cefneithin RFC faithful socialise in Carwyn's shadow, May 2017

Alun Gibbard

1997. A report on the activities appeared in Welsh-language weekly magazine *Golwg* (View), under the heading, '*Nerth yr hedyn a heuodd Carwyn*' (The strength of the seed Carwyn planted). Many talks were given during the Festival exploring the links between Wales and Italy and between the Celts and Northern Italy. A central element of the event was an exhibition of the work of influential Welsh artist, Mary Lloyd Jones, who recalls:

> Dewi, Carwyn's brother, asked me if I would contribute to the Festival. I agreed immediately. I didn't know Carwyn, but I certainly knew of him. I remember I took about 30 paintings with me, many tied to the roof of the car, and we had to go through some snow to get to Rovigo. As I chatted with the people there, it was obvious that they had a great love for Carwyn and what impressed them most was his creativity.

Welsh singer Siân James was also there.

> I went out with my father. I had to borrow a harp as taking one out there would have been difficult. It was a very ornate, imposing harp, I remember. I sang in two concerts. The greatest impression the visit made on me was realising how much they worshipped Carwyn. That was a big surprise to me, coming from the same country as him.

Home

This respect for Carwyn and appreciation of him showed itself in a phrase they would use in referring to him. To them he was: *Un uomo di cultura fatto di semplicità* (A simple, cultured man). This man who had his own private battles made the Italians think that he was a very simple, straightforward man, who fed from the table of Italian culture to his heart's content. The fact that he could create this impression shows how much he benefitted from being in Italy.

But it is Carwyn we are talking of here, a man for whom there is very rarely a 'yes' without a 'no'. Angelo Morello remembers an evening spent with Carwyn at his flat, similar in spirit to the evening when Carwyn gave him his Cardus book.

> He turned to face me, following a lull in a fairly deep conversation about emotions and feelings, and he said, 'If I died tomorrow, no one would be bothered.'

Some clouds didn't leave Carwyn and he took them with him whichever country he was in.

But as we look at his two years in Italy, it was a time when he managed to reclaim some values and to replant some roots that had started to loosen, erode and be chewed away by bitterness and disappointment. As he left the shores of north-eastern Italy, he left lands over which blew the winds called the *maestro*, a sea breeze from the Adriatic which usually brought sunshine and nothing more than light clouds in its wake. For two years, this wind blew through Carwyn's bones, moving a few obstacles, clearing some rot, purifying the blood and restoring a great deal of the artist in the patient.

Chapter 21

Books, suspension and The Priory

> Often in this our life do we begin by cursing men and end
> by loving them. A sense of the common fallibility of all flesh
> makes us kin. No man is lovable who is invincible.
>
> Neville Cardus, *My Life*

THERE WAS NO guarantee that Carwyn would continue to
savour sunshine and light clouds in Wales. The Welsh air was
likely to be less favourable and he could expect crosswinds.
His roots were newly nourished but he was facing a climate
more hostile to their flourishing, and would do well to heed the
warnings of T H Parry-Williams. An Indian summer in Welsh
is called *Haf Bach Mihangel* (Michael's Little Summer) after
the Archangel Michael, whose saint's day Michaelmas is at the
end of September. Parry-Williams warns that there's a need to
be wary of the false comfort of gentle weather:

> *Daw Haf Bach Mihangel trwy weddill yr ŷd*
> *Yn llond ei groen, ac yn gelwydd i gyd.*

> 'Michael's Little Summer comes through the corn's remains
> Full of life, and is nothing but lies.'

Carwyn arrived back in Wales a few months before his
fiftieth birthday. He was back in the BBC corridors in Cardiff,
back picking up his *Guardian* pen and back speaking to groups
and societies throughout England and Wales. A two-year

absence, although he hadn't been away from Wales completely for the entirety of that period, had given him an increased air of detachment and mystery.

He needed a new home, and his contacts in the TV world found him one. HTV Controller of Programmes Aled Vaughan knew of a flat in the Fairwater area of Cardiff, near Rookwood Hospital. Carwyn was delighted with his new home. It was much more like his flat in Rovigo than his previous residence in the Welsh Capital. He set about buying new furniture, but he didn't choose the furniture or have a hand in the interior design either. That responsibility was given to his female friends, who were given some money and asked to go shopping. A grand green leather sofa was one favourite acquisition. Everyone who called to see him would be taken on a guided tour of the flat – Huw Llywelyn Davies for one:

> He delighted in his new little palace. The first time my wife Carol and I went there, with Brian Davies and his wife Enid, he insisted on showing every piece of furniture and every nook and cranny of the flat to the two wives.

Carwyn's return to Wales just about coincided with the formation of the Welsh-language radio service on BBC Wales, Radio Cymru, and he threw himself into the work of the new station. He was asked to present the sports bulletins which were scheduled alongside the news bulletins. That meant that he had to work shifts, as bulletins were broadcast throughout the day, from the early hours of the morning until late at night. He was also the second voice on rugby commentaries. One of the first voices was Huw Llywelyn Davies, who had not only followed Carwyn to Llandovery as Welsh teacher, but also from HTV across to the BBC:

> At the beginning, John Evans and I would share first-voice responsibilities during every match, alternating every 20 minutes. Carwyn would offer his observations every 5–10 minutes or so.

During the 20 minutes I wasn't on air, Carwyn would make many off-air observations as to how he saw the game developing. Those comments were nothing short of an invaluable education for me.

Between two covers

If broadcasting rose to ascendancy in Carwyn's life in the early Seventies, followed by newspaper journalism, his last years would see him entering the book world. He didn't manage to write that autobiography that he had started to write notes for, but he did publish four books between 1978 and 1983. The first, *Y Gamp Lawn* (The Grand Slam) was on the shelves in 1978 while he was still in Italy; the next, *World of Rugby*, was out a year later in 1979; *Injured Pride*, the story of the Lions' tour of South Africa, was published in 1980; and *Focus on Rugby* in 1983, after he had died. These works give us a great deal of Carwyn's rugby philosophy and his opinions about the way the game was developing, especially in Wales. Reading his comments, and between their lines, there's an overwhelming feeling that is best summed up by a line from Leonard Cohen's 'The Tower of Song', when he says that 'I ache in the places where I used to play'. As we read Carwyn deliberating about the game he used to play, the ache is almost tangible.

After Wales won the Grand Slam in 1978, Carwyn got together with some of his old Llandovery colleagues to write a book commemorating that achievement. *Y Gamp Lawn: golwg ar y tîm a'r tymor* (The Grand Slam: a look at the team and the season) was published in 1978 and co-written by former Llandovery Warden R Gerallt Jones, who wrote reports on all the Five Nations matches in 1978; Huw Llywelyn Davies, who wrote profiles of the Welsh players; and Carwyn, who gave his views on the state of the game in Wales in the form of question and answer with R Gerallt Jones.

In response to a question about the Golden Era of the Seventies, he says that a great deal of the credit should go to the coaching system that the WRU initiated in the Sixties.

357

The Union, he said, had succeeded in bringing together two potentially conflicting disciplines into one team:

CJ: I have heard some, like Wilf Wooller and A M Rees, say that it was quite a task in the early days to secure a happy marriage between two types of players – the ones taught in public schools and the Oxbridge colleges, and those who were coalminers or steelworkers.

RGJ: Why?

CJ: Well, their disciplines were different. The college boys would tend instinctively to want to get the ball back to the backs. The others tended instinctively to drive the ball forward. It was difficult to get them to move as a unit.

He had reservations about the way coaching had developed, though. In his writings at this time, he would express the opinion that coaching had taken the wrong turning, and consequently, that individual playing skills had been neglected:

There's a huge emphasis these days on making fewer mistakes. But as a result, the game isn't as adventurous and can be more monotonous for the spectator.

In addition to the coaching system, Wales had also been fortunate in the Seventies to have quite a collection of gifted players, which Carwyn discussed in *Y Gamp Lawn*.

CJ: It's been quite a special conveyor belt, and to an extent, we have depended on their individual genius to win matches, despite the coaching system.

RGJ: And the future? With Gerald and Gareth retiring, and Phil and Cobner as well?

CJ: That will be the test of the nature of the coaching.

RGJ: You don't feel that the coaching system has been tested yet?

CJ: No, it hasn't been under any pressure because of the ability of the stars to save us. The future will tell.

RGJ: Would you agree that the increased professionalism to be seen in the clubs these days has led to a tendency for teams

CJ: to be coached to win at all costs, even against the rules and the spirit of the game?

CJ: That is true – I know of examples. I detest such a thing. I think we have to show this up more and more on the TV and start a public campaign against it.

This attitude is summed up clearly by his friend John Reason, in the obituary he wrote for Carwyn in *The Daily Telegraph*. In it, he writes:

> For those who think that Welsh rugby didn't do too badly through the Seventies, Carwyn would point to the lonely figure of Gerald Davies standing for match after match on the wing and hardly ever receiving a pass, while Gareth Edwards took on the world at the base of the scrum. 'We shall never see Gerald's like again,' said Carwyn, 'and we are letting him rust away. The point about Welsh rugby in the Seventies is not what it has achieved but what it could have achieved.'

R Gerallt Jones then winds up the discussion by going where Carwyn was always happy to look: the future.

RGJ: An era has come to an end; that is obvious. How would you like to see things developing in the next few years?

CJ: Well, without doubt continuing to perfect the play of the forwards, securing clean possession and organising the tight play – but restoring true centres at the same time. But I am not very hopeful about that.

RGJ: Why?

CJ: I'm willing to say that there aren't many people in Wales who are able to coach the three-quarter line. All the emphasis in coaching courses is placed on the forwards. And I certainly agree that good possession is essential. Without possession you have nothing. But we've forgotten how much need there is to develop the basic skills of the backs. Also, we must get rid of the over-planning that leads to calling a move before you've seen the nature of the play.

RGJ: Would you have any sympathy with the view that systematic coaching in itself has brought a new pressure on players, bringing with it an alien spirit of cynicism, an attitude that could harm the spirit of the game itself?

CJ: That is perfectly true. People need to realise that. We must accept it – when coaching came into the game, the door was opened to this tendency. But what you describe isn't inevitable, remember. For me, the future of this amateur game depends on the extent to which the majority of our coaches understand the spirit of the game. The easiest thing in the world to do is to bend a rule; it takes a little bit more perception to understand why that rule is there in the first place, and in doing so, to penetrate through to the true nature and glory of rugby.

The World of Rugby

While in Italy, discussions had begun about Carwyn doing a series on the story of rugby for the BBC and writing a book to coincide with it. BBC Wales' Dewi Griffiths visited Carwyn in Rovigo to discuss this idea. The TV production was run by Opix Films, in a partnership between the BBC, S4C and Ireland's RTÉ. The programmes contained technical analysis of every position on the rugby field, every set-piece, and open-play moves. An accompanying book, *The World of Rugby*, was also published in 1979, co-written by Carwyn and his friend from *The Telegraph*, John Reason. It is a substantial volume that traces the development of rugby across the world. *Focus on Rugby* is a more technical coaching book, whose publication Carwyn didn't see as unfortunately he died before it came out. In that sense, they literally are his last words on the game. He wrote the opening chapter, 'What's wrong with Rugby?' This, in addition to *The World Of Rugby*'s last chapter, entitled 'The Union stumbling into its second century' and the conversation with R Gerallt Jones in *Y Gamp Lawn*, give us the meat of Carwyn's views on coaching.

In *The World of Rugby*, he comments further on the observation made in *Y Gamp Lawn* about increased professionalism in the game.

Players today feel no sense of dishonour or impropriety at receiving the many perquisites which are now regarded as part of the game. They see nothing wrong in playing as semi-professionals in France or Italy or of being paid inflated expenses to play the game in Wales. In this regard, the governing bodies of the game are performing successfully that most difficult of athletic contortions, which is to sit on the fence while sticking their heads firmly into the sand at the same time.

He puts this rugby point into a broader societal context. Society as a whole, he says, has turned far more materialistic, and this has crept into the world of rugby. As innovative as his rugby comments were, this particular observation smacks of an old-fashioned Welsh attitude. As usual, he practised what he preached. He was offered £20,000 to coach a professional World XV, but he turned it down. There was an increasing emphasis at that time on the need to develop professional rugby exhibition matches. Players such as Gerald Davies and J P R Williams had been mentioned, without proof, as being interested in such a development. Carwyn's stance was as resolute as it was traditional: 'It's strictly an amateur game. I don't want their money.'

He has a clear warning for the governing body in English rugby too, and one that shows him back to his prophetic best:

> English Rugby must be reorganised. A regional Championship must be introduced to challenge the club championship in France, the provincial structures of New Zealand and South Africa, the happy geographical accident of South Wales and the flourishing leagues in Scotland. Until England undertakes such a reorganisation, they will never achieve consistent international results and they will never take their place in the world of rugby.

His last book, *Focus on Rugby*, only just saw the light of day. Carwyn had passed away, leaving his co-writer John Reason to see the work through to press. That process involved Max Boyce, Westminster Abbey and a parcel, as Max remembers:

I had a phone call asking if I would deliver a parcel to John Reason as the caller knew I was going to London. The problem was that John Reason was in Westminster Abbey for a service of some kind. So when I approached the Abbey doors, they wouldn't let me in. I pleaded with the man at the door, saying I had an important parcel to give to *The Telegraph*'s John Reason. That didn't work. The man was not for budging. I continued pleading, saying that it was a book co-written by Carwyn James. 'Oh! Carwyn James,' he said. 'Wonderful man!' And then he opened the door for me.

When the book was published, it included an additional extra. Gerald Davies had been asked to write a tribute to Carwyn, who had died only a few weeks earlier. Gerald, who was hewn from the same rock as Carwyn, knew that the life of the Maestro had to be taken back to where it all began:

> A miner's son in socialist West Wales, he subscribed fully to the idea of excellence and he believed passionately, where talent was concerned, in the existence of an elite. He was a product of a community which, given a glimpse of what was possible, yearned for ideas and unprejudiced thinking.

Carwyn's own contribution in the opening chapter expands on the thoughts shared by Gerald Davies. In answering the question he himself had set, 'What's wrong with the game?', he doesn't begin in the present. He roots the answer back in his own formative experiences in Cefneithin. He remembers his father putting him on his shoulders at the age of three to watch the village men play in the park; the boisterous playing on road and pavement – which is where he learned to side-step, because if he hadn't he would have fallen and hurt himself on tarmac or concrete, he says; the kickabouts in the park and playtime rugby at school. He emphasises that the main motivation for all of this was just enjoyment, exemplified by the men of the village organising games just for their own sake, with no league or cup involved at all. That was the beginning of rugby for him, and for him that's what the beginning of rugby should be.

He strongly criticises a new tendency that he feels cuts across the spirit of rugby as he has just outlined it:

> Screaming mums, doting dads and the competitive urge have given it the image of a monster.

Carwyn's early Gwendraeth days were during the war, when all formal inter-school competitions had been abandoned. In that school, as in some others, some of the pitches had been torn up and were being used as allotments to grow vegetables as people dug for victory. The boys therefore organised their own games, which they did purely for enjoyment. In outlining the development of coaching earlier in this book, the point was made that it was thought that coaching was only needed in schools and that it wasn't for adults. Carwyn's experience evidently pre-dates that. Carwyn's view was that formalising rugby training for schoolchildren too early was not a good thing.

Educational developments at the time also challenged Carwyn, as much as the increase of materialism did:

> All children are equal and none is more equal than the other. Comprehensives. The new 'in' word. Big and beautiful.

His contempt is palpable. A consequence of such a development for Carwyn was that the needs of children were being ignored, which included the way in which they were taught sport:

> Choice is the operative word in the comprehensive. A flirtation with half a dozen team games is preferable to the discipline of one. The disciplines of gymnastics are as repugnant as the disciplines of spelling and counting.
>
> The sadness of the age is a lack of understanding of the needs of children. They love discipline. Without it there is chaos, and that is the state of too many of our schools at the present time.

On these pages tradition, establishment and innovation jostle for position, as they did in the mind of the man who wrote the words. As do romanticism and nostalgia. This chapter, more than anything else he wrote on rugby, contains more of the personal Carwyn. The other analyses of rugby and coaching issues are mainly confined between the touchlines. But here he goes outside the stadium and back to the communities that feed it. He hovers on the brink of actually saying, 'Things aren't like they used to be in my day!', but it's definitely implied. The man who achieved so much because he changed so much, and the man whe berated the WRU for opposing change, never welcomed change for change's sake.

Carwyn wrote this chapter in what was undoubtedly the worst year of his life. The winds had risen to gale force, as we will see over the course of the next few pages. Carwyn would have tried to look through the tempest to the safe place, the place where there were certainties. That would have meant the soil of the Gwendraeth Valley and the land of his childhood. Rugby would never give him the assurances he needed – it was far too volatile. Once rugby took over as the mainstay of his career, he lost perspective. As Carwyn's rugby yesterdays and his rugby todays wove through each other, and as his tomorrows looked more uncertain, Dylan Thomas' words echo in Carwyn's writing:

> The ball I threw while playing in the park
> Has not yet reached the ground.

Encroaching shadows

Carwyn continued to back ventures he thought were trying something new and worthwhile. He contributed to a brand new weekly newspaper in Llanelli, *The Llanelli News*, which challenged the long-standing *Llanelli Star*. He was the paper's Sports Editor. He fulfilled the same role in groundbreaking newspaper *Sulyn*, Wales' first Welsh-language Sunday paper.

His work for *The Guardian* continued throughout this period.

His personal life, however, was changing – and not for the better. He started to take gin with some water in it in order to ease the pain of the psoriasis. Soon, he didn't use any water. The drinking increased, and his skin condition worsened. One contributed to the other. He never discussed his skin condition with anyone, but all his friends and family knew that it was getting worse. When he sat down, if he crossed his legs and the bottom of his trousers lifted a little above the socks, flaky red skin was obvious. When wearing a jacket, he would roll the jacket sleeves up to his elbows but leave the shirt sleeves buttoned at the wrist, so that he didn't show what state his arms were in. BBC colleagues testify to mounds of flaky skin around his chair and under his desk in the office, and dried blood stains would be seen on his shirts.

At the BBC he was a part of a culture that centred on the BBC Club, within the BBC grounds in Llandaf. Every lunchtime and at the end of every working day, that was the place to go. They were an august group: dramatist Gwenlyn Parry, author T Glynne Davies, scriptwriter Rhydderch Jones, news anchor Ifan Wyn Williams and many others. Carwyn would occasionally be a lunchtime attendee, but he was always there of an evening. His other haunt was the third floor of Broadcasting House, known as The Gin Palace, where the senior management had their drinks trolleys. A third watering hole, affectionately known as Studio 4, was the Castell Mynach pub in Groesfaen. The picture is clear: work revolved around drink. One of the group, then Head of News and Current Affairs, Gwilym Owen, agrees:

> The BBC was a fairly drunken place at the time, based on the belief that creativity depended on drink. Carwyn fell into this way of thinking, to excess. Many instances come to mind when Carwyn would turn up for work late and worse for wear, or sometimes not turn up at all. At such times, he was not fit enough to broadcast at all, to be honest.

I remember one occasion, arriving at the BBC at 5.30 one morning and Carwyn shuffling in, not looking too good. I'm fairly certain that's the last time I saw him. He reached towards me, a piece of paper in hand, and said, 'Can you send this to *Sulyn*, please? I've got to go somewhere.' It was his article for *Sulyn* newspaper that week and I had to send it off on his behalf.

It was only a matter of time before such a lifestyle caught up with him, and it did: big time. For such a public man, the fall was almost inevitably going to be in public, and it was. He was part of the commentary team for a Bridgend vs. Swansea game, with Huw Llywelyn Davies as the main commentator:

I used to drive him to matches more often than not, and when I picked him up on that day, it was obvious that he wasn't in a good state. He hadn't slept much the night before and he had been drinking. Carwyn slept in the car all the way to Bridgend and when we got to the ground, he went to meet John Dawes in the clubhouse. He was there for the beginning of the programme, and gave his analysis as to how he saw the game going. Swansea, he said, were far too strong a team for Bridgend and they would win comfortably. After a while, I heard the producer Thomas Davies, speaking in my headphones, saying he hadn't heard Carwyn for a while. The truth was that Carwyn was fast asleep by my side. I nudged him to wake him, and half coming round and half-realising that he needed to say something, he proceeded to make some comments, saying that Swansea were really doing well and they were the better team. But at that time in the game, Bridgend were comfortably ahead.

There was no hiding place for Carwyn. On the Monday morning at the BBC there was increasing concern for his well-being. Knowing that he needed both treatment and protection, Thomas Davies went to speak to Gareth Price, BBC Wales Head of Programmes. They discussed what had happened at the Bridgend game, and decided that there was only one course of action. There was no use telling Carwyn off and leaving things be. This is how Gareth Price remembers the next step:

The feeling was that we would have to discipline Carwyn for his own welfare's sake. It was evident to all who would have listened to the game at Bridgend that he had been drinking too much. We needed to tell him the news gently, but firmly, but there was no way he could carry on as he was and he needed to look after himself far better than he was doing. My colleague Teleri Bevan and I went to visit him in his flat that Monday. We explained our thoughts and told him we would have to suspend him from his work for the rest of the season. That would be about six or eight weeks. He took the news like a little lamb. No protestations, no defence; he just consented.

He played no further part in broadcasting in the 1981–82 season. That was not the first break he'd had from work that year. In the January, while in London on *Guardian* duties, he was taken ill on the Tube and had to be rushed to hospital, where he stayed for nearly a week. Not many knew about this minor heart attack, not even some members of his own family. The private Carwyn made sure of that.

Since his return from Italy, there had been much debate as to Carwyn's merits as a broadcaster. Not everyone thought that he was a natural, especially on television. He was more of a radio man they said, where his broadcasting was more analytical and authoritative. That year, 1982, would see the birth of the Welsh-language fourth channel, S4C. Carwyn, possibly aware of the comments of others, or perhaps just sticking to his own preferences, said that he wanted to stay with radio and turned down the opportunity to be a part of the beginnings of S4C.

But there's a question here. Was Carwyn given the best opportunities within the BBC to develop his abilities? It is astonishing that a man of his calibre and stature, for example, was asked to work shifts presenting sports bulletins. Would Sir Clive Woodward be used in the same way today? Carwyn was not used properly by the BBC – this was another Welsh establishment that had let Carwyn down.

His brother Dewi, a quiet man, reserved his strongest animosity for the way the BBC treated his brother. He was to say, in moments more of heat than light, no doubt, but felt none the less for that, that the BBC had killed his brother. Strong words. One who heard Dewi speak in similar terms was the schoolgirl cook at the Llangrannog Urdd Camp, who went on to be one of Wales' foremost broadcasters, Beti George:

> On my weekly radio programme, *Beti a'i Phobol* (Beti and her People), Dewi was a guest one week. He had spoken to me many a time before that about Carwyn's involvement with the BBC. He said that BBC Wales had a huge responsibility for the way in which Carwyn's life ended. There was obvious sincere brotherly bias in his words, but he wasn't one to be dramatic. There's a lot in what he says. Where else but in Wales would someone of Carwyn's ability be used in such a demeaning way? It was a misuse of Carwyn, without a doubt.

Fellow broadcaster, and the man by his side that fateful day in Bridgend, Huw Llywelyn Davies adds to this:

> Carwyn was a contributor and a creator of ideas, not the presenter of reports and facts. As valuable as his rugby contributions were, I'm sure that he felt from time to time that there was something empty about all that, and that the work wasn't substantial enough to satisfy him.

The use made of him at BBC Wales was an insult to him. The WRU had previously failed to utilise his abilities, talent and knowledge, and now the BBC had done the same.

He faced an animosity of a particular kind in BBC corridors too. There was a minority there who resented the Welsh language specifically because those who spoke the language seemed to have a clearer path to the top of the BBC than those who didn't. In such a climate, anyone who became prominent within the BBC and spoke Welsh was deemed a potential threat to their career progress. Carwyn was one towards whom such jealousy was directed. Hopefully, such feelings abated when they realised that Carwyn was not senior management material, any more than he had been MP material.

Drying out

So Carwyn had time on his hands in mid-1982, giving him an opportunity to deal with the cause of him being laid off work in the first place. There was no shortage of friends and family who wanted to help. The help that worked came from Graham Jenkins, brother of Richard Burton. He'd had more than enough experience of the problems Carwyn faced with his hell-raising brother. He arranged for Carwyn to go to the Priory clinic to be dried out. Carwyn went and received the treatment. Beti George remembers him coming back from there:

> He used to come to our house every Sunday almost, for Sunday lunch. That first Sunday after he came back from London we invited him once more. We were very unsure what we were supposed to do. Did we put wine out as usual? We decided not to, and all who were there had water with their meal. The same happened the next week and for a while after. Then some of us decided that we would have wine, but Carwyn stuck to the water. After a while again, Carwyn started on the wine once more.

One of the other guests at that Sunday table was Lorraine Davies, producer of BBC drama and the popular British series, *Children's Hour*. She had also produced some of Dylan Thomas' radio plays when the poet was alive. Beti remembers:

> Carwyn and Lorraine would be engaged in conversation for hours on end, discussing various plays and works of literarure. All the rest of us could do was sit back in amazement and awe, admiring their knowledge and understanding, and delighting in the meeting of two minds.

A picture of the intellectual, socialising Carwyn forms in the days when he was living in Fairwater and there's no doubting its vibrance and stimulation. But, as always with Carwyn, there was a duplicity, as David Foot recalls:

> Once private barriers were broken down, he liked and needed people's company. He was patently happy amongst kindred souls: true rugby addicts, the game's thinkers, fellow journalists and broadcasters, Plaid Cymru devotees, the intellectuals and the gossips. But when he had shaken the last hand of the evening, gulped down the last G & T, run out of untipped cigarettes and remembered where he had left his raincoat, he was once more confronted with the cruel solitude of a clothes-strewn bachelor flat of aching emptiness.

The spirit of the night

This difficult year for Carwyn would have been made more intense by a natural tendency he had to feel the darker emotions – the melancholic and the sad. His poem on not being selected for the Welsh Schoolboys shows that he was a sensitive boy. He gave us a further and more advanced glimpse of this in a radio broadcast for the BBC in 1960, entitled *Llawenydd a Thristwch* (Happiness and Sadness). This talk, almost a meditation, is a combination of Carwyn's own experiences and his reflections on them in the context of both feelings. The Welsh, he says, have an interesting relationship with happiness and sadness, and he quotes one lady he knew from Cefneithin as an example. She would rejoice in her sadness, he says. He then relates his own memory of his first funeral, as a short-trousered boy holding his mother's hand:

> I was there, cosily, in that room holding a warm hand, but I knew that in those few seconds I became conscious of an emptiness, a sadness and an unnatural coldness. When I looked into her eyes, that experience intensified on seeing her distant and melancholic look as she stared through the curtains towards the Cross Colliery. In that instant, I lost the funeral and my mind sped through the confines of time to some invisible world. And there I was, in the centre, at my own funeral...

Thoughts very much embedded in the minor key, made all the more remarkable as they are attributed to a child as young as three. Or at least, that's how Carwyn in 1960, in his thirty-first year, recalls how he felt as a child in that situation. Either way, the feelings are his.

The other side, the major key, is discussed by Carwyn, but it is never an unfettered joy. There's always a 'but', as shown in the story he relates on the occasion of scoring his first points for Wales – a moment of true ecstasy for any rugby player:

> As I made my way back to my own half, tasting the electrifying atmosphere, I felt a hand on my shoulder and Rees Stephens' voice cutting across my thoughts and the voices of 60,000 people: 'Make the most of this moment my boy... it might never happen again.' In the blink of an eye, ecstatic joy turned to sadness with the vivid realisation, right in the middle of a state of excitement, that such moments are fleeting; they disappear, never to return.

For Carwyn, in this frame of mind, every silver lining had a cloud. He was to experience moments of greater ecstasy, in the first half of the Seventies, for example. The disappointments of disappearing moments of joy might well have been greater for him then. And no doubt they also played into the tired and half-hearted way he approached the Welsh coaching vacancy in 1974.

Having his flat in Fairwater, Cardiff did give him that home of his own in a way he had not really experienced previously. But it also isolated him. If sometimes the only voice he heard in his flat in Italy was the voice of the instructor on his 'learn Italian' LP, then in Fairwood he would often hear darker voices in those lonely moments. He would have been familiar with one contemporary Welsh song by pioneering band Edward H Dafis. The song 'Ysbryd y Nos' (Spirit of the Night) was written and sung by one of Carwyn's former Trinity students, Cleif Harpwood, after a time of particular darkness in his life. The song refers to empty whispers on the wind that chill the soul, and it's a plea for the spirit of the night to come and scatter every fear before the dawn arrives.

These characteristics were always a part of Carwyn, but they appeared with increasing frequency as he grew older and they escalated significantly in 1982.

Holidays

The ban lifted, Carwyn resumed his BBC rugby responsibilities at the beginning of the 1982–83 season. His writing had continued throughout the suspension. He made a few TV programmes for Welsh-language feature series *Lloffa* (Gleaning), including one with Swansea centenarian John Llewitha. He was beginning to put the pieces back together again.

After months of psychological and emotional ebb and flow, Carwyn realised that he needed a holiday, a break from the familiar. It's little wonder that he felt like this at the end of a year when he'd suffered a heart attack, been suspended from his work because of his drinking and had to get treatment to dry out.

Needless to say, others saw the same need for Carwyn. Gareth Price's secretary, Brenda Thomas, took it upon herself to arrange a holiday for him. She had already taken some of Carwyn's practical affairs into her own hands, having been appalled to discover how many uncashed cheques there were in his car. She arranged for the BBC to send all Carwyn's payments from that point on to her, so that they would be properly banked. Now she was his holiday organiser.

The first choice was the Caribbean, with the tropical sun being deemed beneficial for Carwyn's skin condition as well. But it proved impossible to book a week's holiday there at such short notice. Someone within the walls of the BBC mentioned that they knew of a good hotel in Amsterdam, the Hotel Krasnapolsky, and added the throwaway line that Hitler had stayed there once. Brenda Thomas made enquiries, and the hotel had a vacancy. The holiday was booked. Carwyn flew to Amsterdam on Monday 3 January 1983.

Chapter 22

Amsterdam and the end

Even the knowledge of my own fallibility cannot keep me from making mistakes. Only when I fall do I get up again.
Vincent Van Gogh

CARWYN'S LAST WEEKEND in Wales was certainly a busy one. On the Friday night, New Year's Eve, he was at a party in Beti George and David Parry-Jones' home. On the Saturday he was watching a rugby game in Cardiff, where he bumped into Clive Rowlands and his wife.

> He didn't look too good that day to be honest. We asked him if he wanted to come and stay with us that evening, as he had done many a time before. We thought this would avoid him going back home on his own. He refused, saying that he was going on holiday the following Monday, to Amsterdam. We never saw him again.

That evening, he was in the BBC Club, where Huw Llywelyn Davies was also:

> We were quite a crowd there that evening. Carwyn shared with us that he was going to Amsterdam on holiday in order to have a break, away from everything. He wanted to go to the sun, but there was nothing available, so Amsterdam was chosen.

His desire for sun no doubt came from memories of the warm Rovigo rays that had done him so much good.

On Sunday 2 January, his brother Dewi and sister Gwen were at his flat in Cardiff, no doubt to make sure that everything was in order for his holiday. Everything was, apart from Carwyn himself. That morning he had been to the BBC club once again, seen by minister and BBC scriptwriter, T James Jones:

> I was on my way home, having been preaching somewhere, and I called into the club. Carwyn was there, on his own. I sat with him and we chatted about everything and nothing really. He mentioned that he was going on holiday the day after, and that was it, the last time I saw him.

From there, Carwyn went home, brother and sister already there. Later in the day, a concerned and worried Gwen phoned the BBC's Gareth Price. Gareth Price recalls:

> I knew Gwen, having been at their home, Hawen, on many an occasion with Carwyn. And as was the order of things, she would prepare food for us and then retreat to the back kitchen. That Sunday, she was really disturbed and asked me to go over the flat. When I got there, Carwyn was there as well and he was not in a good state. Gwen wanted me to try and persuade him not to go on his holiday. It wouldn't be good for him to be on his own for that length of time. But James would have nothing of it. Who was I to tell him otherwise, he challenged me in no uncertain terms. No one was going to persuade him otherwise.

Gareth Price's story includes an account of Gwen and Dewi's response to Carwyn's behaviour and demeanour that day. He says that the two hadn't realised that Carwyn was drunk and were in complete denial. That is difficult to believe. Dewi had been in the Navy for a couple of years and had seen many a variation of drunken behaviour, even if he himself was only a moderate drinker. He was more than aware of the sailor's culture, including its sexual manifestation. Early in his time at sea, Dewi heard a group of sailors discussing one of the younger men nearby, with one saying, 'Leave him alone, he's mine!' Dewi wasn't as sheltered as many believed.

Gwen, as a psychiatric nurse, certainly would not only have seen drunken behaviour but would have experience and knowledge of the related psychological issues of cause and effect as well. She saw many other psychological conditions at their most raw and direct. Many of those in her care were the sons of eminent politicians and judges, put in that private Gloucestershire hospital to be 'cured' of their unnatural sexual tendencies. It is hard to believe, therefore, that neither brother nor sister could recognise a drunken and disturbed Carwyn.

Dewi was so concerned about his brother that he wrote to his son, Llyr, who was to fly out to Zürich to start a new job on the same day that Carwyn was to fly to Amsterdam. Llyr takes up the story:

> My father wrote to me, saying that he was worried about Carwyn, and that we as a family needed to do something about the situation. We knew that he had had a heart attack, or a heart issue, the previous January. That was obviously fresh in my father's mind, knowing that Carwyn was flying to Amsterdam. But because of the nature of international mail in those days, I didn't get the letter until Carwyn was dead.

Over the Friday, Saturday and Sunday of his last weekend in Wales, therefore, Carwyn saw many key individuals in his life. Beti George, David Parry-Jones, Clive Rowlands, Huw Llywelyn Davies, T James Jones and Gareth Price: people from the Welsh-speaking world and the worlds of broadcasting, rugby and religion. Each one feels a sense of frustration and regret that they were there at such a time, they could see what Carwyn was like, but they were completely helpless to do anything to change the situation. It's the exposed, vulnerable and horrible position that friendship can put you in.

Last days in Amsterdam

The details of what Carwyn did during his seven days in Amsterdam have gone with him to his grave. It is not difficult, however, to imagine what this man of culture would have done in such a city: the city of Rembrandt and a school of fine art that influenced the world; of Van Gogh's individual and colourful contribution; of Anne Frank's personal, inspirational suffering; the flowers; the canals in this the Venice of the North; and so much more. This is where he could wander and wonder.

If the Italian culture had seduced him, Amsterdam would have equally. Of all the coffee houses there, no doubt the 'brown cafés' would have been his delight. How easy to picture him sitting within those dark brown walls, nicotine thick on the ceilings above and the pale light of the scattered lamps casting their gentle shadows over those sipping their coffees, chatting and reading their daily papers as many shared their loneliness under the one cloud of smoke.

It was also the city of tolerance, where architectural manifestations showed off attitudes. If drugs and prostitution were going to happen, the thinking went, they might as well be in the open rather than underground, and building design followed this ethos. So different to Carwyn's Wales.

On the Sunday night he was preparing to go out. Where he was going and who he would have been meeting, if anyone, we'll never know. He was aware enough, and responsible enough, to know that he needed to make himself look respectable before going wherever he was going. He had probably been out that day, but knew he had to go back to the hotel in order to prepare himself to go back out again.

He had a bath and then went to shave. Suddenly, almost exactly a year since the same thing had happened to him, he suffered a heart attack. He stumbled against the hand basin, slipped off it and fell into the water he had just stepped out of. And he died. He lay a still and silent corpse in his own dirty water, but almost clean shaven. The *Western Mail* said that he had lain there for several days, but that is not correct. A maid discovered him there the following morning – the day when he would have been flying home. No post mortem was held. The official verdict was that he died as a result of a heart attack.

Carwyn had joined the list of influential Welshmen who loved their mother country, but died abroad. Dylan Thomas and Ryan Davies breathed their last on foreign soil. Just over a year after Carwyn, Richard Burton would join that list and 13 years later, Ray Gravell would suffer the same fate. All of these influential, innovative and mould-breaking Welshmen identified heavily with a definite patch of Welsh soil but ended their lives far, far away from that formative earth. In Carwyn's case, it was a double irony. He came into this world under the shadow of a village, Rhydlewis, he had never lived in but which had shaped the family he was born into. He left this world in a place that was alien to his heritage, far removed from the life he'd carved for himself. In his coming and his going, there was a displacement.

The shock spreads

The news hit everyone in Wales, and in the rugby world generally, very hard. Newspapers and magazines devoted pages and pages to his passing. 'Prince of Coaches', said David Frost in *The Guardian*. 'The Intellectual Welsh legend' was how Clem Thomas described him in the same paper. Wales' *Western Mail* hailed him as 'Carwyn, part of Welsh legend', in John Billot's words, and Mario Basini said he was 'a Bard amongst coaches'. Welsh-language weekly *Y Faner* (The Flag) gave him more than one tribute, including a cartoon on its cover, a poem by Dic Jones and a tribute by Huw Llewelyn Davies under the heading, 'A genius in a heart and soul battle'. In February, there was another tribute to him in *Y Faner*, by James Nicholas. The pioneering Welsh-language Sunday paper that he had championed, *Sulyn*, paid tribute to him in an article headed, 'The Complete Welshman'. Welsh-language weekly *Y Cymro* (The Welshman) commemorated him by publishing an article by Gwynfor Evans entitled 'A Man of Conviction'. Monthly Welsh-language magazine *Barn* (Opinion) printed two tributes in their February edition, one by Barry John and the other by Norah Isaac. Other publications as diverse as the publication of the Union of Welsh Congregationalists, *Y Tyst* (The Witness), and the Welsh Rugby Union publication *Welsh Rugby*, paid their own kind of tribute.

Television and radio gave hours. His contribution to rugby,

The Big Five and a memorial article for Carwyn

both in Wales and worldwide, was evaluated. His literary criticism and comprehension was warmly appreciated. His broadcasting was honoured. His political stand for his country was venerated. His personality weighed and measured. All contributing to, and perpetuating, Alun Richards' quote that everyone knew a lot about him, but who really knew him? There was a perception of knowing. Not that this meant any lack of sincerity, respect or admiration. They were all there in genuine abundance.

As happens when an influence, a champion, passes from this world, people remembered where they were when they heard of that passing. His nephew Llyr was only a few days into his new job in Zürich.

I had a phone message from my head office in Swansea, asking me to ring a Cardiff phone number they gave me. I knew exactly what sort of message would be waiting for me at the other end of that call. I'd been given the phone number of Carwyn's flat, and when I dialled it, my father answered. Gwen was there also, as well as Huw Lewis, from the Gomer Press family. 'Your uncle has died,' were my father's simple words. It was no surprise to me at all.

Bethan, the daughter of Carwyn's sister Eilonwy, was in Cardiff when she heard the news.

My parents had tried more than once to contact me in order to tell me the news. I was working at Cardiff University at the time, but I was staying with a friend, not at my home, because I was recuperating from a bout of measles and wanted company. That Monday evening, the news was on in her house and I suddenly heard the words, 'Carwyn James found dead in Amsterdam'. It was a huge shock and I was quite shaken. I would see Uncle Carwyn fairly often in Cardiff and my mother would go to his flat quite often to help Auntie Gwen with the cleaning and washing for him.

Outside the family circle, others shared how they heard of Carwyn's death – Frank Keating from *The Guardian*, for example, who had previously noted his disappointment that Carwyn hadn't been able to join him at the newspaper's New Year's party.

> I was having a bath. The six o'clock BBC TV news was droning on down the corridor. Suddenly I was standing in the sitting room, dripping and unbelieving. Carwyn James was dead... He had suffered a heart attack in his bath at a hotel in Amsterdam the night before – the evening *The Guardian* had hoped to see him in this very flat at their party... No, I still couldn't believe it.

In summing up the contribution that Carwyn made to every aspect of life that he touched, Keating succinctly touches on Carwyn's disparate qualities:

> Has modern, organised sport thrown up such a man as Carwyn? At one and the same time, poet and pragmatist and preacher, practiser and philosopher, wide-eyed innocent and melancholic optimist.

Gwilym Owen notes the impact the news had on the Welsh Corporation and its staff at BBC Wales' HQ in Llandaff, Cardiff:

> I have never seen a place under so much emotion, feeling the impact of someone's passing so heavily. It was a profound response to Carwyn's death and many were in tears.

Within the same organsation, friend and fellow Welsh international Onllwyn Brace said:

> The sadness that we feel at his passing is shared by Italians, Spaniards, Romanians, Argentines, Japanese, New Zealanders, South Africans and Australians alike – the common language was rugby.

And of course, the sad news reached Italy. The townspeople

of Rovigo felt the loss, but no one more so than his close friend Angelo Morello. He sums up his response, in words put together for this book:

> I only found out about Carwyn's death on Wednesday, 12 January 1983. It was a very cold day, as cold as it usually is in Rovigo in January. No fog, only frost. Carwyn did not like the foggy weather, it made him sad. Nairn MacEwan, the Rovigo RFC coach, said to me when I met him very early that morning: 'Angelo, have you heard?' 'What?' I asked. 'Your friend Carwyn is dead.' I remember I was stunned and too many thoughts jumped into my brain. Nairn understood my feeling and went on to explain how it had happened.
>
> Only a few days later was I informed about his hopeless attempt to spend a quiet Christmas holiday somewhere abroad, alone, far from any of his friends. It was a sudden, terrible blow for me (and surely for many others), because he was a leading man and a true friend. He was always able to give you the right advice simply because he understood the genuine roots of life. My task with him was one of helping him get to know the country he was living in better, the local people's habits, their way of life. It was not just a matter of rugby – we talked about many other aspects related to our experience: art, music, literature, poetry, politics, food, travel, etc.
>
> I was really lucky to be the only man in Italy to be able to listen to Carwyn's ideas, appreciations, projects, judgments, likes and dislikes about all that is life. And because he was such a man, his death was a big loss. The Rovigo people, especially the rugby supporters, were shocked, too. However, their sorrow was mainly related to the great rugby coach or to the guy they were used to eating with at restaurants – in other words something rather superficial, although they sincerely admired the 'guru' in him.
>
> This reminds me of Wordsworth's line from one of the Lucy poems: 'oh, the difference to me!'

Rugby stars offered their praise. A star of the Lions in 1971, Ian McLauchlan, was one:

> I shall always remember his gentleness. In New Zealand, he was

dealing with a fairly rough bunch of blokes, but he never had to utter a harsh word and never had to raise his voice. Our success was entirely due to him.

Cliff Morgan said, simply,

We will never see his like again.

Wiilie John McBride shared how he felt:

He had more to give and the great game will miss him a great deal. Rugby has lost a great friend.

For David Frost it was clear:

There will never be anyone better.

The rugby world was as one in their expression of loss. The varied and multiple tributes could be summed up in the phrase of Delme Thomas, still as heartfelt and meaningful as it was nearly a quarter of a century ago:

I've never ever met anyone like him.

CHAPTER 23

Carwyn *In Memoriam*

...he liked a quiet corner.

Clem Thomas

THE LITTLE CHAPEL of Tabernacl in Carwyn's Cefneithin hadn't seen anything like it before. On the last Saturday morning of January 1983, hundreds filled any space they could inside and outside the chapel, to bid their fond farewells to the man they all loved and revered for many different reasons. Inside, there wasn't an empty seat, with many sitting on the stairs in the gallery and standing in the aisles as well as in the entrance porch. Outside, they filled the path from the main road to the main door and the grass around, standing amongst the tilting gravestones that showed this to be a community shaped by coal. Phil Bennett was one who failed to gain entry to the chapel, which held more than the entire population of the village.

In his last-minute addition to Carwyn's book *Focus on Rugby*, Gerald Davies refers to the memorial service in Tabenacl.

> A week ago at the Tabernacl Cefneithin, where he was a deacon, a remembrance service was held as a tribute. There could have been no better illustration of the range and depth of feeling and friendship which he inspired. Politicians and poets, deacons and doctors of medicine and philosophy were there. Lawyers and lecturers, miners and fellows in faded duffle coats. Rugby men who understood not a word of the all-Welsh service... All loyal friends who came to pay a final homage to Carwyn James, a man who effortlessly bestrode their differing worlds. All in all, we shall not see his like again.

One man succeeded in finding room in the packed chapel, however. Frank Keating arrived relatively late and asked at the door if it would be OK for him to sit inside. When he was told there was no room, he pleaded, saying he was from *The Guardian*. 'Oh, in that case you must come in!' was the reply. As they made their way through the crowd, Keating's chaperone explained why his guest was being allowed in while others were turned away, 'He's from the *Ammanford Guardian* you see! He must come in!' Keating of course worked for *The Guardian* for sale to everyone in Britain, not the local newspaper of the same name. The chaperone had assumed it must be the local one that Keating was from and that was more than enough to grant him access. One paper evidently carried more authority than the other in this patch of land.

An event of this nature in the west of Wales, and in the name or rugby, is sure to create its own folklore. One anecdote that might contribute to that body of stories is to do with a group of people who weren't allowed into the service at all – in fact, they were sent away. The Big Five, the Welsh Rugby Union's selectors, had turned up together only to be given the cold shoulder by the people of Cefneithin and told in no uncertain terms to get out of town. The story ends with the five walking away into the distance. Whether this actually happened or not is almost irrelevant. Its impact is the fact that local people felt so strongly that their hero had been rejected, they wanted the story to be true. It shows the depth of feeling and the nature of loyalty.

The service was entirely in Welsh, quite probably not the result of hours of deliberation, but because those involved wouldn't have even considered holding it in any other language. It was broadcast on BBC radio, with the Corporation allowing the use of their facilities to relay the service to those who had to sit in the adjacent vestry.

Once officially allowed in, the British *Guardian*'s Frank Keating could offer his observations.

The world may have been watching, but this was a private ceremony – the enclosed, exclusive Celtic village paying homage to a favourite villager. I was the interloper, for while the soul was moved, I did not understand one word. I would whisper to my neighbour for an English equivalent. They would crease their brow to help, before apologising, 'All lost in translation, boy.'

Four leading men from different fields were asked to pay tribute to Carwyn during the service. The first was Handel Greville, former Scarlets player and leading Llanelli RFC official. Having established that Carwyn's first game for the club was played under his captaincy in what was one of the worst seasons ever for Llanelli, Greville evaluates Carwyn's contribution:

> It was as a coach that Carwyn made the greatest contribution to Llanelli and to the world of rugby. He had a special gift, and as a club we have a great deal to thank him for. He made our club a special one. Carwyn was one of the boys. When we travelled on the bus, he would be at the back with the players, laughing, arguing, singing. He was in his element. He had a very good singing voice, a tenor, and you should have heard him and say, Bert Peel – another tenor – singing 'Myfanwy' or 'Hywel and Blodwen'.
>
> …The game of rugby as a whole has so much to thank him for. He was years ahead of his time. I remember him speaking to some society a few years back, and he said something like this, in English, 'Rugby is going to be *the* spectator game.' That was quite a statement to make at the time, as the game was not in good shape. Carwyn's contribution, no doubt, is responsible for the good condition the game is in today.

The next up into the pulpit was Head of BBC Wales Sport, Thomas Davies. The two had worked together, he said, for 20 years, and he had been consistently impressed over that period by Carwyn's originality of ideas and his attention to clarity and correctness of language, in both Welsh and English:

> He was a very good listener. That's why he was so good at interviewing people, not just on rugby matters. He would give as

much time to the fool as to the wise man. I remember one meeting, which was a post mortem on some programme or other, and we were discussing interviewing techniques. Carwyn then said, 'Only one question needs to be prepared beforehand. The first one. If that question is right, then every other question should come from the answer to that question.' That's the kind of mind he had. He was on a higher level than the rest of us.

At a time of grief, when sweeter memories can banish darker ones, Thomas Davies didn't pretend that there were no difficulties in Carwyn's life. He had, after all, had to break the news to Carwyn of his suspension from the BBC.

> I can't say that he didn't have his problems, especially on Saturday mornings, when one would say, 'Where's Carwyn?' while another would ask, 'When is he going to turn up?' We know where he is today. And even though those problems have disappeared, one problem more than any other remains: who can fill the gap left in the sports department in Llandaff?

The next eulogy came from the cultural world of Wales, as embodied in its main cultural event, the National Eisteddfod. Its proceedings are overseen by the Gorsedd of Bards, under the leadership of the Archdruid. The Archdruid at the time of Carwyn's death was James Nicholas. Not surprisingly, he used Carwyn's speech as the President of the Day at the Haverfordwest Eisteddfod in 1972 as the basis of his tribute. He refers to it as one of the most notable speeches of its kind. He develops the theme referred to by Carwyn when he used the story of Pwyll from Welsh folk literature, *The Mabinogion*.

> He emphasises that Pwyll belonged to his people. He emphasises belonging and knowing. He asks what knowing is and quotes another Welsh poet, Waldo in his answer, 'Having one root under all the branches.' He magnifies Pwyll because he was one who could identify with the cloud of witnesses. Carwyn had the same ability to recognise who the cloud of witnesses are. By now, he is in their midst. He was horrified by the depersonalisation that goes on

in the world. He brings his speech to an end by glorifying people being close to each other. You felt that closeness when you were speaking to Carwyn.

James Nicholas then tells the story of the last time he saw Carwyn, at BBC Wales in Llandaff.

He introduced someone to me, and to my shame, I didn't recognise that he was Colin Meads. Carwyn asked me what I was doing in the BBC that day and I said I was recording a programme on Niclas y Glais. Carwyn showed great interest in that. That's the last memory I will have of him, the man who was an amalgam of Colin Meads and Niclas y Glais: the culture of the playing fields and the culture of the working people of Wales; the the man who was a bridge between the continents of the South Seas and Wales.

The last to step forward to pay tribute to Carwyn was Gwynfor Evans. He said that when he first met Carwyn, in Carwyn's student days in Aberystwyth, he met a man who had already played for his country at schoolboy level, a cultured man and a member of Plaid Cymru. Carwyn was a man, he said, who stood for his principles, however unpopular that could make him, a man willing to pay for his convictions.

When he stood as candidate for the local council here, he didn't receive honourable support, and despite the fact that he was the greatest authority on rugby in Wales, he wasn't put in any great position of responsibility in that field. He wasn't chosen to be on the Big Five, but he was prepared to pay the price for his convictions. He was a man who was faithful to Wales. He was a unique person. His faithfulness is a source of pride for us today.
…Despite all his talents, his loyalty was his greatest glory. Even though he was famous in many countries, and he had many honours in many countries, yet wherever he was, he would stand as a Welshman. He was a Welshman as solid as a rock. He wasn't a sentimental playing-field Welshman but a Welshman who would stick to Wales with loyalty and steadfastness…He had no shame of his chapel, and no shame either of Jesus as his Lord.

The words spoken by the four bring colours from the main palettes of his life to his portrait, the primary colours of broadcasting, politics, Welsh heritage and rugby. Incidental colours were added by others in between these four speakers. The service was led by the Reverend Elfed Lewys: folk singer, activist and the son of the Minister at Tabernacl through most of Carwyn's life. The choral singing tradition was honoured by Mynydd Mawr Male Voice Choir's contribution, singing the Welsh hymn, *'Tydi a Rhoddaist'* (Thou Gavest). Carwyn had been a vice-president of this choir, along with Barry John. The leaflet printed for the service included references to the Urdd, The Welsh League of Youth, with their pledge on the cover: a promise to be faithful to Wales, to fellow man and to Christ.

This public and, at the same time, intimate act of remembering took place amongst the pews and chapel furniture that Carwyn had been more than familiar with throughout his short life. He had been the youngest ever to be chosen as deacon at Tabernacl, but had not conformed with tradition and taken his place at the front of the chapel in the pew kept specially for the deacons. He had always sat at the back. Consequently he was known, affectionately, as the Back-Seat Deacon. Some say that he did this because he could creep in late if he had to. Others say that he was there because he could sneak out early, to draw heavily on that first post-sermon fag on the side of the road opposite the chapel, near the park. As a deacon, he was given the responsibility of organising the guest preachers from other chapels to come to Tabernacl. In light of this, he would cheekily refer to himself as 'the fixture sec'.

This linking of rugby and religion continued on the day of the memorial service, with devotion at the cathedral of club rugby where Carwyn had been High Priest for so long as much a part of the remembrance as the service in the chapel. The service over, many continued their pilgrimage by going to Stradey Park to watch Llanelli play that afternoon. In the stand that day, having gone there from the chapel, were Gareth Edwards, Gerald Davies, Barry John and so many other stars of the Seventies. Once that Llanelli game was over, the tributes continued in the Social Club – the impromptu, off-the-cuff, spontaneous tributes of the people of the terraces, those to whom Carwyn knew he 'belonged'. The day of remembering ended in random pubs across Llanelli, where men and women would share their thoughts of the one who was one of them, but head and shoulders above them also. These were multiple, colourful branches of various sizes, strengths and health – some strong and tall; others small but well-formed; many average and uniform; one or two misshapen; but all with one thing in common: they came from the same root.

Ashes

Even in death Carwyn didn't take his place in the deacon's pew, the *Sêt Fawr* (Big Seat), as it is called. That's where coffins would usually be placed. But he wasn't at that Tabernacl service. This was not his burial, rather the memorial. Body and soul had left this world a few days before the public ceremony, in a manner that befitted Carwyn so well. No pomp, no ceremony, no proclamation. All was private.

On Monday 17 January, seven days after being found in the bath in Amsterdam, Carwyn's funeral service was held. It was the most appropriate and apposite end to Carwyn James' life. The day began with a simple service on the family hearth at Hawen, Cefneithin, held in the front room – the traditional forum for a Welsh funeral, the room often kept under reverential lock and key all year round, apart from funeral days and the visit of the minister. It was the domestic Welsh sepulchure.

In that small, homely room, chapel ministers and family members gathered, supported by a handful of friends, the mourning led by Gwen, Eilonwy and Dewi. Three ministers took part in that short, simple service and then the coffin was carried out by two men from the village, Cyril Rogers and Wil Morgan, and four stalwarts of Llanelli, Welsh and British rugby: Delme Thomas, Derek Quinnell, Norman Gale and

Ray Gravell. They were the ones who shared that meaningful, final farewell. The funeral procession then made its way to Morriston Crematorium.

They headed in the direction of Rose Villa, where Carwyn was born, and turned left down Heol y Dre towards Garreg Hollt. At the T junction where they would turn left to head on to the main road to Morriston, a policeman was directing traffic. He lifted his right hand and gave a dignified salute to the car that carried Carwyn. Carwyn's cousin, Dai Rees Davies, in a car behind, was overwhelmed by such a gesture:

> It was like he was saluting a king! I'll never forget that mark of respect.

One close friend of Carwyn's wasn't at that funeral service, even though he would have been welcome there. The poet and author Dafydd Rowlands could not face being there, and had decided to go to work at Trinity College as usual. It was too much for him to be emotionally involved in the marking of Carwyn's death. But fate intervened. Having left the saluting policeman behind them, the funeral cortège headed towards the traffic lights on the busy square in the centre of the village of Cross Hands, and slowed down to stop at the red lights. On the other side, coming from Swansea, a car had done the same. In that vehicle, Dafydd Rowlands looked across the square with an instant recognition that his friend Carwyn was in the hearse opposite. He didn't need anyone to tell him that. He knew. The lights changed to green and both vehicles came towards each other. Dafydd Rowlands looked at the coffin that held his friend and raised his hand in one final, poignant farewell before the two friends crossed paths and drove away from each other for ever.

Rowlands' wife testifies that she welcomed home a shaken and emotional husband that evening, a man deeply touched by the almost spiritual significance of that chance meeting at the traffic lights. A week to the following Saturday, Dafydd

Rowlands took his place in the Memorial Service in Tabernacl, and read a selection of verse from one of Carwyn's favourite poets, Gwenallt.

Carwyn has no gravestone. His ashes weren't scattered in a favourite place such as Rhydlewis, Cefneithin or his beloved Stradey. Neither were they scattered in the crematorium grounds and therefore there is no plaque there to note his passing either. The only public acknowledgement of how Carwyn left this world is on the date of his cremation every year, when the book which records all cremation on that day is opened. It was a very private end indeed.

Corporation remembrance

On the Sunday night after the cremation, the people of his chapel had their usual communion service. But this particular one was a further opportunity to mark Carwyn's passing and just like the funeral day itself, it was a quiet occasion, marked by plain simplicity. The breaking of bread and the fellowship of mourning within the only four walls remaining which had seen both Carwyn's arrival and departure.

Once the reserved and homely devotions had been made, the public declarations took place. A week after the Tabernacl service, on Saturday 5 February, there was another one. Carwyn's colleagues at the BBC held a service of rememberance in Llandaff. And just as Cefneithin's commemoration happened on the day of a home match at Stradey, the BBC's took place on the morning of the Five Nations game between England and Wales in Cardiff. This timing was not lost on the man who welcomed everyone gathered that morning, BBC Wales Controller, Geraint Stanley Jones:

> The morning of the match is traditionally a time of anticipation and of excitement; a time, too, for memories. We are gathered here this morning with our memories and with our thanks for having had the privilege of touching a complete Welshman.

391

I GOFIO
CARWYN JAMES
REMEMBERED
1929-1983

CYFARFOD COFFA
YNG NGHANOLFAN Y BBC
LLANDÂF
5ed Chwefror, 1983

MEMORIAL SERVICE
AT
BROADCASTING HOUSE
LLANDAFF
5th February, 1983

"Adnabod nid gwybod yw'n gobaith"

*" . . . the qualities of honour, courage
and pride in performance"*

The BBC remembers

392

Five-times British Lion Willie John McBride took to the podium and read a piece called 'The Soul of a Nation'. There is no reference to its origin, but part of it contains words spoken by Carwyn in one of the voiceovers for the *A Disunited Kingdom?* programme he did for the BBC in the late Sixties. This is the part not in that programme:

> Wales has a soul, a soul which is her own. And she can lose it.
> Education may thrive, religion may increase its hold, freedom may
> be won, the poor may arise from the dust and become powerful,
> the wealthy may be strong and flourish like the green bay, and the
> nation's soul may weaken and fade.
>   The nation may lose itself in the empire, and be a dead member
> and not a living one, her voice never more to be heard. And if that
> calamity were to come about, Wales would be without a soul,
> and the world would be the poorer. But let us not lose sight of
> the nation's soul, lest among much fine building and enthusiastic
> committee-work it vanish from sight.

Three years previously, Clem Thomas had been with Carwyn on the British Lions tour of South Africa, and had had to play a fatherly role in looking after Carwyn while he was out there, because of the latter's fondness for the drink. It was said that on that tour, Clem Thomas, along with John Reason of *The Daily Telegraph*, 'arranged their dear friend's disorder'. Carwyn and Clem had known each other since Schoolboy rugby days, and Clem respected Carwyn very much. His words that morning are given a further significance in the knowledge of that fatherly intervention:

> I do not believe that we have come here today to mourn Carwyn
> or to grieve for him. We have all already done that in our private
> ways. Instead, we have gathered to pay tribute and to honour a
> very special man who had a relevance for all of us, whether we are
> rugby people, academics, politicians or journalists.
>   He was a person who cared little for the material things of
> life. He dealt in the more substantial currencies of friendship,
> kindliness, courtesy, modesty, generosity, dignity and patriotism.

He was famous, but devoted no time to it. He died in a lonely way, but he is one of those, and I quote, 'of those immortal dead who live again in minds made better by their presence'.

The principal thrust of his life was reserved for rugby football, where after being a fine and elegant fly half, he then became a bard amongst coaches. He was without question the greatest rugby coach of all time.

His calm intellectualism, philosophies and vision brought him that essential ingredient – respect – from those players fortunate to find themselves under his command. Together, they translated their rapport into unparalleled success...

However, he was far more than just a rugby man. He was an academic, a bard of the Welsh Gorsedd and a nationalist. But not a nationalist in the narrow sense, for he was also an internationalist.

He would have no part of those who bomb or burn any more than he would be any part of brutality on the rugby field.

He was more concerned that through the democratic processes, Wales should be accorded its rightful stature, and that its culture, language, literature and music should be safeguarded and nourished. He was no saint, but he had saintly qualities.

He was a person who suffered grievously in many ways. The torment of a terrible skin disorder would have made lesser men totally irascible and impossible. But not Carwyn. Having travelled and worked with him for many years, I never knew him to complain. Even *in extremis*, he was always unfailingly courteous and always found time to listen.

We will miss him, especially on occasions such as today, both for his camaraderie and for his definitive comments.

The day after he died I wrote that if I had to write his epitaph I would say of Carwyn that he liked a quiet corner, he only had friends and no enemies and that he possessed the greatest gift of all – friendship. Ladies and gentlemen, I think that you would all agree with me that Carwyn James, rugby man, scholar and patriot, has well earned his quiet corner.

The next contribution was by Alun Richards, author and friend, who would write his own personal memoir of Carwyn a year later. As mentioned earlier, Richards was the man who said that everyone knew of Carwyn, but no one really knew him. He himself came very close:

> He was the kind of man who on ceremonial occasions immediately sympathises with the soldier who drops his rifle. And yet, you know, if this was a service of commemoration for a Welshman of half his distinction, he'd be here. It would have been a must for his crowded diary, and he would have arrived on time, spruce.
>
> If there had been difficulty in parking, he'd have parked – somewhere… somehow… anywhere… anyhow. And if when he had gone, an official, a uniformed figure, happened to look into the back of that car of his, he might have seen on the back seat a small silver statuette of a helmeted constable, with the hand raised in the position of stop, and appropriately inscribed on the bottom of that little silver statuette was this inscription: 'Presented to Mr Carwyn James by the Somersetshire Police Rugby Team on the occasion of their annual dinner.'
>
> What was lovely about Carwyn was the naivety with which he left that little talisman in the back seat. One of hundreds he'd been given, but this one he didn't throw away. Whatever he was, he was not a yellow lines man.
>
> I speak of little things, as a friend should, but he was a very big man, great in little things as well as major achievements. His ideas were straightforward and uncomplicated. You couldn't spend any time with him without him reminding you of the poet Gwenallt's lines bidding you to care for your own country and saying that you cannot care for the nations of the world unless first you care for your own. That is to say, he liked his Irishmen Irish as well as his Welshmen Welsh, and he was aware of all the breedation – he liked his Cardiffians Cardiffian, and after a long period of conversion, his Pontypriddians Pontypriddian.
>
> Another favourite line of his was Milton's: 'Who overcomes by *force*, hath overcome but half his foe.' That tells us a good deal of Carwyn.
>
> Most of all he was interested in the individual; in the essence of another self. This explains his gift of friendship. At the heart of it was his capacity to get to the core of things. He did this by listening. Seldom can so much deserved praise have been uttered for a man who in private said so little and listened so much.

There was something there lurking behind that quizzical countenance that caused a reciprocal spark to ignite. A spark of fellow feeling. It was quite an uncanny and elusive quality. Young people detected it at once because perhaps they have a special way of knowing who is genuinely interested in them...

I said he was a private man and a public man. As a public man, the president of Llanelli [Rugby] Football Club – he was very proud of that, and they honoured him at the right time. As a public man, he took the talents and the riches of his parents, his place and his nation, and used them to enrich the inheritance of us all. As a private man, he had the aspirations of the dodo in *Alice in Wonderland*. He wanted everyone to have prizes.

This was the warmth, the uncomplicated and simple decency of a good and infinitely generous man.

BBC Wales religious programmes producer Meurwyn Williams offered prayers, continuity announcer Frank Lincoln read. This was a bilingual occasion when the establishment recognised a man they had not always succeeded in utilising or understanding, but one who they had always revered and supported in the way they saw was needed.

Poetry by two of his heroes, T H Parry-Williams and Gwenallt was read. Parry-Williams' poem *'Dychwelyd'* (Returning) was read by Huw Llewelyn Davies. It speaks of immortality and a man's place in it, saying that when we flee forever our foolish worldly fussing, we slip back once more into a great tranquility.

In the four weeks after he died, there were four public services where Carwyn was honoured. A diverse range of newspapers, magazines, radio and television programmes, across many countries, communicated tributes regularly. It would have been very difficult not to know that Carwyn James had died. But that was the knowing. The understanding was another matter, as summed up by his rugby and broadcasting colleague, Cliff Morgan:

Carwyn James has died. But you don't have to believe it if you don't want to.

CHAPTER 24

A mirror and a closet

Hay cosas encerradas detrás de los muros
que no pueden cambiar porque nadie las oye.
'There are things locked behind the walls
that can't change as no one hears them.'
Federico García Lorca, *Yerma*

AS THE LAST notes of memorial hymns faded, the last syllables of poetry disappeared and the final echoes of kind words and comments dissipated, a new conversation began. It was one to do with the why of his death, more than the where and the how. His last year on earth could easily be described as his *annus horribilis*. Everyone fairly close to him could see that, but for Carwyn himself it was a living reality. His desire for sun had been so much more than just needing a break at the end of a bad year. It was a critical step on an essential pilgrimage.

When he took that particular step out of his work routine and into the Netherlands' capital city, he walked into a place the Dutch affectionately call Mokum. It comes from the Hebrew world of Carwyn's Old Testament Sunday School days and means place, or safe place. Carwyn found a safe place for seven days early in the process of putting the pieces back together again. Those who have Carwyn's interest at heart can at least take some solace from that. He would have experienced some of the rest he needed. With Mokum under his feet, he would also have been able to open a few windows which were shut to him in Wales – the ones that kept out the light his soul needed.

The cracks in his life were multiple and well established, but the light was only just beginning to filter in through them.

A mirror

In the BBC Memorial Service, Alun Richards, ever the man of words, turned to a literary form to explain Carwyn. A metaphor, he said, would help us understand:

> Of late, he was in many ways like an old-fashioned mirror, wreathed in cigarette smoke very often… And in this mirror, chipped a little at the edges, when you looked into it, you got a better reflection of yourself. This is the gift of a friend indeed.

What he did for others, some did for him at this time, helping him to see and to understand what he saw. Dafydd Huws was one such person – a friend, a fellow nationalist but more relevantly in this case, a psychiatrist. Carwyn went to see him in his professional capacity. After Carwyn's days he shared some of the content of their conversations, although ever mindful of not stepping too far over the patient confidentiality line. Carwyn's family, it must be said, think that he did overstep the mark in making these comments publicly, by literally broadcasting them:

> Carwyn was a man who carried many burdens, which were more than most of us can comprehend, let alone endure. They were psychological burdens and physical burdens and I don't know how he managed to cope so well, and to be such a productive man.

Carwyn's friends had testified to his gypsy, scatty social nature, which was an integral part of both his innocence and his charm. But Huws explains that the reason Carwyn went to see him was that he had got to the point where he knew he needed to stabilise his life, and emphasises that this was a step Carwyn really did need to take for the sake of his own sanity. What Huws saw was a man who'd lost his roots, living from his suitcase or his car. As Huws started to unravel these thoughts, Carwyn interjected. Huws recounts:

> Before I could say anything further, he said, 'You know what I have to do, I need to find home and water my roots!' And I said, 'Yes, you've understood.'

It's from such a position that Carwyn began the process that led to, amongst other things, needing a holiday. The watering process continued in the Venice of the North. Throughout his life, he had succeeded in stretching his roots as he went from place to place, sometimes replanting, sometimes feeding from borrowed nutrients, but the strain was showing more and roots would tear from the soil with increased regularity.

> Living in a city would have been difficult for a man who had the problems Carwyn had. Visiting or living on different continents would have exacerbated the situation. He had come to understand that he needed to settle geographically, to set down firm roots. For him, this included reconnecting with chapel life. He said that he wanted to restore old patterns that would give him firmer and more definite guidelines. But yet, as with a drowning man, these were slipping away from him.

T H Parry-Williams, in one of his poems, refers to a scoundrel all astray, a man on the waters of a nightmare unable to reach the shore. That's where Carwyn was. He could see the shore before the end. But his depression, his psychological battles had isolated him, and in that isolation there was a disconnection.

This desire to re-establish 'home' did not mean a desire to move back to Cefneithin and certainly not Rhydlewis, which would forever be the out-of-reach paradise always needed but never visited. These two villages weren't part of the pattern Carwyn needed to restore. Rather, the values of these two places were the central threads he needed for his new pattern.

It's not only Dafydd Huws who was aware of the help

Carwyn needed. The family were staring into that mirror too, as his nephew Llyr James says:

> There were many discussions within the family at the time about Carwyn's condition. My father's letter to me was only one example of that process. Our family circumstances were changing in a way that was going to be beneficial to Carwyn. Between the end of 1982 and the beginning of 1983, my father was due to retire, I was coming back to Wales from Zürich and my sister Non was to start as a dietician in Glangwili Hospital, Carmarthen. So the three of us would be around to help in different ways. But unfortunately, Carwyn didn't live to see those three things happening.

The situation, therefore, as 1982 journeyed on its way, was that Carwyn was coming to a realisation that things needed to change, his family could see that and their circumstances were changing to help that process. He had professional help from Dafydd Huws and support from some other friends. These people knew not only that help was needed, but why.

Late tributes

Ten years after Carwyn's death, one of the few who knew of his inner battles wrote a moving tribute to him in the form of a letter. It appeared in Welsh-language magazine *Barn* (Opinion) in March 1993 and it was written by Dafydd Rowlands, the man who couldn't face going to Carwyn's funeral and whose last farewell to him had been at the traffic lights on Cross Hands Square. The letter is an apology for his absence that day. Rowlands hadn't written one word about his friend, nor contributed to any TV or radio programme about him, in those ten years.

It's a letter from a friend to a friend, opening with 'Dear Jâms' and ending, 'See you – Rowlands'.

> The truth is that you understand exactly the value of silence between two friends, those moments, sometimes long, sometimes short, when there's no speaking; when words, for their own sake,

can be a burden on friendship. Do you remember those countless lunch hours in the Chestnut Tree Café? The daily ham and chips, the bread and butter pudding drowning in a sea of custard, and us both behind our newspapers enjoying the cigarette smoke and the wordless silence after our peasant lunch. That silence was some sort of a third friend; he belonged to our fellowship.

As he draws his letter to a close, he refers to the time they went to Edgbaston in 1972 to watch Test match cricket. Rowlands refers to the book Carwyn took with him, *Gyda Gwawr y Bore* (With the Morning Dawn) by Aneirin Talfan Davies – the one Carwyn used in preparation for his President of the Day speech at the National Eisteddfod that year. The day Rowlands wrote his apologetic tribute to Carwyn, he had looked through Talfan Davies' volume:

> I looked through that book this morning and I noticed that Aneirin Talfan Davies mentions going to the theatre in Brighton to see one of John Osborne's plays. He names the play: *The Hotel in Amsterdam*. And he says this, 'I had the feeling, as I was watching the performance, that the sound of great suffering could be heard all the way through it.' I cannot begin to tell you, dear Jâms, nor anyone else either, the measure of the depth of such sad irony: an irony that caused you, on one evening of relaxed socialising in the Russell Hotel, to read a book which contained such significant words as those.

Six years later, in his collection of essays on sporting heroes and their philosophy, *Fragments of Idolatry*, David Foot sums up his reaction to Carwyn's contribution:

> Perhaps it's the voice that we remember most of all. It was musical and sweetly-tuned; too calm, one would have thought, for the biting winds of an exposed touchline. The voice, fashioned by the hymnal, was rarely raised in rebuke at the expense of a player; it increased fractionally in decibels only when someone, in his cups, took a sly, insensitive dig at Carwyn's undeviating political zeal, and Welshness. The voice could be mesmeric, full of crotchets and quavers and classical allusions, as his unbridled

conversation weaved joyfully in and out of literature, the arts and the brotherhood of man. He loved talking, philosophising, paying homage to genius, whether he saw it at the time as Beethoven or Phil Bennett. He had a reasoned opinion about most things. Backed by scholarship and a sharp brain, softened by the chuckle that was seldom too far away, he was not easily shifted from his stance. There were moods of silence and torment, often obscured from his friends and the general public. To them, the voice of Carwyn James was never idle. If not articulating the most practical, cunning or ingenious manner of stifling the All Blacks' pack, it was occupied at tenor-pitch in the chapel pews.

The battles of the flesh

Disillusionment at the hands of the WRU and mistreatment at the hands of the BBC have already been discussed. The cumulative effect of these two negative forces had worn Carwyn out. Solely on the rugby front, one of the last pieces he wrote for *The Guardian* ends with the words of a shattered and regretful man:

> In these first weeks of the 1982–1983 season I have watched four of the top English clubs and twice as many Welsh. On most occasions I have been bored to tears…
>
> If I had my time over again I would prefer to be a soccer manager than a coach of a rugby club in which half a dozen or more committee men interfere with selection.

These words have been used in discussion of Carwyn's view of rugby. They say as much about the man as they do about the game.

But these two forces, either individually or accumulatively, weren't the main fire on his skin. A far greater internal battle raged. Questions had surfaced periodically over many years when Carwyn was still alive as to whether he was gay or not. They escalated once he died. No doubt Carwyn would have heard these questions; some sincere enough, some matter-of-fact and some more salacious in motivation.

The stories, allegations, suggestions – whatever form they took – had remained largely as hidden whispers: a comment made behind the back of the hand. But they had spread, and had nearly, so nearly, broken into the public domain in the most sensational way. Carwyn's BBC colleague Martyn Williams tells of an encounter with a journalist in Cardiff.

> British newspapers in those days had what they called stringers: journalists who worked in their particular locality looking for stories that might be of British interest. The *News of the World* had such a stringer in Cardiff. In one of the pubs, The City Arms, he came up to me and started asking me questions about Carwyn. He wanted to know if the stories of him being gay were true. I denied those rumours and after a while, the journalist relented. To be honest, I had no proof that Carwyn actually was gay, so I didn't lie to him. What was completely obvious at that time was that if he was, then he did his best to keep it private but also, it was clear that there was one hell of a battle going on inside his head.

Such rumours had reached the press, then, but timely intervention had prevented the story being printed. It's difficult to imagine what would have happened had that journalist not relented.

No doubt he had heard the stories on the streets, suggesting that Wales', and indeed world rugby's, favourite coach might be gay. There is a need to separate the strands of such gossip, to ignore the chaff and evaluate the wheat. Just as rumours spread like wildfire about Dylan Thomas' drinking, without any attempt to tease fact from fiction, nor to see why he drank as he did when he did, so stories of Carwyn's sexuality have circulated and escalated with scant regard for truth. So what is the case for claiming that Carwyn was gay?

The first point to make is that it's not the responsibility of anyone, biographer included, to stand in judgement on the issue. In an attempt to understand what tensions and battles someone grappling with sexuality would encounter, the advice of world rugby's most prominent gay man, Nigel Owens, was sought. His advice was simple:

> It's not up to you to say that Carwyn was gay if he hadn't come to that decision himself.

The key point there is 'hadn't come to that decision himself'. Death intervened in Carwyn's case before he could decide for himself whether he was gay or not. The point of acceptance hadn't been reached. What he had done was to grapple and battle with his sexuality; being thrown back and forth between accepting and refusing what was happening to him, to the point of torment. Nigel Owens himself went through this same process, which nearly cost him his life. He suffered from bulimia and attempted suicide:

> My life was one big mess. I was feeling very low. I think the biggest challenge anyone can face is accepting who you are, and at this point in my life I couldn't accept who I was. I didn't like who I was and what I was. It affected my performances as a referee and I got very close to being taken off the referee register. Quite simply, I did not want to be gay.

Nigel worked through this dark period and rebuilt his life. Carwyn didn't get the chance to. For him, it would have been like Nigel's story coming to an end in the dark period Nigel describes above. So what are we left with in Carwyn's story? Firstly, the need to establish that many who spread the rumour about Carwyn being gay had no idea why they were saying that. Then we need to look at how and when the more substantiated stories started, before then hearing what they have to say.

The gay Carwyn?

There's no single incident that can be pointed to as the beginning of the 'Carwyn is gay' rumours, no one story broken by the press that started it all. In fact, it was quite the opposite.

The suggestions spread more like smoke under the door than wildfire. Puffs of smoke appearing here, then there, then nothing for a long time before another wisp would drift out.

Looking back over his life, there are many who worked with him, played rugby with him and socialised with him who had a clear opinion on Carwyn's sexuality when the stories or rumours surfaced. From the period in the Navy, through his Llandovery days and the Lions tour in New Zealand, many say they saw no indication of Carwyn being gay at all.

His time doing National Service in the Navy, which itself had a reputation for an active gay culture, and meant living in a segregated world with all male adults, offers no substantiating stories. Tony Cash was there with him.

Nothing about Carwyn at Coulsdon (and we were there together for some ten months) suggested he might be gay, or have any inclinations in that direction. At various times there must have been at least four or five coders who were more or less openly gay. I don't recall him consorting with any of them. Access to girls was pretty limited so very few of us ever struck up amorous relationships. There wasn't much chat about girls. The first time any notion of Carwyn having been gay occurred to me was as a consequence of a conversation I had with my old friend and former BBC colleague, Gwynn Pritchard, who ended his career as BBC Welsh-language supremo in Cardiff. And this must have been some time after Carwyn's death. Both of us thought that Carwyn seemed to have lived a somewhat isolated life, and concealing – perhaps even from himself – a gay disposition may have been a factor in his drinking and therefore untimely demise.

From one male-dominated environment, Carwyn moved to another when he started to teach at Llandovery College. Former Llandovery pupil and now their head of rugby, Iestyn Thomas, is also quite clear on this issue.

We saw no sign of any behaviour from Carwyn that would suggest he was gay. If it was ever there, it was suppressed. We lived in a male-dominated environment, with plenty of scope and opportunity for experimentation, but also a very difficult place to keep any rumours completely hidden. Especially, as in Carwyn's case, if you were there for many years. The closest we got to having to comment on Carwyn's behaviour with the boys was when he would insist on some kind of mock-wrestling with the sixth-formers. He would grab one of them at a time, and wrestle them to the ground. He would do this very often. We thought that this was a kind of play acting which was, at worst, getting on our nerves.

On the rugby circuit, the stars who played for Carwyn were unanimous in the fact that they didn't have any inkling that he might be gay. 1971 Lion Fergus Slatterry sums it up:

> Nothing that came to light after he died, no story or account of any incident made any of us look back and think, 'Ah, yes, maybe that explains such and such now, then.' Nothing of the kind. We weren't aware of any such thing at the time, and hindsight hasn't enlightened us either.

These comments are representative of those spoken to in each situation.

Such stories, however sincere, can not be taken as conclusive proof that Carwyn wasn't gay, however. The issue is far more complex than that for two reasons: the repressive anti-gay climate of the time, and Carwyn's own personality trait of being a very private man.

Throughout his Navy days and the vast majority of his Llandovery days until 1967, homosexuality was illegal, thus making even any casual discussion on the issue difficult, let alone confiding in someone that you might be trying to understand any gay feelings you might have.

The story unfolds

But stories did spread and they need to be noted. The criterion applied to the way these stories have been treated for this book was the same on this issue as for every other story in the book: no story was included if only heard once, unless there was strong justification for doing so. All the following stories relating to the debate about Carwyn's homosexuality were told to the author by more than one person. Further consideration was then given to the relationship between the source of the stories and Carwyn. These sources were all in a situation where they would know first-hand the events they share.

The early Seventies provide us with the first anecdotal references to Carwyn being gay. Three former members of regional WRU committees shared the same story with the author, independently of each other. Such is the fear in Wales of being seen to discuss such a potent mix as rugby and sexuality, each of the three asked to remain anonymous. Their story tells of fellow Committee members, at the time when Carwyn was seeking election to WRU committees, saying that they didn't want to vote 'for a man who slept with other men'. Such a consideration evidently far outweighed any success Carwyn had achieved on the field of play. That is a very early indication that there was a certain perception of Carwyn's preferences. In addition to the other sources, Fergus Slattery, Willie John McBride and Colin Meads all say that as far as they were aware, the stories grew within the grass-roots rugby world of Wales.

A few years after his last attempt to get on to a WRU regional committee, Carwyn met a gay man in Llanelli. Welsh-speaking son of the town Jonathan Thompson was in a gay relationship at the time.

A gay man knows instinctively if someone else is gay, and it was obvious to me from our first meeting that Carwyn was. He asked me if I wanted to go to his flat. This was in 1974. He had just left Llanelli to move into Cardiff. I'm not sure he would have asked me if he hadn't moved away from home. I had to politely decline as I was already in a relationship. We stayed as friends after that and he obviously took a great deal of solace from the fact that he could speak to someone who knew how things were. Having said that, I'm not sure he was ever totally at ease with how he was feeling.

Within the walls of the BBC, in the more liberal, open-to-alternatives, creative world, the stories were more forthcoming. Stories abound of him arriving at work worse for wear, as we've already heard. But other stories add a different twist. More than one of his co-workers, spoken to for this book, tells the same story of him arriving at work one morning with two black eyes. The story was that Carwyn had approached a man near one of the few gay clubs in Cardiff at the time, in the belief that he was gay. It was a case of mistaken sexuality which the man took exception to, and he dealt with Carwyn as he thought he should be dealt with. This was in 1982, after the heart attack, the suspension and the visit to the Priory. Before that, there were also stories about him having a relationship with a male film editor at the BBC.

Former Head of Programmes Gareth Price and another BBC colleague who wishes to remain anonymous testify that amongst the mess in the boot of Carwyn's car were one or two gay videos. These came to light as a result of another of Carwyn's habits: leaving his car at the homes of his friends when he was away.

The earliest reference we have to Carwyn being gay refers to a time way back before the Seventies and before Llandovery. Two individuals, both in the academic world and again wishing to remain nameless, testify that the same man shared with them that he had a relationship with Carwyn back in the tranquil summers of Aberystwyth student days, when they shared secrets most young men at the time would never have admitted to.

So it would appear that the first references to Carwyn being gay go right back to his student days in Aberystwyth. But thereafter there's a complete silence on the issue until the early Seventies. Stories had both accumulated and been suppressed over a long period of time, therefore. There were areas, both geographical and cultural, where the possibility of Carwyn being gay wasn't even considered as an outside chance. There were other areas where people thought he might be and spread the stories as if he was: the rugby world predominantly. And the third, much smaller group, were the people who believed he was. This last group, which knew about Carwyn's internal battle, were a minority within the BBC and a minority within the gay minority. One pattern which can be drawn from this observation is that the stories of Carwyn being gay didn't surface in the JSSL, at Llandovery or in Carmarthen. All the various and diverse component parts of Carwyn's life were in place throughout those periods. The stories surfaced and escalated when those components started to fragment and rugby came to the ascendancy in the early and mid-Seventies. The rumours started in rugby circles, as some of his '71 Lions and local WRU committee men testified. So, did Carwyn not feel the pressure of sexual identity as much when other comforts surrounded him, and when they were gone, the tensions raged? It's more than likely.

Family strain

Gossip and family loyalty came head to head on a night out in Cardiff. The daughter of Carwyn's sister Eilonwy was at a social gathering that Carwyn was due to address. Bethan Cox will not forget that evening:

> I didn't always make it known that I was related to Carwyn. That wasn't because I was ashamed of that fact – I certainly wasn't – but because I didn't think that I was a more special person just because I was related to him, and I didn't like the idea that people might think I was something different because I was. I was embarrassed by the whole idea of fame, as we were as a family.
>
> I was in this gathering where Carwyn was due to speak and the word got out that he was not going to turn up. I knew that happened from time to time. But I didn't expect the reaction that was to follow. Some of the men there had an explanation for Carwyn's non-appearance: 'He's probably sleeping with some man,' they said. That really shook me to the core.

Significantly, Bethan Cox heard this in a rugby event, not

in the Cardiff University circles where she worked. What to do with the comment she'd heard was a further dilemma:

> There's no way in the world that I could share what I'd heard with the family. I couldn't discuss the whole thing because I didn't want to upset anyone. How would people react? What would they say? We must remember the climate of the time, where suggesting that someone was gay would have caused a huge scandal.

Eventually, feeling a compulsion to share with someone, she thought that the best-suited person to discuss the issue with was her aunt Gwen. She felt that Gwen's professional experience as a psychiatric nurse meant it would be easier to speak to her than to Bethan's own mother, a minister's wife. Gwen was instantly defensive.

> 'Lots of people aren't married,' she said, bluntly. It was like a defence of her brother, staying on his side. But behind that, I could feel that she knew more than she was letting on. I think that Carwyn and Gwen had come to understand each other, along the lines of 'I won't say if you don't ask.' Like her brother, she had no children and I think this added to the bond between them.

There's no denying that Gwen had a profound grasp of her brother's emotional and psychological needs. She showed the depth of her understanding quite forcefully in a TV interview. Her words, those of the former psychiatric nurse, taken alongside the observations of psychiatrist Dafydd Huws, are powerfully illuminating:

> Lots of things in Wales are kept quiet. Nobody knows anything about them. Be far better if things were not bottled up. It would give more people a chance to live their life as they would like to.

And then, after a lengthy reflective pause, she adds:

> Of course they say life is what you make it. Not with everybody.

410

Love in a Welsh climate

Gwen's words more than suggest that a specific Welsh problem contributed to her brother's angst: the compulsion to keep things quiet, the fear of sharing feelings. This former psychiatric nurse, having spent all her working life in England, knew of the dangers of keeping things bottled up. The Welsh culture, the Welsh-speaking culture that Carwyn was a part of and which was such a big part of him, was a very firm cap on Carwyn.

Carwyn's beloved Gwenallt wrote a poem referring to Prosser Rhys, a Welsh-language poet in the 1920s and a man who was gay. Rhys' sexuality would have been easier to keep under wraps in pre-mass media Wales, and his fame was not at the same level as Carwyn's. Gwenallt touches on the forces that Rhys would have faced:

> *Cymru a roes i'r Cardi ei foesoldeb,*
> *hyhi a'i cododd uwch cythreuldeb rhyw;*
> *ac anodd yw cerdded un o lwybrau Cymru*
> *heb daro rhywle yn erbyn Duw.*

> 'Wales gave the Cardi his morality,
> it's she who lifted him above the devilment of sex;
> and it's difficult to walk one of the paths of Wales
> without bumping somewhere into God.'

In his battles with his sexuality, Carwyn would have regularly run into the devilment of sex and bumped into God on many street corners.

Nigel Owens felt this acutely as well, in wrestling with his own identity:

> The whole idea of being gay was repulsive and alien to me, cutting across the values of my upbringing and the community in which I lived. I was having feelings and I had no idea what they were, and those are the feelings that sent me to a very dark place.

Identity and formative values came face to face. There's a poignant resonance in these words for Carwyn. A Welsh-speaking rugby man from the Gwendraeth Valley shares his personal battle with sexual identity. It could so easily have been Carwyn, if only he had had the cultural climate, the support network and the self-assurance to articulate such personal thoughts. Nigel Owens speaks for Carwyn James. Those same values of upbringing and community hovered heavily over Carwyn – in fact, they came from exactly the same community. The only difference was time, and what a difference that made.

The silence about his sexuality was at its deepest within these Welsh-language circles. The heritage that shaped Carwyn's nationalism, consisting as it did of chapel values and the need for respectability, would have rendered it impossible for him even to suggest that he had such tendencies. Legalisation had little effect on such responses. His was a heavier chain because of the weight that Welsh chapel life added to it. Not of necessity the tenets of the Christian faith itself, but its legacy – the human, cultural interpretation of that faith – added to his burden. It created a guilt that grew under the shadow of perceived orthodoxy, which led to what members of his own family called the guilt trip. It centred on what other people would think, would say: the need for public respectability that smothered the individual's need to be him or herself. This is where the chapel deacon regularly bumped into God.

But let's not paint only Nonconformist chapel Wales with this brush. The macho rugby world in Wales, and pretty much worldwide, has still to this day seen only two prominent rugby figures coming out as gay: Nigel Owens and Gareth Thomas. Little wonder then that Carwyn wouldn't have uttered a single syllable about feelings he might have had in such an environment. He couldn't talk freely to people in such a world about rugby, so there was no chance he would share anything remotely personal with people who had snubbed him.

Stepping outside Carwyn's world to that of another of

Wales' famous sons gives us a direct counterpoint. Richard Burton, Hollywood actor, drinker, womaniser and hell-raiser, came from a different Wales. He was more than open about the fact that he tried gay sex more than once. On a TV show, he said that this was natural as, in his opinion, all actors were gay anyway. Carwyn would not be able to enjoy such open discussion about the issue as it related to him – acting and rugby are worlds apart. Burton then said something that pulls him right back alongside Carwyn:

> The way this is hidden from the public is through drink.

In one biography of Elizabeth Taylor, the woman he married twice, it's stated that Burton slept with Laurence Olivier and one other man. Burton's brother vehemently denied such allegations, but such vehemence showed the feelings in many quarters about such actions.

The last days of the Seventies pushed gender boundaries only as far as the portrayal of characters such as the famed Mr Humphries in the TV series *Are You Being Served*, with his catchphrase 'I'm free!', and Maldwyn Novello Pugh, Sion Probert's camp character in the classic rugby film *Grand Slam*. Portraying camp and mother's boy characteristics is as far as these portrayals could go, with sexual orientation certainly not made explicit. Those who were campaigning for gay rights at the time felt that characters such as Humphries and Pugh actually harmed their cause.

Traits and tendencies

When Carwyn started to work for the BBC, there was a group within those corridors that he was able to be more open with. But that was scant comfort. Even sharing with the understanding few would been extremely difficult. Those who were openly gay were still in a very small minority, even in 1982. Anyone who would have been more prepared to be open about that was almost certainly considerably younger than Carwyn. He would have faced a lonely battle, even if there were others there who were on the same side as him. Those facing the same internal conflict as Carwyn at the BBC at the time testify to one overwhelming problem – who do you tell? The excruciating dilemma for anyone feeling the need to discuss gay issues was knowing who it was safe to begin such a conversation with. As with Carwyn's niece, this was equally true of those needing to talk about someone they knew who was fighting to understand his or her sexual tendencies.

Against this backdrop of the attitudes of British society in general and his various own communities in particular during the years in which homosexuality was illegal, Carwyn's own personality traits and habits would play their part in his physical and emotional decline.

His fondness for cigarettes is legendary, as was his later equal fondness for gin. As a child, he was a picky eater. He would have been well fed and watered while under the direct care of any one of his three mothers and no doubt at Llandovery, but life in digs and on the road, shift work at the BBC and juggling the responsibilities of serving more than one paymaster at a time would lead to a life of eating on the hoof. Carwyn standing in his suit and tie on the Stradey touchline during training, but with the bottoms of his trousers tucked into his socks and rugby boots on his feet, was a familiar sight. There was not enough time for him to change properly between leaving Trinity and supervising a coaching session with Llanelli.

In later life the weight piled on. The skin condition got worse. This was both a cause and a symptom of his mental turmoil. The psoriasis particularly created the need in him to hide, to choose not to reveal. When he did decide to lift the veil on any personal issue, his choice of words was as critical as his selection of the people to hear them. That's a difficult enough situation for someone to be in, a complexity of issues that destroy and suffocate. But on a deeper level, it created a painful, heart-wrenching dilemma. On the one hand an inner struggle with sexual identity was raging, pulling him in all directions, which no doubt exacerbated his skin condition. But on the other hand, he knew that his torn, bloody skin was a cast-iron reason why he could never take his clothes off in front of someone else if he ever got into the situation where intimacy was a possibility. That is a genuine, authentic burden. Cause becomes effect, which becomes cause and then effect, in a relentless vortex of mental anguish.

His colleague at *The Guardian*, David Foot, says that Carwyn was aware of the talk regarding his sexuality:

> He was conscious that people were inclined to question his sexuality: it annoyed and embarrassed him, doubtless adding to his complexes. There were occasions he withdrew, inexplicably to the unknowing public, almost to the point of anonymity.

People were asking questions of Carwyn that he was still trying to find the answers for, and in this process, they were adding to his burdens.

Sister Gwen remembers the last months with her brother with a selective sisterly affection mixed with a very genuine dose of reality.

> The last year together we had a very happy time. He would go out, and so that I wouldn't be frightened when he came home, he would whistle when he came up the stairs. That was a real comfort for me.
>
> But his health wasn't so good. I know that his skin condition was terrible. But I never heard him say anything about it, even though I was the one who would often treat his lesions.

This must have been in the days after he returned from Italy, when she would stay with him in Fairwater, Cardiff, as she mentions Carwyn coming up the stairs. It couldn't have been in Hawen, Cefneithin, as that was a bungalow. The inherent reluctance to share, to discuss, to offload, is again shown in Gwen's words. The nurse would treat the wounds, but her brother/patient wouldn't discuss his condition. The same family members didn't know, for example, that he had been in Germany or Scotland during his JSSL days, facts that didn't fall under Official Secrets Act jurisdiction, especially in the years after that act had no hold on him. Here was a man who imprisoned his thoughts, and he alone would choose when to unlock the chains, and in whose presence.

The public consequence of the way Carwyn chose to deal with his issues was the creation of those three groups of people who thought they knew what he was going through. Some who would sincerely believe that there was no issue at all; others who would accept that there was an internal battle going on but believed that he never did anything about it; and the last, much smaller group, who were ready to accept that he had gay sex in an attempt to understand his own sexuality. There would be many who would refuse to believe because it offended their sensibilities and because the whole general concept of homosexuality, and the specific possibility that Carwyn was homosexual, was beyond their comprehenison. They didn't think he wasn't gay because of any proof, but because they had no concept that he could be. There were therefore various stages of knowing, consciousness and acceptance.

An indication of Carwyn's unwillingness to disclose his feelings and tendencies is the reaction of those who were kept the other side of that reluctance. Because there was no perception whatsoever on the part of so many in so many significant circles that it was even remotely possible that Carwyn could have been gay, outright denial was the overwhelming response when they first heard of the possibility. It was just too much for so many to take in. Indeed, it was beyond comprehension. That has been shown, for example, in the reaction to the discussion of this issue in the Welsh-language version of this biography. One specific phrase which encapsulates that kind of response is 'Carwyn never practised his problem'. In other words, firstly it was perceived as 'a problem'. Secondly, they maintain that he didn't do anything about it in any way whatsoever. Both are off the mark: firstly, it isn't 'a problem', and secondly, friends' stories show that there was experimenting and exploration in the name of trying to find out. Such a comment, though, is still evidence of the popular perception within certain sections of the Welsh community, nearly four decades after his death.

But what of Carwyn himself? In which group would he have been if he had had to describe himself? The real sadness for Carwyn is that he never got to the point where he could answer his own questions, but he did leave some clues.

CHAPTER 25

Marriage, children
and a photograph

Among the great struggles of man – good/evil,
reason/unreason, etc. – there is also this mighty conflict
between the fantasy of Home and the fantasy of Away,
the dream of roots and the mirage of the journey.

Salman Rushdie, *The Ground Beneath Her Feet*

CARWYN SPOKE OF marriage. In those days, a battle with sexual orientation would often have been hidden by such talk, or even by actually tying the knot in an attempt to conform to a societally-acceptable definition of normality, even though the individual knew they didn't really fit those norms. Carwyn was confronted with this, both in terms of the suggestions of others and in the shape of a direct proposal.

Carwyn got into a conversation with more than one person about him getting married. Usually it was with his family, as they tried their dutiful, genuine best to 'marry him off'. His brother Dewi says this:

> The most unwise thing he did was to not get married and raise a family. He was very fond of children. Even though my sister looked after him, it wasn't the same as if he had been married himself.

His sister Gwen's view was equally clear.

I told him many a time not to let me be an obstacle to him getting married. And all he said to me was that he was glad he hadn't married. After that, what could I say?

His niece, Bethan Cox, remembers being present during some of those conversations between Gwen and Carwyn when marriage was discussed:

Carwyn's attitude, I remember, was that because of his lifestyle – living out of a suitcase, travelling here, there and everywhere – he wouldn't be a good husband to anyone. I remember him asking, 'What kind of a husband would I be, anyway?' But I must say that through the conversations I was party to, and to this day, I had the distinct impression that such posturing was a smokescreen.

Carwyn did discuss marriage with one particular woman. That was in 1972, his year of five milestones. It could well have been a sixth, and if it had been, it would have been more momentous than the other five, with potentially more lasting consequences. BBC producer Ruth Price had been a constant companion to Carwyn since his early days of broadcasting in the late Fifties and early Sixties. She was a regular visitor to Llandovery College. By 1972, things had advanced so much between them that marriage was discussed. There are two versions of the story. Within BBC circles, the story is that Carwyn asked her to marry him. Within the family circle, however, the story is that Carwyn told them that Ruth Price made the first moves. It's difficult to believe that the unassuming Carwyn would have been confident enough to make such a bold move, even if it was during a particularly successful year for him. The family's version is more likely to be accurate. The BBC colleagues' version also includes the addition that a night spent between the sheets was some form of trial in the process of weighing up marital possibilities. The family have no version of this particular aspect of the story.

The inspiration of the flesh

If marriage had been a real issue, children had been also, but in a far, far more complex way. It was an issue on two very raw levels. His natural interest in children and young people was cruelly misinterpreted by the same mindset that spread salacious rumours about his homosexuality. The point came when some claimed that Carwyn had an unnatural interest in young boys. It came from his habit of taking the sons of many friends of his out, to rugby games in particular. R H Williams's son for example, Beti George's, and BBC senior manager Meirion Edwards' boy. He took Gareth Price's son as well:

> I remember my son coming home after seeing a rugby game in Cardiff with Carwyn. He was obviously quite perplexed and out of sorts. I quizzed him carefully as to why, and he eventually said that he'd heard someone in the crowd say something like 'There's Carwyn with another young boy!' The inference was obvious. It was a shock for me to hear such a thing from my own son. But I had absolutely no suspicion at all that there was any substance to those claims and I have none to this day. Not one of the parents of the boys Carwyn took to matches stopped him doing so when stories like that surfaced. It was dangerous and irresponsible talk.

This was a sinister twist on the gossip about Carwyn, which again, came predominantly from rugby circles. It begs the question, was the inability of those within the rugby fraternity to evaluate and interpret Carwyn's difference so great that the only solace they could find was creating prejudicial and injurious falsehoods?

A far more intelligent evaluation of Carwyn's fondness for the company of young boys and men comes from BBC rugby commentator, David Parry-Jones. His summing up of that particular aspect of Carwyn's character was to say that he was very much like Socrates. The evaluation of Socrates' fondness for young male company comes predominantly from Plato's writings. He says clearly that Socrates never expressed his fondness in any sexual manner. His pupil Xenophon also states clearly that Socrates, his teacher, showed no suggestion of the sexual in his enjoyment of the company of young boys. David Parry-Jones' description of Carwyn is therefore very accurate.

One of Carwyn's own literary heroes, Dostoyevsky, said:

The soul is healed by being with children.

Having no children of his own, this could only be expressed by delighting in the children of other people, whether they be his friends' children or the children sent to be educated by him. That's as close as Carwyn could ever get to satisfying the urge in him to produce children and to create life in his own form. This was a force that fed his vocational desire to educate. The welfare and development of young people was the reason he taught, and his genuine interest in young people was a leading virtue in the success of his teaching. It would be irresponsible and incorrect to link this with any sexual motivation.

There was another kind of refuge for Carwyn in the world of children, the spirit of which is unexpectedly caught by Norma Farnes, the manager of comedian Spike Milligan. In dealing with the same issue in the Irishman's life, she says:

He had an affinity with children. They never hurt him.

There was safety and security for Carwyn in the company of children, the healing that Dostoyevsky experienced. Others would hurt him, disappoint him, shame him. Children would never do that.

Back in the world of the experimental Welsh novel *Mae Theomempus yn Hen*, the main character John Rawlins, in Ireland to search for his paternal roots, gets to the point of thinking about his own children back home and then begins to contemplate childhood generally. Knowing that the author's travel companion was Carwyn James, and that the author would have known a great deal about Carwyn's psychological condition, it's very difficult to read the novel's comments on childhood without thinking they speak of Carwyn. One line addresses this dialogue clearly:

> *A yw plant yn ffrwyth awen y cnawd? Fe bery'r tad marw yng ngherddediad byw ei blentyn, fel y bardd mud yn llais ei greadigaeth.*
>
> 'Are children the fruit of the muse of the flesh? The dead father remains in the living walk of his child, like the silent bard in the voice of his creation.'

Carwyn wrestled with the fact that there would be no expression to the inspiration of his own flesh.

In the novel the seagull is a constant image, and it's on the cover of the book as well. *The Seagull* was Carwyn's favourite play by Chekhov, a man not accepted by his own people. Dafydd Rowlands would have known of his friend's love of the Russian playwright's work and its significance. The seagull, in the hands of Chekhov and of Carwyn's author friend Dafydd Rowlands, is a sure metaphor for Carwyn's life. It's a bird that's a symbol of freedom and of artistic expression, but also of sadness and enigma.

Two companions

If Auden referred to books reading us, another quote by author C S Lewis is also relevant. We read, he said, to know we're not alone. Carwyn, a man involved all his life in a team game, needed to know he wasn't alone. Such a reassurance came from his beloved world of books, and in the lives of two specific literary individuals. This again, was at the heart of who Carwyn really was: a man who championed the individual's right to express himself within a collective context. One of those who attended the Memorial Service at the BBC in Llandaff was Oscar-winning director Colin Welland, a good friend of Carwyn's. This northerner from a working class background was known for writing plays that 'championed the individual against the system', as he himself explained when a guest on *Desert Island Discs*. Allowing the individual to be himself when the system or the establishment prohibited that was something which would have united Welland and Carwyn.

But asserting such individuality was a problem for Carwyn in a way that it wasn't for Welland. In this struggle, Carwyn sought the company of two other individuals. Carwyn had two close literary companions during the last days of his pilgrimage on this earth: two books that lift the corner of the veil on the hidden soul that was Carwyn James. His two companions, indeed soulmates, were authors James Baldwin and Federico García Lorca. Two books connected to these two men were on his bookshelf at home when he died. The first was *Giovanni's Room* by Baldwin and the other *The Assassination of Federico García Lorca* by Ian Wilson. He would turn to these two volumes more than any other, and that is an illuminating comment on the last days of Carwyn.

The story of *Giovanni's Room* is the life of David, an American living in Paris. He's asked his girlfriend Susan to marry him and she has gone to Spain to contemplate her answer. Left on his own in Paris, David begins a gay relationship with Giovanni. Baldwin was an American author of Afro-Caribbean origin and was also gay. He published this book in 1956, and insisted upon his right to assert himself as a black gay American at a time when it was almost impossible to do so.

There's a sexual undertone in the writing of Baldwin, and *Giovanni's Room* in particular. In that work, Baldwin connects sexual identiy with the core of ethnic identity: personal identity and national, cultural identity are intertwined. He felt he had to flee America because of the pressures on him.

> To save myself, I finally had to leave for good… I suppose my decision was made when Malcolm X… Martin Luther King… Medgar Evers… were killed. I loved Medgar. I loved Martin and Malcolm. We all worked together and kept the faith together. Now they are all dead. When you think about it, it is incredible. I'm the

last witness – everybody else is dead. I couldn't stay in America. I had to leave.

He fled to France where he spent most of the last 20 years of his life with his lover, Lucien Happersberger. For him, asserting his right to be the black, gay American he was meant leaving the country that gave him that identity. Carwyn's time in Italy is a brief reflection of the same thing.

David, the main character in *Giovanni's Room*, questions his sexuality, which leads to him questioning the heritage into which he was born. The sexual orientation that he felt was his identity would have been denied and rejected by the people he belonged to. The conclusion of this tension is for David to question whether he actually is American after all, as his own people are denying who he is. Carwyn faced the same battle with sexual orientation and he would have faced the same denial and rejection of it from people within his own cultural sphere. Carwyn could well question his own cultural identity, asking if he was gay, but how could he also be a part of an ethnic group that denied the very way he felt inside? Maybe he belonged somewhere else. It was a question that would have faced him on the pages of *Giovanni's Room*.

On the eve of the release of a brand new film documentary and book on Baldwin's life, both titled *I Am Not Your Negro*, respected Irish author Colm Toibin's essay in *The Daily Telegraph* sums up Baldwin's *raison d'être*.

Part of Baldwin's enduring power is that he was not a political thinker. He was interested in the soul's dark spaces much more than in the body politic. His essays are riveting because he insists on being personal, on forcing the public and the political to submit to his voice and the test of his experience...

All art is a kind of confession, more or less oblique. All artists, if they are to survive, are forced, at last, to tell the whole story, to vomit the anguish up.

Carwyn's life is more to do with what happens when you cannot vomit anguish.

Federico García Lorca, Carwyn's other travelling companion, fought on the side of the Socialists in the Spanish Civil War. He was killed during the first few months of that conflict and his body has never been recovered. The fact that the man hailed as Spain's national poet was also gay was kept secret for many years. He lived his public life while hiding his inner feelings. He was a popular artist, musician, dramatist and poet with a high profile in his motherland. He would not have been accepted, however, if his sexuality had been known. He therefore had to live his life on two levels. It's easy to see Carwyn identifying with a man whose public persona was a significant influencing factor in his battle with sexuality. For both, the battle would have been so different had they not been in the public eye.

Lorca's identifying himself with the fight against Fascism in his homeland's Civil War was as public as he got in his stand for values he held dear – freedom of expression and a liberal outlook. He stood against the macho and suffocating interpretation of traditional Spanish values of manhood of Franco and his followers and of the Catholic Church; values which denied the existence of Lorca's own feelings and experience.

Some of Lorca's work touches Carwyn's experience also. One poem and one play relate to Carwyn's reality on the issue of children, as in Dafydd Rowlands' *Mae Theomemphus yn Hen*. Lorca wrote the play *Yerma*, which recently ran in London. *Yerma* is the Spanish word for 'barren' and it's a powerful exploration of people who have to live without being able to have children. Four lines in Lorca's poem 'The Barren Orange Tree' make the same point:

Leÿador.
Córtame la sombra.
Líbrame del suplicio
de verme sin toronjas.

425

'Woodcutter.
Chop away my shadow.
Let me escape the pain of seeing
myself with no fruit.'

Another central element of Lorca's work and attitude is a concept called *duende*, described as a haunting and inexplicable sadness that lives at the heart of certain works of art. It means having soul, a heightened state of emotion, expression and authenticity. The word originally comes from an elf-type creature in Spanish mythology, named Duende.

Lorca gave a famous and influential lecture on this concept, called 'The Theory and Play of the *Duende*', in Buenos Aires in 1933. His talk has influenced artists and musicians across the generations ever since. In Carwyn's own experience, *duende* would resonate with many layers of his own heritage: the minor key of his Welsh hymns, the heavy sense of longing and belonging permeating the literature of his motherland, the spirit that identifies with the Welsh concept of *hiraeth* – that indescribable feeling of wanting a connection with the Welshness that no longer exists. On many levels, Lorca was the soulmate that Carwyn never met.

In Baldwin and Lorca, sexual orientation and a deep-rooted awareness of national and ethnic identity, the influence of heritage, the role of faith and man-made traditions of religion mix in one emotional, psychological cauldron, sometimes simmering, sometimes boiling over. Such were the thoughts accompanying Carwyn in the last years of his life, aired between the covers of what he loved so much more than the oval ball: books.

In his efforts to wrestle with such tensions, a phrase used by his friend Dafydd Rowlands describes his approach. In his Welsh-language novel, he describes the character based on Carwyn as one who draws close from a distance. He sought intimacy from afar, treading carefully towards it, afraid that he would die a little if he got too close. But he still knew that he needed that process of drawing near. He needed to reconnect with his roots, as he'd told psychiatrist Dafydd Huws. He needed to weave new patterns from old threads. But he was afraid to do so because of the battle inside.

Baldwin, in *Giovanni's Room*, says:

Perhaps home is not a place but simply an irrevocable condition.

And then he says again, in another part of the novel:

You will go home and then you will find that home is not home anymore. Then you will really be in trouble. As long as you stay here, you can always think: One day I will go home.

Carwyn read those words during the period when he was talking to his psychiatrist; when he expressed his new-found realisation of wanting to draw near, to find what T S Eliot called the return. He wanted to arrive back at where he had started from, and to know that place for the first time.

Living reality for him was a stark awareness that he could only seem to do so from a distance, and even that, tentatively. Seemingly insurmountable barriers of prejudice, the dense, thick fog of insecurity, and the physical ailment he wore on his body might have made him think that wanting to go home was enough in itself, without having to go through all the turmoil and the tribulations of the actual journey to get there. It was doomed to remain a tension. He did not get to the point of decision.

A photograph

In those first few days of a brand new year, 1983, as Carwyn sank beneath the churning waters of the lowlands, a slightly-curling photograph lay propped up on the mantelpiece of his Cardiff home. It was of a newborn baby; the first grandson of Dai Dolanog, Carwyn's friend from the sun-shining days of school summer holidays in 1940s Rhydlewis. Carwyn had sent some money to the proud parents and they had sent the photograph in return. With Carwyn a dead Welshman in a foreign land, that one small photograph looking out over his empty living room back home became a symbol of new life in the old country, which did exist but which Carwyn would never know.

Carwyn's other favourite painting at the Accademia, Rovigo: Giovanni Bellini, *Cristo Portacroce*

Bibliography

Carwyn's own writing

Rupert Cherry, Carwyn James, Chris Rea, *Injured Pride* (Arthur Baker, 1980)

Huw Llewelyn Davies, Carwyn James, R Gerallt Jones *Y Gamp Lawn* (Y Lolfa, 1978)

Carwyn James, John Reason *The World Of Rugby* (BBC, 1979)

Carwyn James *Focus on Rugby* (Stanley Paul, 1983)

John Reason (ed.) *The Lions Speak* (Rugby Books, 1972) – republished as *How We Beat The All Blacks* (Aurum, 2013)

Biographies of Carwyn

John Jenkins (*gol.*) *Un o 'Fois y Pentre'* (Gomer, 1983)

Alun Richards *Carwyn* (Christopher Davies, 1984)

Rugby

Gerald Davies *Gerald Davies: An Autobiography* (Allen and Unwin, 1979)

Rhodri Davies *Undefeated: The Story of the 1974 Lions* (Y Lolfa, 2015)

David Foot *Fragments of Idolatry* (Fairfield Books, 2001)

Alun Gibbard *Who Beat the All Blacks?* (Y Lolfa, 2012)

Gareth Hughes *One Hundred Years of Scarlet* (Llanelli RFC, 1983)

Barry John *The Barry John Story* (Collins, 1973)

Frank Keating *Up and Under: A Rugby Diary* (Hodder & Stoughton Ltd., 1983)

Howard Lloyd *Crysau Cochion* (Llyfrau'r Dryw, 1958)

Willie John McBride with Peter Bills *Willie John: The Story of My Life* (Piatkus, 2004)

Ian McLauchlan *Mighty Mouse: an autobiography* (Stanley Paul, 1980)

Terry McLean *They Missed the Bus: Kirkpatrick's All Blacks of 1972/73* (AH & AW Reed Limited, 1973)

Geoffrey Nicholson, Clem Thomas *Welsh Rugby: The Crowning Years 1968–80* (Collins, 1980)

Roger G K Penn *Three Feathers and a Silver Fern* (Gomer, 2013)

Ross Reyburn *The Man Who Changed the World of Rugby: John Dawes* (Y Lolfa, 2013)

Huw Richards *A Game for Hooligans: The History of Rugby Union* (Mainstream, 2007)

Richards, Stead and Williams (ed.) *Heart and Soul: The Character of Welsh Rugby* (UWP, 1998)

David Smith, Gareth Williams *Fields of Praise: Official History of the Welsh Rugby Union 1881–1981* (UWP, 1980)

Delme Thomas with Alun Gibbard *Delme* (Y Lolfa, 2013)

J B G Thomas *Rugby in Focus 1978: A review of rugby union football* (Pelham Books, 1979)

David Tossell *Nobody Beats Us: The Inside Story of the 1970s Wales Rugby Team* (Mainstream Publishing, 2010)

J J Williams with Peter Jackson *JJ Williams: the life and times of a rugby legend* (Y Lolfa, 2015)

Llandovery

W Gareth Evans *A History of Llandovery College* (Trustees of Llandovery College, 1981)

R Brinley Jones *Floreat Landubriense* (Trustees of Llandovery College, 1998)

Gwendraeth Valley and Llanelli

Glyn Anthony *Coal Dust and Dogma* (Alun Books, 1988)

Aneirin Talfan Davies *Crwydro Sir Gâr* (Llyfrau'r Dryw, 1955)

Hywel Teifi Edwards (gol.) *Cwm Gwendraeth* (*Cyfres y Cymoedd*) (Gomer, 2000)

Jon Gower *Real Llanelli* (Seren, 2009)

James Griffiths and his Times (The Labour Party Wales, 1976)

James Griffiths *Pages from Memory* (Littlehampton Book Services Ltd., 1969)

Hywel Gwynfryn *Ryan a Ronnie* (Gomer, 2013)

Gareth Hughes *A Llanelli Chronicle* (Cyngor Bwrdeisdref Llanelli, 1984)

Gareth Hughes (ed.) *Looking Around Llanelli with Harry Davies* (Cyngor Bwrdeistref Llanelli, 1985)

Elwyn Jenkins *Pwll, Pêl a Phulpud* (Gomer, 2008)

D Huw Owen *Hanes Cymoedd y Gwendraeth a Llanelli* (Y Lolfa, 2014)

T W Pearce (*gol.*) *Gwendraeth 1925–1975* (Christopher Davies, 1975)

D Ben Rees *Arwr Glew y Werin: Cofiant James Griffiths* (Y Lolfa, 2014)

Ann Gruffydd Rhys *Cwm Gwendraeth/Llanelli* (*Cyfres Broydd Cymru*) (Carreg Gwalch, 2000)

K C Treharne *Glofeydd Cwm Gwendraeth* (Cyngor Bwrdeistref Llanelli, 1995)

Politics and History

Kate Bosse-Griffiths *Trem ar Rwsia a Berlin* (Gomer, 1962)

Mike Benbough-Jackson *Cardiganshire and the Cardi c.1760–c.2000: Locating a Place and its People* (UWP, 2011)

Tony Cash, Mike Gerrard *The Coder Special Archive* (Hodgson Press, 2012)

John Davies *Broadcasting and the BBC in Wales* (UWP, 1994)

John Davies *Hanes Cymru* (Penguin, 2007)

Russell Davies *People, Places and Passions* (UWP, 2015)

Evans, Jarman, Jones, Pierce, Thomas, Wade-Evans *Seiliau Hanesyddol Cenedlaetholdeb Cymru* (Plaid Cymru, 1950)

Rhys Evans *Rhag pob Brad: Cofiant Gwynfor Evans* (Y Lolfa, 2005)

Katie Gramich *Narrating the Nation: Telling Stories of Wales* (North American Journal of Welsh Studies Vol. 6, 1 Winter 2011)

Ieuan Gwynedd Jones *Ar Drywydd Hanes Cymdeithasol yr Iaith Gymraeg* (Prifysgol Cymru Aberystwyth, 1994)

W J Lewis *Atlas Hanesyddol Ceredigion* (Cymdeithas Llyfrau Ceredigion, 1955)

Elystan Morgan *Elystan: Atgofion Oes* (Y Lolfa, 2012)

Kenneth O Morgan *Rebirth of a Nation: A History of Modern Wales 1880–1980* (OUP, 1987)

Roger Turvey *Cymru Mewn Oes o Newidiadau 1815–1918* (Y Ganolfan Astudiaethau Addysg, Aberystwyth, 2002)

Literature

James Baldwin *Giovanni's Room* (Delta, 2000)

Cyfansoddiadau a Beirniadaethau, Eisteddfod Hwlffordd 1972 (Gomer/Llys yr Eisteddfod, 1972)

Bryan Martin Davies *Cerddi Bryan Martin Davies: Y Casgliad Cyflawn* (Barddas, 2003)

Walford Davies *The Loud Hill of Wales* (Dent, 1991)

T S Eliot *T.S. Eliot Collected Poems 1909–1935* (Faber and Faber, 1946)

Bernard Evans *Glaw Tyfiant* (Carreg Gwalch, 1990)

Bernard Evans *Y Meini'n Siarad* (Carreg Gwalch, 1992)

Caradoc Evans *My People* (Seren, 1995)

Ian Gibson *The Assassination of Federico García Lorca* (Penguin Books Ltd., 1983)

Christine James (*gol.*) *Cerddi Gwenallt: Y Casgliad Cyflawn* (Gomer, 2001)

T James Jones *Cymanfa* (Gomer, 2014)

R Gerallt Jones *T.H. Parry-Williams* (*Cyfres Dawn Dweud*) (Gwasg Prifysgol Cymru, 1999)

Bethan Mair (*gol.*) *Cerddi Sir Gâr* (Gomer, 2004)

Moelona *Teulu Bach Nantoer* (Hughes a'i Fab, 1913)

T H Parry-Williams *Cerddi T.H. Parry-Williams* (Gomer, 2011)

Angharad Price *Ffarwél i Freiburg: Crwydriadau Cynnar T.H.* Parry-Williams (Gomer, 2013)

Dafydd Rowlands Mae Theomemphus yn hen (Christopher Davies, 1977)

General

Teleri Bevan Years on Air (Y Lolfa, 2004)

Neville Cardus My Life: Neville Cardus (Collins, 1965)

John Cosslett (ed.) The Century Collection: An anthology of best writing in the Western Mail throughout the 20th Century (The Breedon Books Publishing Company, 1999)

T I Ellis *Crwydro Ceredigion* (Llyfrau'r Dryw, 1953)

The books Carwyn left in Italy

M H Abrams (ed.) *English Romantic Poets* (OUP, 1977)

Y Caniedydd (Undeb yr Annibynwyr Cymraeg, 1960)

Neville Cardus *My Life: Neville Cardus* (Collins, 1965)

Benvenuto Cellini *Memoirs* (Unit Library Ltd, 1903)

Colin Cowdrey *M.C.C.: The Autobiography of a Cricketer* (Hodder & Stoughton Ltd., 1976)

T J Davies *Cyfle i Nabod* (Christopher Davies, 1977)

Owen M Edwards *Tro yn yr Eidal* (Hughes a'i Fab, 1921)

Stewart Harris *Political Football – The Springbok Tour of Australia, 1971* (Gold Star Publications, Melbourne, 1972)

Ernest Hemingway *A Hemingway Selection* (Longman, 1977)

Anne Hooper (ed.) *More Sex Life Letters* (HarperCollins, 1977)

Helen MacInnes *The Venetian Affair* (Fontana Books, Collins, 1968)

Laddie Marshack *Crowd of Lovers* (Corgi Children's, 1978)

W Somerset Maugham *A Writer's Notebook* (Heinemann, 1978)

Anaïs Nin *Delta of Venus* (W.H. Allen & Co, 1978)

The Oxford Pocket Dictionary (OUP, 1961)

Various *Kontinent 2 – The Alternative Voice of Russia & Eastern Europe* (Hodder & Stoughton, 1978)

Marcia Williams *Inside Number 10* (New English Library., 1975)

There was also a volume of English quotations.